GTK+/Gnome Application Development

New
Riders

GTK+/Gnome Application Development

New Riders

201 West 103rd Street,
Indianapolis, Indiana 46290

Havoc Pennington

GTK+/Gnome Application Development

Havoc Pennington

Copyright © 1999 by New Riders Publishing

This material may be distributed only subject to the terms and conditions set forth in the Open Publication License, v1.0 or later (the latest version is presently available at http://www.opencontent.org/openpub/).

For Version 1.0 of the Open Publication License see Appendix F.

International Standard Book Number: 0-7357-0078-8

Library of Congress Catalog Card Number: 99-63032

Printed in the United States of America

First Printing: August, 1999

03 02 01 00 99   7 6 5 4 3 2 1

Interpretation of the printing code: The rightmost double-digit number is the year of the book's printing; the right-most single-digit number is the number of the book's printing. For example, the printing code 99-1 shows that the first printing of the book occurred in 1999.

Trademarks

Warning and Disclaimer

Publisher
David Dwyer

Executive Editor
Laurie Petrycki

Acquisitions Editor
Katie Purdum

Development Editor
Jim Chalex

Managing Editor
Gina Brown

Project Editors
Laura Loveall
Clint McCarty

Copy Editors
Gayle Johnson
Audra McFarland

Indexer
Joy Dean Lee

Technical Reviewers
Jeff Garzik
James Henstridge
Raph Levien
Federico Mena Quintero
Marius Vollmer

Proofreader
Laura Loveall

Layout Technician
Amy Parker

About the Author

Havoc Pennington started programming with GTK+ before version 1.0 was released and became an active Gnome developer a few months after the project began. He is the author of several components of the Gnome libraries and some small Gnome utilities; his current free software projects include a data analysis program called Guppi and a Gnome frontend to the Debian GNU/Linux package management tool. Havoc is also the author of a free tutorial for new Debian users and a frequent contributor to the GTK and Gnome mailing lists. He is currently employed by EMC Capital Management, Inc., and writes Gnome software for internal use.

About the Reviewers

Jeff Garzik has been working on various free software projects for over a decade, in additional to many years in the Unix industry, both as a developer and as a system administrator. Current free software projects he contributes to include autoconf, automake, Gnome, and the Linux kernel. When not basking in the glow of monitor radiation, Jeff enjoys loud music, rock climbing, backpacking, and all things green.

James Henstridge lives in Perth, Western Australia. He is currently studying at the University of Western Australia, working toward a combined Bachelor of Science/Bachelor of Engineering degree (doing a mixture of computer science, pure mathematics and electrical/electronic engineering). He has been using Linux since 1995 and first started looking at Gnome in early 1998. Since then, he has contributed to a number of Gnome packages, and he is responsible for a few, including the Python language bindings for Gnome.

Raph Levien has been doing GTK+ and Gnome development since 1996, the prehistory of the project. He has implemented much of the high-performance graphics code in Gnome, including the antialiased canvas renderer. He is currently responsible for Gnome's printing architecture, in addition to general hacking on GTK+, Gimp, and Gnome. Raph is close to completing his Ph.D. in Computer Science from the University of California at Berkeley (hopefully by the time you're reading this!), and he plans to do consulting and independent technology development of free software after graduating.

Federico Mena Quintero was born in Mexico City in 1976. He has been programming since he was 7 years old. He is an undergraduate student of computer science at the Universidad Nacional Autónoma de México (UNAM) and is currently in a training program to work on Gnome for Red Hat, Inc. Miguel de Icaza and Federico founded the Gnome project in August 1997. It has been going on since then. He likes good coffee and dislikes messy code.

Marius Vollmer was born in Germany in 1971. He studied Electrical Engineering until 1998 and is now working towards his Ph.D. He became interested in Gnome through the GTK+ toolkit, which he was trying to connect to the programming language Guile. He did some low-level changes to GTK+ to make it work better with interpreted languages, but fortunately he wasn't there when his changes broke the Gimp.

To my parents and grandparents, for inspiration.

Contents

Foreword by Miguel de Icaza   xiii

I Overview   1

1 Introduction   3
1.1   What is Gnome?   3
1.2   The Gnome Development Framework   4
1.3   Structure of the Book   9

2 glib: Portability and Utility   11
2.1   Basics   11
2.2   Data Structures   21
2.3   Other Features   35

3 GTK+ Basics   37
3.1   A Whirlwind Tour of GTK+   37
3.2   Containers and Widget Layout   44
3.3   Widget Concepts   57
3.4   The Main Loop   63

II Building a Gnome Application   69

4 Creating Your Source Tree   71
4.1   Overview of a Gnome Source Tree   72
4.2   Source Tree Checklist   73
4.3   `configure.in`   74
4.4   `Makefile.am`   77
4.5   Relevant GNU Documentation   79
4.6   Installing Support Files   80

5 Gnome Application Basics   85
5.1   Initializing the Libraries   85
5.2   Internationalization   86
5.3   Argument Parsing with `popt`   88

5.4   Saving Configuration Information   95

5.5   Session Management   104

6   The Main Window: *GnomeApp*   107

6.1   The `GnomeApp` Widget   107

6.2   Menus and Toolbars with `GnomeUIInfo`   109

6.3   Adding a Status Bar   113

6.4   Online Help   117

6.5   Finishing Touches   120

7   User Communication: Dialogs   123

7.1   The `GnomeDialog` Widget   123

7.2   Modal Dialogs   129

7.3   A Dialog Example   131

7.4   Special Dialog Types   132

7.5   Convenience Routines   136

8   Gnome Application Checklist   137

III   Advanced GTK+/Gnome Techniques   139

9   The GTK+ Object and Type System   141

9.1   Object and Class Structures   142

9.2   Type Checking and New Types   142

9.3   Initializing a New Class   145

9.4   `GtkArg` and the Type System   149

9.5   Object Arguments   153

9.6   Signals   160

9.7   Object Finalization   173

9.8   Attaching Data to Objects   179

10   Gdk Basics   181

10.1   Gdk and Xlib   181

10.2   `GdkWindow`   182

10.3   Visuals and Colormaps   188

10.4   Drawables and Pixmaps   193

10.5   Events   195

10.6   The Mouse Pointer   216

10.7   Fonts   219

10.8   Graphics Contexts   224

10.9   Drawing   231

10.10   Gdk Resource Management   238

10.11   GtkStyle and Themes   239

11   Writing a *GtkWidget*   243

11.1   Overview   244

11.2   The `GtkWidget` Base Class   245

11.3   An Example: The `GtkEv` Widget   250

11.4   `GtkWidget` In Detail   268

11.5   `GtkVBox`: A Windowless Container   281

11.6   `GnomeAppBar`: A Trivial Composite Widget   289

11.7   Other Examples   292

12   *GnomeCanvas*   293

12.1   Introduction to the Canvas   293

12.2   Basic Canvas Architecture   294

12.3   Using the Canvas   299

12.4   Standard Canvas Item Reference   311

13   Writing a *GnomeCanvasItem*   321

13.1   Overview   321

13.2   Drawing Methods   324

13.3   Other Methods   336

IV   Appendices   341

A   GTK+/Gnome Object Hierarchy   343

A.1   Hierarchy Summary   344

A.2   `GtkObject`   347

A.3   Widgets   347

A.4   Canvas Items   403

A.5   Miscellaneous Objects   406

B Table of Header Files 411

C Frequently Asked Questions 419
    C.1 Index of Questions 419
    C.2 Questions, with Answers 420

D Online Resources 433
    D.1 Obtaining and Compiling the Libraries 433
    D.2 Web Sites 434
    D.3 Mailing Lists 434
    D.4 Internet Relay Chat 435
    D.5 This Book 435

E Code Listings 437
    E.1 The GnomeHello Application 437
    E.2 The GtkEv Widget 448

F Open Publication License Version 1.0 471
    F.1 Requirements on Both Unmodified and Modified Versions 471
    F.2 Copyright 472
    F.3 Scope of License 472
    F.4 Requirements on Modified Works 472
    F.5 Good-Practice Recommendations 473
    F.6 License Options 473
    F.7 Open Publication Policy Appendix 474

Index 477

Foreword

The Importance of Free Software

When we started the GNOME Project in 1997, we were trying to address a number of shortcomings in the UNIX world—specifically, in the area of the free UNIXes.

The original aim of the GNU Project was to build a completely free operating system, bundled with free tools and applications. For years, programmers worked to make this happen. The work was simple to organize: Given that the goal was to clone UNIX, the GNU programmers just needed to pick a specific component they were interested in and implement it. Given UNIX's modularity, this was a good approach to the problem.

But UNIX had its deficiencies. The UNIX market was divided by the major vendors, and they each extended, improved, and fixed their operating systems in different ways. Sometimes they would add entirely new subsystems. Sometimes they would incorporate third-party proprietary technology from other companies. And sometimes they would extend the kernel and library APIs to give the users of their systems a larger feature set.

This was done to increase the added value of their specific version of UNIX, or to address the needs of a particular market sector. New technologies that emerged seldom became part of mainstream UNIX, and when they did, it took a long time for the various vendors to adopt them.

This division in the UNIX world was disastrous for UNIX on the desktop. Although vendors had tried to address some problems by standardizing the system APIs, and the free X Window System was successful, they fell short of creating a standard GUI toolkit and a free desktop environment.

At the beginning of 1997, UNIX lacked a standard open-source user interface with a consistent look and feel. It lacked desktop applications as well as all the tools and components required to build these applications. The infrastructure was just not there.

This lag in desktop technology was disastrous for application developers. For example, UNIX had no printing infrastructure, so each application had to roll its own. Component programming appeared on other operating systems, but it did not exist on UNIX.

The GNOME Project was created to address these problems.

- We created a free (open-source) standard for writing consistent graphical applications for UNIX systems. Anyone can use our libraries and infrastructure, without licensing fees or vendor lock-in.

- Our libraries are designed to be exported to programming languages other than C. This allows programmers to write GNOME applications in the language most appropriate for a given task.

- We are developing a suite of applications along with our infrastructure and desktop environment. As we develop real-world applications, we identify genuine problems with existing UNIX standards and create solutions to them.

The GNOME Development Process

Contributors to the GNOME Project come from a variety of backgrounds and have a wide range of interests. Everyone has their own reasons for contributing.

GNOME has been an exciting project for all of us. It has given us the opportunity to design a system from the ground up. We have learned how to build a large software system, we have learned how to work as a team, we have learned how to write better software, and we have learned from the wizardry and experience of other programmers. We have also learned a lot by making mistakes and fixing them.

All of us are driven by the desire to write free software that will benefit people around the world, giving them useful software that comes with the freedoms enumerated by the Free Software Foundation.

The GNOME team uses several different open-source licenses. We use the GNU General Public License for most applications (GNU GPL), and we use the GNU Lesser General Public License (GNU LGPL) for most libraries. We tend to use the GNU licenses because they protect the software code from being proprietarized: We do our best to ensure that the GNOME source code will always remain free.

I used to use a proprietary system and computers that had only proprietary software. As a programmer, I became very frustrated that I could never find out exactly how some of this software worked its magic. I could guess, but as a novice programmer, it was very hard for me to understand how it worked. Free software gave me a chance to explore how real applications are written and how they work. I can now read other people's code, and I have become a better programmer because of it.

From a programmer's point of view, this is one of the most important gifts that free software has provided. Reading the source code for a good application is like reading a good book. Now, there is a difference: Programs and software create a computational model, and tinkering with this model is always fun. Creating new programming models and watching them work and interconnect is one of the most enjoyable tasks I have performed.

This feeling is at the core of GNOME: creating interesting, powerful, reusable models—and, furthermore, exciting models to work on and with. GNOME ships these models to other people; we give them the freedom to use our software as they see fit. But this just adds bonus points to the overall pleasure of programming and hacking software.

Learning is a powerful reason to work on GNOME. Many GNOME contributors work on the system because they want to learn more about a GNOME component or some aspect of programming. As they learn, they write code for and contribute code to the GNOME Project. Everyone gains from this.

The Hacking Process

The launch of GNOME was motivated by two different desires: the desire to create a component model of interoperable, reusable components, and the moral desire to provide a free desktop environment for people to use.

These original desires are still part of the day-to-day work of GNOME development. People are interested in writing better tools—tools that can be used in more situations, that are compliant to more standards, and that are more useful than the existing tools. They also want to write reusable code and see it used over and over. Both our coding style and our licenses are designed to make the software as beneficial and widely used as possible.

It took us quite a while to get where we are now, but we have enjoyed every minute of it. I hope you will enjoy working with GNOME and in GNOME as much as we have enjoyed creating it.

We have observed that some ideas and code snippets have a life of their own. People use these pieces over and over in a number of different setups and in various places. When a piece of code is useful, people will cut and paste it and reuse it in different setups. (This is for cases in which the code snippet is not in a library function or when it doesn't make much sense to make it a library function.)

If an early useful setup is used, many applications will use it. We failed in one regard: The original GNOME setup didn't include a framework for documentation, and the idea of documentation just didn't propagate. We are now fixing this problem. It is something to keep in mind for the future.

Free Documentation

I still remember the very first days when Havoc Pennington got involved in the GNOME Project. He was among the first batch of hackers who got involved.

You might recognize Havoc's name because he constantly helps other users and programmers on the GTK+ and GNOME mailing lists. This book is another step in that direction.

This book is the result of many months of work from Havoc to provide a good tutorial on the infrastructure behind GNOME, and the result is outstanding. Even better than this is the fact that this book is distributed under a free license that allows both modification and redistribution of the modifications.

This is important given that GNOME is evolving at a very rapid pace. We can maintain this book. The GNOME community will benefit from it. We can extend it to cover new topics or topics that are not part of this first edition. We can improve the contents, extending the descriptions and improving the examples. We can keep this document up-to-date and incorporate descriptions of new GNOME technologies.

Whether you want to write your own applications or you want to get directly involved in the GNOME Project, I hope you enjoy this book as much as I enjoyed reading it.

I am very thankful to New Riders Publishing, and especially to Laurie Petrycki and Havoc, for making this all happen. They have given the free software community a free text that we can use to document the GNOME system.

If you want to join the team, or if you want to get up-to-date information on GNOME development, check the `http://developer.gnome.org` Web site.

Miguel de Icaza
June 22, 1999
Mexico City, Mexico

Acknowledgments

Many, many thanks to everyone who reviewed the book for technical accuracy. Federico Mena Quintero mercilessly critiqued almost every chapter; he made the book ten times better than it was before. Jeff Garzik, Gnome hacker and author of the `glib` test suite, reviewed the `glib` chapter; James Henstridge and Marius Vollmer (authors of *The Python* and *Guile bindings for GTK+/Gnome*, respectively) reviewed the chapter on the type and object system; official Gnome rocket scientist, Raph Levien, reviewed the chapter on GDK.

Everyone at New Riders should be mentioned; Jim Chalex, my development editor, cleaned up the manuscript, kept me organized, and fixed bunches of embarrassing errors. Laura Loveall and Clint McCarty put the final polish on the book. Katie Purdum expertly coordinated the whole writing process. Laurie Petrycki tirelessly talks to the free software community and may be one of the few non-computer-geeks that understands what we're up to. She deserves credit for the book's free license.

My co-workers were patient with my groggy Monday mornings after long book-writing weekends. They deserve thanks for making EMC Capital Management a great place to work.

This book was only possible because of all the free software hackers who've spent years patiently working on their vision of a free operating system and application suite. At the Gnome Project we're building on (and trying to live up to) an incredible legacy. Every day I learn from the GTK+ and Gnome hackers; I couldn't have written this book without all the information they've shared with me.

Most of all, thanks to my parents and grandparents, and to Amy.

Tell Us What You Think

As the reader of this book, you are our most important critic and commentator. We value your opinion and want to know what we're doing right, what we could do better, what areas you'd like to see us publish in, and any other words of wisdom you're willing to pass our way.

As the Executive Editor for the Open Source team at New Riders Publishing, I welcome your comments. You can fax, email, or write me directly to let me know what you did or didn't like about this book—as well as what we can do to make our books stronger.

Please note that I cannot help you with technical problems related to the topic of this book, and that due to the high volume of mail I receive, I might not be able to reply to every message. When you write, please be sure to include this book's title and author, as well as your name and phone or fax number. I will carefully review your comments and share them with the author and editors who worked on the book.

Fax: 317-581-4663
Email: newriders@mcp.com
Mail: Laurie Petrycki
               Executive Editor
               Open Source
               New Riders Publishing
               201 West 103rd Street
               Indianapolis, IN 46290 USA

I

Overview

1 Introduction

2 glib: Portability and Utility

3 GTK+ Basics

Introduction

THIS CHAPTER GIVES YOU AN OVERVIEW of the technologies described in this book.

1.1 What Is Gnome?

Gnome is a free (or "open source") software development project started in 1997 by Miguel de Icaza of the Mexican Autonomous National University and a small team of programmers from around the world. Inspired by the success of the similar K Desktop Environment (KDE) project, the burgeoning popularity of the GNU/Linux operating system, and the power of the GTK+ graphical toolkit, Gnome grew quickly. Within a year, hundreds of programmers were involved with it, and many thousands of lines of code had been written. Gnome has become a powerful framework for GUI application development, which runs on any modern variety of UNIX.

"Gnome" is actually an acronym for GNU Network Object Model Environment. Originally, the project was intended to create a framework for application objects, similar to Microsoft's OLE and COM technologies. However, the scope of the project rapidly expanded, and it became clear that substantial groundwork was required before the "network object" part of the name could become reality. The latest development versions of Gnome include an object embedding architecture called Bonobo, and Gnome 1.0 included a fast, light CORBA 2.2 ORB called ORBit.

Gnome is a part of the GNU Project, whose overall goal is developing a free operating system (named GNU) plus applications to go with it. GNU stands for "GNU's Not UNIX," a humorous way of saying that the GNU operating system is UNIX-compatible. You can learn more about GNU at http://www.gnu.org. Gnome has two important faces. From the user's perspective, it is an integrated desktop environment and application suite. From the programmer's perspective, it is an application development framework (made up of numerous useful libraries). Applications written with the Gnome libraries run fine even if the user isn't running the desktop environment, but they integrate nicely with the Gnome desktop if it's available.

The desktop environment includes a file manager; a "panel" for task switching, launching programs, and docking applets; a "control center" for configuration; and several smaller bells and whistles. These programs hide the traditional UNIX shell behind an easy-to-use graphical interface.

Gnome's development framework makes it possible to write consistent, easy-to-use, interoperable applications. The X Window System designers made a deliberate decision not to impose any user interface policy on developers; Gnome adds a "policy layer," creating a consistent look and feel. Finished Gnome applications work well with the Gnome desktop and can also be used "standalone"—users need to install only Gnome's shared libraries. It's even possible to write Gnome applications that do not rely on the X Window System; you might want to provide a non-graphical CORBA service, for example.

This book is about Gnome from a developer's point of view; it describes how to write a Gnome application using the Gnome libraries and tools.

1.2   The Gnome Development Framework

Gnome's application development framework centers around a suite of libraries, all written in portable ANSI C and intended to be used on UNIX-like systems. Libraries that involve graphics rely on the X Window System. Wrappers are available to export the Gnome API to nearly any language you can think of, including Ada, Scheme, Python, Perl, Tom, Eiffel, Dylan, and Objective C. In addition, there are at least three different C++ wrappers.

This book will cover the C interface to the libraries; however, it should be useful for users of any language binding because the mapping from C to your preferred language is typically straightforward. The book covers version 1.0 of the Gnome libraries (including the compatible bug fix releases, such as 1.0.9—all 1.0.x versions are compatible).

1.2.1 Non-Gnome Libraries

Taking full advantage of the free software tradition, Gnome didn't start from scratch. It uses several libraries, which are maintained separately from the Gnome project. These are part of the Gnome application development framework, and you can count on their presence in a Gnome environment.

1.2.1.1 glib

glib is the base of the Gnome infrastructure. It's a C utility library, providing routines for creating and manipulating common data structures. It also addresses portability issues; for example, many systems lack the `snprintf()` function, but glib contains an implementation called `g_snprintf()`, which is guaranteed to exist on all platforms and is slightly safer than `snprintf()` (because it always NULL-terminates the target buffer).

Gnome 1.0 uses glib version 1.2 and works with any glib in the 1.2 series (1.2.1, 1.2.2, etc.). All glib versions beginning with 1.2 are compatible bug-fix releases.

1.2.1.2 GTK+

GTK+, or the Gimp Tool Kit, is the GUI toolkit used in Gnome applications. GTK+ was originally written for the Gimp (GNU Image Manipulation Program— `http://www.gimp.org`), but it has become a general-purpose library. GTK+ depends on glib.

The GTK+ package includes Gdk, the Gimp Drawing Kit, which is a simplification and abstraction of the low-level X Window System libraries. Because GTK+ uses Gdk rather than calling X directly, a port of Gdk permits GTK+ to run on windowing systems other than X with relatively few modifications. GTK+ and the Gimp have already been ported to the Win32 platform in this way.

GTK+ provides several features for Gnome applications:

- A dynamic type system.
- An object system written in C, complete with inheritance, type checking, and a signal/callback infrastructure. The type and object systems are not GUI-specific.
- A `GtkWidget` object written using the object system, which defines the interface GTK+'s graphical components implement.
- A large collection of useful `GtkWidget` subclasses (*widgets*); this collection forms the bulk of GTK+'s code.

Gnome adds a number of additional widgets to the basic GTK+ collection.

Gnome 1.0 is based on GTK+ version 1.2. All GTK+ versions beginning with 1.2 (1.2.1, for example) are compatible bug-fix releases.

1.2.1.3   ORBit

ORBit is a CORBA 2.2 ORB written in C. It was designed to be small and fast compared to other ORBs, and it supports the C language mapping. ORBit is implemented as a suite of libraries.

CORBA, or Common Object Request Broker Architecture, is a specification for Object Request Brokers, or *ORBs*. An ORB is much like a dynamic linker, but it works with objects rather than subroutines. At runtime, a program can request the services of a particular object; the ORB locates the object and creates a connection between it and the program. For example, an email program might request an "addressbook" object and use it to look up a person's name. Unlike dynamic linking, CORBA works fine across a network and even allows different programming languages and operating systems to interact. If you're familiar with DCOM on the Windows operating system, CORBA is analogous.

1.2.1.4   Imlib

Imlib ("Image Library") provides routines for loading, saving, displaying, and scaling images in a variety of popular formats (including GIF, JPEG, PNG, and TIFF). It comes in two versions; an Xlib-only version and a Gdk-based version. Gnome uses the Gdk version.

1.2.2   Gnome Libraries

The libraries in this section are a part of the `gnome-libs` package and were developed specifically for the Gnome project.

1.2.2.1   *libgnome*

`libgnome` is a collection of non-GUI-related routines for use by Gnome applications. It includes code for parsing configuration files, for example. It also includes interfaces to some external facilities, such as internationalization (via the GNU `gettext` package), argument parsing (via the `popt` package), and sound (via the Enlightenment Sound Daemon, `esound`). The `gnome-libs` package takes care of interacting with these external libraries. So, the programmer does not need to concern herself with their implementation or availability.

1.2.2.2   *libgnomeui*

`libgnomeui` collects GUI-related Gnome code. It consists primarily of widgets designed to enhance and extend GTK+. Gnome widgets generally impose user interface policy, which permits a more convenient API (because there is less for the programmer to specify). It also results in applications with more consistent interfaces, of course.

Highlights of `libgnomeui` include the following:

- The `GnomeApp` widget, which makes it easy to create a nice main window for your application. It uses another widget called `GnomeDock` that enables users to rearrange and "undock" toolbars.
- The `GnomeCanvas` widget, which makes it easy to write intricate flicker-free custom displays.
- The Gnome stock pixmaps (icons for open, close, save, and other operations).
- Convenient routines for creating and using dialog boxes.
- The `GnomePixmap` widget, which is more versatile than `GtkPixmap`.

1.2.2.3 *libgnorba*

`libgnorba` provides CORBA-related facilities, including a security mechanism and object activation. Object activation is the process of obtaining a reference to an object that implements a given interface; it can involve executing a server program, loading a shared library module, or asking an existing program for a new object instance.

1.2.2.4 *libzvt*

This small library contains a terminal widget (`ZvtTerm`) you can use in your Gnome programs.

1.2.2.5 *libart_lgpl*

This library contains graphics rendering routines by Raph Levien. The routines included here are released under the GNU Library General Public License and used in the `GnomeCanvas` widget. `libart_lgpl` provides antialiasing, microtile refresh regions, and other magic. In essence, it is a vector graphics rasterization library, functionally analogous to the PostScript language.

1.2.3 Other Libraries

These libraries are commonly used in Gnome applications but are not a part of `gnome-libs` proper.

1.2.3.1 *gnome-print*

`gnome-print` is still somewhat experimental but very promising. It uses `libart_lgpl` and works nicely with `GnomeCanvas`. It provides virtual output devices (called "print contexts"); so, a single codebase can output to a print preview widget, to PostScript, and eventually to other printer formats. `gnome-print` also includes printing-related GUI elements, like a print setup dialog box, and a virtual font interface (to deal with the problem that X fonts are not printable).

1.2.3.2 *gnome-xml*

gnome-xml is a non-validating XML engine written by Daniel Veillard of the World Wide Web Consortium. It can parse XML into a tree structure and output a tree structure as XML. It's useful for any application that needs to load and save structured data; many Gnome applications use it as a file format. This library does not depend on any of the others, not even glib—so it is tied to Gnome in name only. However, you can expect most Gnome users to have it installed. So, it should not inconvenience your users if your application uses this library.

1.2.3.3 Guile

Guile is an implementation of the Scheme programming language in a library so that any application can have an embedded Scheme interpreter. It is the official extension language of the GNU Project and is used by several Gnome applications. Adding an extension language to your application might sound complex, but Guile makes it almost trivial. (Several Gnome applications support Perl and Python as well; it is usually easy to support several languages after you implement the first. But Guile has a special place in the Gnome developer's hearts.)

1.2.3.4 Bonobo

At press time, the Gnome hackers were putting the finishing touches on Bonobo. Bonobo is a compound document architecture in the tradition of Microsoft's OLE. It allows you to embed charts in spreadsheets, for example. It will be used pervasively throughout Gnome; any application will be able to display MIME-typed data such as plain text, HTML, or images, by asking the Gnome libraries for an appropriate Bonobo component. Look for Bonobo technology in the next major Gnome release.

1.2.4 A Word About Header Files

Throughout the book, the exact header file that declares each function is given alongside the function prototype. This is to facilitate your exploration of the source code. However, you probably don't want to manually include the hundreds of headers found in GTK+ and Gnome. You can include all GTK+ headers *en masse* by including the gtk/gtk.h header file. gtk/gtk.h also includes gdk/gdk.h for you. You can include all Gnome headers by including gnome.h; gnome.h includes gtk/gtk.h for you. Most Gnome application files simply include gnome.h.

1.3   Structure of the Book

This book is divided into several parts:

- Right now you're reading Part I, "Overview." This chapter gives you an overview of the Gnome application development framework. The following two chapters quickly introduce glib and GTK+. If you're already familiar with GTK+ programming, you may want to move directly to Part II, "Building a Gnome Application."

- Part II, "Building a Gnome Application," guides you through the development of a skeletal Gnome application. It starts with the creation of the source tree and then explains how to write menus, dialog boxes, and other essential application components. At the end of Part II is a checklist of features every application should have.

- Part III, "Advanced GTK+/Gnome Techniques," describes some advanced topics, including the internals of the GTK+ object and type system, writing a custom `GtkWidget` subclass, and using the `GnomeCanvas` widget. It also covers Gdk.

- Part IV, "Appendices," includes a map of the GTK+ and Gnome object hierarchy, with a short description of each object; a map of the GTK+ and Gnome header files; and some pointers to online programming resources.

This book assumes some knowledge of GTK+ programming. Chapter 2, "glib: Portability and Utility," and Chapter 3, "GTK+ Basics," will give you a quick overview if your knowledge is minimal, but they move very quickly. Most of the specific widgets in GTK+ are not covered. The book is intended to introduce Gnome programming and some advanced GTK+ topics; it is a supplement to an introductory GTK+ book.

Due to time and space limitations, only the central Gnome libraries are covered; in particular, CORBA, printing, XML, plug-ins, and scripting are not covered. Most large applications will use these features in addition to the core libraries.

2

glib: Portability and Utility

gLIB IS A C PORTABILITY AND UTILITY LIBRARY for UNIX-like systems and
Windows. This chapter covers some of the most commonly-used library features in
GTK+ and Gnome applications. glib is simple, and the concepts are familiar, so we'll
move quickly. For more complete coverage of glib, see `glib.h` or the free glib reference manual that comes with the library. (By the way, don't be afraid of using the glib,
GTK+, or Gnome header files. They are very clean, easy to read, and handy as a quick
reference. For that matter, don't be afraid to look at the source code if you have very
specific questions about the implementation.)

glib's various facilities are intended to have a consistent interface. The coding style
is semi-object-oriented, and identifiers are prefixed with "g" to create a kind of namespace.

glib has a single header file, `glib.h`.

2.1 Basics

glib provides substitutes for many standard and commonly-used C language constructs.
This section describes glib's fundamental type definitions, macros, memory allocation
routines, and string utility functions.

2.1.1   Type Definitions

Rather than using C's standard types (such as int and long), glib defines its own. These serve a variety of purposes. For example, gint32 is guaranteed to be 32 bits wide, something no standard C type can ensure. guint is simply easier to type than unsigned. A few of the typedefs exist only for consistency. For example, gchar is always equivalent to the standard char.

The following primitive types are defined by glib:

- gint8, guint8, gint16, guint16, gint32, guint32, gint64, and guint64 give you integers of a guaranteed size. Not all platforms provide 64-bit integers. If a platform has them, glib will define G_HAVE_GINT64. (If it isn't obvious, the guint types are unsigned, and the gint types are signed.)

- gboolean is useful for making your code more readable because C has no bool type.

- gchar, gshort, glong, gint, gfloat, and gdouble are purely cosmetic.

- gpointer may be more convenient to type than void *. gconstpointer gives you const void*. (const gpointer will *not* do what you typically want it to. You probably want a pointer to a constant object rather that a constant pointer.)

2.1.2   Frequently Used Macros

glib defines a number of familiar macros used in many C programs; these are shown in Macro Listing 2.1. All of these should be self-explanatory. TRUE/FALSE/NULL are the usual 1/0/((void*)0); MIN()/MAX() return the smaller or larger of their arguments. ABS() returns the absolute value of its argument. CLAMP(x, low, high) means x, unless x is outside the range [low, high]. If x is below the range, low is returned; if x is above the range, high is returned.

Macro Listing 2.1   **Familiar C macros**   *#include <glib.h>*

```
TRUE

FALSE

NULL

MAX(a, b)

MIN(a, b)

ABS(x)

CLAMP(x, low, high)
```

There are also many macros unique to glib, such as the portable gpointer-to-gint and gpointer-to-guint conversions shown in Macro Listing 2.2.

Most of glib's data structures are designed to store a gpointer. If you want to store pointers to dynamically allocated objects, this is the right thing. However, sometimes you want to store a simple list of integers without having to dynamically allocate them. Although the C standard doesn't strictly guarantee it, it is possible to store a gint or guint in a gpointer variable on the wide range of platforms glib has been ported to. In some cases, an intermediate cast is required. The macros shown in Macro Listing 2.2 abstract the presence of the cast.

Here's an example:

```
gint my_int;
gpointer my_pointer;

my_int = 5;
my_pointer = GINT_TO_POINTER(my_int);
printf("We are storing %d\n", GPOINTER_TO_INT(my_pointer));
```

Be careful, though: These macros allow you to store an integer in a pointer, but storing a pointer in an integer will *not* work. To do that portably, you must store the pointer in a long. (It's undoubtedly a bad idea to do so, however.)

Macro Listing 2.2   **Macros for storing integers in pointers**   *#include <glib.h>*

```
GINT_TO_POINTER(p)

GPOINTER_TO_INT(p)

GUINT_TO_POINTER(p)

GPOINTER_TO_UINT(p)
```

2.1.3 Debugging Macros

glib has a nice set of macros that you can use to enforce invariants and preconditions in your code. GTK+ uses these liberally. This is one of the reasons it's so stable and easy to use. They all disappear when you define G_DISABLE_CHECKS or G_DISABLE_ASSERT; so, there's no performance penalty in production code. Using these liberally is a very good idea. You'll find bugs much faster if you do. You can even add assertions and checks whenever you find a bug to be sure that the bug doesn't reappear in future versions—this complements a regression suite. Checks are especially useful when the code you're writing will be used as a black box by other programmers; users will immediately know when and how they've misused your code.

Of course, you should be very careful to ensure that your code isn't subtly dependent on debug-only statements to function correctly. Statements that will disappear in production code should *never* have side effects.

Macro Listing 2.3 shows glib's precondition checks. g_return_if_fail() prints a warning and immediately returns from the current function if condition is FALSE. g_return_val_if_fail() is similar but allows you to return a retval. These macros are incredibly useful. If you use them liberally, especially in combination with GTK+'s runtime type checking, you'll halve the time you spend looking for bad pointers and type errors.

Macro Listing 2.3   **Precondition checks**   *#include <glib.h>*

```
g_return_if_fail(condition)


g_return_val_if_fail(condition, retval)
```

Using these functions is simple. Here's an example from the glib hash table implementation:

```
void
g_hash_table_foreach (GHashTable *hash_table,
                      GHFunc func,
                      gpointer user_data)
{
  GHashNode *node;
  gint i;

  g_return_if_fail (hash_table != NULL);
  g_return_if_fail (func != NULL);

  for (i = 0; i < hash_table->size; i++)
    for (node = hash_table->nodes[i]; node; node = node->next)
      (* func) (node->key, node->value, user_data);
}
```

Without the checks, passing NULL as a parameter to this function would result in a mysterious segmentation fault. The person using the library would have to figure out where the error occurred with a debugger and maybe even dig into the glib code to see what was wrong. With the checks, the person will get a nice error message telling him/her that NULL arguments are not allowed.

glib also has more traditional assertion macros, as shown in Macro Listing 2.4. g_assert() is basically identical to assert(), but it responds to G_DISABLE_ASSERT and behaves consistently across all platforms. g_assert_not_reached() is also provided; this is an assertion that always fails. Assertions call abort() to exit the program and (if your environment supports it) dump a core file for debugging purposes.

Macro Listing 2.4   ***#include* assertions**   *#include <glib.h>*

```
g_assert(condition)

g_assert_not_reached()
```

Fatal assertions should be used to check the *internal consistency* of a function or library, while g_return_if_fail() is intended to ensure that sane values are passed to the public interfaces of a program module. In other words, if an assertion fails, you typically look for a bug in the module containing the assertion; if a g_return_if_fail() check fails, you typically look for the bug in the code that invokes the module. This code from glib's calendrical calculations module shows the difference:

```
GDate*
g_date_new_dmy (GDateDay day, GDateMonth m, GDateYear y)
{
  GDate *d;
  g_return_val_if_fail (g_date_valid_dmy (day, m, y), NULL);

  d = g_new (GDate, 1);

  d->julian = FALSE;
  d->dmy = TRUE;

  d->month = m;
  d->day = day;
  d->year = y;

  g_assert (g_date_valid (d));

  return d;
}
```

The precondition check at the beginning ensures that the user passes in reasonable values for the day, month, and year. The assertion at the end ensures that glib constructed a sane object, given sane values.

g_assert_not_reached() should be used to mark "impossible" situations. A common use is to detect switch statements that don't handle all possible values of an enumeration:

```
switch (val)
  {
    case FOO_ONE:
      break;
    case FOO_TWO:
      break;
    default:
      /* Invalid enumeration value */
      g_assert_not_reached();
      break;
  };
```

All the debugging macros print a warning using glib's `g_log()` facility. This means that the warning includes the name of the originating application or library, and you can optionally install a replacement warning-printing routine. For example, you might send all warnings to a dialog box or log file instead of printing them on the console.

2.1.4   Memory

glib wraps the standard `malloc()` and `free()` with its own `g_` variants, `g_malloc()` and `g_free()`, as shown in Function Listing 2.1. These are nice in several small ways:

- `g_malloc()` always returns a `gpointer`, never a `char*`, so there's no need to cast the return value.
- `g_malloc()` aborts the program if the underlying `malloc()` fails, so you don't have to check for a `NULL` return value.
- `g_malloc()` gracefully handles a `size` of `0` by returning `NULL`.
- `g_free()` will ignore any `NULL` pointers you pass to it.

In addition to these minor conveniences, `g_malloc()` and `g_free()` can support various kinds of memory debugging and profiling. If you pass the `—enable-mem-check` option to glib's configure script, the compiled `g_free()` will warn you whenever you free the same pointer twice. The `—enable-mem-profile` option enables code that keeps memory use statistics. When you call `g_mem_profile()`, they are printed to the console. Finally, you can define `USE_DMALLOC`, and the glib memory wrappers will use the `MAL-LOC()` (and other) debugging macros available in `dmalloc.h` on some platforms.

Function Listing 2.1   *#include* **glib memory allocation**

```
gpointer
g_malloc(gulong size)

void
g_free(gpointer mem)

gpointer
g_realloc(gpointer mem,
          gulong size)

gpointer
g_memdup(gconstpointer mem,
         guint bytesize)
```

It's important to match `g_malloc()` with `g_free()`, plain `malloc()` with `free()`, and (if you're using C++) new with `delete`. Otherwise, bad things could happen as these allocators may use different memory pools (and new/`delete` call constructors and destructors).

Of course, there's a g_realloc() equivalent to realloc(). The g_malloc0() convenience function returns allocated memory filled with Os. g_memdup() copies a block of bytes into newly allocated memory. g_realloc() and g_malloc0() will both return NULL if you request 0 bytes of memory, for consistency with g_malloc(). However, g_memdup() will not.

g_malloc0() fills raw memory with unset bits, not the value 0 for whatever type you intend to put there. Occasionally someone expects to get an array of floating-point numbers initialized to 0.0, but this will *not* work.

Finally, there are type-aware allocation macros, as shown in Macro Listing 2.5. The type argument to each of these is the name of a type, and the count argument is the number of type-size blocks to allocate. These macros save you some typing and multiplication and thus are less error-prone. They automatically cast to the target pointer type. So, attempting to assign the allocated memory to the wrong kind of pointer should trigger a compiler warning (if you have warnings turned on, as a responsible programmer should!).

Macro Listing 2.5 **Allocation macros** *#include <glib.h>*

```
g_new(type, count)

g_new0(type, count)

g_renew(type, mem, count)
```

2.1.5 String Handling

glib provides a number of functions for string handling. Some are unique to glib, and some solve portability concerns. They all interoperate nicely with the glib memory allocation routines.

If you're interested in a better string than gchar*, there's also a GString type. It isn't covered in this book, but documentation is available at http://www.gtk.org/. Function Listing 2.2 shows some substitutes that glib provides for commonly implemented but unportable extensions to ANSI C.

Function Listing 2.2 **Portability wrappers** *#include <glib.h>*

```
gint
g_snprintf(gchar* buf,
           gulong n,
           const gchar* format,
           ...)

gint
g_strcasecmp(const gchar* s1,
             const gchar* s2)
```

continues

Function Listing 2.2 **Continued**

```
gint
g_strncasecmp(const gchar* s1,
              const gchar* s2,
              guint n)
```

One of the annoying things about C is that it provides the crash-causing, security-hole-creating, generally evil `sprintf()`, but the relatively safe and widely implemented `snprintf()` is a vendor extension. `g_snprintf()` wraps native `snprintf()` on platforms that have it and provides an implementation on those that don't. So you can say goodbye to `sprintf()` forever. Even better: classically, `snprintf()` doesn't guarantee that it will NULL-terminate the buffer it fills, but `g_snprintf()` does.

`g_strcasecmp()` and `g_strncasecmp()` perform a case-insensitive comparison of two strings, optionally with a maximum length. `strcasecmp()` is available on many platforms, but not universally. So, using glib instead is advisable.

The functions shown in Function Listing 2.3 modify a string in-place. The first two convert the string to lowercase or uppercase, respectively, and `g_strreverse()` reverses the string's characters. `g_strchug()` and `g_strchomp()` "chug" the string (remove leading spaces) or "chomp" it (remove trailing spaces). These last two return the string in addition to modifying it in-place. In some cases, it may be convenient to use the return value. There is a macro, `g_strstrip()`, that combines both functions to remove both leading and trailing spaces. It is used just as the individual functions are.

Function Listing 2.3 **In-place string modifications** *#include <glib.h>*

```
void
g_strdown(gchar* string)

void
g_strup(gchar* string)

void
g_strreverse(gchar* string)

gchar*
g_strchug(gchar* string)

gchar*
g_strchomp(gchar* string)
```

Function Listing 2.4 shows a few more semi-standard functions' glib wraps. g_strtod is like strtod(). It converts string nptr to a double, and it also attempts to convert the double in the "C" locale if it fails to convert it in the user's default locale. *endptr is set to the first unconverted character (any text after the number representation). If conversion fails, *endptr is set to nptr. endptr may be NULL, causing it to be ignored. g_strerror() and g_strsignal() are like their non-g_ equivalents, but they are portable. (They return a string representation for an errno or a signal number.)

Function Listing 2.4 **String conversions** *#include <glib.h>*

```
gdouble
g_strtod(const gchar* nptr,
         gchar** endptr)

gchar*
g_strerror(gint errnum)

gchar*
g_strsignal(gint signum)
```

Function Listing 2.5 shows glib's rich array of functions for allocating strings. Unsurprisingly, g_strdup() and g_strndup() produce an allocated copy of str or the first *n* characters of str. For consistency with the glib memory allocation functions, they return NULL if passed a NULL pointer. The printf() variants return a formatted string. g_strescape escapes any \ characters in its argument by inserting another \ before them, returning the escaped string. g_strnfill() returns a string of size length filled with fill_char.

g_strdup_printf() deserves a special mention. It is a simpler way to handle this common piece of code:

```
gchar* str = g_malloc(256);
g_snprintf(str, 256, "%d printf-style %s", 1, "format");
```

Instead you could write this more concise code and avoid having to guess the required buffer length:

```
gchar* str = g_strdup_printf("d printf-style s", 1, "format");
```

Function Listing 2.5 **Allocating strings** *#include <glib.h>*

```
gchar*
g_strdup(const gchar* str)

gchar*
g_strndup(const gchar* format,
          guint n)

gchar*
g_strdup_printf(const gchar* format,
                ...)
```

continues

Function Listing 2.5   **Continued**

```
gchar*
g_strdup_vprintf(const gchar* format,
                 va_list args)

gchar*
g_strescape(gchar* string)

gchar*
g_strnfill(guint length,
           gchar fill_char)
```

glib provides some convenient functions for concatenating strings, as shown in Function Listing 2.6. g_strconcat() returns a newly-allocated string created by concatenating each of the strings in the argument list. The last argument must be NULL so that g_strconcat() knows when to stop. g_strjoin() is similar, but separator is inserted between each string. If separator is NULL, no separator is used.

Function Listing 2.6   **Concatenating strings**   *#include <glib.h>*

```
gchar*
g_strconcat(const gchar* string1,
            ...)

gchar*
g_strjoin(const gchar* separator,
          ...)
```

Finally, Function Listing 2.7 summarizes a few routines that manipulate NULL-terminated arrays of strings. g_strsplit() breaks string at each delimiter, returning a newly-allocated array. g_strjoinv() concatenates each string in the array with an optional separator, returning an allocated string. g_strfreev() frees each string in the array and then the array itself.

Function Listing 2.7   **Manipulating *NULL*-terminated string vectors**
#include <glib.h>

```
gchar**
g_strsplit(const gchar* string,
           const gchar* delimiter,
           gint max_tokens)

gchar*
g_strjoinv(const gchar* separator,
           gchar** str_array)

void
g_strfreev(gchar** str_array)
```

2.2 Data Structures

glib implements many common data structures so that you don't have to reinvent the wheel every time you want a linked list. This section covers glib's implementation of linked lists, sorted binary trees, N-ary trees, and hash tables.

2.2.1 Lists

glib provides generic singly and doubly linked lists—GSList and GList, respectively. These are implemented as lists of gpointer. You can use them to hold integers with the GINT_TO_POINTER and GPOINTER_TO_INT macros. GSList and GList have identical APIs, except that there is a g_list_previous() function and no g_slist_previous(). This section discusses GSList, but everything also applies to the doubly linked list.

In the glib implementation, the empty list is simply a NULL pointer. It's always safe to pass NULL to list functions because it's a valid list of length 0. Code to create a list and add one element might look like this:

```
GSList* list = NULL;
gchar* element = g_strdup("a string");
list = g_slist_append(list, element);
```

glib lists have a noticeable Lisp influence: The empty list is a special "nil" value for that reason. g_slist_prepend() works much like cons—it's a constant-time operation that adds a new cell to the front of the list.

Notice that you must replace the list passed to list-modifying functions with their return value in case the head of the list changes. glib will handle memory issues, deallocating and allocating list links as needed.

For example, the following code would remove the just-added element and empty the list:

```
list = g_slist_remove(list, element);
```

list is now NULL. You still have to free element yourself, of course. To clear an entire list, use g_slist_free(), which removes all the links in one fell swoop. g_slist_free() has no return value because it would always be NULL. So, you can simply assign that value to your list if you like. Obviously, g_slist_free() frees only the list cells; it has no way of knowing what to do with the list contents.

To access a list element, you refer to the GSList struct directly:

```
gchar* my_data = list->data;
```

To iterate over the list, you might write code like this:

```
GSList* tmp = list;
while (tmp != NULL)
  {
    printf("List data: %p\n", tmp->data);
    tmp = g_slist_next(tmp);
  }
```

Function Listing 2.8 shows the basic functions for changing GSList contents. For all of these, you must assign the return value to your list pointer in case the head of the list changes. Note that glib does *not* store a pointer to the tail of the list; so prepending is a constant-time operation, while append, insert, and remove are proportional to the list's size.

Function Listing 2.8 **Changing linked list content** *#include <glib.h>*

```
GSList*
g_slist_append(GSList* list,
               gpointer data)

GSList*
g_slist_prepend(GSList* list,
                gpointer data)

GSList*
g_slist_insert(GSList* list,
               gpointer data,
               gint position)

GSList*
g_slist_remove(GSList* list,
               gpointer data)
```

Because appends are a relatively expensive operation, constructing a list using g_slist_append() is a *terrible* idea. Use g_slist_prepend() and then call g_slist_reverse() if you need items in a particular order. If you anticipate frequently appending to a list, you can also keep a pointer to the last element. The following code can be used to perform efficient appends:

```
void
efficient_append(GSList** list, GSList** list_end, gpointer data)
{
  g_return_if_fail(list != NULL);
  g_return_if_fail(list_end != NULL);
  if (*list == NULL)
    {
      g_assert(*list_end == NULL);

      *list = g_slist_append(*list, data);
      *list_end = *list;
    }
  else
    {
      *list_end = g_slist_append(*list_end, data)->next;
    }
}
```

To use this function, you would store the list and its end somewhere and pass their address to `efficient_append()`:

```
GSList* list = NULL;
GSList* list_end = NULL;
efficient_append(&list, &list_end, g_strdup("Foo"));
efficient_append(&list, &list_end, g_strdup("Bar"));
efficient_append(&list, &list_end, g_strdup("Baz"));
```

Of course, you have to be careful not to use any list functions that might change the end of the list without updating `list_end`. To access list elements, the functions in Function Listing 2.9 are provided.

Function Listing 2.9   **Accessing data in a linked list**   *include <glib.h>*

```
GSList*
g_slist_find(GSList* list,
             gpointer data)

GSList*
g_slist_nth(GSList* list,
            guint n)

gpointer
g_slist_nth_data(GSList* list,
                 guint n)

GSList*
g_slist_last(GSList* list)

gint
g_slist_index(GSList* list,
              gpointer data)

void
g_slist_foreach(GSList* list,
                GFunc func,
                gpointer user_data)
```

None of these changes the list's structure. `g_slist_foreach()` applies a `GFunc` to each element of the list. A `GFunc` is defined as follows:

```
typedef void (*GFunc)(gpointer data, gpointer user_data);
```

Used in g_slist_foreach(), your GFunc will be called on each list->data in list, passing the user_data you provided to g_slist_foreach(). g_slist_foreach() is comparable to Scheme's "map" function.

For example, you might have a list of strings, and you might want to be able to create a parallel list with some transformation applied to the strings. Here is some code, using the efficient_append() function from an earlier example:

```
typedef struct _AppendContext AppendContext;
struct _AppendContext {
  GSList* list;
  GSList* list_end;
  const gchar* append;
};

static void
append_foreach(gpointer data, gpointer user_data)
{
  AppendContext* ac = (AppendContext*) user_data;
  gchar* oldstring = (gchar*) data;

  efficient_append(&ac->list, &ac->list_end,
                   g_strconcat(oldstring, ac->append, NULL));
}

GSList*
copy_with_append(GSList* list_of_strings, const gchar* append)
{
  AppendContext ac;

  ac.list = NULL;
  ac.list_end = NULL;
  ac.append = append;

  g_slist_foreach(list_of_strings, append_foreach, &ac);
  return ac.list;
}
```

glib and GTK+ use the "function pointer and user data" idiom heavily. If you have functional programming experience, this is much like using lambda expressions to create a *closure*. (A closure combines a function with an *environment*—a set of name-value bindings. In this case the "environment" is the user data you pass to append_foreach(), and the "closure" is the combination of the function pointer and the user data.)

There are some handy list-manipulation routines, listed in Function Listing 2.10. With the exception of g_slist_copy(), all of these affect the lists in-place. This means you must assign the return value and forget about the passed-in pointer, just as you do when adding or removing list elements. g_slist_copy() returns a newly-allocated list, so you can continue to use both lists. You must free both lists eventually.

Function Listing 2.10   **Manipulating a linked list**   *#include <glib.h>*

```
guint
g_slist_length(GSList* list)

GSList*
g_slist_concat(GSList* list1,
               GSList* list2)

GSList*
g_slist_reverse(GSList* list)

GSList*
g_slist_copy(GSList* list)
```

Finally, there are some provisions for sorted lists, as shown in Function Listing 2.11. To use these, you must write a GCompareFunc, which is just like the comparison function in the standard C qsort(). Using glib types, this becomes:

```
typedef gint (*GCompareFunc) (gconstpointer a, gconstpointer b);
```

If a < b, the function should return a negative value. If a > b, it should return a positive value. If a == b, it should return 0.

Once you have a comparison function, you can insert an element into an already-sorted list or sort an entire list. Lists are sorted in ascending order. You can even recycle your GCompareFunc to find list elements, using g_slist_find_custom(). (A word of caution: GCompareFunc is used inconsistently in glib. Sometimes glib expects an equality predicate instead of a qsort()-style function. However, the usage is consistent within the list API.)

Be careful with sorted lists; misusing them can rapidly become very inefficient. For example, g_slist_insert_sorted() is an O(n) operation, but if you use it in a loop to insert multiple elements, the loop runs in exponential time. It's better to simply prepend all your elements and then call g_slist_sort().

Function Listing 2.11   **Sorted lists**   *include <glib.h>*

```
GSList*
g_slist_insert_sorted(GSList* list,
                      gpointer data,
                      GCompareFunc func)

GSList*
g_slist_sort(GSList* list,
             GCompareFunc func)

GSList*
g_slist_find_custom(GSList* list,
                    gpointer data,
                    GCompareFunc func)
```

2.2.2 Trees

There are two different kinds of trees in glib. GTree is your basic balanced binary tree, useful for storing key-value pairs sorted by key. GNode stores arbitrary tree-structured data, such as a parse tree or taxonomy.

2.2.2.1 GTree

To create and destroy a GTree, use the constructor-destructor pair shown in Function Listing 2.12. GCompareFunc is the same qsort()-style comparison function described for GSList. In this case, it's used to compare keys in the tree.

Function Listing 2.12   **Creating and destroying balanced binary trees**
#include <glib.h>

```
GTree*
g_tree_new(GCompareFunc key_compare_func)

void
g_tree_destroy(GTree* tree)
```

Functions for manipulating the contents of the tree are shown in Function Listing 2.13. All are very straightforward. g_tree_insert() overwrites any existing value; so be careful if the existing value is your only pointer to a chunk of allocated memory. If g_tree_lookup() fails to find the key, it returns NULL. Otherwise, it returns the associated value. Both keys and values have type gpointer, but the GPOINTER_TO_INT() and GPOINTER_TO_UINT() macros allow you to use integers instead.

Function Listing 2.13   **Manipulating *GTree* contents**   *#include <glib.h>*

```
void
g_tree_insert(GTree* tree,
              gpointer key,
              gpointer value)

void
g_tree_remove(GTree* tree,
              gpointer key)

gpointer
g_tree_lookup(GTree* tree,
              gpointer key)
```

The two functions shown in Function Listing 2.14 give you an idea how large the tree is.

Function Listing 2.14   **Determining the size of a GTree**   #include <glib.h>

```
gint
g_tree_nnodes(GTree* tree)

gint
g_tree_height(GTree* tree)
```

Using g_tree_traverse(), shown in Function Listing 2.15, you can walk the entire tree. To use it, you provide a GTraverseFunc, which is passed each key-value pair and a data argument you give to g_tree_traverse(). Traversal continues as long as GTraverseFunc returns FALSE. If it ever returns TRUE, traversal stops. You can use this to search the tree by value. Here is the definition of GTraverseFunc:

```
typedef gint (*GTraverseFunc)(gpointer key, gpointer value, gpointer data);
```

GTraverseType is an enumeration; there are four possible values. Here are their meanings with respect to GTree:

- G_IN_ORDER first recurses the left child of the node (the "lower" key according to your GCompareFunc), calls the traversal function on the key-value pair of the current node, and then recurses the right child. This traversal is in order from lowest to highest, according to your GCompareFunc.

- G_PRE_ORDER calls the traversal function on the key-value pair of the current node, recurses the left child, and then recurses the right child.

- G_POST_ORDER recurses the left child, recurses the right child, and finally calls the traversal function on the current node's key-value pair.

- G_LEVEL_ORDER is meaningful only for GNode. It is not allowed with GTree.

Function Listing 2.15   **Traversing Gtree**   #include <glib.h>

```
void
g_tree_traverse(GTree* tree,
                GTraverseFunc traverse_func,
                GTraverseType traverse_type,
                gpointer data)
```

2.2.2.2 GNode

A GNode is an N-way tree, implemented as a doubly linked list with parent and child lists. Thus, most list operations have analogues in the GNode API. You can also walk the tree in various ways. Here's the declaration for a node:

```
typedef struct _GNode GNode;

struct _GNode
{
  gpointer data;
  GNode *next;
  GNode *prev;
  GNode *parent;
  GNode *children;
};
```

There are macros to access GNode members, as shown in Macro Listing 2.6. As with GList, the data member is intended to be used directly. These macros return the next, prev, and children members, respectively. They also check whether their argument is NULL before dereferencing it and return NULL if it is.

Macro Listing 2.6 **Accessing *GNode* members**   *#include <glib.h>*

```
g_node_prev_sibling(node)

g_node_next_sibling(node)

g_node_first_child(node)
```

To create a node, the usual _new() function is provided (see Function Listing 2.16). g_node_new() creates a childless and parentless node containing data. Typically, g_node_new() is used only to create the root node. Convenience macros are provided that automatically create new nodes as needed.

Function Listing 2.16 **Creating a *GNode***   *#include <glib.h>*

```
GNode*
g_node_new(gpointer data)
```

The fundamental operations shown in Function Listing 2.17 are used to build a tree. Each operation returns the just-added node for convenience when writing loops or recursing the tree. Unlike GList, it is safe to ignore the return value.

Function Listing 2.17 **Building a *GNode* tree**   *#include <glib.h>*

```
GNode*
g_node_insert(GNode* parent,
              gint position,
              GNode* node)

GNode*
g_node_insert_before(GNode* parent,
                     GNode* sibling,
                     GNode* node)

GNode*
g_node_prepend(GNode* parent,
               GNode* node)
```

The convenience macros shown in Macro Listing 2.7 are implemented in terms of the fundamental operations. g_node_append() is analogous to g_node_prepend(). The rest take a data argument, automatically allocate a node for it, and call the corresponding basic operation.

Macro Listing 2.7 **Building a *GNode***   *#include <glib.h>*

```
g_node_append(parent, node)

g_node_insert_data(parent, position, data)

g_node_insert_data_before(parent, sibling, data)

g_node_prepend_data(parent, data)

g_node_append_data(parent, data)
```

The two functions shown in Function Listing 2.18 are used to remove a node from the tree. g_node_destroy() removes the node from a tree, destroying it and all its children. g_node_unlink() removes a node and makes it into a root node. In other words, it converts a subtree into an independent tree.

Function Listing 2.18 **Destroying a *GNode***   *#include <glib.h>*

```
void
g_node_destroy(GNode* root)

void
g_node_unlink(GNode* node)
```

There are two macros for detecting the top and bottom of a GNode tree, as shown in Macro Listing 2.8. A root node is defined as a node with no parent or siblings. A leaf node has no children.

Macro Listing 2.8   **Predicates for *GNode***   *#include <glib.h>*

```
G_NODE_IS_ROOT(node)

G_NODE_IS_LEAF(node)
```

You can ask glib to report useful information about a GNode, including the number of nodes it contains, its root node, its depth, and which node contains a particular data pointer. These functions are shown in Function Listing 2.19.
GTraverseType was introduced earlier, with respect to GTree. Here are the possible values for GNode:

- G_IN_ORDER first recurses the leftmost child of the node, and visits the node itself, then recurses the rest of the node's children. This isn't very useful; mostly it is intended for use with GTree.

- G_PRE_ORDER visits the current node and then recurses each child in turn.

- G_POST_ORDER recurses each child in order and then visits the current node.

- G_LEVEL_ORDER first visits the node itself, then each of the node's children, then the children of the children, then the children of the children of the children, and so on. That is, it visits each node of depth 0, then each node of depth 1, then each node of depth 2, and so on.

GNode's tree-traversal functions have a GTraverseFlags argument. This is a bitfield used to change the nature of the traversal. Currently there are only three flags. You can visit only leaf nodes, only nonleaf nodes, or all nodes:

- G_TRAVERSE_LEAFS means to traverse only leaf nodes.

- G_TRAVERSE_NON_LEAFS means to traverse only nonleaf nodes.

- G_TRAVERSE_ALL is simply a shortcut for (G_TRAVERSE_LEAFS ¦ G_TRAVERSE_NON_LEAFS).

Function Listing 2.19   ***GNode* properties**   *#include <glib.h>*

```
guint
g_node_n_nodes(GNode* root,
                GTraverseFlags flags)

GNode*
g_node_get_root(GNode* node)

gboolean
g_node_is_ancestor(GNode* node,
```

```
                          GNode* descendant)

guint
g_node_depth(GNode* node)

GNode*
g_node_find(GNode* root,
            GTraverseType order,
            GTraverseFlags flags,
            gpointer data)
```

The remaining GNode functions are straightforward; most of them are simply operations on the node's list of children. Function Listing 2.20 lists them. Two function
typedefs are unique to GNode:

```
typedef gboolean (*GNodeTraverseFunc) (GNode* node, gpointer data);
typedef void (*GNodeForeachFunc) (GNode* node, gpointer data);
```

These are called with a pointer to the node being visited and the user data that you
provide. A GNodeTraverseFunc can return TRUE to stop whatever traversal is in progress;
thus, you can use GNodeTraverseFunc in combination with g_node_traverse() to
search the tree by value.

Function Listing 2.20   **Accessing a GNode**   *#include <glib.h>*

```
void
g_node_traverse(GNode* root,
                GTraverseType order,
                GTraverseFlags flags,
                gint max_depth,
                GNodeTraverseFunc func,
                gpointer data)

guint
g_node_max_height(GNode* root)

void
g_node_children_foreach(GNode* node,
                        GTraverseFlags flags,
                        GNodeForeachFunc func,
                        gpointer data)

void
g_node_reverse_children(GNode* node)

guint
g_node_n_children(GNode* node)

GNode*
g_node_nth_child(GNode* node,
                 guint n)
```

continues

Function Listing 2.20 **Continued**

```
GNode*
g_node_last_child(GNode* node)

GNode*
g_node_find_child(GNode* node,
                  GTraverseFlags flags,
                  gpointer data)

gint
g_node_child_position(GNode* node,
                      GNode* child)

gint
g_node_child_index(GNode* node,
                   gpointer data)

GNode*
g_node_first_sibling(GNode* node)

GNode*
g_node_last_sibling(GNode* node)
```

2.2.3 Hash Tables

GHashTable is a simple hash table implementation that provides an associative array with constant-time lookups. To use the hash table, you must provide a GHashFunc, which should return a positive integer when passed a hash key:

```
typedef guint (*GHashFunc) (gconstpointer key);
```

Each returned guint (modulus the size of the table) corresponds to a "slot" or "bucket" in the hash. GHashTable handles collisions by storing a linked list of key-value pairs in each slot. Thus, the guint values returned by your GHashFunc must be fairly evenly distributed over the set of possible guint values, or the hash table will degenerate into a linked list. Your GHashFunc must also be fast because it is used for every lookup.

In addition to GHashFunc, a GCompareFunc is required to test keys for equality. Somewhat unpleasantly, GHashTable doesn't use GCompareFunc in the same way GSList and GTree do although the function signature is the same. Here GCompareFunc is expected to be an equality operator, returning TRUE if its arguments are equal. It should *not* be a qsort()-style comparison function. The key comparison function is used to find the correct key-value pair when hash collisions result in more than one pair in the same hash slot.

To create and destroy a `GHashTable`, use the constructor and destructor shown in Function Listing 2.21. Remember that glib has no way of knowing how to destroy the data contained in your hash table; it destroys only the table itself.

Function Listing 2.21   ***GHashTable***   *#include <glib.h>*

```
GHashTable*
g_hash_table_new(GHashFunc hash_func,
                 GCompareFunc key_compare_func)

void
g_hash_table_destroy(GHashTable* hash_table)
```

Ready-to-use hash and comparison functions are provided for the most common keys: integers, pointers, and strings. These are listed in Function Listing 2.22. The functions for integers accept a pointer to a `gint` rather than the `gint` itself. If you pass `NULL` as the hash function argument to `g_hash_table_new()`, `g_direct_hash()` is used by default. If you pass `NULL` as the key equality function, simple pointer comparison is used (equivalent to `g_direct_equal()`, but without a function call).

Function Listing 2.22   **Prewritten hashes/comparisons**   *#include <glib.h>*

```
guint
g_int_hash(gconstpointer v)

gint
g_int_equal(gconstpointer v1,
            gconstpointer v2)

guint
g_direct_hash(gconstpointer v)

gint
g_direct_equal(gconstpointer v1,
               gconstpointer v2)

guint
g_str_hash(gconstpointer v)

gint
g_str_equal(gconstpointer v1,
            gconstpointer v2)
```

Manipulating the hash is simple. The routines are summarized in Function Listing 2.23. Insertions do *not* copy the key or value; these are entered into the table exactly as you provide them, overwriting any preexisting key-value pair with the same key (remember that "same" is defined by your hash and equality functions). If this is a problem, you must do a lookup or remove before you insert. Be especially careful if you dynamically allocate keys or values.

The simple g_hash_table_lookup() returns the value it finds associated with key, or NULL if there is no value. Sometimes this won't do. For example, NULL may be a valid value in itself. If you're using strings as keys, especially dynamically allocated strings, knowing that a key is in the table might not be enough. You might want to retrieve the exact gchar the hash table is using to represent key "foo." A second lookup function is provided for cases like these. g_hash_table_lookup_extended() returns TRUE if the lookup succeeded. If it returns TRUE, it places the key and value it found in the locations it's given.

Function Listing 2.23   **Manipulating *GHashTable***   *#include <glib.h>*

```
void
g_hash_table_insert(GHashTable* hash_table,
                    gpointer key,
                    gpointer value)

void
g_hash_table_remove(GHashTable * hash_table,
                    gconstpointer key)
gpointer
g_hash_table_lookup(GHashTable * hash_table,
                    gconstpointer key)

gboolean
g_hash_table_lookup_extended(GHashTable* hash_table,
                             gconstpointer lookup_key,
                             gpointer* orig_key,
                             gpointer* value)
```

GHashTable keeps an internal array whose size is a prime number. It also keeps a count of the number of key-value pairs stored in the table. If the average number of pairs per available slot drops below 0.3 (or so), the array is made smaller; if it goes above 3, the array is made larger to reduce collisions. Resizing happens automatically whenever you insert or remove pairs from the table. This ensures that the hash table's memory use is optimal. Unfortunately, it is inefficient to rebuild the hash table repeatedly if you're doing a large number of insertions or removals. To solve the problem, the hash table can be *frozen,* meaning that resizing is temporarily suppressed. When you're done adding and removing items, you simply *thaw* the table, resulting in a single optimal-size calculation. (Be careful, though. A frozen table can end up with many hash collisions if you add large quantities of data. This should be fine as long as you thaw before you do any lookups.) These functions are shown in Function Listing 2.24.

Function Listing 2.24   **Freezing and thawing *GHashTable***   *#include <glib.h>*

```
void
g_hash_table_freeze(GHashTable* hash_table)

void
g_hash_table_thaw(GHashTable* hash_table)
```

2.3   Other Features

There simply isn't enough space in this book to cover all of glib's features. It's worth looking at glib whenever you find yourself thinking, "There really *should* be a function that..." glib.h and the glib documentation on http://www.gtk.org/ are excellent resources.

Here's a brief list of features not already mentioned:

- FLOAT_MAX equivalents for many numeric types.
- Byte-order conversions.
- g_memmove() is more portable than memmove().
- G_DIR_SEPARATOR handles Windows/UNIX differences.
- G_VA_COPY copies a va_list in a portable way.
- Numerous macros permit the use of compiler extensions (especially gcc extensions) in a portable way.
- Portable g_htonl() and other host-to-network conversions.
- A GCache generic cache facility.
- "Callback maintenance" routines register and unregister callbacks.
- The g_log() facility allows you to print warnings, messages, and so on with configurable log levels and pluggable print routines.
- GMemChunk allows you to allocate a large pool of small memory chunks, for efficiency gains compared to g_malloc(). Used in the GList implementation, for example.
- A timer facility.
- Convenience/portability routines let you get the user's home directory, get the name of a /tmp directory, and similar tasks.
- Filename manipulation, such as g_basename() and g_path_is_absolute().

- Bitfield manipulation.
- Enhanced string and array classes.
- Pointer and byte arrays.
- GQuark: Two-way mapping from strings to integer identifiers.
- Routines to associate data with strings or arbitrary pointers.
- A lexical scanner.
- Tab completions.
- Calendrical/date-arithmetic functions.
- A generic event loop abstraction used to implement GTK+'s event loop.
- A portable threads abstraction.

If you need a generally-useful routine that's not in glib already, consider writing it in glib style and contributing it to the library! You get free assistance with design, debugging, and maintenance. Plus, other programmers benefit from the facility you've written. By the time you read this, it's also possible that the feature you want is already in the latest version of glib.

3

GTK+ Basics

T HIS CHAPTER DOES THE USUAL "HELLO, WORLD" to give you an overview of GTK+ and then moves on to discuss some of the essential details that you need to start developing GTK+ applications.

If you've already read the *GTK+ Tutorial* from `http://www.gtk.org/`, or the book by Eric Harlow, *Developing Linux Applications with GTK+ and GDK* (also from New Riders), you may be able to skip or just skim this chapter. If you haven't used GTK+ before, read this chapter carefully.

3.1 A Whirlwind Tour of GTK+

GTK+'s object-oriented coding style, clean design, and carefully followed API naming conventions make programs simple to write and understand. To make the point, here's a complete "Hello, World" in GTK+ (see Figure 3.1). You probably can guess what 80 percent of the code does with no GTK+ experience whatsoever.

Figure 3.1   "Hello, World."

3.1.1   A Complete "Hello, World"

```
#include <gtk/gtk.h>

static gint delete_event_cb(GtkWidget* w, GdkEventAny* e, gpointer data);
static void button_click_cb(GtkWidget* w, gpointer data);

int
main(int argc, char* argv[])
{
  GtkWidget* window;
  GtkWidget* button;
  GtkWidget* label;

  gtk_init(&argc, &argv);

  window = gtk_window_new(GTK_WINDOW_TOPLEVEL);

  button = gtk_button_new();

  label = gtk_label_new("Hello, World!");

  gtk_container_add(GTK_CONTAINER(button), label);
  gtk_container_add(GTK_CONTAINER(window), button);

  gtk_window_set_title(GTK_WINDOW(window), "Hello");
  gtk_container_set_border_width(GTK_CONTAINER(button), 10);

  gtk_signal_connect(GTK_OBJECT(window),
                     "delete_event",
                     GTK_SIGNAL_FUNC(delete_event_cb),
                     NULL);

  gtk_signal_connect(GTK_OBJECT(button),
                     "clicked",
                     GTK_SIGNAL_FUNC(button_click_cb),
                     label);

  gtk_widget_show_all(window);

  gtk_main();

  return 0;
```

```
}

static gint
delete_event_cb(GtkWidget* window, GdkEventAny* e, gpointer data)
{
  gtk_main_quit();
  return FALSE;
}

static void
button_click_cb(GtkWidget* w, gpointer data)
{
  GtkWidget* label;
  gchar* text;
  gchar* tmp;

  label = GTK_WIDGET(data);

  gtk_label_get(GTK_LABEL(label), &text);

  tmp = g_strdup(text);

  g_strreverse(tmp);

  gtk_label_set_text(GTK_LABEL(label), tmp);

  g_free(tmp);
}
```

3.1.1.1   Compiling Hello, World

GTK+ comes with a shell script called `gtk-config`; this script is created when GTK+ is built. Its purpose is to report the compiler flags that you need to compile GTK+ programs. The following shell session demonstrates its features:

```
$ gtk-config --version
1.2.0
$ gtk-config --prefix
/home/hp/local
$ gtk-config --exec-prefix
/home/hp/local
$ gtk-config --libs
-L/home/hp/local/lib -L/usr/X11R6/lib -lgtk -lgdk -rdynamic -lgmodule
➥-lglib -ldl -lXext -lX11 -lm
$ gtk-config --libs gthread
-L/home/hp/local/lib -L/usr/X11R6/lib -lgtk -lgdk -rdynamic -lgmodule
➥-lgthread -lglib -lpthread -ldl -lXext -lX11 -lm
$ gtk-config --cflags
-I/usr/X11R6/include -I/home/hp/local/lib/glib/include -I/home/hp/local/include
$
```

If you're using a Bourne shell variant, such as `bash`, you can use backticks (*not* single quotes!) to execute `gtk-config` and substitute its output. A simple `Makefile` for compiling Hello, World might look like this:

```
CC=gcc

all: hello.c
        $(CC) `gtk-config --libs` `gtk-config --cflags` -o hello hello.c
clean:
        /bin/rm -f *.o *~
```

Of course, this `Makefile` is far too simple for real-world applications. Chapter 4, "Creating Your Source Tree," describes how to set up a more realistic build using `automake` and `autoconf`.

`gtk-config` allows you to locate GTK+ on the user's system instead of hard-coding a location in your `Makefile`. It also comes in handy if you have two versions of GTK+ on your own system. If you install each one in a dedicated directory tree, you can choose one or the other by placing the correct `gtk-config` in your shell's search path.

3.1.2 How It Works

This simple program contains all the essential elements of a GTK+ application. It does not contain any Gnome features, but because Gnome builds on GTK+, the same concepts will apply.

3.1.2.1 Initialization

First, GTK+ must be initialized:

```
gtk_init(&argc, &argv);
```

This call connects to an X server and parses some default arguments understood by all GTK+ programs. Parsed arguments are removed from `argv`, and `argc` is decremented accordingly. `gtk_init()` also registers a "cleanup function" using `atexit()`. In practice, this is important only when you `fork()`; the child process must exit with `atexit()` rather than `exit()` to avoid shutting down GTK+ in the parent.

3.1.2.2 Widgets

Next, any program will have some user interface elements. In the X tradition, these are called *widgets*. All widgets are subclasses of the `GtkWidget` base class; so you can use a `GtkWidget*` to refer to them. (Because C has no native support for object inheritance, GTK+ has its own mechanism. Chapter 9, "The GTK+ Object and Type System," describes this.)

```
window = gtk_window_new(GTK_WINDOW_TOPLEVEL);

button = gtk_button_new();

label  = gtk_label_new("Hello, World!");
```

```
gtk_container_add(GTK_CONTAINER(button), label);
gtk_container_add(GTK_CONTAINER(window), button);

gtk_window_set_title(GTK_WINDOW(window), "Hello");
gtk_container_set_border_width(GTK_CONTAINER(button), 10);
```

Each widget has a function called `gtk_widgetname_new()`, which is analogous to a constructor in C++ or Java. This function allocates a new object, initializes it, and returns a pointer to it. All of the `new()` routines return a `GtkWidget*`, even though they allocate a subclass; this is for convenience.

Once you have a `GtkWidget*` representing an object, you can manipulate the object using its methods. All GTK+ widget functions begin with the name of the type they operate on and accept a pointer to that type as the first argument. In the preceding code, `gtk_container_add()` accepts a `GtkContainer*` as the first argument. The macro `GTK_CONTAINER()` casts the `GtkWidget*` and also performs a runtime type check. Casting is required because C doesn't understand the inheritance relationship.

As you might imagine, `GtkButton` and `GtkWindow` are both subclasses of `GtkContainer`. A `GtkContainer` can hold any other widget. The code creates a top-level window, places a button inside it, and places a label (line of text) inside the button. Then it sets the window title and adds a small cosmetic border around the button.

3.1.2.3 Signals

Next, you'll want to arrange to respond when users manipulate the widgets. In this simple application, two interesting things can happen: The user can click the button or close the window using a window manager decoration. Widgets (actually, all `GtkObjects`) emit *signals* when something interesting happens that a program might want to respond to. To respond to a signal, you "connect a callback" to it—that is, you register a function to be called when the signal is emitted. Here's that code again:

```
gtk_signal_connect(GTK_OBJECT(window),
                   "delete_event",
                   GTK_SIGNAL_FUNC(delete_event_cb),
                   NULL);

gtk_signal_connect(GTK_OBJECT(button),
                   "clicked",
                   GTK_SIGNAL_FUNC(button_click_cb),
                   label);
```

`gtk_signal_connect()` specifies the `GtkObject` to monitor, which signal to connect to, the callback to connect, and finally a `user_data` argument—an arbitrary `gpointer` that will be passed to the callback. The macro `GTK_SIGNAL_FUNC()` casts the callback to a standard function signature. Because callbacks have a variety of type signatures, the alternative would be dozens of `gtk_signal_connect()` variants.

GTK+ performs copious runtime sanity checks. The `GTK_OBJECT()` macro includes a runtime type check in addition to a C cast, and `gtk_signal_connect()` will verify that the object can actually emit the signal you've specified.

3.1.2.4   Entering the Main Loop

Once everything is set up, two steps remain: You need to show the window on the screen and wait for user input.

```
gtk_widget_show_all(window);

gtk_main();

return 0;
```

`gtk_widget_show_all()` recursively calls `gtk_widget_show()` on a container and its children. The following code would have the same effect in this case:

```
gtk_widget_show(label);
gtk_widget_show(button);
gtk_widget_show(window);
```

It's necessary to show every widget that you want to appear on the screen. The opposite operation is called `gtk_widget_hide()`; widgets start their life hidden and can be rehidden or reshown any number of times. It's good practice to show all child widgets before showing the outermost container; otherwise, the user will see the container first, followed by its children. Widgets are not actually visible on the screen until their parent container is shown. The exception to this rule is `GtkWindow` because it has no parent.

Once your widgets have been shown, you want to wait for the user to do something with them. `gtk_main()` enters the GTK+ main loop; the main loop is event-driven. That is, user actions trigger *events* that generally result in signals being emitted and your callbacks being called. `gtk_main()` blocks indefinitely, waiting for and responding to user input. The main loop is described in more detail in Section 3.4. Events and their relation to the main loop are described in Section 10.5.

3.1.2.5   More on Signals and Callbacks

If either of the signals the program connects to is emitted, the corresponding callback is called. Our `"delete_event"` callback ends the `gtk_main()` event loop by calling `gtk_main_quit()`; this causes `gtk_main()` to return, ending the program. The `"clicked"` callback replaces the text from the label with the same text in reverse. Notice that the label was passed to the callback as the `user_data` parameter to `gtk_signal_connect()`.

A common mistake is to assume that all signals use the same kind of callback. This isn't true. Each signal requires a callback with a particular type signature and behavior. The `"clicked"` signal has a very common callback type. Its callback receives a pointer to the widget emitting the signal and any `user_data` provided by the programmer. This callback *must* return `void`, or memory corruption is likely to occur.

"delete_event", on the other hand, is something of a special case. It accepts three arguments. The first and last are analogous to "clicked," and the second is a pointer to the event that triggered the signal. (*Events* are messages from X to the application, reporting mouse movements, key presses, and the like.) The "delete_event" callback returns a "magic" value: If FALSE is returned, GTK+ will destroy the window; if TRUE is returned, GTK+ will do nothing. Return TRUE if you need to do something other than destroy the window. For example, you might want to warn the user about an unsaved document.

Widget header files are the best quick reference for callback signatures. The widget's "class structure" will have a space for a default signal handler; your handler will be modeled on the default one. For example, in gtk/gtkbutton.h the GtkButton class struct looks like this:

```
struct _GtkButtonClass
{
  GtkBinClass  parent_class;

  void (* pressed) (GtkButton *button);
  void (* released) (GtkButton *button);
  void (* clicked) (GtkButton *button);
  void (* enter) (GtkButton *button);
  void (* leave) (GtkButton *button);
};
```

Chapter 9 explains exactly what a class struct is for. For now, just pay attention to the function pointers, and note that they correspond to signals. To get from this:

```
void (* clicked) (GtkButton *button);
```

to this:

```
static void button_click_cb(GtkWidget* w, gpointer data);
```

simply add a gpointer data to the class struct function's signature. In "Hello, World" I've also changed the type from GtkButton* to GtkWidget*. This implicit cast is common because it can be more convenient to have a GtkWidget*. The argument will always be the GtkButton emitting the signal.

Another example may be useful. Here is "delete_event" from gtk/gtkwidget.h:

```
gint (* delete_event)  (GtkWidget   *widget,
                        GdkEventAny *event);
```

and the callback from Hello, World:

```
static gint delete_event_cb(GtkWidget* w, GdkEventAny* e, gpointer data);
```

That's all there is to it. You can write simple GTK+ applications using only the information presented in this section. GTK+ and Gnome are powerful application development tools, because you can think about real functionality instead of struggling to get a window on the screen.

3.2   Containers and Widget Layout

There are two kinds of container widgets in GTK+. Both of them are subclasses of the abstract `GtkContainer`. The first type of container widget always descends from `GtkBin`, another abstract base class. Descendents of `GtkBin` can contain only one child widget; these containers add some kind of functionality to the child. For example, `GtkButton` is a `GtkBin` that makes the child into a clickable button. `GtkFrame` is a `GtkBin` that draws a relieved border around the child. `GtkWindow` places a top-level window around the child.

The second type of container widget often has `GtkContainer` as its immediate parent. These containers can have more than one child, and their purpose is to manage layout. "Manage layout" means that these containers assign *sizes* and *positions* to the widgets they contain. For example, `GtkVBox` arranges its children in a vertical stack. `GtkFixed` allows you to position children at arbitrary coordinates. `GtkPacker` gives you Tk-style layout management.

This section is about the second kind of container. To produce the layout you want without hard-coding any sizes, you'll need to understand how to use these. The goal is to avoid making assumptions about window size, screen size, widget appearance, fonts, and so on. Your application should automatically adapt if these factors change.

3.2.1   Size Allocation

To understand layout containers, you first have to understand how GTK+ widgets negotiate their size. It's quite simple, really. There are only two concepts: *requisition* and *allocation*. These correspond to the two phases of layout.

3.2.1.1   Requisition

A widget's *requisition* consists of a width and a height—the size the widget would like to be. This is represented by a `GtkRequisition` struct:

```
typedef struct _GtkRequisition GtkRequisition;

struct _GtkRequisition
{
  gint16 width;
  gint16 height;
};
```

Different widgets choose what size to request in different ways. `GtkLabel`, for example, requests enough room to display all the text in the label. Most container widgets base their size request on the size requests of their children. For example, if you place several buttons in a box, the box will ask to be large enough to hold all the buttons.

The first phase of layout starts with a top-level widget such as `GtkWindow`. Because it's a container, `GtkWindow` asks its child widget for a size request. That child might ask its own children, and so on recursively. When all child widgets have been queried, `GtkWindow` will finally get a `GtkRequisition` back from its child. Depending on how it was configured, `GtkWindow` may or may not be able to expand to accommodate the size request.

3.2.1.2   Allocation

Phase two of layout begins at this point. `GtkWindow` decides how much space is actually available for its child and then communicates its decision to the child. This is known as the child's *allocation* and is represented by the following struct:

```
typedef struct _GtkAllocation  GtkAllocation;

struct _GtkAllocation
{
  gint16 x;
  gint16 y;
  guint16 width;
  guint16 height;
};
```

The `width` and `height` elements are identical to `GtkRequisition`; they represent the widget's size. A `GtkAllocation` also includes the child's coordinates with respect to its parent. `GtkAllocations` are assigned to children by their parent container.

Widgets are required to honor the `GtkAllocation` given to them. `GtkRequisition` is only a request; widgets must be able to cope with any size.

Given the layout process, it's easy to see what role containers play. Their job is to assemble each child's requisition into a single requisition to be passed up the widget tree and then to divide the allocation they receive between their children. Exactly how this happens depends on the particular container.

3.2.2   *GtkBox*

A `GtkBox` manages a row (`GtkHBox`) or column (`GtkVBox`) of widgets. For `GtkHBox`, all the widgets are assigned the same height; the box's job is to distribute the available width between them. `GtkHBox` optionally uses some of the available width to leave gaps (called "spacing") between widgets. `GtkVBox` is identical, but in the opposite direction (it distributes available height rather than width). `GtkBox` is an abstract base class; `GtkVBox` and `GtkHBox` can be used almost entirely via its interface. Boxes are the most useful container widget.

To create a `GtkBox`, you use one of the constructors shown in Function Listings 3.1 and 3.2. The box constructor functions take two parameters. If `TRUE`, `homogeneous` means that all children of the box will be allocated the same amount of space. `spacing` specifies the amount of space between each child. There are functions to change spacing and toggle homogeneity after the box is created.

Function Listing 3.1   *GtkHBox* **constructor**   *#include <gtk/gtkhbox.h>*

```
GtkWidget*
gtk_hbox_new(gboolean homogeneous,
             gint spacing)
```

Function Listing 3.2   *GtkVBox* **constructor**   *#include <gtk/gtkvbox.h>*

```
GtkWidget*
gtk_vbox_new(gboolean homogeneous,
             gint spacing)
```

There are two basic functions to add a child to a GtkBox; they are shown in Function Listing 3.3.

Function Listing 3.3   **Packing** *GtkBox*   *#include <gtk/gtkbox.h>*

```
void
gtk_box_pack_start(GtkBox* box,
                   GtkWidget* child,
                   gboolean expand,
                   gboolean fill,
                   gint padding)

void
gtk_box_pack_end(GtkBox* box,
                 GtkWidget* child,
                 gboolean expand,
                 gboolean fill,
                 gint padding)
```

A box can contain two sets of widgets. The first set is packed at the "start" (top or left) of the box, and the second is at the "end" (bottom or right). If you pack three widgets into the start of a box, the first widget you pack appears topmost or leftmost. The second follows the first, and the third appears closest to the center of the box. If you then pack three widgets into the end of the same box, the first appears bottommost or rightmost, the second follows it, and the third appears closest to the center. With all six widgets packed, the order from top/left to bottom/right is 1, 2, 3, 3, 2, 1. Figure 3.2 shows this for GtkVBox. The order of packing is important only within each end of the box. For example, we could have switched the packing start and packing end, with the same results.

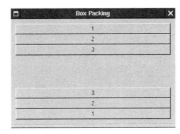

Figure 3.2   Buttons packed into a `GtkVBox`.

3.2.2.1 *GtkBox* Layout Details

Packing is affected by three parameters, which are the same for both start and end packing. The meaning of these parameters is somewhat complicated, because they interact with the box's `homogeneous` setting and with each other.

Here's how a `GtkBox` computes its size request for the "interesting" direction (width for `GtkHBox`, height for `GtkVBox`):

1. The total requested size of each child is considered to be the child's size request plus two times the `padding` value used to pack the child. A child's `padding` is the amount of blank space on either side of it. In short, Child Size = Child Widget's Size Request + (2 × Child Padding).

2. If the box is homogeneous, the base size request for the entire box is equal to the size (request + padding) of the largest child times the number of children. In a homogeneous box, all children are as large as the largest child.

3. If the box is not homogeneous, the base size request for the entire box is the sum of the size (request + padding) of each child.

4. The box-wide `spacing` setting determines how much blank space to leave between children. This value is multiplied by the number of children minus 1 and is added to the base size request. Note that *spacing* does not belong to a child; it is blank space between children and is unaffected by the `expand` and `fill` parameters. *Padding,* on the other hand, is the space around each child and *is* affected by the child's packing parameters.

5. All containers have a "border width" setting. Two times the border width is added to the request, representing a border on either side. Thus, the total size requested by a `GtkBox` is Sum of Child Sizes + (Spacing × (Number of Children - 1)) + (2 × Border Width).

After computing its size request and delivering it to its parent container, GtkBox will receive its size allocation and distribute it among its children as follows:

1. Enough space for the border width and inter-child spacing is subtracted from the allocation; the remainder is the available space for children themselves. This space is divided into two chunks: the amount actually requested by the children (child requisitions and padding), and the "extra." Extra = Allocation Size - Sum of Child Sizes.

2. If the box is not homogeneous, the "extra" space is divided among those children with the expand parameter set to TRUE. These children can expand to fit the available space. If no child can expand, the extra is used to add more space to the center of the box, between the start-packed widgets and the end-packed widgets.

3. If the box is homogeneous, the extra is distributed according to need. Children who requested more space get less extra so that everyone ends up with the same amount of space. The expand parameter is ignored for homogeneous boxes. Extra is distributed to all children, not just the expandable ones.

4. When a child gets some extra space, there are two possibilities. More padding can be added around the child, or the child widget itself can be expanded. The fill parameter determines which will happen. If fill is TRUE, the child widget expands to fill the space. In other words, the entire space becomes the child's allocation. If fill is FALSE, the child's padding is increased to fill the space, and the child is allocated only the space it requested. Note that fill has no effect if expand is set to FALSE and the box is not homogeneous because the child will never receive any extra space to fill.

Whew! Who wants to think about all that? Fortunately, there are some common patterns of usage, so you don't need to solve a multivariate equation to figure out how to use the widget. The authors of the *GTK+ Tutorial* boil things down nicely to five cases that occur in practice; we'll follow in their footsteps here.

3.2.2.2 Non-Homogeneous Box Packing Patterns

There are three interesting ways to pack a nonhomogeneous box. First, you can pack all the widgets into the end of the box with their natural size. This means setting the expand parameter to FALSE:

```
gtk_box_pack_start(GTK_BOX(box),
                   child,
                   FALSE, FALSE, 0);
```

The result is shown in Figure 3.3. The expand parameter is the only one that matters in this case; no children are receiving extra space, so they wouldn't be able to fill it even if fill were TRUE.

Figure 3.3   Nonhomogeneous with `expand` = `FALSE`.

Second, you can spread widgets throughout the box, letting them keep their natural size, as shown in Figure 3.4. This means setting the `expand` parameter to `TRUE`:

```
gtk_box_pack_start(GTK_BOX(box),
                   child,
                   TRUE, FALSE, 0);
```

Figure 3.4   Nonhomogeneous with `expand` = `TRUE` and `fill` = `FALSE`.

Finally, you can fill the box with widgets (letting larger children have more space) by setting the `fill` parameter to `TRUE` as well:

```
gtk_box_pack_start(GTK_BOX(box),
                   child,
                   TRUE, TRUE, 0);
```

This configuration is shown in Figure 3.5.

Figure 3.5   Nonhomogeneous with `expand` = `TRUE` and `fill` = `TRUE`.

3.2.2.3   Homogeneous Box Packing Patterns

There are only two interesting ways to pack a homogeneous box. Recall that the `expand` parameter is irrelevant for homogeneous boxes, so the two cases correspond to the `fill` parameter's setting.

If `fill` is `FALSE`, you get Figure 3.6. Notice that the box is logically divided into three equal parts, but only the largest child widget occupies its entire space. The others are padded to fill their third of the area. If `fill` is `TRUE`, you get Figure 3.7, in which all the widgets are the same size.

Figure 3.6   Homogeneous with `fill = FALSE`.

Figure 3.7   Homogeneous with `fill = TRUE`.

3.2.2.4 Box-Packing Summary

Figure 3.8 shows all five box-packing techniques together. (They are packed into a homogeneous `GtkVBox` with `fill` set to `TRUE` and an interchild spacing of two pixels.) This should give you a sense of their relative effects. Keep in mind that you can also tweak the `padding` and `spacing` parameters to increase or decrease the amount of blank space between widgets. However, you can easily create an ugly layout by using inconsistent spacing. It's a good idea to try to keep widgets "lined up" and consistently spaced.

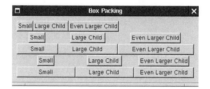

Figure 3.8   All five ways to pack a box.

A final point: Note that the `expand` and `fill` parameters are relevant only when a box's size allocation is larger than its size request. That is, these parameters determine how *extra* space is distributed. Typically, extra space appears when a user resizes a window to make it larger than its default size. Thus, you should always try resizing your windows to be sure your boxes are packed correctly.

3.2.3 *GtkTable*

The second most common layout container is `GtkTable`. `GtkTable` divides a region into cells; you can assign each child widget to a rectangle made up of one or more cells. You can think of `GtkTable` as a sheet of graph paper (with more flexibility because the grid lines don't have to be equidistant, but they can be).

GtkTable comes with the usual constructor and some functions to attach children to it; these are shown in Function Listing 3.4. When creating a table, you specify the number of cells you plan to use; this is purely for efficiency. The table will automatically grow if you place children in cells outside its current area. Like boxes, tables can be homogeneous or not.

Function Listing 3.4   **GtkTable**   *#include <gtk/gtktable.h>*

```
GtkWidget*
gtk_table_new(guint rows,
              guint columns,
              gboolean homogeneous)

GtkWidget*
gtk_table_attach(GtkTable* table,
                 GtkWidget* child,
                 guint left_side,
                 guint right_side,
                 guint top_side,
                 guint bottom_side,
                 GtkAttachOptions xoptions,
                 GtkAttachOptions yoptions,
                 guint xpadding,
                 guint ypadding)
```

The first two arguments to gtk_table_attach() are the table and the child to place in the table. The next four specify which imaginary grid lines should form the child's bounding box. Grid lines are numbered from the top-left (northwest) corner of the table, starting with 0. For example, a 2-by-3 table would have vertical lines 0, 1, 2 and horizontal lines 0, 1, 2, 3. The last two arguments are the amount of padding to put on the left and right sides of the child (xpadding) and the top and bottom sides (ypadding). This is analogous to padding in boxes.

The GtkAttachOptions arguments require some explanation. Here's a summary of possible values. The values are bitmasks, so you can specify more than one by ORing them together.

- GTK_EXPAND specifies that this section of the table will expand to fit the available space, much like the expand option does when you're packing boxes.

- GTK_FILL specifies that the child widget will expand to fill available space. This is important only if GTK_EXPAND is set because GTK_EXPAND permits extra space to exist.

- GTK_SHRINK determines what will happen if there is insufficient space to meet the child's size request. If GTK_SHRINK is set, the child is given a smaller allocation that reflects available space—that is, the table shrinks the child. If it isn't set, the child is given its requested size. This may result in overlapping children within the table, and children will be "chopped off" at the table edges (because they'll try to draw outside the table's GdkWindow).

It's possible to set spacing between rows and columns in addition to padding around particular children; the terms "spacing" and "padding" mean the same thing with respect to tables and boxes. See gtk/gtktable.h for a complete list of available GtkTable functions.

3.2.3.1 *GtkTable* Example

The following code creates a table with four cells and three children; one child covers two cells. The children are packed using different parameters:

```
GtkWidget* window;
GtkWidget* button;
GtkWidget* container;

window = gtk_window_new(GTK_WINDOW_TOPLEVEL);

container = gtk_table_new(2, 2, FALSE);

gtk_container_add(GTK_CONTAINER(window), container);

gtk_window_set_title(GTK_WINDOW(window), "Table Attaching");

gtk_container_set_border_width(GTK_CONTAINER(container), 10);

/* This would be a bad idea in real code, but it lets us
 * experiment with window resizing.
 */
gtk_window_set_policy(GTK_WINDOW(window), TRUE, TRUE, TRUE);

gtk_signal_connect(GTK_OBJECT(window),
                   "delete_event",
                   GTK_SIGNAL_FUNC(delete_event_cb),
                   NULL);

button = gtk_button_new_with_label("1. Doesn't shrink\nor expand");
gtk_table_attach(GTK_TABLE(container),
                 button,
                 0, 1,
                 0, 1,
                 GTK_FILL,
                 GTK_FILL,
                 0,
                 0);
```

```
button = gtk_button_new_with_label("2. Expands and shrinks\nvertically");
gtk_table_attach(GTK_TABLE(container),
                 button,
                 0, 1,
                 1, 2,
                 GTK_FILL,
                 GTK_FILL ¦ GTK_EXPAND ¦ GTK_SHRINK,
                 0,
                 0);

button = gtk_button_new_with_label("3. Expands and shrinks\nin both directions");
gtk_table_attach(GTK_TABLE(container),
                 button,
                 1, 2,
                 0, 2,
                 GTK_FILL ¦ GTK_EXPAND ¦ GTK_SHRINK,
                 GTK_FILL ¦ GTK_EXPAND ¦ GTK_SHRINK,
                 0,
                 0);
```

It's instructive to observe the resulting table as the window is resized. First, here's a quick summary of how the children are attached:

1. The first child will always receive its requested size; it neither expands nor shrinks.

2. The second child can expand and shrink only in the Y direction.

3. The third child can expand and shrink in either direction.

The window's natural size is shown in Figure 3.9. Notice that some cells are given more space than the widgets inside them requested because table cells have to remain aligned. (Recall that a button with a label will request only enough space to display the entire label.) The GTK_FILL flag causes GtkTable to allocate extra space to the widgets themselves instead of leaving blank padding around them.

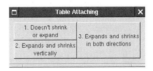

Figure 3.9   GtkTable before resizing.

Now imagine that the user expands the window vertically. As shown in Figure 3.10, extra space is given to the widgets with GTK_EXPAND turned on in the Y direction—namely, widgets 2 and 3—while the widget in the top-left corner remains unchanged.

Figure 3.10 `GtkTable` after expanding the window vertically.

Next, imagine that the user expands the window horizontally. Only child widget 3 can expand horizontally, as shown in Figure 3.11.

Figure 3.11 `GtkTable` after expanding the window horizontally.

Figure 3.12 shows the result if the user shrinks the table vertically. There isn't enough vertical space to give all the widgets their size requests. Child 2 gets shortchanged, while child 1 gets all the vertical space it needs.

Figure 3.12 `GtkTable` after shrinking the window vertically.

Finally, Figure 3.13 shows the result if the user shrinks the table horizontally. Child 3 gets the short end of the stick in this situation.

Figure 3.13 `GtkTable` after shrinking the window horizontally.

It's not a bad idea to try resizing your window like this whenever you're designing a layout, just to be sure that something sane happens. The definition of "sane" varies with the exact widgets you've placed in the layout.

3.2.3.2 Using *gtk_table_attach_defaults()*

Because `gtk_table_attach()` is somewhat cumbersome, there's a simpler version called `gtk_table_attach_defaults()`, shown in Function Listing 3.5. This version attaches the child with the options `GTK_EXPAND` and `GTK_FILL`, and no padding.

It's tempting to use `gtk_table_attach_defaults()` all the time to save typing, but really you shouldn't. In fact, it's probably fair to say that it's rarely used. This function is useful only if the defaults happen to be exactly the settings you want. Most of the time, you need to carefully tweak your table attachment parameters to get really nice behavior when your window is resized. Always try resizing your window to be sure that you've designed your layout well.

Function Listing 3.5 **Attaching with defaults**   *#include <gtk/gtktable.h>*

```
GtkWidget*
gtk_table_attach_defaults(GtkTable* table,
                          GtkWidget* child,
                          guint left_side,
                          guint right_side,
                          guint top_side,
                          guint bottom_side)
```

3.2.4 Other Layout Widgets

Boxes and tables are the most commonly-used layout widgets by far. However, there are a few others for special situations:

- `GtkButtonBox` is a special kind of box appropriate for a dialog's "action area."
- `GtkPacker` supports `Tk`-style packing, which is useful if you're familiar with `Tk`.
- `GtkLayout` provides an infinite scrolling area. In general, scrolling areas in GTK+ are limited to just over 30,000 pixels, because that is the maximum size of an X window.
- `GtkFixed` allows you to manually position widgets at fixed coordinates.

3.2.5   Manually Affecting Layout

It's possible to manually override GTK+'s geometry management. This is a bad idea most of the time, because GTK+'s geometry is essentially the user's preferred geometry, determined by the theme and resizing top-level windows. If you find yourself wanting to do things manually, it's probably because you're using the wrong layout container, or you really should be writing a custom container widget.

You can force a size or position on a widget with the functions shown in Function Listing 3.6. However, it is rarely a good idea to use them. In particular, `gtk_widget_set_usize()` shouldn't be used to set a top-level window's default size. Usually you want to set window size because you've saved the application's state and you're restoring it, or because the user specified a window geometry on the command line. Unfortunately, if you use `gtk_widget_set_usize()`, the user will be unable to shrink the window, and you'll get hate mail. Rather than force a size, you want to specify an initial size with `gtk_window_set_default_size()`, shown in Function Listing 3.7. `gtk_widget_set_usize()` is almost never a good idea for non-top-level widgets either. Most of the time, you can get better results using the proper layout widget.

`gtk_widget_set_uposition()` is useful only for top-level windows. It borders on nonsensical for other widgets, and it will most likely cause bad things to happen. It's primarily used to honor a `--geometry` command-line argument.

All three of these functions can accept `-1` for the `x`, `y`, `width`, or `height` argument. The functions ignore any `-1` argument. This allows you to set only one of the two arguments, leaving the default value for the other.

Function Listing 3.6   **Forcing allocations**   *#include <gtk/gtkwidget.h>*

```
void
gtk_widget_set_uposition(GtkWidget* widget,
                         gint x,
                         gint y)

void
gtk_widget_set_usize(GtkWidget* widget,
                     gint width,
                     gint height)
```

Function Listing 3.7   **Default window size**   *#include <gtk/gtkwindow.h>*

```
void
gtk_window_set_default_size(GtkWindow* window,
                            gint width,
                            gint height)
```

3.3   Widget Concepts

This section discusses concepts that apply to all widgets, including memory management and certain special states widgets can be in. It's a "conceptual" section; however, the concepts are very important to practical topics covered later in the book.

3.3.1   Widget Life Cycle

Widget resource and memory management is mostly automatic. However, there are a couple of "gotchas" to keep in mind if you're doing more complicated things.

A widget can be destroyed at any time by calling `gtk_widget_destroy()` (shown in Function Listing 3.8); destroying a widget frees any associated memory and other resources. If the widget is inside a container, it is automatically removed from the container before it's destroyed. It's worth noting that `gtk_widget_destroy()` is simply another name for `gtk_object_destroy()`; `GtkObjects` have "virtual destructors," so `gtk_object_destroy()` will always do the right thing.

Function Listing 3.8   **Widget destruction**   *#include <gtk/gtkwidget.h>*

```
void
gtk_widget_destroy(GtkWidget* widget)
```

Internally, a reference count is maintained for all widgets (actually, all `GtkObjects`). Objects begin their life with a reference count of 1, even though they haven't yet been referenced. At this stage the object is said to be *floating* and is flagged as such. It is possible to remove the object's initial reference; this is called *sinking* the floating object and will destroy the object if the floating reference was the only one.

Containers first reference, and then sink, any floating widgets that are added to them. By sinking a widget, a container "takes ownership" of it for resource-management purposes. Thus, the reference count of the widget remains 1, but the object is no longer flagged as floating. When a widget is removed from a container—or the container is destroyed—the reference count is decremented to 0. When an object's reference count reaches 0, it is destroyed.

In practice, this means that you have to destroy only top-level widgets; any widgets that are inside a container will be destroyed along with the container.

There's a danger here, however. Sometimes you want to remove a widget from a container; perhaps some element of your interface is optional or appears only under certain circumstances. When you remove the widget (using `gtk_container_remove()`), it will be unreferenced, its reference count will drop to 0, and it will be destroyed. To avoid this situation, you should add a reference to the widget before you remove it. Function Listing 3.9 lists the functions that manipulate reference counts.

Function Listing 3.9 **Reference counting** *#include <gtk/gtkobject.h>*

```
void
gtk_object_ref(GtkObject* object)

void
gtk_object_unref(GtkObject* object)

void
gtk_object_sink(GtkObject* object)
```

`gtk_object_ref()` and `gtk_object_unref()` have widget-specific variants (such as `gtk_widget_ref()`), but the object and widget versions are completely synonymous. The widget-specific versions are leftovers from earlier versions of GTK+. So, to safely remove a widget from a container, you might do this:

```
gtk_widget_ref(widget);
gtk_container_remove(container, widget);
```

The widget now has one reference, held by your code. At some point you'll need to release the reference, destroying the widget. (It would make sense to do so after re-adding the widget to some other container, for example.)

It's worth pointing out that removing widgets from containers is uncommon. In general, it's faster to simply hide the widget with `gtk_widget_hide()` and then `gtk_widget_show()` it later.

`gtk_object_sink()` is used almost exclusively in widget implementations, when you expect to be the primary "owner" of an object. If an object is not "floating," `gtk_object_sink()` has no effect. To claim ownership of a widget, do this:

```
gtk_widget_ref(widget);
gtk_object_sink(GTK_OBJECT(widget));
```

This code adds one reference to the widget. If the widget was "floating," it also subtracts one reference. If the widget was not floating, `gtk_widget_sink()` has no effect.

It's important to understand the details, because in some cases they can be vital. But most of the time, you can get by with a few simple rules:

- You must destroy any top-level widgets when you are done with them, but child widgets are destroyed automatically.

- If you want to remove a widget from a container without destroying it, you must first add a reference to the widget.

- If you add a reference to a widget, you are responsible for unreferencing the widget again when you're done with it.

3.3.2 Realizing, Mapping, and Showing

Fully understanding GTK+ requires a minimal understanding of the X Window System. This book assumes you have a user-level understanding—you know what an X server is, that X is network-transparent, what a window manager does, and so on. A few more details are needed to write programs, however.

One detail is particularly important: the X Window System maintains a tree of *windows.* "Window" in this sense refers to an X window, not a `GtkWindow`. `GtkWindow` is a GTK+-specific concept, a widget that corresponds to an application's top-level X window. An X window is not the user-visible concept "window" represented by `GtkWindow`; rather, it's an abstraction used by the X server to partition the screen. The "background" displayed by your X server is the *root window,* which has no parent. Application windows are typically near-children of the root window. Most window managers create a child of the root window to hold the window's title bar and other decorations, and place the application window inside. Window managers have total control over application windows: They can reposition them, reparent them, and iconify them at will. In turn, application windows can contain subwindows, which are controlled by the application. Note that GTK+ uses the Gdk library rather than using X directly; in Gdk, there is a thin X window wrapper called `GdkWindow`. Don't confuse `GdkWindow` and `GtkWindow`.

An X window, or a `GdkWindow`, gives the X server hints about the structure of the graphics being displayed. Because X is network-transparent, this helps reduce network traffic. The X server knows how to show windows on the screen, hide them, move them around (keeping children in a position relative to their parents), capture events such as mouse movements on a per-window basis, and so on. A `GdkWindow` is also the fundamental unit for drawing graphics. You can't draw to "the screen" as a whole; you must draw on a `GdkWindow`.

Most GTK+ widgets have a corresponding GdkWindow. There are exceptions, such as GtkLabel; these are referred to as "no-window widgets" and are relatively lightweight. Widgets with no associated GdkWindow draw into their parent's GdkWindow. Some operations, such as capturing events, require a GdkWindow; thus, they are impossible on no-window widgets.

Widgets pass through a number of states related to their GdkWindow:

- A widget is said to be *realized* if its corresponding GdkWindow has been created. Widgets are realized via gtk_widget_realize() and unrealized via gtk_widget_unrealize(). Because an X window must have a parent, if a widget is realized, its parent must also be.

- A widget is *mapped* if gdk_window_show() has been called on its GdkWindow. This means the server has been asked to display the window on the screen. Obviously, the GdkWindow must exist, implying that the widget is realized.

- A widget is *visible* if it will automatically be mapped when its parent is mapped. This means that gtk_widget_show() has been called on the widget. A widget can be rendered invisible by calling gtk_widget_hide(); this will either unschedule the pending map or unmap the widget (hide its GdkWindow). Because top-level widgets have no parent, they are mapped as soon as they are shown.

In typical user code, you only need to call gtk_widget_show(); this implies realizing and mapping the widget as soon as its parent is realized and mapped. It's important to understand that gtk_widget_show() has no immediate effect; it merely schedules the widget to be shown. This means you don't have to worry about showing widgets in any particular order. It also means you can't immediately access a widget's GdkWindow. Sometimes you need to access the GdkWindow; in those cases, you'll want to manually call gtk_widget_realize() to create it. gtk_widget_realize() will also realize a widget's parents if appropriate. It's uncommon to need gtk_widget_realize(). If you find that you do, perhaps you are approaching the problem incorrectly.

Destroying a widget automatically reverses the entire sequence of events, recursively unrealizing the widget's children and the widget itself.

Function Listing 3.10 summarizes the functions discussed in this section.

Function Listing 3.10   **Showing/realizing widgets**   *#include <gtk/gtkwidget.h>*

```
%void
gtk_widget_realize(GtkWidget* widget)

void
gtk_widget_unrealize(GtkWidget* widget)

void
gtk_widget_map(GtkWidget* widget)
```

```
void
gtk_widget_unmap(GtkWidget* widget)

void
gtk_widget_show(GtkWidget* widget)

void
gtk_widget_hide(GtkWidget* widget)
```

Macro Listing 3.1 summarizes macros for querying the states discussed in this section.

Macro Listing 3.1 **Widget predicates**   *#include <gtk/gtkwidget.h>*

```
GTK_WIDGET_NO_WINDOW(widget)

GTK_WIDGET_REALIZED(widget)

GTK_WIDGET_MAPPED(widget)

GTK_WIDGET_VISIBLE(widget)
```

3.3.3   Other Widget Concepts

This section describes a few other concepts associated with the GtkWidget base class, including *sensitivity*, *focus*, and *widget states*.

3.3.3.1   Sensitivity

Widgets can be *sensitive* or *insensitive*. Insensitive widgets do not respond to input. (On other platforms, this is termed "ghosted" or "inactive.")

gtk_widget_set_sensitive(), shown in Function Listing 3.11, changes a widget's sensitivity.

Function Listing 3.11 **Changing sensitivity**   *#include <gtk/gtkwidget.h>*

```
void
gtk_widget_set_sensitive(GtkWidget* widget,
                         gboolean setting)
```

By default, sensitivity is set to TRUE. A widget is only "really" sensitive if all its parents are sensitive. That is, you can make an entire container full of widgets (in)sensitive by setting the container's sensitivity. A widget's "real" sensitivity, including its parent's state, can be tested with the GTK_WIDGET_IS_SENSITIVE() macro. The sensitivity of the widget itself, which matters only if the widget's parent is sensitive, can be queried using GTK_WIDGET_SENSITIVE(). These are shown in Macro Listing 3.2.

Macro Listing 3.2 **Sensitivity** *#include <gtk/gtkwidget.h>*

```
GTK_WIDGET_IS_SENSITIVE(widget)

GTK_WIDGET_SENSITIVE(widget)
```

3.3.3.2 Focus

Within each top-level window, one widget at a time may have the *keyboard focus*. Any key events received by the top-level window are forwarded to the focused widget. This is important, because typing something on the keyboard should have only one effect—changing only one text entry field, for example.

Most widgets will give some visual indication that they have the current focus. Using the default GTK+ theme, the focused widget is typically surrounded by a thin black frame. The user can move the focus between widgets, using the arrow keys or the Tab key. Focus can also move to a widget if the user clicks it.

The concept of focus is important for keyboard navigation. For example, pressing Enter or the Spacebar "activates" many widgets if they have the focus.

3.3.3.3 Grabs

Widgets can *grab* the pointer and keyboard away from other widgets. This essentially means that the widget becomes "modal:" Input goes only to that widget, and the focus can't be changed to another widget. A typical reason to grab input is to create a modal dialog. If a window has the grab, interaction with other windows is blocked. Note that there is another, Gdk-level "grab": A Gdk keyboard or pointer grab occurs on an X-server-wide basis. That is, other applications are unable to receive keyboard or mouse events. A widget grab is a GTK+ concept; it grabs events away from other widgets only in the same application.

3.3.3.4 Default

Each window may have at most one *default* widget. For example, dialogs typically have a default button that is activated when the user presses the Enter key.

3.3.3.5 Widget States

Widgets have *states* that determine their appearance:

- Normal: Just like it sounds.
- Active: A button is currently pressed in, or a check box is currently checked, for example.

- Prelight: The mouse is over the widget (typically, clicking would have some effect). Buttons become "highlighted" when you move over them, for example.

- Selected: The widget is in a list or another set of alternatives and is the currently selected option.

- Insensitive: The widget is "ghosted," inactive, or unresponsive; it will not respond to input.

The exact meaning and visual representation of a given state depends on the particular widget and the current theme. You can access the state of the widget using `GTK_WIDGET_STATE()`, as shown in Macro Listing 3.3. This macro returns one of the constants `GTK_STATE_NORMAL`, `GTK_STATE_ACTIVE`, `GTK_STATE_PRELIGHT`, `GTK_STATE_SELECTED`, or `GTK_STATE_INSENSITIVE`.

Macro Listing 3.3   **State accessor**   *#include <gtk/gtkwidget.h>*

```
GTK_WIDGET_STATE(widget)
```

3.4   The Main Loop

The GTK+ main loop's primary role is to listen for events on a file descriptor connected to the X server and forward them to widgets. Section 10.5.3 describes the main loop's event handling in more detail. This section explains the main loop in general terms and describes how to add new functionality to the main loop. It explains, for example, callbacks to be invoked when the loop is idle and at a specified interval, when a file descriptor is ready for reading or writing, and when the main loop exits.

3.4.1   Main Loop Basics

The main loop is primarily implemented by glib, which has a generic main loop abstraction. GTK+ attaches the glib main loop to Gdk's X server connection and presents a convenient interface (the glib loop is slightly lower level than the GTK+ loop). The core GTK+ main loop interface is shown in Function Listing 3.12.

`gtk_main()` runs the main loop. `gtk_main()` will not return until `gtk_main_quit()` is called. `gtk_main()` can be called recursively; each call to `gtk_main_quit()` exits one instance of `gtk_main()`. `gtk_main_level()` returns the level of recursion; that is, it returns zero if no `gtk_main()` is on the stack, one if one `gtk_main()` is running, and so forth.

All instances of `gtk_main()` are functionally identical; they are all watching the same connection to the X server and working from the same event queue. `gtk_main()` instances are used to block, halting a function's flow of control until some conditions are met. All GTK+ programs use this technique to keep `main()` from exiting while the application is running. The `gnome_dialog_run()` function (see Section 7.2) uses a recursive main loop so that it doesn't return until the user clicks a dialog button.

Sometimes you want to process a few events without handing the flow of control to
gtk_main().You can perform a single iteration of the main loop by calling
gtk_main_iteration().This might process a single event, for example; it depends on
what tasks are pending.You can check whether any events need to be processed by
calling the gtk_events_pending() predicate.Together, these two functions allow you
to temporarily return control to GTK+ so that the GUI can "catch up." For example,
during a long computation, you will want to display a progress bar; you must allow the
GTK+ main loop to run periodically so that GTK+ can redraw the progress bar. Use
this code:

```
while (gtk_events_pending())
  gtk_main_iteration();
```

Function Listing 3.12   **Main Loop**   *#include <gtk/gtkmain.h>*

```
void
gtk_main()
void
gtk_main_quit()
void
gtk_main_iteration()
gint
gtk_events_pending()
guint
gtk_main_level()
```

3.4.2   Quit Functions

A *quit function* is a callback to be invoked when gtk_main_quit() is called. In other
words, the callback runs just before gtk_main() returns.The callback should be a
GtkFunction, defined as follows:

```
typedef gint (*GtkFunction) (gpointer data);
```

Quit functions are added with gtk_quit_add() (refer to Function Listing 3.13).When
adding a quit function, you must specify a main loop level as returned by
gtk_main_level().The second and third arguments specify a callback and callback
data.

The callback's return value indicates whether the callback should be invoked again.
As long as the callback returns TRUE, it will be repeatedly invoked.As soon as it returns
FALSE, it is disconnected.When all quit functions have returned FALSE, gtk_main() can
return.

gtk_quit_add() returns an ID number that can be used to remove the quit
function with gtk_quit_remove().You can also remove a quit function by passing
its callback data to gtk_quit_remove_by_data().

Function Listing 3.13   **Quit Functions**   *#include <gtk/gtkmain.h>*

```
guint
gtk_quit_add(guint main_level,
             GtkFunction function,
             gpointer data)
void
gtk_quit_remove(guint quit_handler_id)
void
gtk_quit_remove_by_data(gpointer data)
```

3.4.3   Timeout Functions

Timeout functions are connected and disconnected exactly as quit functions are; the expected callback is the same. gtk_timeout_add() expects an interval argument; the callback is invoked every interval milliseconds. If the callback ever returns FALSE, it is removed from the list of timeout functions just as if you had called gtk_timeout _remove(). It is not safe to call gtk_timeout_remove() from within a timeout function; this modifies the timeout list while GTK+ is iterating over it, causing a crash. Instead, return FALSE to remove a function.

Function Listing 3.14   **Timeout Functions**   *#include <gtk/gtkmain.h>*

```
guint
gtk_timeout_add(guint32 interval,
                GtkFunction function,
                gpointer data)
void
gtk_timeout_remove(guint timeout_handler_id)
```

3.4.4   Idle Functions

Idle functions run continuously while the GTK+ main loop has nothing else to do. Idle functions run only when the event queue is empty and the main loop would normally sit idly, waiting for something to happen. As long as they return TRUE, they are invoked over and over; when they return FALSE, they are removed just as if gtk_idle_remove() had been called.

The idle function API, shown in Function Listing 3.15, is identical to the timeout and quit function APIs. Again, gtk_idle_remove() should not be called from within an idle function because it will corrupt GTK+'s idle function list. Return FALSE to remove the idle function.

Idle functions are mostly useful to queue "one-shot" code, which is run after all events have been handled. Relatively expensive operations such as GTK+ size negotiation and GnomeCanvas repaints take place in idle functions that return FALSE. This ensures that expensive operations are performed only once, even though multiple consecutive events independently require the recalculation.

The GTK+ main loop contains a simple scheduler; idle functions actually have priorities assigned to them just as UNIX processes do. You can assign a non-default priority to your idle functions, but it's a complicated topic and outside the scope of this book.

Function Listing 3.15   **Idle Functions**   *#include <gtk/gtkmain.h>*

```
guint
gtk_idle_add(GtkFunction function,
             gpointer data)
void
gtk_idle_remove(guint idle_handler_id)
void
gtk_idle_remove_by_data(gpointer data)
```

3.4.5   Input Functions

Input functions are handled on the Gdk level; strictly speaking they are independent of the GTK+ main loop. They are invoked when a given file descriptor is ready for reading or writing. They are especially useful for networked applications.

To add an input function, you specify the file descriptor to monitor, the state you want to wait for (ready for reading or writing,) and a callback/data pair. Function Listing 3.16 shows the API. Functions can be removed using the tag returned by gdk_input_add(). Unlike quit, timeout, and idle functions, it should be safe to call gdk_input_remove() from inside the input function; GTK+ will not be in the midst of iterating over the list of input functions.

To specify the condition(s) to wait for, use the GdkInputCondition flags: GDK_INPUT_READ, GDK_INPUT_WRITE, and GDK_INPUT_EXCEPTION. You can use one or more flags together. These correspond to the three file descriptor sets passed to the select() system call. (Consult a good UNIX programming book for details.) If any condition is met, the input function is invoked.

The callback should look like this:

```
typedef void (*GdkInputFunction) (gpointer data,
                                  gint source_fd,
                                  GdkInputCondition condition);
```

It receives your callback data, the file descriptor being watched, and the conditions that were met (possibly a subset of those you were watching for).

Function Listing 3.16 **Input Functions** *#include <gdk/gdk.h>*

```
gint
gdk_input_add(gint source_fd,
              GdkInputCondition condition,
              GdkInputFunction function,
              gpointer data)
void
gdk_input_remove(gint tag)
```

Building a Gnome Application

4   Creating Your Source Tree

5   Gnome Application Basics

6   The Main Window: GnomeApp

7   User Communication: Dialogs

8   Gnome Application Checklist

4

Creating Your Source Tree

ALMOST ALL GNOME APPLICATIONS USE THE SAME build system based on the GNU tools `automake`, `autoconf`, and `libtool`. GTK+ and Gnome provide a set of `autoconf` macros that make it easy to create a portable, standards–compliant build setup. Due to the bewildering array of tools involved, it can be difficult to figure out how Gnome source trees work; there are manuals available for each tool, but none describes the "big picture." This chapter gives you a simple overview that should help you get started. It also covers some Gnome-specific details and tells you how to ship and install your application's icons, translations, and documentation.

If you're writing a large application or a library, this chapter won't have all the information you need; you will probably need to consult the GNU tools' manuals to get more details. A complete discussion would fill the entire book.

Beginning with this chapter and continuing throughout Part II of the book, a sample application called GnomeHello will be used to demonstrate Gnome features. The GnomeHello source code is listed in Appendix E, "Code Listings," and the entire GnomeHello source tree is available online. It may be convenient to use it as a template for your own application's source code.

You may miss the simple `Makefile` made possible by the `gtk-config` script; there is an equivalent `gnome-config` script (use `gnome-config---help` to learn how to use it). However, these simple makefiles are not adequate for any real–world application.

4.1 Overview of a Gnome Source Tree

Gnome application build trees and distributed tarballs follow a set of conventions, most of which are widespread in the free software community. Aspects of these conventions are formalized in documents such as the GNU Project's Coding Standards (`http://www.gnu.org/prep/standards_toc.html`) and the Linux Filesystem Hierarchy Standard (`http://www.pathname.com/fhs/`). It's worth using these standards even with non-free software—partially because they are very good from a technical standpoint, and partially because "going with the flow" will save you a lot of trouble, especially if you're using the GNU toolset. Besides, you might want to free your software someday.

The GNU toolset, including `automake` and `autoconf`, will make it easy for you to comply with these standards. However, sometimes there are reasons not to use the GNU tools; for example, you may want a unified build that works on platforms such as Windows and MacOS. (Some of the tools do work with Windows using the Cygnus "Cygwin" environment; see `http://sourceware.cygnus.com/cygwin` for more information.)

If you use `autoconf` and `automake`, you should know that users are not required to have these tools in order to build your software. The purpose of the tools is to build portable shell scripts and makefiles that will work in the user's environment.

The `autoconf` package encompasses the `aclocal`, `autoheader`, and `autoconf` executables. Together, these tools are used to create a portable shell script called `configure`; `configure` is distributed to users with your software package. It explores the compilation system and creates makefiles and a special header called `config.h`. The files created by `configure` are adapted to the specifics of the user's system.

`configure` creates each `Makefile` from a template, called `Makefile.in`. `automake` is a tool for creating these templates. `automake` generates `Makefile.in` from a hand-written `Makefile.am`. You distribute `Makefile.in` with your software, and users create a `Makefile` when they run `configure`.

The `libtool` package is the third important GNU tool; its purpose is to abstract the idiosyncrasies of shared libraries. (Static library behavior is fairly uniform across UNIX-like systems, but shared libraries present major portability issues.)

The following list informally outlines some of the characteristics most Gnome packages have in common:

- A file called `README` that describes the package.

- A file called `INSTALL` that explains how to compile and install the package.

- A script called `configure` that automatically adapts the program to platform-specific features (or the lack thereof). `configure` is expected to take an argument `--prefix`, specifying where to install the package.

- Standard `make` targets, such as `clean` and so on.

- A file called `COPYING` that contains the package's copyright.

- A `ChangeLog`, in which changes to the software are recorded.

- Tar files are traditionally compressed with `gzip`, and their name includes the package version (for example, `foo-0.2.1.tar.gz`). They should unpack into a single directory, named with package and version—`foo-0.2.1`.

- *Internationalization* is provided via the GNU `gettext` package. A copy of `gettext` is shipped along with the application, so the user does not have to acquire one.

4.2   Source Tree Checklist

As an initial overview, here are the important steps in creating a skeletal Gnome source tree. If you are starting a new program, follow this list so that you won't forget anything. The rest of this chapter explains the checklist in more detail. It might also be helpful to download a Gnome package or two to look at as you follow the discussion (in particular, the "GnomeHello" source tree is intended to illustrate a proper build setup).

1. Create a toplevel directory to hold all the components of your application, including build files, documentation, and translations.

2. It's often nice to create a `src` subdirectory within this toplevel directory to keep source code separate from everything else.

3. In the toplevel directory, create `AUTHORS`, `NEWS`, `COPYING`, and `README` files. If desired, also create an empty `ChangeLog`.

4. Write a `configure.in`. The main purpose of `configure.in` is to determine which compiler, compiler flags, and linker flags to use. `configure.in` can also `#define` symbols to reflect features of the current platform, placing these definitions in the automatically generated file `config.h`.

5. Write `acconfig.h`, which is a template for `config.h.in`. This file should `#undef` each symbol you will potentially `#define` in `config.h`. The `autoheader` program creates `config.h.in` based on `acconfig.h`, and `autoconf` creates `config.h`. `autoheader` comes with `autoconf`.

6. Create an empty file called `stamp.h.in`; this is used by the `AM_CONFIG_HEADER` macro in `configure.in`.

7. Write a `Makefile.am` in the toplevel directory, listing each subdirectory that contains source code. In each subdirectory, also write a `Makefile.am`.

8. Run the gettextize program that comes with the gettext package. This creates the intl and po directories, which are needed for internationalization (gettextize is documented in the gettext manual). The intl directory contains the GNU gettext source code; if users compiling the program do not have gettext, they can pass the --with-included-gettext option to configure to automatically compile a static version in the intl directory. The po directory holds the translation files; gettextize will also create a file called po/Makefile.in.in, which is used to build the translations.

9. Create a file called po/POTFILES.in to list source files that should be scanned for strings to translate. POTFILES.in can be empty at first.

10. Copy autogen.sh and the macros directory from another Gnome module. You must modify autogen.sh to reflect the name of your package. Running autogen.sh will invoke libtoolize, aclocal, autoheader, automake, and autoconf.

11. autogen.sh invokes automake with the --add-missing argument. This will add some files, such as INSTALL, with generic installation instructions. You can (and should) edit INSTALL to include any specific instructions for your application. autogen.sh will also create a Makefile in each directory.

4.3 *configure.in*

autoconf processes configure.in to produce a configure script. configure is a portable shell script that examines the build environment to determine which libraries are available, which features the platform has, where libraries and headers are located, and so on. Based on this information, it modifies compiler flags, generates makefiles, and/or outputs the file config.h with appropriate preprocessor symbols defined. Again, configure does not require autoconf to run; because you generate it before distributing your software, users do not have to have autoconf.

Your job is to write configure.in. The file is basically a series of m4 macros, which expand to snippets of shell script according to the parameters you pass them. You can also write shell code manually. Really understanding how to write a configure.in requires some knowledge of m4 (which is pretty simple) and some knowledge of the Bourne shell (which is a black art). Fortunately, you can cheat: Start with an existing configure.in and modify it slightly to suit your application. You can also use the extensive autoconf manual, which describes the many pre-written macros shipped with autoconf.

The GTK+ and Gnome developers have simplified things still further by providing macros to locate GTK+ and Gnome on the user's system.

Here is a sample `configure.in` from a Gnome version of "Hello, World":

```
AC_INIT(src/hello.c)

AM_CONFIG_HEADER(config.h)

AM_INIT_AUTOMAKE(GnomeHello, 0.1)

AM_MAINTAINER_MODE

AM_ACLOCAL_INCLUDE(macros)

GNOME_INIT

AC_PROG_CC
AC_ISC_POSIX
AC_HEADER_STDC
AC_ARG_PROGRAM
AM_PROG_LIBTOOL

GNOME_COMPILE_WARNINGS

ALL_LINGUAS="es"
AM_GNU_GETTEXT

AC_SUBST(CFLAGS)
AC_SUBST(CPPFLAGS)
AC_SUBST(LDFLAGS)

AC_OUTPUT([
Makefile
macros/Makefile
src/Makefile
intl/Makefile
po/Makefile.in
pixmaps/Makefile
doc/Makefile
doc/C/Makefile
doc/es/Makefile
])
```

Before describing each macro, we should make some general points. First, those macros that begin with AC come with autoconf, and those that begin with AM usually come with automake. (This is useful knowledge when you're trying to find documentation for them.) The macros that begin with GNOME come in the Gnome macros directory. These macros are written in m4; the standard ones from autoconf and automake reside in /usr/share/aclocal—if you installed autoconf and automake under /usr. (An aside: the macros directory is not a good thing; each Gnome package should install its own m4 files to /usr/share/aclocal. Newer Gnome versions attempt to fix the problem.)

The following list describes each macro in detail:

- `AC_INIT` is always the first macro in `configure.in`. It expands to a lot of boiler-plate code shared by all `configure` scripts; this code parses the command line arguments to `configure`. The macro's one argument is a file that should be present in the source directory; it is used as a sanity check, to make sure `configure` has correctly located the source directory.

- `AM_CONFIG_HEADER` specifies a header file to create; this will almost always be `config.h`. The created header file will contain C preprocessor symbols defined by `configure`. At a minimum, the symbols `PACKAGE` and `VERSION` will be defined, which makes it easy to put the name and version of your program in your code without hard-coding them. (Your non-public source files should `#include <config.h>` to take advantage of its definitions; however, `config.h` should never be installed because it would conflict with other packages.)

- `AM_INIT_AUTOMAKE` initializes `automake`. The arguments to this macro are the name and version of the package being compiled. (These arguments become the values of `PACKAGE` and `VERSION`, defined in `config.h`.)

- `AM_MAINTAINER_MODE` turns off maintainer-only makefile targets by default and changes `configure` to understand an `--enable-maintainer-mode` option. `--enable-maintainer-mode` turns the maintainer-only targets back on. The maintainer-only makefile targets permit end users to clean automatically generated files such as `configure`, which means they have to have `autoconf` and `automake` installed to repair the damage. `AM_MAINTAINER_MODE` makes it a bit harder for a user to shoot herself/himself in the foot. Note, however, that the `autogen.sh` script used in Gnome automatically passes `--enable-maintainer-mode` to `configure` because `autogen.sh` is intended for developers to use.

- `AM_ACLOCAL_INCLUDE` specifies an additional directory in which to search for `m4` macros. In this case, it specifies the `macros` subdirectory, to which you should have copied the Gnome macros.

- `GNOME_INIT` adds a number of Gnome-related command-line arguments to `configure` and defines makefile variables containing the necessary preprocessor and linker flags for Gnome programs. These flags are obtained from a `gnome-config` script installed by the `gnome-libs` package.

- `AC_PROG_CC` locates the C compiler.

- `AC_ISC_POSIX` adds some flags needed for POSIX compatibility on certain platforms.

- `AC_HEADER_STDC` checks whether the present system has the standard ANSI header files and defines `STDC_HEADERS` if so.

- `AC_ARG_PROGRAM` adds options to `configure` so the user can modify the name of an installed program. (This is useful if your program happens to have the same name as some locally installed program on their system.)

- `AM_PROG_LIBTOOL` is used by `automake` to set up its use of `libtool`. This is required only if you are planning to build a shared library or dynamically loadable modules; it is unnecessary for this early version of GnomeHello, but we're planning ahead for the deluxe version.

- `GNOME_COMPILE_WARNINGS` adds a number of warning options to the `gcc` command line, but does nothing for most other compilers.

- `ALL_LINGUAS="es"` is not a macro, just a bit of shell code. It contains a space-separated list of language abbreviations, corresponding to `.po` files in the po subdirectory. (`.po` files contain translations into other languages, so `ALL_LINGUAS` should list all languages your program has been translated into.)

- `AM_GNU_GETTEXT` is used by `automake`, but the macro itself is distributed with the `gettext` package. It causes `automake` to perform a number of internationalization-related tasks.

- `AC_SUBST` "exports" a variable into the files generated by `configure`. More on this later.

- `AC_OUTPUT` lists the files to be created by the `configure` script. These will be created from a file with the same name, with `.in` appended. For example, the output file `src/Makefile` is generated from `src/Makefile.in`, and `config.h` comes from `config.h.in`.

In the `AC_OUTPUT` stage, `configure` processes files containing variables marked with two @ symbols (for example, `@PACKAGE@`). It recognizes such variables only if `AC_SUBST` was used to "export" the variable (many of the pre-written macros discussed above use `AC_SUBST` to define variables). Most commonly, this feature is used to convert a `Makefile.in` to a `Makefile`. `Makefile.in` is typically generated by `automake` from `Makefile.am`. (However, you can use `autoconf` without `automake` and write `Makefile.in` yourself.)

4.4 *Makefile.am*

`automake` processes `Makefile.am` to produce a standards-compliant `Makefile.in`. `automake` does a lot of work for you: It keeps up with dependencies between source files, for example, and it creates all the standard targets, such as `install` and `clean`. It also creates more complex targets. Simply typing `make dist` creates a standard `.tar.gz` file if your `Makefile.am` is correct.

The `Makefile.am` in the top source directory is generally very simple; here is an example:

```
SUBDIRS = macros po intl src pixmaps doc

EXTRA_DIST = \
        gnome-hello.desktop

Applicationsdir = $(datadir)/gnome/apps/Applications
Applications_DATA = gnome-hello.desktop
```

The `SUBDIRS` line instructs `automake` to recursively look for `Makefile.am` files in the given subdirectories. (Section 4.6.2 describes the remainder of the file; ignore it for now.)

The `Makefile.am` in the `src` directory is a little more interesting:

```
INCLUDES = -I$(top_srcdir) -I$(includedir) $(GNOME_INCLUDEDIR) \
        -DG_LOG_DOMAIN=\"GnomeHello\" -
DGNOMELOCALEDIR=\""$(datadir)/locale"\" \
        -I../intl -I$(top_srcdir)/intl

bin_PROGRAMS = hello

hello_SOURCES =         \
        app.c          \
        hello.c        \
        menus.c        \
        app.h          \
        hello.h        \
        menus.h

hello_LDADD = $(GNOMEUI_LIBS) $(GNOME_LIBDIR) $(INTLLIBS)
```

`automake` understands a number of "magic variables" and can use them to create `Makefile.in`. In the short example above, the following variables are used:

- `INCLUDES` specifies flags to pass to the C compiler during the compile phase (as opposed to the link phase). The variables used in this line come from the `configure.in` shown in the previous section.
- `bin_PROGRAMS` lists the programs to be compiled.
- `hello_SOURCES` lists the files to be compiled and linked to create the program called `hello`; `hello` must be listed in `bin_PROGRAMS`. All files in this variable are automatically included in the distribution.
- `hello_LDADD` lists flags to be passed to the linker (in this case, Gnome library flags determined by `configure`).

Several elements of the `INCLUDES` line should be used in all Gnome programs. `G_LOG_DOMAIN` should always be defined; error messages from checks and assertions will report this value so that you can determine where the error occurred (either in your code or in a library). `GNOMELOCALEDIR` is used to locate translation files. The `intl` directory is added to the header search path so the application can find the `intl` headers.

You can do many more complex things in `Makefile.am`. In particular, you can add @-bounded variables to be substituted by `configure`, you can conditionally include portions of the `Makefile` based on `configure` checks, and you can build libraries. The `automake` manual gives more details.

Table 4.1 summarizes the most interesting targets generated by automake. Of course the default target is all, which compiles the program. The GNU Coding Standards (http://www.gnu.org/prep/standards_toc.html) have more information about these targets and GNU makefiles in general.

Table 4.1 **Standard make targets**

Target	Description
dist	Builds a tarball (.tar.gz) for distribution.
distcheck	Builds a tarball and then tries to compile it.
clean	Deletes the results of compilation (object files and executables), but may not delete some generated files that come with the distribution.
install	Creates installation directories if needed and copies the software into them.
uninstall	Reverses the install (deletes installed files).
distclean	Reverses the effects of the configure script and the all target; that is, reverts a tarball to its pristine state.
mostlyclean	Nearly the same as clean, but this leaves some object files that most likely don't need to be rebuilt.
maintainer-clean	More thorough than clean; may delete some files that require special tools to rebuild, such as machine-generated source code.
tags	Creates a tag table for use with Emacs.
check	Runs a test suite if you have one.

4.5 Relevant GNU Documentation

A number of GNU manuals are relevant to the topics discussed in this chapter and will give you a deeper understanding. It is worth reading the tutorial sections of each of these. The following GNU manuals come with the software and are also available from http://www.gnu.org/doc/doc.html.

- The libtool manual explains the intermediate.lo and .la files created while your program or library is compiling; automake generates makefiles that use libtool.

- The autoconf manual explains how to write configure.in and its associated files.

- The automake manual explains how to write a Makefile.am.

- The gettext manual has sections titled "Programmers" and "Maintainers." You should read those sections to learn how the intl and po subdirectories work.

- The GNU coding standards describe how GNU packages should behave; `autoconf` and `automake` try to implement these standards.

- The GNU `hello` package is intended to demonstrate the GNU packaging standards and is an excellent source of examples. "GnomeHello" and other Gnome packages are good sources of Gnome-specific examples, of course.

- The manuals for `make`, the Bourne shell, and `m4` are essential if you need to write custom `configure` checks or add `Makefile` targets outside of `automake`'s capabilities.

4.6   Installing Support Files

Complete Gnome applications consist of more than just code. They have online help, are listed on the Gnome panel's menu, have translations, and have a desktop icon. They might come with pixmaps as well, such as a logo for the "about" dialog box, a graphic for a "wizard," or small icons to help the user rapidly distinguish menu items or list elements. This section tells you how to ship some of these files.

4.6.1   Installing Datafiles: Documentation and Pixmaps

Documentation and pixmaps are installed in much the same way. `automake` allows you to install datafiles to arbitrary locations, and you can use variables defined by `configure` to decide where they should go.

4.6.1.1   Pixmaps

To install datafiles from your `Makefile.am`, you simply come up with a name for the install target—`pixmap` seems good—and then create a variable for the directory and a corresponding variable for the files to be installed there. Here's an example:

```
EXTRA_DIST = gnome-hello-logo.png

pixmapdir = $(datadir)/pixmaps

pixmap_DATA = gnome-hello-logo.png
```

The "pixmap" string connects the `pixmapdir` variable with the `pixmap_DATA` variable. `automake` interprets the `_DATA` suffix and generates appropriate rules in `Makefile.in`. This `Makefile.am` segment installs `gnome-hello-logo.png` into `$(datadir)/pixmaps`; `$(datadir)` is a variable filled in by `configure`. Typically `$(datadir)` is `/usr/local/share` (more precisely, `$(prefix)/share`), which is the standard location for architecture-independent datafiles (that is, files that can be shared between several systems with different binary file formats).

Section 4.6.3 describes the `EXTRA_DIST` variable.

The standard location for Gnome pixmaps is `$(datadir)/pixmaps`, so we used that in the example. The Gnome Project encourages the use of PNG format for all pixmaps. This format is supported by `gdk_imlib`, the Gnome image-loading library. It is also small, fast, and unencumbered by patents.

4.6.1.2 Documentation

Installing documentation uses the same principles, with a little more complication. Gnome documentation is typically written in DocBook. DocBook is an SGML DTD ("Document Type Definition") like HTML. However, DocBook's tags are designed for technical documentation. Documentation written in DocBook can be converted to several other formats, including PostScript and HTML. As a standard, you want to install the HTML format so users can read it with their Web browsers or the Gnome help browser.

The Gnome libraries and help browser understand a file called `topic.dat`, which is simply a list of help topics with corresponding URLs. It serves as an index of help topics for your application. Here's an example, with only two entries:

```
gnome-hello.html      GnomeHello manual
advanced.html         Advanced Topics
```

URLs are relative to the directory where you install your help files.

You should consider in advance that your documentation will be translated into other languages. It is nice to make a subdirectory in your source tree for each locale (for example, the default `C` locale or the `es` (Spanish) locale). That way, translations don't cause clutter. Gnome expects help to be installed in a directory named after the locale, so this arrangement is convenient from that point of view as well. Your documentation directory might look like this one from the `GnomeHello` example application:

```
doc/
  Makefile.am
  C/
    Makefile.am
    gnome-hello.sgml
    topic.dat
  es/
    Makefile.am
    gnome-hello.sgml
    topic.dat
```

Here is doc/C/Makefile.am:

```
gnome_hello_helpdir = $(datadir)/gnome/help/gnome-hello/C

gnome_hello_help_DATA =          \
        gnome-hello.html         \
        topic.dat

SGML_FILES =                     \
        gnome-hello.sgml

# files that aren't in a binary/data/library target have to be listed
here
# to be included in the tarball when you 'make dist'
EXTRA_DIST = \
        topic.dat                \
        $(SGML_FILES)


## The - before the command means to ignore it if it fails.  that way
## people can still build the software without the docbook tools

all:

gnome-hello.html: gnome-hello/gnome-hello.html
        -cp gnome-hello/gnome-hello.html .

gnome-hello/gnome-hello.html: $(SGML_FILES)
        -db2html gnome-hello.sgml

## when we make dist, we include the generated HTML so people don't
## have to have the docbook tools
dist-hook:
        mkdir $(distdir)/gnome-hello
        -cp gnome-hello/*.html gnome-hello/*.css $(distdir)/gnome-hello
        -cp gnome-hello.html $(distdir)

install-data-local: gnome-hello.html
        $(mkinstalldirs) $(gnome_hello_helpdir)/images
        -for file in $(srcdir)/gnome-hello/*.html $(srcdir)/gnome-hello/*.css; do \
        basefile=`basename $$file`; \
        $(INSTALL_DATA) $(srcdir)/$$file $(gnome_hello_helpdir)/$$basefile; \
        done

gnome-hello.ps: gnome-hello.sgml
        -db2ps $<


gnome-hello.rtf: gnome-hello.sgml
        -db2rtf $<
```

In particular, notice the install directory for the generated HTML files: `$(datadir)/gnome/help/gnome-hello/C`. The Gnome libraries look for help here. Each application's help goes in its own directory under `$(datadir)/gnome/help`. Each locale's documentation is installed in its own subdirectory of the application directory. Other rules in `Makefile.am` run the DocBook-to-HTML converter, include HTML in the distribution tarball, and create PostScript and Rich Text Format targets. (Users can create PostScript by typing `make gnome-hello.ps` explicitly.)

4.6.2 *.desktop* **Entries**

Gnome programs come with ".`desktop` entries," which are simply small files describing how the application should appear in menus. When you install a .`desktop` entry, your application shows up in the Gnome panel menu. Here is `gnome-hello.desktop`:

```
[Desktop Entry]
Name=Gnome Hello
Name[es]=Gnome Hola
Comment=Hello World
Comment[es]=Hola Mundo
Exec=gnome-hello
Icon=gnome-hello-logo.png
Terminal=0
Type=Application
```

The file consists of key-value pairs. The `Name` key specifies the name of your application in the default (`C`) locale; any key can have translations with a locale appended in brackets, such as `Name[es]`. The `Comment` key is a "tooltip" or hint describing the application in more detail. `Exec` is the command line to use to execute the program. `Terminal` is a boolean value; if non-zero, the program will be run inside a terminal. `Type` should always be "Application" in this context.

Installing a .`desktop` entry is simple; here is the toplevel `Makefile.am` from GnomeHello again:

```
SUBDIRS = macros po intl src pixmaps doc

EXTRA_DIST = \
        gnome-hello.desktop

Applicationsdir = $(datadir)/gnome/apps/Applications
Applications_DATA = gnome-hello.desktop
```

Notice that there is a directory tree under `$(datadir)/gnome/apps/` with subdirectories that arrange programs into categories. GnomeHello installs itself in the "Applications" category; other programs might choose "Games," "Graphics," "Internet," or whatever is appropriate. Try to choose a category that already exists instead of inventing your own.

4.6.3 *EXTRA_DIST*

The EXTRA_DIST variable in a Makefile.am lists files to be included in the distribution (tarball). Most important files are automatically included (for example, all files listed as source files for binaries or libraries). However, automake does not know about .desktop files or SGML documentation; so these files must be listed in EXTRA_DIST. If you leave files out of EXTRA_DIST, make distcheck's attempt to build the distribution will probably fail.

5

Gnome Application Basics

THIS CHAPTER DESCRIBES THE MOST RUDIMENTARY aspects of a Gnome application, including initializing the libraries, marking strings for translation, parsing command-line arguments, saving configuration files, and responding to requests from the session manager. From here on, the book assumes you know how to write a simple GTK+-only application.

5.1 Initializing the Libraries

On startup, your application must initialize the GTK+ and Gnome libraries with a call to gnome_init(). gnome_init(), shown in Function Listing 5.1, takes the place of gtk_init() for Gnome apps (it calls gtk_init() for you).

The first argument to gnome_init() is a short name for your application, and the second is a string representing the application's version. These are used internally by the Gnome libraries (in some default messages provided by the argument parser, for example).

Function Listing 5.1 **Initializing Gnome**   *#include <libgnomeui/gnome-init.h>*

```
int
gnome_init(const char* app_id,
           const char* app_version,
           int argc,
           char** argv)
```

Like `gtk_init()`, `gnome_init()` parses the command-line arguments; unlike `gtk_init()`, it will not change `argc` and `argv`. If you want to parse application-specific options, you should use `gnome_init_with_popt_table()`, described in Section 5.3.

The return value from `gnome_init()` is supposed to be nonzero if initialization fails, but the current implementation always returns 0[†]. (`gnome_init()` will simply abort if there's a problem, such as a missing X server.) Common practice is to ignore this return value, at least in Gnome 1.0, but it's a good idea to check it anyway in case future versions do return an error.

5.2 Internationalization

All user-visible strings in a Gnome application should be marked for translation. Translation is achieved using the GNU `gettext` facility. `gettext` is simply a message catalog; it stores key-value pairs, where the key is the string hard-coded into the program, and the value is a translated string (if appropriate) or simply the key (if there's no translation or if the key is already in the correct language).

As a programmer, it's not your responsibility to provide translations. However, you must make sure strings are marked for translation—so that `gettext`'s scripts can extract a list of strings to be translated—and you must call a special function on each string when the catalog lookup should take place.

Gnome makes this easy by defining the two macros shown in Macro Listing 5.1. The macro `_()` both marks the string for translation and performs the message-catalog lookup. You should use it in any context where C permits a function call. The `N_()` macro is a no-op but marks the string for translation. You can use it when C doesn't permit a function call—for example, in static array initializers. If you mark a string for translation with `N_()`, you must eventually call `_()` on it to actually perform the lookup.

[†] Most people consider this a misfeature, but `gtk_init()` had the same problem until just before Gnome 1.0, so little could be done. Future versions will hopefully fix this problem.

Macro Listing 5.1 **Translation Macros** *#include <libgnome/gnome-i18n.h>*

```
_(string)
N_(string)
```

Here's a simple example:

```
#include <config.h>
#include <gnome.h>

static char* a[] = {
  N_("Translate Me"),
  N_("Me Too")
};

int main(int argc, char** argv)
{
  bindtextdomain(PACKAGE, GNOMELOCALEDIR);
  textdomain(PACKAGE);

  printf(_("Translated String\n"));
  printf(_(a[0]));
  printf(_(a[1]));

  return 0;
}
```

Notice that the string literals "Translate Me" and "Me Too" are marked so that gettext can find them and produce a list of strings to be translated. Translators will use this list to create the actual translations. Later, _() includes a function call to perform the translation lookup on each member of the array. Since a function call is allowed when the string literal "Translated String" is introduced, everything can happen in a single step.

At the beginning of your program, you have to call bindtextdomain() and textdomain(), as shown in the example. In the preceding code, PACKAGE is a string representing the package the program is found in, typically defined in config.h (see Chapter 4, "Creating Your Source Tree"). You must arrange to define GNOMELOCALEDIR, typically in your Makefile.am ($(prefix)/share/locale, or $(datadir)/locale, is the standard value). Translations are stored in GNOMELOCALEDIR.

When marking strings for translation, you must make sure that the strings are translatable. Avoid constructing a string at runtime via concatenation. For example, do not do this:

```
gchar* message = g_strconcat(_("There is an error on device "),
                             device, NULL);
```

The problem is that in some languages it may be correct to put the name of the device first (or in the middle). If you use g_snprintf() or g_strdup_printf() instead of concatenation, the translator can change the word order. Here's the right way to do it:

```
gchar* message = g_strdup_printf(_("There is an error on device %s"),
                                 device);
```

Now the translator can move %s as needed.

Complicated syntax-on-the-fly should be avoided whenever possible. For example, translating this is a major problem:

```
printf(_("There %s %d dog%s\n"),
        n_dogs > 1 ? _("were") : _("was"),
        n_dogs,
        n_dogs > 1 ? _("s") : "");
```

It is better to move the conditional out of the printf():

```
if (n_dogs > 0)
  printf(_("There were %d dogs\n"), n_dogs);
else
  printf(_("There was 1 dog\n"));
```

However, as the gettext manual points out, even this will not always work. Some languages distinguish more categories than "exactly one" and "more than one" (that is, they might have a word form for "exactly two" in addition to English's singular and plural forms). That manual suggests that a lookup table indexed by the number you plan to use might work in some cases:

```
static const char* ndogs_phrases[] = {
  N_("There were no dogs.\n"),
  N_("There was one dog.\n"),
  N_("There were two dogs.\n"),
  N_("There were three dogs.\n")
};
```

As you can see, this rapidly becomes unpleasant to deal with. Avoid it if you can. The gettext documentation has more examples, if you find yourself in a hairy situation.

Internationalization must also be considered when parsing or displaying certain kinds of data, including dates and decimal numbers. In general, the C library provides sufficient facilities to deal with this. Use strftime(), strcoll(), and so on to handle these cases; a good C or POSIX book will explain them. The glib GDate facility handles dates using strftime() internally.

Here's one common mistake to avoid: Don't use locale-dependent functions when reading and writing files. For example, printf() and scanf() adjust their decimal number format for the locale, so you can't use this format in files. Users in Europe won't be able to read files created in the United States.

5.3 Argument Parsing with *popt*

Gnome uses a powerful option-parsing library called popt. popt handles all the default Gnome options. To see the default options, pass the --help option to any Gnome application. You can add a "popt table" with your custom options. To do so, replace gnome_init() with the gnome_init_with_popt_table() variant, shown in Function Listing 5.2.

Function Listing 5.2   **Init with Argument Parsing**
#include <libgnomeui/gnome-init.h>

```
int
gnome_init_with_popt_table(const char* app_id,
                           const char* app_version,
                           int argc,
                           char** argv,
                           const struct poptOption* options,
                           int flags,
                           poptContext* return_ctx)
```

A popt table is simply an array of struct poptOption, defined as follows:

```
struct poptOption {
  const char* longName;
  char shortName;
  int argInfo;
  void* arg;
  int val;
  char* descrip;
  char* argDescrip;
};
```

The first two components are the long and short names for the option. For example, "help" and 'h' would correspond to the command-line options --help and -h. These can be NULL and '\0', respectively, if you want only one name for the option.

The arginfo member tells you what kind of table entry this is. Here are the possible values:

- POPT_ARG_NONE means that the option is a simple switch; it takes no argument.
- POPT_ARG_STRING means that the option takes a string argument, as in --geometry="300x300+50+100".
- POPT_ARG_INT means that the option takes an int argument, as in --columns=10.
- POPT_ARG_LONG means that the option takes a long argument.
- POPT_ARG_INCLUDE_TABLE means that this struct poptOption doesn't specify an option, but rather another popt table to be included.
- POPT_ARG_CALLBACK means that this struct poptOption doesn't specify an option, but rather a callback function to be used for parsing options in this table. This kind of entry should be at the beginning of your table.
- POPT_ARG_INTL_DOMAIN means that this struct poptOption specifies the translation domain for this table and any subtables.

The meaning of arg depends on the arginfo member. For options that take an argument, arg should point to a variable of the argument type. popt will fill the pointed-to variable with the argument. For POPT_ARG_NONE, *arg is set to TRUE if the option is found on the command line. In all cases, arg may be NULL, causing popt to ignore it.

For POPT_ARG_INCLUDE_TABLE, arg points to the table to include; for POPT_ARG_
CALLBACK, it points to the callback to invoke; for POPT_ARG_INTL_DOMAIN, it should be
the translation domain string.

The val member serves as an identifier for each option. Typically, it isn't that useful
in Gnome applications, but if you use a callback, it will be available in the callback. If
you aren't going to use it, set it to 0.

The final two members are used to automatically generate output for the --help
option. descrip describes an option; argDescrip describes the argument to that
option, if applicable. For example, the help for the --display option looks like this:

```
--display=DISPLAY            X display to use
```

Here argDescrip is "DISPLAY" and descrip is "X display to use." Remember to
mark these two strings for translation.

descrip has a slightly different meaning for POPT_ARG_INCLUDE_TABLE. In this case, it
titles a "group" of options in the help output—for example, "Help options" in the
following output:

```
Help options
  -?, --help                 Show this help message
  --usage                    Display brief usage message
```

If you place an entry of type POPT_ARG_CALLBACK at the beginning of a popt table, a
user-defined callback will be invoked with information about each option found on
the command line. Here is the type that your callback is expected to have:

```
typedef void (*poptCallbackType)(poptContext con,
                                 enum poptCallbackReason reason,
                                 const struct poptOption* opt,
                                 const char* arg,
                                 void* data);
```

The opaque poptContext object contains all of popt's state. This makes it possible to
use popt more than once in the same program or to parse more than one set of
options simultaneously. You can also extract information about the current parsing
state from poptContext using functions provided by popt.

Here are possible poptCallbackReason values:

- POPT_CALLBACK_REASON_PRE
- POPT_CALLBACK_REASON_POST
- POPT_CALLBACK_REASON_OPTION

Your callback is called once for each option found on the command line with
POPT_CALLBACK_REASON_OPTION as the reason argument. If you request, it can
also be called before and after argument parsing. In these cases, reason will be

POPT_CALLBACK_REASON_PRE or POPT_CALLBACK_REASON_POST. To specify that you want your callback to be called before or after parsing, you have to combine a pair of flags with POPT_ARG_CALLBACK. For example, the following struct poptOption initializer specifies a callback to be invoked both before and after argument parsing:

```
{ NULL, '\0', POPT_ARG_CALLBACK¦POPT_CBFLAG_PRE¦POPT_CBFLAG_POST,
  &parse_an_arg_callback, 0, NULL}
```

The opt argument to the callback is the struct poptOption that corresponds to the most recently-seen command-line option. (You can access the val member of this struct to determine which option you're looking at.) The arg argument is the text of any argument passed to the command-line option. The data argument is the callback data, given as the descrip member of the struct poptOption that specified the callback.

The flags argument to gnome_init_with_popt_table() can basically be ignored in a Gnome context; the available flags are not very useful.

If you pass a non-NULL pointer for return_ctx, the final argument to gnome_init_with_popt_table(), the current context will be returned; you can use this to extract the non-option components of the command line, such as filenames. This is done with the function poptGetArgs(). Here's an example:

```
char** args;
poptContext ctx;
int i;

bindtextdomain (PACKAGE, GNOMELOCALEDIR);
textdomain (PACKAGE);

gnome_init_with_popt_table(APPNAME, VERSION, argc, argv,
                           options, 0, &ctx);

args = poptGetArgs(ctx);

if (args != NULL)
  {
    i = 0;
    while (args[i] != NULL)
      {
        /* Do something with each argument */
        ++i;
      }
  }

poptFreeContext(ctx);
```

Notice that you must free the poptContext if you ask for it. However, if you pass NULL for return_ctx, the library will free it for you. Also keep in mind that poptGetArgs() will return NULL if there are no arguments on the command line.

5.3.1   Argument Parsing in GnomeHello

The GnomeHello application outputs the following if you invoke it with the
--help option:

```
$ ./hello --help
Usage: hello [OPTION...]

GNOME Options
  --disable-sound            Disable sound server usage
  --enable-sound             Enable sound server usage
  --espeaker=HOSTNAME:PORT   Host:port on which the sound server to use is
                             running

Help options
  -?, --help                 Show this help message
  --usage                    Display brief usage message

GTK options
  --gdk-debug=FLAGS          Gdk debugging flags to set
  --gdk-no-debug=FLAGS       Gdk debugging flags to unset
  --display=DISPLAY          X display to use
  --sync                     Make X calls synchronous
  --no-xshm                  Don't use X shared memory extension
  --name=NAME                Program name as used by the window manager
  --class=CLASS              Program class as used by the window manager
  --gxid_host=HOST
  --gxid_port=PORT
  --xim-preedit=STYLE
  --xim-status=STYLE
  --gtk-debug=FLAGS          Gtk+ debugging flags to set
  --gtk-no-debug=FLAGS       Gtk+ debugging flags to unset
  --g-fatal-warnings         Make all warnings fatal
  --gtk-module=MODULE        Load an additional Gtk module

GNOME GUI options
  -V, --version

Help options
  -?, --help                 Show this help message
  --usage                    Display brief usage message

Session management options
  --sm-client-id=ID          Specify session management ID
  --sm-config-prefix=PREFIX  Specify prefix of saved configuration
  --sm-disable               Disable connection to session manager

GnomeHello options
  -g, --greet                Say hello to specific people listed on the
                             command line
  -m, --message=MESSAGE      Specify a message other than "Hello, World!"
  --geometry=GEOMETRY        Specify the geometry of the main window
$
```

Almost all of these options are common to all Gnome applications; only the last three, labeled "GnomeHello options," are specific to GnomeHello. The --greet or -g option turns on "greet mode": GnomeHello will expect a list of names on the command line and will create a dialog to say hello to each person named. The --message option expects a string argument that replaces the usual "Hello, World!" message. The --geometry option expects a standard X geometry string, specifying the position and size of the main application window.

Here are the variables and popt table that GnomeHello uses to do its argument parsing:

```
static int greet_mode = FALSE;
static char* message  = NULL;
static char* geometry = NULL;

struct poptOption options[] = {
  {
    "greet",
    'g',
    POPT_ARG_NONE,
    &greet_mode,
    0,
    N_("Say hello to specific people listed on the command line"),
    NULL
  },
  {
    "message",
    'm',
    POPT_ARG_STRING,
    &message,
    0,
    N_("Specify a message other than \"Hello, World!\""),
    N_("MESSAGE")
  },
  {
    "geometry",
    '\0',
    POPT_ARG_STRING,
    &geometry,
    0,
    N_("Specify the geometry of the main window"),
    N_("GEOMETRY")
  },
  {
    NULL,
    '\0',
    0,
    NULL,
    0,
    NULL,
    NULL
  }
};
```

And here's the first part of `main()`, where GnomeHello checks that the arguments are properly combined and assembles a list of people to greet:

```
GtkWidget* app;

poptContext pctx;

char** args;
int i;

GSList* greet = NULL;

GnomeClient* client;

bindtextdomain(PACKAGE, GNOMELOCALEDIR);
textdomain(PACKAGE);

gnome_init_with_popt_table(PACKAGE, VERSION, argc, argv,
                           options, 0, &pctx);

/* Argument parsing */

args = poptGetArgs(pctx);

if (greet_mode && args)
  {
    i = 0;
    while (args[i] != NULL)
      {
        greet = g_slist_prepend(greet, args[i]);
        ++i;
      }
    /* Put them in order */
    greet = g_slist_reverse(greet);
  }
else if (greet_mode && args == NULL)
  {
    g_error(_("You must specify someone to greet."));
  }
else if (args != NULL)
  {
    g_error(_("Command line arguments are only allowed with --greet."));
  }
else
  {
    g_assert(!greet_mode && args == NULL);
  }

poptFreeContext(pctx);
```

Complete source code for GnomeHello is included in Appendix E, "Code Listings."

5.4 Saving Configuration Information

`libgnome` has the ability to store simple key-value pairs in plain-text configuration files. Convenience routines are provided for numeric and boolean types that transparently convert to and from a text representation of each type. The standard location for Gnome configuration files is `~/.gnome`, and the library will use that location by default. However, the library can be used with any file. There are also variants of each function that save to `~/.gnome_private`, a directory with user permissions only. The basic functions to store and retrieve data are listed in Function Listings 5.3 and 5.4. This module of `libgnome` is often referred to as `gnome-config`. Don't confuse this usage of "gnome-config" with the `gnome-config` script that reports the compile and link flags for Gnome programs.

The `gnome-config` functions work with a *path*. A path has three components:

- The *filename* to use, underneath the `~/.gnome` or `~/.gnome_private` directory. By convention, this is the name of your application.

- A *section*—a logical subcategory of related configuration information.

- A *key*—the key half of a key-value pair. The key is actually associated with a piece of configuration data.

A path is passed to Gnome as a string, with the form `"/filename/section/key"`. If you want to use a filename that is *not* in the standard Gnome directories, you can bracket the entire path with the `=` character, and it will be interpreted as absolute. You can even use this as a simple datafile format (it is used for the `.desktop` files programs install in order to appear on the Gnome panel menu). However, XML (perhaps using the `gnome-xml` package) is almost certainly a better choice for that. XML may also be a better choice for storing some kinds of configuration information; the primary advantage of the `libgnome` configuration library is its simplicity.

`gnome-config` has a long history. It was first written for the WINE Windows emulator project. Then it was used in the GNU Midnight Commander file manager. Finally, it was migrated into the Gnome libraries. The plan is to replace `gnome-config` with something more powerful in the next version of Gnome; we want to support per-host configuration, back-ends such as LDAP, and other features. However, the `gnome-config` API will almost certainly be supported even if the underlying engine changes dramatically.

5.4.1   Reading Stored Config Data

Retrieving data from files is simple. You simply call a function to retrieve the value for a given key. The value-retrieving functions, shown in Function Listing 5.3, accept a path as their argument. For example, you might ask whether the user wants to see a dialog box:

```
gboolean show_dialog;

show_dialog =
  gnome_config_get_bool("/myapp/General/dialog");
```

If the config file doesn't exist yet, or there is no key matching the path you provide, these functions return 0, FALSE, or NULL. The functions that return a string return allocated memory; you should g_free() the returned string. The string vector functions return an allocated vector full of allocated strings (g_strfreev() is the easiest way to free this vector).

You can specify a default value to be returned if the key doesn't exist; to do so, append an "=*value*" to the path. For example:

```
gboolean show_dialog;

show_dialog =
  gnome_config_get_bool("/myapp/General/dialog=true");
```

Each function has a with_default variant; these tell you whether the return value was taken from a config file or from the default you specified. For example:

```
gboolean show_dialog;
gboolean used_default;

show_dialog =
  gnome_config_get_bool_with_default("/myapp/General/dialog=true",
                                     &used_default);

if (used_default)
  printf("Default value used for show_dialog\n");
```

gnome_config_push_prefix() and gnome_config_pop_prefix() (discussed in Section 5.4.3.3) can be used to avoid specifying the entire path each time. For example:

```
gboolean show_dialog;

gnome_config_push_prefix("/myapp/General/");

show_dialog =
  gnome_config_get_bool("dialog=true");

gnome_config_pop_prefix();
```

These functions also work when you're saving values.

Configuration functions that have private in their name use a .gnome_private directory with restricted permissions, as discussed in the previous section. The translated_string functions qualify the provided key with the name of the current

locale. These are used when Gnome reads .desktop files (see Section 4.6.2) and probably aren't useful to applications.

Function Listing 5.3   **Retrieving data from configuration files**
#include <libgnome/gnome-config.h>

```
gchar*
gnome_config_get_string(const gchar* path)
gchar*
gnome_config_get_translated_string(const gchar* path)
gint
gnome_config_get_int(const gchar* path)
gdouble
gnome_config_get_float(const gchar* path)
gboolean
gnome_config_get_bool(const gchar* path)
void
gnome_config_get_vector(const gchar* path,
                        gint* argcp,
                        gchar*** argvp)
gchar*
gnome_config_private_get_string(const gchar* path)
gchar*
gnome_config_private_get_translated_string(const gchar* path)
gint
gnome_config_private_get_int(const gchar* path)
gdouble
gnome_config_private_get_float(const gchar* path)
gboolean
gnome_config_private_get_bool(const gchar* path)
void
gnome_config_private_get_vector(const gchar* path,
                                gint* argcp,
                                gchar*** argvp)
gchar*
gnome_config_get_string_with_default(const gchar* path,
                                     gboolean* was_default)
gchar*
gnome_config_get_translated_string_with_default(const gchar* path,
                                                gboolean* was_default)
gint
gnome_config_get_int_with_default(const gchar* path,
                                  gboolean* was_default)
gdouble
gnome_config_get_float_with_default(const gchar* path,
                                    gboolean* was_default)
gboolean
gnome_config_get_bool_with_default(const gchar* path,
                                   gboolean* was_default)
void
```

continues

Function Listing 5.3 **Continued**

```
gnome_config_get_vector_with_default(const gchar* path,
                                     gint* argcp,
                                     gchar*** argvp,
                                     gboolean* was_default)
gchar*
gnome_config_private_get_string_with_default(const gchar* path,
                                             gboolean* was_default)
gchar*
gnome_config_private_get_translated_string_with_default(const gchar* path,
                                                        gboolean* was_default)
gint
gnome_config_private_get_int_with_default(const gchar* path,
                                          gboolean* was_default)
gdouble
gnome_config_private_get_float_with_default(const gchar* path,
                                            gboolean* was_default)
gboolean
gnome_config_private_get_bool_with_default(const gchar* path,
                                           gboolean* was_default)
void
gnome_config_private_get_vector_with_default(const gchar* path,
                                             gint* argcp,
                                             gchar*** argvp,
                                             gboolean* was_default)
```

5.4.2 Storing Data in Configuration Files

Saving data is simply the inverse of loading it: You provide a /file/section/key path
in just the same way, along with the value to store (see Function Listing 5.4). Data isn't
written immediately; you must call gnome_config_sync() to ensure that the file is
written to disk.

Function Listing 5.4 **Saving data to configuration files**
#include <libgnome/gnome-config.h>

```
void
gnome_config_set_string(const gchar* path,
                        const gchar* value)
void
gnome_config_set_translated_string(const gchar* path,
                                   const gchar* value)
void
gnome_config_set_int(const gchar* path,
                     gint value)
void
gnome_config_set_float(const gchar* path,
                       gdouble value)
```

```
void
gnome_config_set_bool(const gchar* path,
                      gboolean value)
void
gnome_config_set_vector(const gchar* path,
                        gint argc,
                        const gchar* const argv[])
void
gnome_config_private_set_string(const gchar* path,
                                const gchar* value)
void
gnome_config_private_set_translated_string(const gchar* path,
                                           const gchar* value)
void
gnome_config_private_set_int(const gchar* path,
                             gint value)
void
gnome_config_private_set_float(const gchar* path,
                               gdouble value)
void
gnome_config_private_set_bool(const gchar* path,
                              gboolean value)
void
gnome_config_private_set_vector(const gchar* path,
                                gint argc,
                                const gchar* const argv[])
```

5.4.3   Config File Iterators

Iterators are used to scan the sections in a given file or the keys in a given section.
Applications can use this feature to store lists of data by dynamically generating key or
section names to save and later iterating over them to discover what was saved. These
functions are summarized in Function Listing 5.5.

An iterator is an opaque data type; you pass gnome_config_init_iterator() the
name of a section to iterate over and receive an iterator in return. You then call
gnome_config_iterator_next() to obtain key-value pairs from the section. The key
and value returned from gnome_config_iterator_next() must be freed with
g_free(), and the return value of gnome_config_iterator_next() is a pointer to the
next iterator. When gnome_config_iterator_next() returns NULL, all key-value pairs
have been
traversed.

5.4.3.1   An Iteration Example from *gnome-apt*

Here's an example from gnome-apt, a C++ application used to manage packages on
Debian systems. gnome-apt loads and saves the position of some columns in a tree

display. The columns are identified by the GAptPkgTree::ColumnType enumeration. GAptPkgTree::ColumnTypeEnd is the last element in the column type enumeration and is equal to the number of valid column types. This example is frighteningly "real-world" and checks for a number of error conditions.

```
static void
load_column_order(vector<GAptPkgTree::ColumnType> & columns)
{
  gpointer config_iterator;
  guint loaded = 0;

  config_iterator = gnome_config_init_iterator("/gnome-apt/ColumnOrder");

  if (config_iterator != 0)
    {
      gchar * col, * pos;
      columns.reserve(GAptPkgTree::ColumnTypeEnd);

      loaded = 0;
      while ((config_iterator =
              gnome_config_iterator_next(config_iterator,
                                         &col, &pos)))
      {
        // shouldn't happen, but I'm paranoid
        if (pos == 0 || col == 0)
          {
            if (pos) g_free(pos);
            if (col) g_free(col);
            continue;
          }

        GAptPkgTree::ColumnType ct = string_to_column(col);

        gint index = atoi(pos);

        g_free(pos); pos = 0;
        g_free(col); col = 0;

        // the user could mangle the config file to make this happen
        if (static_cast<guint>(index) >= columns.size())
          continue;

        columns[index] = ct;

        ++loaded;
      }
    }

  if (loaded != static_cast<guint>(GAptPkgTree::ColumnTypeEnd))
    {
      // Either there was no saved order, or something is busted - use
      // default order
      columns.clear();
```

```
     int i = 0;
     while (i < GAptPkgTree::ColumnTypeEnd)
       {
         columns.push_back(static_cast<GAptPkgTree::ColumnType>(i));
         ++i;
       }

     // Clean the section - otherwise an old entry could
     // remain forever and keep screwing us up in the future.
     gnome_config_clean_section("/gnome-apt/ColumnOrder");
     gnome_config_sync();
   }

  g_return_if_fail(columns.size() ==
                   static_cast<guint>(GAptPkgTree::ColumnTypeEnd));
}
```

It might be helpful to see the function that saves the column positions:

```
static void
save_column_order(const vector<GAptPkgTree::ColumnType> & columns)
{
  g_return_if_fail(columns.size() ==
                   static_cast<guint>(GAptPkgTree::ColumnTypeEnd));

  int position = 0;
  vector<GAptPkgTree::ColumnType>::const_iterator i = columns.begin();
  while (i != columns.end())
    {
      gchar key[256];
      g_snprintf(key, 255, "/gnome-apt/ColumnOrder/%s", column_to_string(*i));
      gchar val[30];
      g_snprintf(val, 29, "%d", position);
      gnome_config_set_string(key, val);

      ++position;
      ++i;
    }

  gnome_config_sync();
}
```

When writing this code, the decision was made to store enumeration values as strings
rather than as integers. The column_to_string() and string_to_column() functions
use a simple array of column names indexed by the enumeration values to convert
back and forth. There are two reasons to do this: It won't break when the enumeration
is altered in future versions of the program, and it keeps the configuration file human-
editable.

You may also notice that the column positions are stored with gnome_config_
set_string() instead of gnome_config_set_int(). This is because gnome_config_
iterator_next() returns a string representation of the stored information, as found in
the file. Most likely, gnome_config_set_int() stores integers as strings that atoi()
would understand (in fact, it does), but technically this isn't guaranteed by the API. If
the code used gnome_config_set_int(), it would have to obtain only the key from
gnome_config_iterator_next() and then call gnome_config_get_int() to obtain the
integer value. Using atoi() on the string value would make unwarranted assumptions
about gnome-config's implementation.

5.4.3.2   Section Iterators

gnome_config_init_iterator_sections() allows you to iterate over the sections
in a file, rather than over the keys in a section. When iterating over sections,
gnome_config_iterator_next() ignores its value argument and places the section
name in the key argument.

Function Listing 5.5   **Configuration file iterators**
#include <libgnome/gnome-config.h>

```
void*
gnome_config_init_iterator(const gchar* path)
void*
gnome_config_private_init_iterator(const gchar* path)
void*
gnome_config_init_iterator_sections(const gchar* path)
void*
gnome_config_private_init_iterator_sections(const gchar* path)
void*
gnome_config_iterator_next(void* iterator_handle,
                           gchar** key,
                           gchar** value)
```

5.4.3.3   Other Config File Operations

Function Listing 5.6 lists some additional operations available for manipulating config
files. The most important of these have already been mentioned in passing. gnome_
config_sync() writes the configuration file to disk, and gnome_config_push_prefix()
allows you to shorten the path passed to the other gnome-config functions. There are
also boolean tests, to ask gnome-config whether a given section exists.

Two new operations are introduced. To *drop* a file or section means to forget any
information about it stored in memory, including cached values loaded from the file
and values not yet saved to the file with gnome_config_sync(). To *clean* a file, section,
or key means to unset its value(s) so that the file, section, or key will not exist once
gnome_config_sync() is called.

gnome_config_sync() automatically calls gnome_config_drop_all() to free all gnome-config resources, since the information is safely stored on disk.

Functions are also provided to get the "real" (filesystem) path of a configuration file from a gnome-config path. These are unlikely to be useful in application code.

Function Listing 5.6   **Miscellaneous configuration file functions**
#include <libgnome/gnome-config.h>

```
gboolean
gnome_config_has_section(const gchar* path)
gboolean
gnome_config_private_has_section(const gchar* path)
void
gnome_config_drop_all()
void
gnome_config_sync()
void
gnome_config_sync_file(const gchar* path)
void
gnome_config_private_sync_file(const gchar* path)
void
gnome_config_drop_file(const gchar* path)
void
gnome_config_private_drop_file(const gchar* path)
void
gnome_config_clean_file(const gchar* path)
void
gnome_config_private_clean_file(const gchar* path)
void
gnome_config_clean_section(const gchar* path)
void
gnome_config_private_clean_section(const gchar* path)
void
gnome_config_clean_key(const gchar* path)
void
gnome_config_private_clean_key(const gchar* path)
gchar*
gnome_config_get_real_path(const gchar* path)
gchar*
gnome_config_private_get_real_path(const gchar* path)
void
gnome_config_push_prefix(const gchar* path)
void
gnome_config_pop_prefix()
```

5.5 Session Management

The term *session* refers to a snapshot of the state of a user's desktop: what applications are open, where their windows are located, what windows each application has open, what size those windows are, what documents are open, what the current cursor position is, and so on. Users should be able to save their session before logging out and have it automatically restored as closely as possible the next time they log in. For this to work, applications must cooperate by having the ability to record and restore those aspects of their state not controlled by the window manager.

A special program called the *session manager* notifies applications when they should save their state. The Gnome desktop environment comes with a session manager called `gnome-session`, but Gnome uses the X session management specification, which is several years old. CDE uses the same specification, and at the time this book was published, KDE was planning to adopt it as well. An application that implements session management via the Gnome interfaces should work on any session-managed desktop. Gnome does implement some extensions to the basic specification (notably, startup "priorities"), but these shouldn't break other session managers and will likely be implemented in KDE as well.

It's worthwhile to read the session management documentation that comes with X; it's a good introduction to what's going on "behind the scenes." The Gnome libraries also come with a useful document called `session-management.txt`. Have a look at it, and the heavily-commented `gnome-client.h` header file, for additional details not covered in this section.

5.5.1 Using the *GnomeClient* Object

Gnome shields you from the raw session management interface that comes with X. This is done via a `GtkObject` called `GnomeClient`. `GnomeClient` represents your application's connection to the session manager.

Gnome manages most of the details of session management. For most applications, you have to respond to only two requests:

- When a session is saved, the session manager will ask each client to save enough information to restore its state the next time the user logs in. Your application should save as much interesting state information as possible: the current open documents, cursor position, command histories, and so on. Applications should *not* save their current window geometries; the window manager is responsible for that.

- Sometimes the session manager will ask your client to shut down and exit (typically when the user logs out). When you receive this request, you should do whatever is necessary to exit the application.

When the session manager requests action from your application, the GnomeClient object emits an appropriate signal. The two important signals are "save_yourself" and "die". "save_yourself" is emitted when an application should save its state, and "die" is emitted when an application should exit. A "save_yourself" callback is fairly complex and has quite a few arguments; a "die" callback is trivial.

GnomeHello obtains a pointer to the GnomeClient object and connects to its signals as follows:

```
client = gnome_master_client ();
gtk_signal_connect (GTK_OBJECT (client), "save_yourself",
                    GTK_SIGNAL_FUNC (save_session), argv[0]);
gtk_signal_connect (GTK_OBJECT (client), "die",
                    GTK_SIGNAL_FUNC (session_die), NULL);
```

argv[0] will be used in the "save_yourself" callback.

First, here's the "die" callback from GnomeHello:

```
static gint
session_die(GnomeClient* client, gpointer client_data)
{
  gtk_main_quit ();
  return TRUE;
}
```

This is straightforward; the application just exits.

Now here's the "save_yourself" callback:

```
static gint
save_session (GnomeClient *client, gint phase, GnomeSaveStyle save_style,
              gint is_shutdown, GnomeInteractStyle interact_style,
              gint is_fast, gpointer client_data)
{
  gchar** argv;
  guint argc;

  /* allocate 0-filled, so it will be NULL-terminated */
  argv = g_malloc0(sizeof(gchar*)*4);
  argc = 1;

  argv[0] = client_data;

  if (message)
    {
      argv[1] = "--message";
      argv[2] = message;
      argc = 3;
    }

  gnome_client_set_clone_command (client, argc, argv);
  gnome_client_set_restart_command (client, argc, argv);

  return TRUE;
}
```

This is a bit more complex. A `"save_yourself"` must tell the session manager how to restart and "clone" (create a new instance of) the application. The restarted application should remember as much state as possible. In GnomeHello's case, it will remember the message being displayed. The simplest way to store the application state is to generate a command line, as GnomeHello does. It's also possible to ask `GnomeClient` for a prefix to be used with the gnome-config API. You can then save information to a per-session configuration file. Applications with significant state will need to use this method.

6

The Main Window: *GnomeApp*

THIS CHAPTER DESCRIBES GNOME'S FEATURES for creating your application's main window, complete with menus and a toolbar.

6.1   The *GnomeApp* Widget

All Gnome applications, excluding a few with special needs, use the GnomeApp widget for their main window. GnomeApp is a subclass of GtkWindow; it extends the basic toplevel window with convenient menu and toolbar handling. A GnomeApp window is automatically user-configurable in several ways:

- Menu and toolbars can be detached from the window or rearranged in relation to one another and the main window contents.
- Users can elect to disable detachable bars for all Gnome applications.
- Users can choose whether to display small icons in the application's menus.

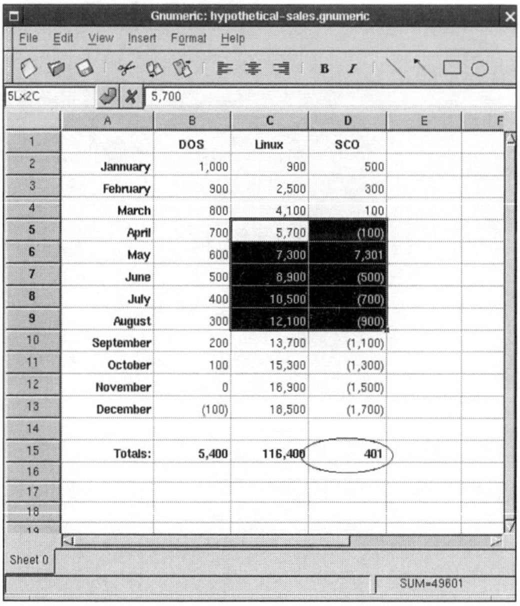

Figure 6.1 The Gnumeric spreadsheet, which uses the GnomeApp widget.

GnomeApp has the usual constructor function, shown in Function Listing 6.1. The first argument, app_id, is an internal name Gnome can use to work with this application. It should be the same as the app_id passed to gnome_init(); the name of the executable is a good choice. The second argument is simply a title for the application window; if you use NULL here, the title will not be set.

Function Listing 6.1   *GnomeApp* **Constructor**   *#include <libgnomeui/gnome-app.h>*

```
GtkWidget*
gnome_app_new(gchar* app_id,
              gchar* title)
```

GnomeApp has a single "content area" in the center where you place the main functionality of your application. On all four sides of this central area, you can add toolbars, menubars, and statusbars. Function Listing 6.2 lists the relevant functions.

These functions should be self-explanatory. They simply install the widget you give them in the appropriate place on the GnomeApp. There are easy ways to create the menubar, toolbar, and statusbar; the remainder of this chapter describes them.

Function Listing 6.2   **Adding Widgets to *GnomeApp***
#include <libgnomeui/gnome-app.h>

```
void
gnome_app_set_contents(GnomeApp* app,
                       GtkWidget* contents)

void
gnome_app_set_menus(GnomeApp* app,
                    GtkMenuBar* menubar)

void
gnome_app_set_toolbar(GnomeApp* app,
                      GtkToolbar* toolbar)

void
gnome_app_set_statusbar(GnomeApp* app,
                        GtkWidget* statusbar)
```

6.2   Menus and Toolbars with *GnomeUIInfo*

It's tedious to create large menus, especially if they have features such as icons and keyboard accelerators. Gnome provides a simple solution. You assemble a `GnomeUIInfo` struct as a template for each menu item, listing only its characteristics: name, icon, accelerator, and so on. The Gnome libraries can automatically create menus from arrays of `GnomeUIInfo` templates. The same method works with toolbars.

Here's the declaration of `struct GnomeUIInfo`.

```
typedef struct {
  GnomeUIInfoType type;
  gchar* label;
  gchar* hint;
  gpointer moreinfo;
  gpointer user_data;
  gpointer unused_data;
  GnomeUIPixmapType pixmap_type;
  gpointer pixmap_info;
  guint accelerator_key;
  GdkModifierType ac_mods;
  GtkWidget* widget;
} GnomeUIInfo;
```

A static initializer is the most convenient way to fill in the struct (but of course you can create it dynamically if you prefer). Gnome's routines accept an array of GnomeUIInfo, and macros are provided to simplify and standardize the most common static initializers. Here's a typical example, a File menu:

```
static GnomeUIInfo file_menu[] = {
  GNOMEUIINFO_MENU_NEW_ITEM(N_("_New Window"),
                          N_("Create a new text viewer window"),
                          new_app_cb, NULL),
  GNOMEUIINFO_MENU_OPEN_ITEM(open_cb,NULL),
  GNOMEUIINFO_MENU_SAVE_AS_ITEM(save_as_cb,NULL),
  GNOMEUIINFO_SEPARATOR,
  GNOMEUIINFO_MENU_CLOSE_ITEM(close_cb,NULL),
  GNOMEUIINFO_MENU_EXIT_ITEM(exit_cb,NULL),
  GNOMEUIINFO_END
};
```

There isn't always a nice macro for the menu item you want, so sometimes you must manually specify each element of the struct, as in this example:

```
{
  GNOME_APP_UI_ITEM, N_("_Select All"),
  N_("Select all cells in the spreadsheet"),
  select_all_cb, NULL,
  NULL, 0, 0, 'a', GDK_CONTROL_MASK
}
```

By now you're probably wondering what the struct members mean. Simple enough. Here's a breakdown:

- type is a type marker from the GnomeUIInfoType enumeration (see Table 6.1).

- label is the text of the menu or toolbar button. It should be marked for internationalization with the N_() macro.

- hint is a long description of the item's function. For toolbar buttons, it will appear in a tooltip; for menus, it can be made to appear in the statusbar.

- moreinfo depends on the type of the item (see Table 6.1).

- user_data will be passed to your callback function if the item type has a callback.

- unused_data should be set to NULL and is not used yet. It may be used in future versions of Gnome.

- pixmap_type is a value from the GnomeUIPixmapType enumeration; its purpose is to specify the type of the next member, pixmap_info.

- pixmap_info can be raw pixmap data, a filename, or the name of a Gnome stock pixmap.

- accelerator_key is the key to be used as an accelerator for this item. You can use a character such as 'a' or a value from gdk/gdkkeysyms.h.

- **ac_mods** is a modifier mask to be used with the accelerator.
- **widget** should be NULL. Gnome fills it in when it creates the menu item or tool-bar button. You can then retrieve it if you need to manipulate the widget in some way.

You might also be wondering why each menu item name contains an underscore. The underscore is used to mark the key shortcut for the menu item. Translators can move it around as needed to make it intuitive in their language. Gnome will parse the menu item name to obtain the accelerator and will then remove the underscore.

Table 6.1 summarizes the possible values for the `type` field of a GnomeUIInfo struct. See `libgnomeui/gnome-app-helper.h` for more details. There are actually a few more possible values, but the others are used internally by the library. The values in Table 6.1 should be sufficient for application code.

Table 6.1   *GnomeUIIngo Type* **Values**

GnomeUIInfoType	Description	moreinfo **Field**
GNOME_APP_UI_ENDOFINFO	Terminates a table of GnomeUIInfo	None
GNOME_APP_UI_ITEM	Normal item (or radio item inside radio group)	Callback function
GNOME_APP_UI_TOGGLEITEM	Toggle/check item	Callback function
GNOME_APP_UI_RADIOITEMS	Radio item group	Array of radio items in the group
GNOME_APP_UI_SUBTREE	Submenu	Array of GnomeUIInfo in the subtree
GNOME_APP_UI_SEPARATOR	Separator	None
GNOME_APP_UI_HELP	Help item	Help node to load

To create an entire menu tree, you include pointers to previous menu tables using the GNOMEUIINFO_SUBTREE() macro:

```
static GnomeUIInfo main_menu[] = {
  GNOMEUIINFO_SUBTREE(N_("_File"), file_menu),
  GNOMEUIINFO_END
};
```

In this particular case, there is a better macro to use, however:

```
static GnomeUIInfo main_menu[] = {
  GNOMEUIINFO_MENU_FILE_TREE(file_menu),
  GNOMEUIINFO_END
};
```

The main advantage of using this macro is standardization; it ensures that all Gnome file menus use the same key shortcut and have the same name. Quite a few macros are analogous; see `libgnomeui/gnome-app-helper.h` for the complete list.

6.2.1 Converting *GnomeUIInfo* to a Widget

After you have created a menu table, Gnome will process it and convert it to a widget. The functions are listed in Function Listing 6.3.

Function Listing 6.3 **Creating Widgets from GnomeUIInfo**
#include <libgnomeui/gnome-app-helper.h>

```
void
gnome_app_create_menus(GnomeApp* app,
                       GnomeUIInfo* uiinfo)

void
gnome_app_create_menus_with_data(GnomeApp* app,
                                 GnomeUIInfo* uiinfo,
                                 gpointer user_data)

void
gnome_app_create_toolbar(GnomeApp* app,
                         GnomeUIInfo* uiinfo)

void
gnome_app_create_toolbar_with_data(GnomeApp* app,
                                   GnomeUIInfo* uiinfo,
                                   gpointer user_data)

void
gnome_app_fill_toolbar(GtkToolbar* toolbar,
                       GnomeUIInfo* uiinfo,
                       GtkAccelGroup* accel_group)

void
gnome_app_fill_toolbar_with_data(GtkToolbar* toolbar,
                                 GnomeUIInfo* uiinfo,
                                 GtkAccelGroup* accel_group,
                                 gpointer data)

void
gnome_app_fill_menu(GtkMenuShell* menushell,
                    GnomeUIInfo* uiinfo,
                    GtkAccelGroup* accel_group,
                    gboolean uline_accels,
                    gint pos)
```

```
void
gnome_app_fill_menu_with_data(GtkMenuShell* menushell,
                              GnomeUIInfo* uiinfo,
                              GtkAccelGroup* accel_group,
                              gboolean uline_accels,
                              gint pos,
                              gpointer user_data)
```

If you are using the `GnomeApp` widget, `gnome_app_create_menus()`, and `gnome_app_create_toolbar()`, create a menubar or toolbar from the `GnomeUIInfo` table you provide and then attach that to the `GnomeApp`. Most of the time these are the functions you want to use, and they do everything automatically. A `_with_data()` variant of each function overrides the `user_data` field of `GnomeUIInfo`.

If you have more specialized needs, you can manually fill a menubar or toolbar and then add it to the container of your choice. The `fill` functions require you to specify the accelerator group you want to add accelerators to; for `GnomeApp`, an accelerator group already exists in the widget struct (the `accel_group` member). The `fill` functions for menus take two additional arguments: You can toggle whether to parse the underscores in menu item labels to extract accelerators, and you can specify at which position in the `GtkMenuShell` the function will begin inserting menu items. (`GtkMenuShell` is simply the base class for `GtkMenuBar` and `GtkMenu`. In other words, it is a widget that contains menu items. An accelerator group is just a collection of accelerators, normally attached to a `GtkWindow`; use `GNOME_APP(widget)->accel_group` in this case.)

When you use a `GnomeUIInfo` table to create a menubar or toolbar, pointers to the individual menu item or toolbar button widgets are placed in the `widget` member of each `GnomeUIInfo` struct. You can use these pointers to access the individual widgets; for example, if you create a check menu item, you might want to set the state of the check. The pointer is also useful if you want to manually create some part of the menu. You can create an empty subtree item, for example, and manually build the contents of the subtree.

6.2.2 GnomeHello: An Example

The GnomeHello application contains menus and a toolbar created using the `GnomeUIInfo` method; the relevant code is in a separate file, `menus.c`. Appendix E lists this file in its entirety.

6.3 Adding a Status Bar

Adding a status bar is simple enough. Simply call the aptly named `gnome_app_set_statusbar` function (see Function Listing 6.4) with your statusbar widget as the second argument.

However, you need to keep some additional things in mind. First, you can use either GtkStatusbar or GnomeAppBar as a statusbar. Second, you probably want to use the statusbar to display help about menu items as the user moves over them. Gnome comes with convenience functions for doing this. This section describes the two status bar widgets; Section 6.4 discusses using the statusbar to display menu item help.

Function Listing 6.4   **Installing a Statusbar**   *#include <libgnomeui/gnome-app.h>*

```
void
gnome_app_set_statusbar(GnomeApp* app,
                        GtkWidget* statusbar)
```

6.3.1   *GnomeAppBar*

There's no real reason to prefer GnomeAppBar or GtkStatusbar; they simply have different APIs. The GnomeAppBar widget was written later, with the following goals in mind:

- To simplify the GtkStatusbar API
- To support an optional progress bar next to the status bar (similar to Netscape's)
- To eventually add support for "interactive" use in the tradition of the Emacs "minibuffer" (this is unfinished in Gnome 1.0, however)

To create a GnomeAppBar, use gnome_appbar_new() (see Function Listing 6.5). The constructor lets you configure the capabilities of GnomeAppBar. It can have a progress bar (or not), have a status text area (or not), and be interactive (or not). You must have either a status text area or a progress bar. GnomePreferencesType is a kind of extended boolean value:

- GNOME_PREFERENCES_NEVER means the bar is never interactive.
- GNOME_PREFERENCES_USER means the bar is interactive if the user has activated that feature as a Gnome-wide preference.
- GNOME_PREFERENCES_ALWAYS means the bar is always interactive.

In Gnome 1.0, interactivity is incomplete, so you should avoid GNOME_PREFERENCES_ ALWAYS. Some experimental Gnome functions provide an abstraction of certain user interactions, allowing users to choose between dialog boxes and the Emacs-style minibuffer approach. When these are more developed, GNOME_PREFERENCES_USER will make sense even if you don't explicitly use the interactivity. Therefore, GNOME_PREFERENCES_USER is the recommended setting.

Function Listing 6.5 **GnomeAppBar Constructor**
#include <libgnomeui/gnome-appbar.h>

```
GtkWidget*
gnome_appbar_new(gboolean has_progress,
                 gboolean has_status,
                 GnomePreferencesType interactivity)
```

Using a `GnomeAppBar` is simple. The progress bar element presents a `GtkProgress` interface; to use it, extract the `GtkProgress` with `gnome_appbar_get_progress()` (see Function Listing 6.6), and then use the `GtkProgress` functions. Note that you should not make assumptions about the specific subclass of `GtkProgress`; in particular, do not cast it to `GtkProgressBar`.

Function Listing 6.6 **Extracting GtkProgress**
#include <libgnomeui/gnome-appbar.h>

```
GtkProgress*
gnome_appbar_get_progress(GnomeAppBar* appbar)
```

Status texts are stored in a stack. When the bar is refreshed, the top item of the stack is displayed. The bar is refreshed anytime you manipulate the stack. So pushing some text onto the status stack displays that text.

There are two other sources for the status text. You can set some "default" text; this is displayed if the stack is empty. The default default text is `""`. You can also set the status text without changing the stack; this "transient" text is immediately displayed but is not stored. On the next refresh (the next time you push, pop, or set the default), the text disappears forever, replaced by the text from the top of the stack.

Function Listing 6.7 lists the functions for manipulating the status text. `gnome_appbar_set_status()` is used to set the transient status text; `gnome_appbar_refresh()` forces a refresh without changing the stack—this is useful to be sure any transient text has been cleared. The other functions should be obvious.

Note that you can use the `GnomeAppBar` as a simple label—one message at a time, always replacing the previous message. Just stick to either setting the default or setting the transient text, and never use the stack.

Function Listing 6.7 **Setting GnomeAppBar Text**
#include <libgnomeui/gnome-appbar.h>

```
void
gnome_appbar_set_status(GnomeAppBar* appbar,
                        const gchar* status)
void
gnome_appbar_set_default(GnomeAppBar* appbar,
                         const gchar* default_status)
```

continues

Function Listing 6.7   **Continued**

```
void
gnome_appbar_push(GnomeAppBar* appbar,
                  const gchar* status)
void
gnome_appbar_pop(GnomeAppBar* appbar)
void
gnome_appbar_clear_stack(GnomeAppBar* appbar)
void
gnome_appbar_refresh(GnomeAppBar* appbar)
```

6.3.2   *GtkStatusbar*

GtkStatusbar has no default text or "transient" text, as GnomeAppBar does; it has only a message stack. However, each message is tagged with a "context" identified by a string. When you pop a message off the stack, you must specify a context, and the topmost message *in that context* is popped. If there are no messages in the context you specify, no text is popped. In essence, the GtkStatusbar "pop" operation works only within namespaces. There's no way to unconditionally pop all messages or unconditionally pop the topmost message.

In principle, this lets different parts of the program use the statusbar without interfering with one another. However, in my experience there's no need for this. For example, Netscape doesn't even have a stack for its statusbar; its statusbar is simply a label. In general, it is poor interface design to make anything *essential* appear in the statusbar because the user might not notice it. Accidentally deleting a message should not be a major worry.

Function Listing 6.8 shows the GtkStatusbar functions.

Function Listing 6.8   **GtkStatusbar**   *#include <gtk/gtkstatusbar.h>*

```
GtkWidget*
gtk_statusbar_new()
guint
gtk_statusbar_get_context_id(GtkStatusbar* statusbar,
                             const gchar* context_description)
guint
gtk_statusbar_push(GtkStatusbar* statusbar,
                   guint context_id,
                   const gchar* text)
void
gtk_statusbar_pop(GtkStatusbar* statusbar,
                  guint context_id)
void
gtk_statusbar_remove(GtkStatusbar* statusbar,
                     guint context_id,
                     guint message_id)
```

To use the statusbar, follow these steps:

1. First obtain a context ID with `gtk_statusbar_get_context_id()`; the `context_description` argument can be any string you like.

2. Push a message onto the statusbar using `gtk_statusbar_push()`; the message is tagged with the given context ID. The return value is a message ID you can use to remove the message. (Unlike `GnomeAppBar`, `GtkStatusbar` lets you remove a message that isn't on top of the stack.)

3. Eventually remove the message with `gtk_statusbar_remove()` or `gtk_statusbar_pop()`. The former refers to a specific message by ID; the latter removes the topmost message in the specified context.

Note that `gtk_statusbar_push()` pushes a message on top of all other messages, even those in other contexts. But `gtk_statusbar_pop()` will pop from the specified context only. Contexts do not refer to separate stacks, they merely restrict which messages you are permitted to pop.

6.4   Online Help

Finished applications should provide online help and documentation. Of course, the first line of defense is to have an intuitive interface in the first place. But you should give users a way to get more information if they need it.

This section describes the two primary ways you can explain your interface to users:

- By writing documentation and providing buttons and menu items that jump to relevant sections. For example, the "Help" button in a properties dialog box should bring up a help window describing the dialog box.

- By adding *tooltips*, explanatory text that appears if the mouse remains motionless over a widget for a short time. For menu items, explanatory text appears in the window's status bar as the user moves over the item.

6.4.1   Gnome Documentation and Help Menu Items

The Gnome documentation installation process was described in Section 4.6.1. Recall that applications install documentation in HTML format in directories named after locales. Each locale directory contains both help files and a `topic.dat` file indexing the available help topics.

Gnome makes it ridiculously easy to create menu items for the nodes in `topic.dat`. Simply create a help menu using the `GNOMEUIINFO_HELP()` macro, like this:

```
static GnomeUIInfo help_menu [] = {
  GNOMEUIINFO_HELP ("gnome-hello"),
  GNOMEUIINFO_MENU_ABOUT_ITEM(about_cb, NULL),
```

```
    GNOMEUIINFO_END
  };
```

The single argument to `GNOMEUIINFO_HELP()` is the name of the directory where you've installed your help files. The Gnome libraries will read `topic.dat` for the user's locale (or the C locale if there is no translation) and create a menu item for each topic. Activating these menu items will launch a help browser to display the appropriate URL. (Users can configure the exact browser Gnome will launch.) If `topic.dat` isn't found, Gnome creates no menu items.

In other contexts, you will have to manually set up widgets and callbacks to open your help files. Gnome provides some helper functions; the two most important ones are shown in Function Listing 6.9. `gnome_help_file_find_file()` returns the complete path to a help file, given the name of your help directory and the name of a help file (relative to one of the locale directories). If the help file is not found, `NULL` is returned. For example:

```
gchar* helpfile;

helpfile = gnome_help_file_find_file("gnome-hello",
                                     "gnome-hello.html");

if (helpfile != NULL)
  {
    gchar* url;

    url = g_strconcat("file:", helpfile, NULL);

    gnome_help_goto(NULL, url);

    g_free(url);
    g_free(helpfile);
  }
else
  {
    gnome_error_dialog(_("Couldn't find the GnomeHello manual!"));
  }
```

`gnome_help_file_find_file()` takes the user's locale into account when generating the help file's pathname.

`gnome_help_goto()` simply directs the help browser to a URL. You must prepend `"file:"` to a path to make it a valid URL before calling this function. The first argument to `gnome_help_goto()` is ignored; this makes it convenient to connect `gnome_help_goto()` as a callback function (for example, to a button's `"clicked"` signal).

`libgnome/gnome-help.h` contains a few other variants of `gnome_help_goto()` suited for connection to signals with different signatures. In particular, there's a callback there for the `GnomePropertyBox`'s `"help"` signal.

One caveat: the Gnome libraries look for files in the Gnome installation prefix, not in your application's installation prefix. For now, users should install Gnome applications and libraries in the same place. This was done for simplicity's sake when Gnome was much smaller. However, it's clearly the wrong behavior and will be fixed in a future version. If you use Gnome library functions such as `gnome_help_file_find_file()`, your application will automatically take advantage of this future Gnome enhancement.

Function Listing 6.9   **Help Files**   *#include <libgnome/gnome-help.h>*

```
gchar*
gnome_help_file_find_file(const gchar* app,
                          const gchar* filename)

void
gnome_help_goto(void* ignore,
                const gchar* url)
```

6.4.2   Menu Hints

As the user moves over your application menus, a short description of each menu item should appear in the statusbar. Gnome makes this very easy; just call the `gnome_app_install_menu_hints()` (see Function Listing 6.10) after you create your menus and statusbar. The `GnomeUIInfo` struct passed to this function must have its `widget` fields filled in by one of the menu-creation functions, and the `GnomeApp` must have a `GnomeAppBar` or `GtkStatusbar` in its statusbar slot.

Function Listing 6.10   **Installing Menu Hints**
#include <libgnomeui/gnome-app-helper.h>

```
void
gnome_app_install_menu_hints(GnomeApp* app,
                             GnomeUIInfo* uiinfo)
```

6.4.3   Tooltips

GTK+ provides tooltip functionality; you simply create a `GtkTooltips` and attach it to a widget. I like to use the following convenience function in my applications:

```
void
set_tooltip(GtkWidget* w, const gchar* tip)
{
  GtkTooltips* t = gtk_tooltips_new();

  gtk_tooltips_set_tip (t, w, tip, NULL);
}
```

The GtkTooltips will be destroyed along with the widget. Make your tooltips long rather than short; there's no reason to skimp on the amount of information you provide here. You should get in the habit of calling set_tooltip() every time you create a button or other widget that could benefit from it.

Note that toolbars created from a GnomeUIInfo template will have tooltips installed automatically.

6.5 Finishing Touches

Really polished application windows behave well on small screens and set hints so the window manager can keep track of them.

6.5.1 Adapting to Screen Size

The functions in Function Listing 6.11 allow you to query the size of the screen in pixels. You can use this information to adjust the layout of your application window; for example, if you know your usual application window is too large for a 640 by 480 display, you could provide an alternative widget layout for small screens. Applications that automatically adapt to the screen size are very impressive.

Of course, you should leave control in the hands of the user; users with large screens might want the small version of your application anyway, and you should always try to respond sensibly if the user resizes the window. Use the screen size to select the best default from among your application's possible configurations.

Function Listing 6.11 **Querying Screen Size** *#include <gdk/gdk.h>*

```
gint
gdk_screen_width()

gint
gdk_screen_height()
```

6.5.2 Setting Window Class Hints

The "class hint" is a property of GtkWindow that window managers can read to decide how to treat the window. Most window managers allow you to set icons and other properties based on the class hint. Two elements make up the hint. The wmclass_name field should be unique for each kind of toplevel window in an application (such as the main window or a tools dialog box). The wmclass_class field is conventionally set to the name of the application, capitalized. For example, xterm windows set these properties to xterm (name) and XTerm (class). The GIMP toolbox sets its name to toolbox and its class to Gimp. The gtk_window_set_wmclass() function sets these hints for GtkWindow (see Function Listing 6.12).

Function Listing 6.12 **Setting Class Hints**   *#include <gtk/gtkwindow.h>*

```
void
gtk_window_set_wmclass(GtkWindow* window,
                       const gchar* wmclass_name,
                       const gchar* wmclass_class)
```

7

User Communication: Dialogs

DIALOGS ARE A CONTINUOUS ANNOYANCE IN PLAIN GTK+. Every time you want to tell the user anything, you have to create a window, some buttons, and a label, pack the buttons and label into the window, set up callbacks, remember to capture "`delete_event`", and so on. It's a pain. Gnome saves you from this pain with an easy-to-use general-purpose dialog widget and several subclasses of it that implement common dialog types. Gnome also has easy functions for using modal dialogs.

7.1   The *GnomeDialog* Widget

Because dialogs in plain GTK+ are painstakingly constructed from scratch, there are at least as many ways to write a dialog as there are programmers. The programmer must decide where to place the dialog on the screen, how much padding to have, whether to put a separator above the buttons, what container to put the buttons in, what the keyboard shortcuts are, and so on. The premise of `GnomeDialog` is that the programmer shouldn't have to care about these things; if they're variable at all, the user should configure them the way she/he wants. From the programmer's perspective, dialogs "just work."

7.1.1 Creating a Dialog

A `GnomeDialog` is easy to create. Here's a summary of the basic steps. You'll read more details later.

1. Read Section 7.4 and decide whether one of the special dialog subclasses is appropriate. If so, skip the following steps and create that subclass instead.

2. Create the widget with `gnome_dialog_new()`. Pass this function the title of the dialog (displayed by the window manager) and the name of each button you'd like to have.

3. Populate `GNOME_DIALOG(dialog)->vbox` with the contents of your dialog.

4. Plan how your dialog will work. You can connect to the `"close"` or `"clicked"` signals, as appropriate. You can have the dialog hide or destroy itself when closed. You can also have the dialog automatically close when clicked, or handle this yourself. There are a number of ways the user can interact with a dialog, so it's important to be sure the combination of settings you choose will work no matter what the user does.

To create a dialog, use `gnome_dialog_new()`, shown in Function Listing 7.1. The argument list is a `NULL`-terminated list of buttons to insert in the dialog. For example, you might say:

```
GtkWidget* dialog;
dialog = gnome_dialog_new(_("My Dialog Title"),
                          _("OK"),
                          _("Cancel"),
                           NULL);
```

This creates a dialog called "My Dialog Title" with OK and Cancel buttons; the strings are marked for translation with the `_()` macro. The OK button will be the leftmost button in the dialog.

Function Listing 7.1   ***GnomeDialog* constructor**   *#include <libgnomeui/gnome-dialog.h>*

```
GtkWidget*
gnome_dialog_new(const gchar* title,
                 ...)
```

The `GnomeDialog` API numbers the buttons you add starting with 0. You use these numbers to refer to the buttons later, because you don't have a pointer to the automatically created button widgets. In this case, the OK button is button 0, and the Cancel button is button 1. (Note that this is standard Gnome practice—OK and Yes are first, and Cancel and No are second. In fact, `libgnomeui/gnome-uidefs.h` contains the macros `GNOME_YES`, `GNOME_OK`, `GNOME_NO`, and `GNOME_CANCEL`, which represent the dialog button numbers for these items in a two-button dialog.)

This example, which specifies buttons called OK and Cancel, is not quite correct for production code. Gnome provides a set of "stock buttons" for common button names. These ensure that everyone uses "OK" instead of "Ok" or "OK!"; they allow translators to translate common strings only once; and they often insert icons in the buttons, making them more attractive and recognizable to users. You should always use stock buttons if possible.

You can use stock buttons in `gnome_dialog_new()`. Simply substitute the stock button macros for the button names:

```
dialog = gnome_dialog_new(_("My Dialog Title"),
                GNOME_STOCK_BUTTON_OK,
                GNOME_STOCK_BUTTON_CANCEL,
                NULL);
```

Gnome includes many stock buttons, stock menu items, and stock pixmaps. It's a good idea to check these out so that you don't reinvent the wheel. A complete list is in `libgnomeui/gnome-stock.h`.

7.1.2 Filling in the Dialog

After creating a dialog, you'll want to put something inside. If you just want a label inside, you probably should use `GnomeMessageBox` or one of the convenience routines (such as `gnome_ok_dialog()`) instead of constructing the dialog manually. Otherwise, filling a dialog is very simple:

```
GtkWidget* button;
/* ... create dialog as shown earlier ... */
button = gtk_button_new_with_label(_("Push Me"));
gtk_box_pack_start(GTK_BOX(GNOME_DIALOG(dialog)->vbox),
                button,
                TRUE,
                TRUE,
                0);
```

Of course, you can pack the contents of `dialog->vbox` using the packing options of your choice. The preceding code is just an example.

Figure 7.1 shows a dialog from the Gnumeric spreadsheet, with its components labeled.

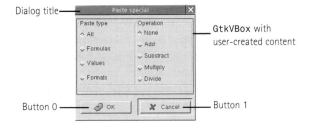

Figure 7.1 A `GnomeDialog` from the Gnumeric spreadsheet.

7.1.3   Handling *GnomeDialog* Signals

Now for the tricky part. You have to prepare yourself to handle anything the user might do to your dialog. Here's a brief list of possibilities that you should review whenever you create a dialog:

- Closing the dialog by pressing the Esc key
- Closing the dialog by clicking the window manager's close decoration
- Clicking one of the dialog's buttons
- Interacting with the dialog's contents
- If the dialog is not modal, interacting with other parts of the application

GnomeDialog emits two signals in addition to those it inherits from parent classes. If the user clicks one of the dialog's buttons, a "clicked" signal is emitted. (This is *not* the "clicked" signal from GtkButton; it's a different signal, emitted by GnomeDialog.) A GnomeDialog "clicked" handler should have three arguments: the dialog emitting the signal, the number of the button clicked, and your callback data.

GnomeDialog also has a "close" signal. It is emitted when gnome_dialog_close() is called; all the built-in event handlers (such as for the Escape shortcut) call this function to close the dialog. GnomeDialog's default handler for "close" has two possible behaviors: It can call either gtk_widget_hide() or gtk_widget_destroy() on the dialog. The behavior can be configured by calling gnome_dialog_close_hides(), as shown in Function Listing 7.2.

Function Listing 7.2   **Closing *GnomeDialog***   *#include <libgnomeui/ gnome-dialog.h>*

```
void
gnome_dialog_close_hides(GnomeDialog* dialog,
                         gboolean setting)


void
gnome_dialog_set_close(GnomeDialog* dialog,
                       gboolean setting)
```

By default, "close" destroys the dialog. This is what you usually want. However, if a dialog is noticeably time-consuming to create, you might want to merely hide and reshow it between uses without ever destroying it. You might also want to hide the dialog from the user, extract the state of any widgets inside it, and then destroy it with gtk_widget_destroy(). The decision depends on the structure of your code. However, in general it is simpler and less error-prone to let the dialog be destroyed when clicked. You can connect to the "clicked" signal if you need to query the state of widgets in the dialog.

If you connect a handler to `"close"`, that handler should return a boolean value. If it returns TRUE, the hide or destroy will not take place. You can use this to keep the user from closing the dialog, such as when she/he didn't fill in all of a form's fields.

The `"close"` signal is designed to collect several possible user actions into a single handler. It should be emitted when the user presses Esc or the window manager's window close button is clicked. It's often convenient to emit `close` when the dialog's buttons are clicked as well. You can ask `GnomeDialog` to emit `close` whenever a button is clicked with `gnome_dialog_set_close()` (see Function Listing 7.2). If its `setting` argument is TRUE, the dialog will emit `"close"` in addition to `"clicked"` if any of its buttons are clicked. By default, this setting is FALSE for `GnomeDialog`, but for many of the special dialog types, the default is TRUE (the inconsistency is an unfortunate feature).

Note that the `"close"` signal is emitted when the dialog receives `"delete_event"`. This means you have to write only one signal handler to deal with all dialog closings. There is no need to handle `"delete_event"` as a separate case.

7.1.4 Finishing Touches

The difference between a good dialog and a great dialog is in the details. `GnomeDialog` has a number of features to make that final polish easy. Function Listing 7.3 sums them up.

Function Listing 7.3   *GnomeDialog* **polish**   *#include <libgnomeui/gnome-dialog.h>*

```
void
gnome_dialog_set_parent(GnomeDialog* dialog,
                        GtkWindow* parent)

void
gnome_dialog_set_default(GnomeDialog* dialog,
                         gint button)

void
gnome_dialog_editable_enters(GnomeDialog* dialog,
                             GtkEditable* editable)

void
gnome_dialog_set_sensitive(GnomeDialog* dialog,
                           gint button,
                           gboolean setting)
```

Dialogs have a logical *parent,* usually the main application window. You can tell the library about this parent-child relationship. Doing so lets Gnome honor certain user preferences and in turn indicates the relationship to the window manager. Most window managers will minimize child dialogs when the parent window is minimized and will keep child dialogs on top of their parent.

It's important to use `gnome_dialog_set_parent()` only with *transient* dialogs. A transient dialog is one that appears and is dismissed relatively quickly. (`GnomeDialog` is really meant for transient dialogs.) Some "dialogs" are just small windows, such as the tool palette in the Gimp. These persistent ("floating") dialogs should be able to be minimized without minimizing the parent, and they should not be forced to stay above the parent window.

Your dialog should have a sensible *default button* the button activated when the user presses the Enter key. `gnome_dialog_set_default()` specifies the default button. It's a judgment call which button should be the default. Often the best choice is the least-destructive action (such as Cancel rather than OK), but if neither is destructive, user convenience might guide your decision.

Typically, operations such as deleting data or quitting an application have Cancel or No as the default; dialogs that ask the user to enter text or other information typically have OK as the default. Remember that many window managers will focus windows when they pop up, so keystrokes users intend to go to their current application might go to your dialog instead. If your dialog has "delete all my files" as the default button, you will get hate mail.

Editable widgets emit the `"activate"` signal when Enter is pressed. Typically, users expect Enter to activate the default dialog button, but if you have an editable widget such as `GtkEntry` in your dialog, it will capture any Enter presses and keep the dialog's buttons from responding to them. `gnome_dialog_editable_enters()` activates the dialog's default button when the `GtkEditable` is activated, solving the problem.

`gnome_dialog_set_sensitive()` calls `gtk_widget_set_sensitive()` on a dialog button. If clicking a button makes no sense at a given time, it should be desensitized.

Finally, you should make sure you don't create multiple instances of a dialog. Many applications allow you to display multiple Preferences or About dialogs. Users will not trigger this bug very often, but it's nice to avoid the problem. The following code deals with it in a simple way. (Note that the details of creating and showing the dialog have been omitted.)

```
void
do_dialog()
{
  static GtkWidget* dialog = NULL;
  if (dialog != NULL)
    {
      /* This code tries to de-iconify and raise the dialog.
       * It assumes the dialog is realized; if you can't
       * ensure that, check that dialog->window != NULL.
       */

      gdk_window_show(dialog->window);
      gdk_window_raise(dialog->window);
    }
  else
    {
```

```
  dialog = gnome_dialog_new();        /* Arguments elided. */

  gtk_signal_connect(GTK_OBJECT(dialog),
                     "destroy",
                     GTK_SIGNAL_FUNC(gtk_widget_destroyed),
                     &dialog);

  /* Show the dialog, connect callbacks, etc. here */
    }
  }
```

gtk_widget_destroyed() is defined in gtk/gtkwidget.h and simply assigns NULL to its
second argument. The code resets the dialog variable each time the user closes the
dialog and raises/de-iconifies the dialog if the user tries to open it while another one
is active. Note that the window manager has some say in whether the raise/de-iconify
is successful, so it is not guaranteed to happen.

7.2   Modal Dialogs

Sometimes you need to prevent interaction with the rest of your application while the
user manipulates a dialog. Dialogs that freeze the rest of the application in this way are
called *modal* dialogs.

There is much debate about when to use modal dialogs. Some users hate them pas-
sionately, but there are times when they are necessary. Unfortunately, it is somewhat
easier to write code using modal dialogs, because you can stop in the middle of a
function, wait for a user response, and then continue. With nonmodal dialogs, you have
to return the flow of control to the main application and arrange callbacks to pick up
where you left off when the user finally deals with the dialog. With a complex
sequence of dialogs, the result is ugly spaghetti code. This tempts many programmers
to use modal dialogs all the time, or at least a little too often. Avoid the temptation.
Your users will thank you.

Avoid modal dialogs if users might want to refer back to information in the main
application as they use the dialog, or if they might want to cut and paste between the
application and the dialog. Properties dialogs should usually be nonmodal because
users will want to experiment with the effects of the changes they make without having to close the dialog. And there's no reason to make trivial message boxes modal,
because clicking on them has no effect on the rest of the application.

Do not be afraid to use a modal dialog if it makes sense, however. For example, I
wrote a front end for the Debian package manager called gnome-apt. The main application allows the user to select software packages for installation and removal. A series
of dialogs ask for confirmation and perform the requested changes. These dialogs are
modal, because it would make no sense to change a request in the middle of performing it. Changing the request should imply restarting the request-fulfillment process and

asking for confirmation a second time. Another example: the File Properties dialog for the Gnome file manager is modal, because otherwise the user could delete the file while its properties were being edited—a strange situation. There are no hard and fast rules; you'll have to use your judgment on a dialog-by-dialog basis.

All that said, it is very easy to create a modal dialog. In GTK+, any window can be made modal with `gtk_window_set_modal()`, as shown in Function Listing 7.4.

Function Listing 7.4 **Modal windows** *#include <gtk/gtkwindow.h>*

```
gtk_window_set_modal(GtkWindow* window,
                     gboolean modality)
```

Because `GnomeDialog` is a `GtkWindow` subclass, this function works fine. It simply blocks all interaction with windows other than the modal one.

Typically you want to go a step further by waiting for the user to click one of the dialog buttons without setting up a lot of callbacks. In GTK+ this is done by running a second instance of `gtk_main()`, entering another, nested event loop. When the second loop exits, the flow of control returns to just after your `gtk_main()` call. However, there are a host of complications and race conditions, due to the large number of ways to close a dialog. The resulting code is somewhat unpleasant and error-prone. The two functions shown in Function Listing 7.5 save you from the mess.

Function Listing 7.5 **"Running" a dialog** *#include <libgnomeui/gnome-dialog.h>*

```
gint
gnome_dialog_run(GnomeDialog* dialog)

gint
gnome_dialog_run_and_close(GnomeDialog* dialog)
```

These two functions block until the user clicks a dialog button, clicks the window manager's close decoration, or does the equivalent with a key shortcut. If a button was clicked, the functions return that button's number; recall that `GnomeDialog` buttons are numbered from left to right starting with `0`. If no button was clicked (the dialog was closed via window manager), they return `-1` instead.

The dialog is automatically made modal for the duration of the call; otherwise, chaos would reign. (For example, calling `gtk_main_quit()` from your main application code would quit the nested `gtk_main()` rather than the primary one.) However, if you plan to leave the dialog open after `gnome_dialog_run()` returns, and you want it to be modal, you should manually make it modal; `gnome_dialog_run()` will change the dialog's modality only temporarily.

It is your responsibility to figure out how the dialog will be closed or destroyed before you call `gnome_dialog_run()`. You can set the dialog up so that no user actions destroy it and then destroy it yourself after `gnome_dialog_run()` returns. Or you can

set the dialog up so that all user actions destroy it and then forget about it after
`gnome_dialog_run()` returns. You could also write a loop, calling `gnome_dialog_run()`
repeatedly until the user gives valid input, and then close the dialog only after the loop
ends. If you write a loop, be careful to manually make the dialog modal; otherwise,
there will be short intervals where it is not.

   `gnome_dialog_run_and_close()` monitors the dialog's `"close"` and `"destroy"` signals and closes the dialog if and only if it doesn't close "naturally" in response to user
clicks or keystrokes. Using this function guarantees that `gnome_dialog_close()` will be
called exactly once before it returns, unless you connect truly malicious callbacks to
sabotage the process. `gnome_dialog_run_and_close()` is not very useful, in my opinion; it is little more than a way to avoid thinking about how the dialog will be closed.

7.3   A Dialog Example

Here's a piece of code from the Gnome plot and chart component, Guppi. It is used
for an Open File dialog. Future versions of Gnome will have a `GnomeFileSelection`
widget, which would be more appropriate for this particular task than a custom dialog,
but the example is nonetheless instructive.

```
GtkWidget * dialog;

dialog = gnome_dialog_new(_("Guppi: Open"),
                          GNOME_STOCK_BUTTON_OK,
                          GNOME_STOCK_BUTTON_CANCEL,
                          NULL);

gnome_dialog_set_close(GNOME_DIALOG(dialog), TRUE);
gnome_dialog_close_hides(GNOME_DIALOG(dialog), TRUE);

guppi_setup_dialog(dialog);

GtkWidget* fileentry =
  gnome_file_entry_new("guppi:guppi_loadsave_history",
                       _("Guppi: Browse Files For Open"));

gnome_dialog_editable_enters(GNOME_DIALOG(dialog),
                             GTK_EDITABLE(gnome_file_entry_gtk_entry(
➥GNOME_FILE_ENTRY(fileentry))));
gnome_dialog_set_default(GNOME_DIALOG(dialog), GNOME_OK);

gtk_box_pack_start(GTK_BOX(GNOME_DIALOG(dialog)->vbox),
                   fileentry,
                   TRUE, TRUE, GNOME_PAD);

gtk_widget_show_all(dialog);

int reply = gnome_dialog_run(GNOME_DIALOG(dialog));
```

```
if (reply == GNOME_OK)
  {
    gchar* s =
      gnome_file_entry_get_full_path(GNOME_FILE_ENTRY(fileentry),
                                     TRUE);
    /* Application-specific details of actually
     * loading the file omitted.
     */
  }

gtk_widget_destroy(dialog);
```

gnome_dialog_set_close() is called, so this dialog will close if any of its buttons are
clicked. However, closing the dialog only calls gtk_widget_hide() rather than destroying it; gnome_dialog_close_hides() configures this behavior. guppi_setup_dialog() is
a wrapper function that calls gnome_dialog_set_parent() to set the main application
window as the dialog's parent.

Because the purpose of the dialog is to get a filename, it will be convenient to have
pressing the Enter key as the equivalent to pressing the OK button; thus, the OK button should be the default. However, the text entry box would normally steal the Enter
key press; gnome_dialog_editable_enters() fixes the problem. gnome_dialog_run()
waits for the user to take an action. If OK is clicked, the contents of the text entry
are retrieved, and the file is loaded. Note that the dialog is *not* destroyed after
gnome_dialog_run() returns, because we called gnome_dialog_close_hides().
However, the dialog is *closed* after gnome_dialog_run() returns, because the code
ensures that all user actions will close it (using gnome_dialog_set_close() and
relying on the default behavior for the window manager's close button). Finally,
gtk_widget_destroy() is necessary, because the dialog was not destroyed when it was
closed.

7.4   Special Dialog Types

This section describes some special kinds of dialogs that exist for your convenience
and for UI consistency. Of course, nearly everything said so far about GnomeDialog also
applies to its subclasses.

7.4.1   *GnomeAbout*

Gnome applications should have an "About *xxx*" menu item that displays this widget
(where *xxx* is the name of your application). Using it is easy. The only function
involved is gnome_about_new() (see Function Listing 7.6). The arguments are, respectively, the title of your application, the version of your application, a one-line copyright notice, a NULL-terminated vector of authors' names, a short paragraph saying
anything you want to say, and an image filename to display as your application's logo.
Only the authors argument is required; the others can be NULL. However, your dialog
will look fairly strange if all the other arguments are NULL.

Function Listing 7.6 ***GnomeAbout***   *#include<libgnomeui/gnome-about.h>*

```
GtkWidget*
gnome_about_new(const gchar* title,
                const gchar* version,
                const gchar* copyright,
                const gchar** authors,
                const gchar* comments,
                const gchar* logo)
```

GnomeAbout automatically closes when clicked, so you don't really need to worry about it; just create and show the dialog. Remember to ensure that only one instance exists at any given time, as explained in Section 7.1.4.

Here's a menu item callback to show an about dialog, from the Gnome calendar application:

```
static void
about_calendar_cmd (GtkWidget *widget, void *data)
{
   GtkWidget *about;
   const gchar *authors[] = {
     "Miguel de Icaza <miguel@kernel.org>",
     "Federico Mena <federico@gimp.org>",
     "Arturo Espinosa <arturo@nuclecu.unam.mx>",
     NULL
   };

   about = gnome_about_new (_("Gnome Calendar"), VERSION,
                            "(c)1998 the Free Software Foundation",
                            authors,
                            _("The GNOME personal calendar and schedule
➥manager."),
                            NULL);
   gtk_window_set_modal (GTK_WINDOW (about), TRUE);

   gtk_widget_show (about);
}
```

Note that the authors give both their name and email address; that way people can use the dialog to decide where to send hate mail and bug reports. (Or thank-you notes!) The VERSION macro comes from config.h and is defined by configure. The Gnome Calendar authors chose to prevent multiple dialog instances by making the dialog modal—the user can't reselect the menu item while the dialog is open. It is probably better to use the technique described in Section 7.1.4 so that the dialog is de-iconified and raised if the user reselects the menu item.

7.4.2   *GnomePropertyBox*

GnomePropertyBox is used for application preferences or to edit the properties of a user-visible object. It's a dialog with a GtkNotebook inside and four buttons: OK, Apply, Close, and Help. The OK button is equivalent in all respects to clicking Apply followed by Close. Apply should immediately make any changes the user has requested using the widgets you've placed in the GnomePropertyBox. Unsurprisingly, Help should display help. OK and Close are handled automatically by the property box, so you can ignore them.

You don't need to deal with the property box's buttons directly; instead, GnomePropertyBox emits "apply" and "help" signals. Their handlers should look like this:

```
void handler(GtkWidget* propertybox, gint page_num, gpointer data);
```

page_num is the currently-active page of the GtkNotebook inside the dialog. (GtkNotebook pages are numbered from front to back, starting with 0; the front page is the first one you add to the notebook.) For "help", the page number lets you provide context-sensitive help. When the user clicks the Apply or OK button, the "apply" signal is emitted once per page and is then emitted a final time with -1 as the page_num value. The multiple emissions of "apply" are something of an anachronism, because it has become the de facto standard to simply apply all pages when the -1 page number is received.

To create a property box, you first create the dialog and then create each page and add it. Creating a GnomePropertyBox is straightforward; gnome_property_box_new() takes no arguments.

You then create a widget for each page (probably a container with a number of controls inside) and append it to the property box with gnome_property_box_append_page() (see Function Listing 7.7). Its page argument is the widget to place inside the new notebook page, and tab is a widget to use on the notebook tab. The page number of the newly-added page is returned, so you don't have to keep a count yourself.

Function Listing 7.7   ***GnomePropertyBox***   *#include <libgnomeui/gnome-propertybox.h>*

```
GtkWidget*
gnome_property_box_new()

gint
gnome_property_box_append_page(GnomePropertyBox* pb,
                               GtkWidget* page,
                               GtkWidget* tab)
```

It's your responsibility to keep track of any user interaction with the contents of each page. When the user changes a setting, you must notify the property box; it uses this information to set the Apply and OK buttons sensitive if and only if there are unapplied changes. The relevant routines are shown in Function Listing 7.8.

Function Listing 7.8 **Property box state** *#include <libgnomeui/gnome-propertybox.h>*

```
%void
gnome_property_box_changed(GnomePropertyBox* pb)

void
gnome_property_box_set_state(GnomePropertyBox* pb,
                            gboolean setting)
```

gnome_property_box_changed() tells the property box about changes. The property box will automatically unset its internal "changes pending" flag when "apply" is emitted. If you need to change that internal flag for some reason (this is unlikely), you can use gnome_property_box_set_state().

7.4.3 *GnomeMessageBox*

A GnomeMessageBox is a GnomeDialog subclass that conveys a short message or asks a simple question. Gnome provides several types of message boxes. They have different icons next to the text, and corresponding titles. The icons look nice and let users quickly classify the message being presented.

The API is very simple; there are no functions specific to GnomeMessageBox other than the constructor, as shown in Function Listing 7.9. The first argument is the message to display; the second is a string encoding the message box type. Then you can list any buttons, just as you would with gnome_dialog_new(). Unlike the unadorned GnomeDialog, GnomeMessageBox closes on any button click by default. Of course, you can change this behavior by using gnome_dialog_set_close().

Function Listing 7.9 **Message box constructor** *#include <libgnomeui/gnome-messagebox.h>*

```
GtkWidget*
gnome_message_box_new(const gchar* message,
                      const gchar* messagebox_type,
                      ...)
```

Macros are provided for the available message box types:

- GNOME_MESSAGE_BOX_INFO should be used for "FYI" messages.
- GNOME_MESSAGE_BOX_WARNING should be used for nonfatal errors.
- GNOME_MESSAGE_BOX_ERROR should be used if an operation fails entirely.
- GNOME_MESSAGE_BOX_QUESTION should be used if your dialog asks a question.
- GNOME_MESSAGE_BOX_GENERIC should be used if none of the other types apply.

Here's how you might use `GnomeMessageBox`:

```
GtkWidget * mbox;

mbox = gnome_message_box_new (message,
                             GNOME_MESSAGE_BOX_INFO,
                             GNOME_STOCK_BUTTON_OK,
                             NULL);

gtk_widget_show (mbox);
```

Notice that `GnomeMessageBox`, like most `GnomeDialog` subclasses but not like `GnomeDialog` itself, automatically closes when clicked. So there is no need to destroy it by hand.

7.5 Convenience Routines

Because message boxes almost always have the same button (a single OK), there are convenience routines covering that case. Each routine has a `_parented()` variant that calls `gnome_dialog_set_parent()`. The three function pairs shown in Function Listing 7.10 display an info box, a warning box, and an error box, respectively. They create and show the widget, so you can ignore the return value if you like.

The only purpose of these functions is to save you typing. They are pure syntactic sugar. I find it much easier to remember them than to use `gnome_message_box_new()`, though; I always forget the order of the arguments to `gnome_message_box_new()`.

Function Listing 7.10 **Convenience dialogs**
#include <libgnomeui/gnome-dialog-util.h>

```
GtkWidget*
gnome_ok_dialog(const gchar* message)

GtkWidget*
gnome_ok_dialog_parented(const gchar* message,
                         GtkWindow* parent)

GtkWidget*
gnome_warning_dialog(const gchar* warning)

GtkWidget*
gnome_warning_dialog_parented(const gchar* warning,
                              GtkWindow* parent)

GtkWidget*
gnome_error_dialog(const gchar* error)

GtkWidget*
gnome_error_dialog_parented(const gchar* error,
                            GtkWindow* parent)
```

8

Gnome Application Checklist

ALMOST ALL GNOME APPLICATIONS SHOULD SUPPORT a common set of features. This checklist summarizes the most important ones. Always remember that Gnome is a direct response to the problem of application heterogeneity in the X environment. One of the most important goals of any Gnome application should be to offer a look and feel that's consistent with other Gnome applications, starting with the source code seen by programmers and ending with the spiffy GUI presented to users.

- ❏ Create a standards-compliant source tree. Use the Gnome `autoconf` macros or the `gnome-config` script to reliably locate the Gnome libraries and header files.
- ❏ Include a `README` file describing the package.
- ❏ Include the standard `INSTALL` file describing how to compile and install the package; change the standard file to reflect anything specific to your application.
- ❏ Include a copyright in a file called `COPYING`.
- ❏ Internationalize your application with GNU `gettext` and the standard C library functions.
- ❏ Include the `intl` directory with your application so that users can build the application without having `gettext`. Include `intl` in your header file search path.
- ❏ Define the `G_LOG_DOMAIN` preprocessor symbol to identify the origin of glib error messages.

❏ Define the GNOMELOCALEDIR preprocessor symbol so that Gnome can find translation files.

❏ Include config.h *before* gnome.h in each source file, or internationalization will not work properly.

❏ Install a .desktop file so that your application will appear on the Gnome desktop's menus.

❏ Install help files along with topic.dat files so that the Gnome help browser can locate them.

❏ Be sure the make distcheck target works; this will catch many common makefile errors.

❏ Set up a popt argument parser. At a minimum, you will probably want to support a --geometry option.

❏ All configurations should be possible via the GUI. The easiest way to achieve this is with the Gnome configuration library.

❏ Your application should support session management. At a minimum, it should save and restore the currently open documents.

❏ If appropriate, use the GnomeApp for your main document windows; this widget gives Gnome applications a consistent look and feel.

❏ Call gtk_window_set_wmclass() to set the class hint on your windows so that users can customize how window managers treat them.

❏ Use GnomeUIInfo to create menus and toolbars. When appropriate, use the Gnome macros for standard menu items.

❏ Add a status bar to display hints for the menu items and any other status that your application has to report.

❏ Use GnomeDialog and its subclasses for your dialog boxes.

❏ Add online help, including tooltips and documentation for display in the help browser.

❏ Keep a ChangeLog detailing changes you make to your source code. This will help other people understand the evolution of the application and help you understand why you made certain changes years later.

Advanced GTK+/Gnome Techniques

9   The GTK+ Object and Type System

10 Gdk Basics

11 Writing a *GtkWidget*

12 *GnomeCanvas*

13 Writing a *GnomeCanvasItem*

The previous part got you started with a skeletal application. This part of the book describes features available to the Gnome developer as she begins to implement the main functionality of the program. The first few chapters in this part cover some useful GTK+ details. The later chapters branch out to describe facilities unique to Gnome. You may not use all the tools described here for a given application, but you will probably use many of them.

9

The GTK+ Object and Type System

P EOPLE OFTEN ASK WHY GTK+ WAS WRITTEN IN C rather than an object-oriented language. The answer is that C is more portable and commonly available than any other language. However, although C lacks syntactic sugar for object-oriented programming, it does not prohibit an object-oriented approach.

GTK+ implements its own custom object system, which offers standard object-oriented features such as inheritance and virtual functions. In the tradition of languages such as Lisp, Smalltalk, and Java, the GTK+ object system is more runtime-centric than that of C++, which allows it to interact with interpreted language bindings and GUI builders in powerful ways.

You may recall from Chapter 3, "GTK+ Basics," that widgets are a special type of GtkObject. Any object with GtkWidget in its ancestry is a widget. Widgets represent a region on the screen; most of them are user interface elements, such as buttons or menus. There's nothing GUI-specific about GtkObject. The object system can be used in non-graphical programs.

This chapter dives right into the details of GTK+'s object system, giving you an idea of what's happening "behind the scenes" in any GTK+ program. Sooner or later, you'll need this information whether it's to write your own objects, debug existing objects, or just understand GTK+ code on a conceptual level.

9.1   Object and Class Structures

Each GtkObject has two essential components: a struct representing an *instance* of the object, and a struct representing the *class*. In general, the instance struct contains the data members for each instance, and the class struct contains class function pointers (which can be overridden by subclasses). The class struct can also contain class data members. However, it's more typical to use static variables in the .c file implementing the object. If you're familiar with C++, the class struct is equivalent to a vtable, except the class struct is written by hand. It stores virtual functions for an object type.

Here are the structs used in GtkButton:

```
typedef struct _GtkButton       GtkButton;
typedef struct _GtkButtonClass  GtkButtonClass;

struct _GtkButton
{
  GtkBin bin;

  GtkWidget *child;

  guint in_button : 1;
  guint button_down : 1;
  guint relief : 2;
};

struct _GtkButtonClass
{
  GtkBinClass        parent_class;

  void (* pressed)  (GtkButton *button);
  void (* released) (GtkButton *button);
  void (* clicked)  (GtkButton *button);
  void (* enter)    (GtkButton *button);
  void (* leave)    (GtkButton *button);
};
```

Notice that the first member of struct _GtkButton is GtkBin. That's because GtkButton is a subclass of GtkBin. (GtkBin is a GtkContainer that can hold one child.) Because GtkBin is the first member, we can safely cast a GtkButton to GtkBin. In struct _GtkButtonClass, the same principle applies, and GtkBinClass is the first member.

9.2   Type Checking and New Types

GTK+ has an extensive type system, which is (to some extent) independent of its object system. However, the object system makes use of the larger type system. Every object has a type, and every type has a unique integer identifier. When you're writing a GtkObject, it's customary to provide a function that returns the type's identifier.

In the case of `GtkButton`, the relevant function is as follows:

```
GtkType gtk_button_get_type();
```

The first time this function is invoked, it will register a `GtkButton` type with the object system and, in the process, obtain a type identifier. On subsequent calls, the type identifier is simply returned. `GtkType` is a typedef (`unsigned int` is the actual type of GTK+'s type identifiers).[1]

The type system allows GTK+ to check the validity of casts. To facilitate this, objects customarily provide macros like these in their header file:

```
#define GTK_TYPE_BUTTON           (gtk_button_get_type ())
#define GTK_BUTTON(obj)           (GTK_CHECK_CAST ((obj), \
                                   GTK_TYPE_BUTTON, GtkButton))
#define GTK_BUTTON_CLASS(klass)   (GTK_CHECK_CLASS_CAST ((klass), \
                                   GTK_TYPE_BUTTON, GtkButtonClass))
#define GTK_IS_BUTTON(obj)        (GTK_CHECK_TYPE ((obj), \
                                   GTK_TYPE_BUTTON))
#define GTK_IS_BUTTON_CLASS(klass) (GTK_CHECK_CLASS_TYPE ((klass), \
                                   GTK_TYPE_BUTTON))
```

Instead of simply casting an object, you can use the `GTK_BUTTON()` macro. If `GTK_NO_CHECK_CASTS` is defined, these macros are equivalent to simple casts. Otherwise, they retrieve the type of the object and compare it to the type you're attempting to cast to.[2]

GTK+ also provides convenient runtime type checking with the `GTK_IS_BUTTON()` macro. This is often used in preconditions; for example, a function expecting a button as an argument might have this check at the beginning:

```
g_return_if_fail(GTK_IS_BUTTON(widget));
```

The GTK+ and Gnome library functions have many such checks. You can also use the macro to make code conditional on an object's type, although this is most likely a poor idea from a design standpoint.

1. You should not make assumptions about `GtkType` values. However, each `GtkType` has a unique sequence number associated with it; sequence numbers are optimized to be array indices (that is, they are densely packed and as small as possible). You can extract sequence numbers with the `GTK_TYPE_SEQNO()` macro and use them to index a table containing information about types.

2. When you compile GTK+, use the `--enable-debug` option to `configure` to enable type checking.

To give you an idea what sort of information GTK+ stores about each object type, here's the implementation of gtk_button_get_type():

```
GtkType
gtk_button_get_type (void)
{
  static GtkType button_type = 0;

  if (!button_type)
    {
      static const GtkTypeInfo button_info =
      {
        "GtkButton",
        sizeof (GtkButton),
        sizeof (GtkButtonClass),
        (GtkClassInitFunc) gtk_button_class_init,
        (GtkObjectInitFunc) gtk_button_init,
        /* reserved_1 */ NULL,
        /* reserved_2 */ NULL,
        (GtkClassInitFunc) NULL,
      };

      button_type = gtk_type_unique (GTK_TYPE_BIN, &button_info);
      gtk_type_set_chunk_alloc (button_type, 16);
    }

  return button_type;
}
```

The code fills in a struct with information about the class and then hands that struct to GTK+ to get a type identifier (GtkType). Only six components of the GtkTypeInfo struct are important. GtkButton gives GTK+ a human-readable name for the class (which is used in error messages and the like), the size of the instance and class structs, and one function to initialize the class struct and another to initialize each new instance. The sixth and seventh members of the struct (reserved_1 and reserved_2) are obsolete and preserved only for compatibility. The final member is a pointer to a base class initialization function, which is used to initialize the class struct of any sub-classes.

gtk_type_unique() registers the new type and obtains a type identifier. The GTK_TYPE_BIN argument is a macro containing the type of GtkButton's parent class, GtkBin. The call to gtk_type_set_chunk_alloc() optimizes memory allocation for this type; it is never required and should be used only for frequently allocated types like GtkButton.

Given a registered `GtkButton` type, the following code creates a type instance:

```
GtkWidget*
gtk_button_new (void)
{
  return GTK_WIDGET (gtk_type_new (gtk_button_get_type ()));
}
```

The newborn `GtkButton` will be initialized by its instance initializer. The instance initialization function is called each time an instance of the type is created; it gives the object's data members reasonable default values:

```
static void
gtk_button_init (GtkButton *button)
{
  GTK_WIDGET_SET_FLAGS (button, GTK_CAN_FOCUS);
  GTK_WIDGET_UNSET_FLAGS (button, GTK_NO_WINDOW);

  button->child = NULL;
  button->in_button = FALSE;
  button->button_down = FALSE;
  button->relief = GTK_RELIEF_NORMAL;
}
```

Remember that `gtk_button_init()` was passed to `gtk_type_unique()` when the `GtkButton` type was created. GTK+ stores the function pointer and uses it to create `GtkButton` instances.

Instance structs are created with all bits set to zero. So setting members to zero or `NULL` is not strictly necessary. Still, most GTK+ code does initialize the members for clarity.

To fully understand the class initialization and base class initialization functions, you need some background information. You will know how to write them after you read this chapter.

9.3   Initializing a New Class

When a type is first used, GTK+ creates an instance of its class struct (using the information supplied to `gtk_type_unique()`). To initialize the class struct for a type, GTK+ first verifies that all parent classes are initialized and initializes them if not. Then it fills the top portion of the class struct with a byte-for-byte copy of the parent's class struct. This means the subclass inherits any function pointers found in the parent class.

Next, the base class initialization functions of each parent class and that of the class itself are called in order, starting with `GtkObject`. (The base class init function is the last argument to `gtk_type_unique()`. A base class initializer is optional; in the `GtkButton` case, there is none. If present, the base class initializer supplements the byte-for-byte copy of the class struct. For example, some functions should not be inherited. To prevent class function inheritance, the base class initializer can zero certain function pointers. Normally, you do not need a base class initializer.

Finally, GTK+ calls the type's own class init function. The class init function can override functions from the parent class by replacing them in the class struct. It should also fill in any functions unique to the subclass and register signals and object arguments (discussed later in the chapter).

A concrete example should make the class creation process clear. The class hierarchy for GtkButton is shown in Figure 9.1. When the GtkButton type is registered, an empty GtkButtonClass is created. This class struct is initialized as described here:

1. The class struct for GtkBin, GtkButton's immediate parent, is copied into it. This means GtkButton inherits class functions from GtkBin.

2. The base class initialization function for GtkObject is called on it. This zeroes some GtkObject class functions that should not be inherited.

3. There is no base class initializer for GtkWidget; if there were one, it would be called.

4. The base class initializer for GtkContainer is called. This zeroes some GtkContainer class functions that should not be inherited and initializes a GtkContainerClass data member.

5. There is no base class initializer for GtkBin; if there were one, it would be called.

6. There is no base class initializer for GtkButton; if there were one, it would be called.

7. The class initializer is called for GtkButton. This fills in the GtkButtonClass structure, registers signals, and registers object arguments.

When writing a new class, you only need to concern yourself with the final two steps: You should consider whether a base class initializer is needed and supply it if so; you must supply a class initializer in all cases.

```
GtkObject
    |
GtkWidget
    |
GtkContainer
    |
GtkBin
    |
GtkButton
```

Figure 9.1 GtkButton ancestry.

Here is the `GtkButton` class initialization function, which will give you an initial sense of things. Read on to learn what this code does.

```
static void
gtk_button_class_init (GtkButtonClass *klass)
{
  GtkObjectClass *object_class;
  GtkWidgetClass *widget_class;
  GtkContainerClass *container_class;

  object_class = (GtkObjectClass*) klass;
  widget_class = (GtkWidgetClass*) klass;
  container_class = (GtkContainerClass*) klass;

  parent_class = gtk_type_class (GTK_TYPE_BIN);

  gtk_object_add_arg_type ("GtkButton::label",
                           GTK_TYPE_STRING,
                           GTK_ARG_READWRITE,
                           ARG_LABEL);
  gtk_object_add_arg_type ("GtkButton::relief",
                           GTK_TYPE_RELIEF_STYLE,
                           GTK_ARG_READWRITE,
                           ARG_RELIEF);


  button_signals[PRESSED] =
    gtk_signal_new ("pressed",
                    GTK_RUN_FIRST,
                    object_class->type,
                    GTK_SIGNAL_OFFSET (GtkButtonClass, pressed),
                    gtk_marshal_NONE__NONE,
                    GTK_TYPE_NONE, 0);
  button_signals[RELEASED] =
    gtk_signal_new ("released",
                    GTK_RUN_FIRST,
                    object_class->type,
                    GTK_SIGNAL_OFFSET (GtkButtonClass, released),
                    gtk_marshal_NONE__NONE,
                    GTK_TYPE_NONE, 0);
  button_signals[CLICKED] =
    gtk_signal_new ("clicked",
                    GTK_RUN_FIRST | GTK_RUN_ACTION,
                    object_class->type,
                    GTK_SIGNAL_OFFSET (GtkButtonClass, clicked),
                    gtk_marshal_NONE__NONE,
                    GTK_TYPE_NONE, 0);
  button_signals[ENTER] =
    gtk_signal_new ("enter",
                    GTK_RUN_FIRST,
                    object_class->type,
```

```
                            GTK_SIGNAL_OFFSET (GtkButtonClass, enter),
                            gtk_marshal_NONE__NONE,
                            GTK_TYPE_NONE, 0);
    button_signals[LEAVE] =
      gtk_signal_new ("leave",
                            GTK_RUN_FIRST,
                            object_class->type,
                            GTK_SIGNAL_OFFSET (GtkButtonClass, leave),
                            gtk_marshal_NONE__NONE,
                            GTK_TYPE_NONE, 0);


    gtk_object_class_add_signals (object_class, button_signals,
LAST_SIGNAL);


    object_class->set_arg = gtk_button_set_arg;
    object_class->get_arg = gtk_button_get_arg;

    widget_class->activate_signal = button_signals[CLICKED];
    widget_class->realize = gtk_button_realize;
    widget_class->draw = gtk_button_draw;
    widget_class->draw_focus = gtk_button_draw_focus;
    widget_class->draw_default = gtk_button_draw_default;
    widget_class->size_request = gtk_button_size_request;
    widget_class->size_allocate = gtk_button_size_allocate;
    widget_class->expose_event = gtk_button_expose;
    widget_class->button_press_event = gtk_button_button_press;
    widget_class->button_release_event = gtk_button_button_release;
    widget_class->enter_notify_event = gtk_button_enter_notify;
    widget_class->leave_notify_event = gtk_button_leave_notify;
    widget_class->focus_in_event = gtk_button_focus_in;
    widget_class->focus_out_event = gtk_button_focus_out;

    container_class->add = gtk_button_add;
    container_class->remove = gtk_button_remove;
    container_class->child_type = gtk_button_child_type;

    klass->pressed = gtk_real_button_pressed;
    klass->released = gtk_real_button_released;
    klass->clicked = NULL;
    klass->enter = gtk_real_button_enter;
    klass->leave = gtk_real_button_leave;
  }
```

The following sections will return to this code; you should understand all of it by the end of the chapter.

9.4 *GtkArg* and the Type System

Before delving further into GtkObject, you will need more details on GTK+'s type system. The type system is used in many contexts:

- It allows signals and callbacks with any signature to be dynamically registered and dynamically queried. Function argument lists can be constructed at runtime.

- It allows object attributes (values that you can "get" or "set") to be dynamically queried and manipulated.

- It exports information about enumerations and bitfields (lists of permitted values and human-readable names).

- It is possible to identify types at runtime and traverse the object class hierarchy.

Because of its type system, GTK+ is particularly easy to manipulate from dynamically typed interactive languages. Bindings are available for nearly all popular languages, and the bindings can be lightweight (because GTK+ already includes much of the needed functionality, and types can be handled generically, which reduces the amount of glue code). You can find a complete list of functions for querying and using GTK+'s type system in gtk/gtktypeutils.h. Most of the functions are not useful in applications. Only the functions of general interest are described in this book.

GTK+ has a number of so-called *fundamental* types that are automatically registered during gtk_init() (or gnome_init()). The fundamental types include all the primitive C types, some GTK+ types (such as GTK_TYPE_SIGNAL), and GTK_TYPE_OBJECT. Fundamental types are essentially the "base classes" understood by the GTK+ type system. For example, the fundamental type of any enumeration is GTK_TYPE_ENUM, and the fundamental type of any GtkObject subclass is GTK_TYPE_OBJECT. Fundamental types are supposed to cover all the "special cases" in the GTK+ type system. All types ultimately derive from some fundamental type. A type's fundamental type is extracted from a GtkType with the GTK_FUNDAMENTAL_TYPE() macro. The fundamental types are listed in Table 9.1.

Table 9.1 **The GTK+ Fundamental Types**

GtkType **Constant**	**Corresponding C Type**
GTK_TYPE_INVALID	None
GTK_TYPE_NONE	void
GTK_TYPE_CHAR	gchar
GTK_TYPE_UCHAR	guchar
GTK_TYPE_BOOL	gboolean
GTK_TYPE_INT	gint
GTK_TYPE_UINT	guint
GTK_TYPE_LONG	glong
GTK_TYPE_ULONG	gulong

continues

Table 9.1 **Continued**

GtkType **Constant**	**Corresponding C Type**
GTK_TYPE_FLOAT	gfloat
GTK_TYPE_DOUBLE	gdouble
GTK_TYPE_STRING	gchar*
GTK_TYPE_ENUM	Any enumeration
GTK_TYPE_FLAGS	guint
GTK_TYPE_BOXED	gpointer
GTK_TYPE_POINTER	gpointer
GTK_TYPE_SIGNAL	GtkSignalFunc, gpointer
GTK_TYPE_ARGS	gint, GtkArg*
GTK_TYPE_CALLBACK	GtkCallbackMarshal, gpointer, GtkDestroyNotify
GTK_TYPE_C_CALLBACK	GtkFunction, gpointer
GTK_TYPE_FOREIGN	gpointer, GtkDestroyNotify
GTK_TYPE_OBJECT	GtkObject*

There is a second category of GtkType values: *Built-in* types are registered by GTK+ and libgnomeui during library initialization and are, therefore, always available. Built-in types include enumerations, flags, and some structs (GdkWindow and GdkImlibImage, for example). Built-in types are distinct from fundamental types because the GTK+ type system does not have to understand them. For the purposes of getting and setting argument values, they can be treated as fundamental types. They are somewhat arbitrarily distinguished from user-registered enumeration or flag types. (The difference between built-in types and user types is merely the time of registration.)

Built-in types are all accessible via macros that come with GTK+ and Gnome. These begin with GTK_TYPE_, as in: GTK_TYPE_WINDOW, GTK_TYPE_GDK_WINDOW, GTK_TYPE_RELIEF_STYLE, and GTK_TYPE_GNOME_DIALOG. As you can see, the name of the type macro is derived from the name of the GtkObject, struct, or enumeration. If the object name begins with "GTK," the "GTK" is dropped. The above examples map to the GtkWindow widget, GdkWindow struct, GtkReliefStyle enumeration, and GnomeDialog widget, respectively.

The final major category of GtkType values contains the registered GtkObject types. These are registered the first time the _get_type() routine for each object is called.

Some of the fundamental types require further explanation. Here's a brief list of those:

- GTK_TYPE_INVALID: Used to signal errors.
- GTK_TYPE_NONE: Used to indicate a void return value when specifying the signature of a signal.
- GTK_TYPE_BOXED: Subtypes of GTK_TYPE_BOXED are used to mark the type of a pointer; language bindings will special case these types. Most Gdk types, such as GdkWindow, are registered as boxed types.

- GTK_TYPE_SIGNAL: Special-cased in GtkObject; it allows users to connect signal handlers with gtk_object_set(). It should not be useful in application code.

- GTK_TYPE_ARGS: Type of an array of GtkArg. (When used with gtk_object_set(), an integer array length followed by the array itself is expected as arguments.)

- GTK_TYPE_CALLBACK: Interpreted language bindings can use this to pass signal callbacks around.

- GTK_TYPE_C_CALLBACK: This is used for other kinds of callbacks, such as callbacks that are not attached to signals (for example, the argument to a _foreach() function).

- GTK_TYPE_FOREIGN: Unused in current GTK+ code. Represents a pointer plus a function used to destroy the pointed-to resource; intended to represent object data, for example (see Section 9.8).

A fundamental type describes not only the data layout but also how memory is managed. For values passed in as arguments, the called function is not allowed to retain the pointer beyond the duration of the call. For returned values, the caller assumes ownership of the memory. GTK_TYPE_BOXED, GTK_TYPE_ARGS, and GTK_TYPE_STRING obey this rule.

Note that you should almost always use the most informative type available. Notably, GTK_TYPE_POINTER should be used only for generic pointers (gpointer). Whenever possible, you should use a "subclass" of GTK_TYPE_BOXED such as GTK_TYPE_GDK_WINDOW or GTK_TYPE_GDK_EVENT. Similarly, it is better to use a specific enumeration type than to use GTK_TYPE_ENUM. GTK_TYPE_CALLBACK is normally preferred over GTK_TYPE_C_CALLBACK and GTK_TYPE_SIGNAL because GTK_TYPE_CALLBACK includes information about how to marshal the function and destroy the callback data.

GTK+ has a consistent interface for passing typed values around; to do that, however, it needs a data structure that stores a type tag and a value. GtkArg fills the bill. Here is its definition, from gtk/gtktypeutils.h:

```
typedef struct _GtkArg GtkArg;

struct _GtkArg
{
  GtkType type;
  gchar *name;

  union {
    gchar char_data;
    guchar uchar_data;
    gboolean bool_data;
    gint int_data;
    guint uint_data;
    glong long_data;
    gulong ulong_data;
    gfloat float_data;
```

```
        gdouble double_data;
        gchar *string_data;
        gpointer pointer_data;
        GtkObject *object_data;

        struct {
          GtkSignalFunc f;
          gpointer d;
        } signal_data;
        struct {
          gint n_args;
          GtkArg *args;
        } args_data;
        struct {
          GtkCallbackMarshal marshal;
          gpointer data;
          GtkDestroyNotify notify;
        } callback_data;
        struct {
          GtkFunction func;
          gpointer func_data;
        } c_callback_data;
        struct {
          gpointer data;
          GtkDestroyNotify notify;
        } foreign_data;
      } d;
    };
```

The type field contains the value's GtkType, as you might expect. The name field is an object argument name (more on arguments in a moment). The final union stores a value of the appropriate type, and there is one union member for each fundamental type. This value field should be accessed using a special set of macros provided for the purpose, as listed in Macro Listing 9.1. Each macro corresponds to a fundamental type. These macros are defined so that you can use the & operator on them (as in &GTK_VALUE_CHAR(arg)).

Macro Listing 9.1 **Macros for Accessing *GtkArg* Values**   *#include <gtk/gtktypeutils.h>*

```
GTK_VALUE_CHAR(arg)
GTK_VALUE_UCHAR(arg)
GTK_VALUE_BOOL(arg)
GTK_VALUE_INT(arg)
GTK_VALUE_UINT(arg)
GTK_VALUE_LONG(arg)
GTK_VALUE_ULONG(arg)
GTK_VALUE_FLOAT(arg)
GTK_VALUE_DOUBLE(arg)
GTK_VALUE_STRING(arg)
GTK_VALUE_ENUM(arg)
```

```
GTK_VALUE_FLAGS(arg)
GTK_VALUE_BOXED(arg)
GTK_VALUE_POINTER(arg)
GTK_VALUE_OBJECT(arg)
GTK_VALUE_SIGNAL(arg)
GTK_VALUE_ARGS(arg)
GTK_VALUE_CALLBACK(arg)
GTK_VALUE_C_CALLBACK(arg)
GTK_VALUE_FOREIGN(arg)
```

To print a `GtkArg`'s value, you might write code like this:

```
GtkArg arg;

/* ... */

switch (GTK_FUNDAMENTAL_TYPE (arg.type))
  {
  case GTK_TYPE_INT:
    printf("arg: %d\n", GTK_VALUE_INT(arg));
    break;
  /* ... case for each type ... */
  }
```

9.5   Object Arguments

Arguments are one of the more interesting features of `GtkObject`. Arguments offer a mechanism for handling what CORBA's Interface Definition Language (IDL) calls an "attribute:" a value with a "getter" and a "setter." In concrete terms, object arguments pair a key (which is a string) with a value (represented as a `GtkArg`). Each `GtkObject` subclass can register permissible keys and the `GtkTypes` of their associated values.

By using object arguments, one can discover at runtime what attributes an object has and then get or set their values. This is very useful for people implementing GUI builders because some of the widget configuration dialog boxes can be automated. Similarly, it makes it much easier to write GTK+ bindings for scripting languages. It can also be convenient for programmers because it lets them avoid writing get/set functions. The `GnomeCanvas`, for example, uses object arguments for almost all of its API. Finally, object arguments may be configurable via the `gtkrc` configuration mechanism in a future version of GTK+, making it possible for users to extensively customize GTK+ software.

9.5.1   Setting Object Arguments

Most commonly, arguments are used as an API to set attributes of widgets. However, not all of the GTK+ API has been exported via arguments. So, it is not always possible.[1]

To set widget attributes, the most convenient interface is gtk_object_set(). Here's an example:

```
gtk_object_set(GTK_OBJECT(vbox),
               "GtkContainer::border_width", (gulong) 10,
               NULL);
```

The above code is identical in effect to the following:

```
gtk_container_set_border_width(GTK_CONTAINER(vbox), 10);
```

It's up to you which one you use; it depends on the context. Typically, you would use the argument mechanism if you have a reason to, such as if you are using its dynamic, runtime-oriented features. However, if you are setting several attributes, it may be easier to type and read.

gtk_object_set() takes a GtkObject as the first argument, followed by any number of key-value pairs. If a key is not defined for the object you pass in, a runtime error will be triggered. The list of key-value pairs must be terminated with a NULL key. When a GtkObject registers itself with GTK+, it tells GTK+ what type of value to expect after each key. For the aggregate fundamental types, gtk_object_set() will expect more than one C function argument after the key. For example, first a signal function and then a user data pointer will be expected after GTK_TYPE_SIGNAL arguments. (Table 9.1 gives the types of the expected arguments.)

It is permissible to leave off the object class portion of an argument name. For example, "GtkContainer::border_width" can be simply "border_width", as shown here:

```
gtk_object_set(GTK_OBJECT(vbox),
               "border_width", (gulong) 10,
               NULL);
```

If you do not specify the class name as part of the argument name, GTK+ will start with the real type of the object and look up the argument name in the argument table for each superclass until it finds the right one (GtkContainer in this case). If you do specify the class name, GTK+ will look for the argument in the specified class's argument table only.

Because gtk_object_set() uses C variable argument lists, it has limited type safety. This can be a real problem in your code. You may have noticed the cast to gulong in the sample call to gtk_object_set(). The argument GtkContainer::border_width has type GTK_TYPE_ULONG. GTK+ will extract sizeof(gulong) bytes from the argument list when it encounters this argument. If you leave out the cast, C will probably pass only sizeof(gint) bytes to the function. As you might imagine, this causes memory corruption on many platforms. A similar problem arises with arguments of type

---

1. This is due to lack of time rather than lack of will; patches to add argument support to objects that don't have it are welcome.

GTK_TYPE_DOUBLE. If you type 5 instead of 5.0, C will pass an integer to
gtk_object_set(). These bugs are very hard to find after you introduce them.

gtk_object_set() is syntactic sugar for a more fundamental function call:
gtk_object_setv(). gtk_object_setv() takes a vector of GtkArg (gtk_object_set()
converts each key-value pair in its argument list to GtkArg internally).

```
GtkArg args[1];
args[0].name = "GtkContainer::border_width";
args[0].type = GTK_TYPE_ULONG;
GTK_VALUE_ULONG(args[0]) = 10;
gtk_object_setv(GTK_OBJECT(button),
                1,
                args);
```

The second argument to gtk_object_setv() is the length of the array of GtkArg.
gtk_object_set() is plainly easier to use when you are typing the code manually,
but gtk_object_setv() can be passed a dynamically constructed argument array—
which is convenient if you're exporting GTK+ functionality to an interpreted
environment.

It is also possible to set object arguments when objects are created. You can create
most objects using the gtk_object_new() function, and you can create most widgets
with the gtk_widget_new() function. The routines take a GtkType as their first argument and create an object or widget of that type. They then take a list of argument-
value pairs, just as gtk_object_set() does. There are also gtk_object_newv() and
gtk_widget_newv() variants.

9.5.2 Reading Object Arguments

To get the value of one or more arguments, you simply create an array of GtkArg, filling in the name field of each GtkArg. gtk_object_getv() fills in the type fields and
the argument values. If an error occurs, the type field is set to GTK_TYPE_INVALID. If
the fundamental type of the returned value is GTK_TYPE_STRING, GTK_TYPE_BOXED, or
GTK_TYPE_ARGS, you are responsible for freeing it.

Here's a simple example:

```
GtkArg args[2];

args[0].name = "GtkContainer::border_width";
args[1].name = "GtkContainer::resize_mode";
gtk_object_getv(GTK_OBJECT(button),
                2,
                args);

g_assert(args[0].type == GTK_TYPE_ULONG);
g_assert(args[1].type == GTK_TYPE_RESIZE_MODE);
g_assert(GTK_FUNDAMENTAL_TYPE(args[1].type) == GTK_TYPE_ENUM);

printf("Border width: %lu Resize mode: %d\n",
       GTK_VALUE_ULONG(args[0]), GTK_VALUE_ENUM(args[1]));
```

9.5.3   Using Object Arguments in Your Own *GtkObject* Subclass

If you're writing a custom GtkObject or a custom subclass of some existing object, you can register your own object arguments in the class initialization function at the same time you register your object's signals. To do this, call gtk_object_add_arg_type(). Here's an example from GtkContainer:

```
gtk_object_add_arg_type("GtkContainer::border_width",
                        GTK_TYPE_ULONG,
                        GTK_ARG_READWRITE,
                        ARG_BORDER_WIDTH);
```

The first argument must be a static string constant because GTK+ does not copy it. It must also begin with the name of your new class, separated from the name of the argument by two colons (reminiscent of the C++ scope operator). The second argument should be the type of the argument; this can be any GtkType that GTK+ knows about. The third argument contains one or more flags, defined in gtk/gtkobject.h. Available flags include the following:

- GTK_ARG_READABLE means the argument's value can be read using gtk_object_getv().
- GTK_ARG_WRITABLE means the argument's value can be written using gtk_object_set() or gtk_object_setv().
- GTK_ARG_CONSTRUCT means the argument should be initialized with a default value. This applies to numeric and pointer types; they are set to 0 or NULL, respectively. (This happens within gtk_object_new() or gtk_widget_new(), which call gtk_object_default_construct().)
- GTK_ARG_CONSTRUCT_ONLY means the argument is used *only* for object construction; it cannot be read or written later. That is, you can't use these arguments with gtk_object_set().
- GTK_ARG_CHILD_ARG is used by subclasses of GtkContainer; GtkContainer implements a specialized variation on the argument system to permit setting the attributes of child-container pairs (such as packing flags for GtkBox; the flags are not a property of the child or the container, but of the pair). You will use this flag only if you're writing a new type of container or some other kind of object with similar semantics.
- GTK_ARG_READWRITE is shorthand for (GTK_ARG_READABLE | GTK_ARG_WRITABLE).

The following list outlines some limitations for flag use:

- All arguments must be either readable or writable.
- GTK_ARG_CONSTRUCT arguments must be both readable and writable.
- GTK_ARG_CONSTRUCT_ONLY arguments must be writable.
- GTK_ARG_CHILD_ARG should not be used outside of container-style object implementations; it is used internally by the GtkContainer child argument functions.

The fourth and final argument to gtk_object_add_arg_type() is an argument ID to be used by the object subclass to identify this argument. This can be any integer except 0, but it is customary to use a private enumeration in the object implementation's .c file. GtkObject has two class functions that any subclass with arguments must implement: one to get arguments specific to the subclass and one to set them. These functions are passed the argument ID so that they know which argument to get or set. Argument IDs reduce the need for string comparisons, increasing the efficiency of argument manipulation.

For example, GtkContainer defines these functions:

```
static void gtk_container_get_arg(GtkObject* object,
                                  GtkArg* arg,
                                  guint arg_id);
static void gtk_container_set_arg(GtkObject* object,
                                  GtkArg* arg,
                                  guint arg_id);
```

It uses this enumeration to create its argument IDs:

```
enum {
  ARG_0,                    /* Skip 0, an invalid argument ID */
  ARG_BORDER_WIDTH,
  ARG_RESIZE_MODE,
  ARG_CHILD
};
```

It registers its arguments in gtk_container_class_init() as shown here:

```
gtk_object_add_arg_type("GtkContainer::border_width",
                        GTK_TYPE_ULONG,
                        GTK_ARG_READWRITE,
                        ARG_BORDER_WIDTH);
gtk_object_add_arg_type("GtkContainer::resize_mode",
                        GTK_TYPE_RESIZE_MODE,
                        GTK_ARG_READWRITE,
                        ARG_RESIZE_MODE);
gtk_object_add_arg_type("GtkContainer::child",
                        GTK_TYPE_WIDGET,
                        GTK_ARG_WRITABLE,
                        ARG_CHILD);
```

gtk_container_set_arg() and gtk_container_get_arg() are installed in the class struct:

```
object_class->get_arg = gtk_container_get_arg;
object_class->set_arg = gtk_container_set_arg;
```

gtk_container_set_arg() and gtk_container_get_arg() are then implemented like this:

```
static void
gtk_container_set_arg (GtkObject    *object,
                       GtkArg       *arg,
                       guint        arg_id)
{
  GtkContainer *container;

  container = GTK_CONTAINER (object);

  switch (arg_id)
    {
    case ARG_BORDER_WIDTH:
      gtk_container_set_border_width (container, GTK_VALUE_ULONG (*arg));
      break;
    case ARG_RESIZE_MODE:
      gtk_container_set_resize_mode (container, GTK_VALUE_ENUM (*arg));
      break;
    case ARG_CHILD:
      gtk_container_add (container, GTK_WIDGET (GTK_VALUE_OBJECT (*arg)));
      break;
    default:
      break;
    }
}

static void
gtk_container_get_arg (GtkObject    *object,
                       GtkArg       *arg,
                       guint        arg_id)
{
  GtkContainer *container;

  container = GTK_CONTAINER (object);

  switch (arg_id)
    {
    case ARG_BORDER_WIDTH:
      GTK_VALUE_ULONG (*arg) = container->border_width;
      break;
    case ARG_RESIZE_MODE:
      GTK_VALUE_ENUM (*arg) = container->resize_mode;
      break;
    default:
      arg->type = GTK_TYPE_INVALID;
      break;
    }
}
```

Notice that the type must be set to `GTK_TYPE_INVALID` if your subclass doesn't understand the argument ID. This is used as an error indicator; users who call `gtk_object_getv()` will check for it.

If you flip back to the end of Section 9.3 and take another look at the `GtkButton` class initialization function, you should find that you now understand what is going on with respect to object arguments.

9.5.4 Discovering the Available Object Arguments

You can easily find out at runtime what arguments a given `GtkObject` understands by using `gtk_object_query_args()`. Here is a nifty piece of code that prints out the arguments for the entire class hierarchy of a given `GtkObject`:

```
void
print_arguments(GtkObject* object)
{
  GtkType type;

  type = GTK_OBJECT_TYPE(object);

  do {
    GtkArg* args;
    guint32* flags;
    guint n_args;
    guint i;

    args = gtk_object_query_args(type,
                                 &flags,
                                 &n_args);

    printf("Displaying arguments for object type `%s'\n",
           gtk_type_name(type));

    i = 0;
    while (i < n_args)
      {
        printf(" - Argument %u is called `%s' and has type `%s'\n",
               i,
               args[i].name,
               gtk_type_name(args[i].type));

        ++i;
      }

    g_free(args);
    g_free(flags);

    type = gtk_type_parent(type);
  }
  while (type != GTK_TYPE_INVALID);
}
```

Notice that a type's parent type can be obtained using the `gtk_type_parent()` function and that you can extract the `GtkType` tag from a `GtkObject` using the `GTK_OBJECT_TYPE()` macro. `GTK_OBJECT_TYPE()` is defined as follows:

```
#define GTK_OBJECT_TYPE(obj) (GTK_OBJECT (obj)->klass->type)
```

An object's type is stored in its class structure, and a pointer to an object's class structure is stored in each instance of the object. (The class structure pointer is called `klass` rather than `class` to avoid confusing C++ compilers.)

Function Listing 9.1 summarizes the functions for reading, writing, and querying object arguments.

Function Listing 9.1   **Manipulating Object Arguments**   *#include <gtk/gtkobject.h>*

```
void
gtk_object_getv(GtkObject* object,
                guint n_args,
                GtkArg* args)
void
gtk_object_set(GtkObject* object,
                const gchar* first_arg_name,
                ...)
void
gtk_object_setv(GtkObjec* object,
                guint n_args,
                GtkArg* args)
void
gtk_object_add_arg_type(const gchar* arg_name,
                        GtkType arg_type,
                        guint arg_flags,
                        guint arg_id)
GtkArg*
gtk_object_query_args(GtkType class_type,
                        guint32** arg_flags,
                        guint* n_args)
```

9.6   Signals

A `GtkObject` can emit a *signal*. Signals are stored in a global table by GTK+. *Handlers* or *callbacks* can be *connected* to signals; when a signal is *emitted*, its callbacks are invoked. The process of invoking all handlers for a signal is called *emission*.

Abstractly, a signal is a *kind* of message that an object wants to broadcast. The kind of message is associated with certain conditions (such as the user selecting a list item) and with message-specific parameter types that are passed to connected callbacks (such as the index of the row the user selected). User callbacks are connected to a particular signal and to a particular object instance. That is, you do not connect callbacks to the "clicked" signal of all buttons; rather, you connect to the "clicked" signal of a particular one. (However, there is a way to monitor all emissions of a signal; these callbacks are called "emission hooks.")

Signals are typically associated with a class function pointer that is invoked every time the signal is emitted. If non-NULL, the pointed-to class function serves as a default handler for the signal. It is up to the author of each GtkObject subclass to decide whether to provide a space in the class struct for a default handler and whether to implement the default handler in the base class. Conventionally, signals have the same name as the class function they are associated with.

For example, the GtkButtonClass struct has a member called clicked, which is registered as the default handler for the "clicked" signal. However, the GtkButton base class does not implement a default handler and leaves the clicked member set to NULL. Subclasses of GtkButton could optionally fill it in with an appropriate function. If GtkButton did implement a default "clicked" handler subclasses could still override it with a different one.

Note that GTK+ signals have nothing to do with UNIX signals. Sometimes new GTK+ users confuse the two.

9.6.1 Adding a New Signal

When you understand the GTK+ type system and GtkArg, signal registration is fairly transparent. Here is the signal registration code from GtkButton again:

```
button_signals[PRESSED] =
  gtk_signal_new ("pressed",
                  GTK_RUN_FIRST,
                  object_class->type,
                  GTK_SIGNAL_OFFSET (GtkButtonClass, pressed),
                  gtk_marshal_NONE__NONE,
                  GTK_TYPE_NONE, 0);
button_signals[RELEASED] =
  gtk_signal_new ("released",
                  GTK_RUN_FIRST,
                  object_class->type,
                  GTK_SIGNAL_OFFSET (GtkButtonClass, released),
                  gtk_marshal_NONE__NONE,
                  GTK_TYPE_NONE, 0);
button_signals[CLICKED] =
  gtk_signal_new ("clicked",
                  GTK_RUN_FIRST | GTK_RUN_ACTION,
                  object_class->type,
                  GTK_SIGNAL_OFFSET (GtkButtonClass, clicked),
                  gtk_marshal_NONE__NONE,
                  GTK_TYPE_NONE, 0);
```

```
button_signals[ENTER] =
  gtk_signal_new ("enter",
                 GTK_RUN_FIRST,
                 object_class->type,
                 GTK_SIGNAL_OFFSET (GtkButtonClass, enter),
                 gtk_marshal_NONE__NONE,
                 GTK_TYPE_NONE, 0);
button_signals[LEAVE] =
  gtk_signal_new ("leave",
                 GTK_RUN_FIRST,
                 object_class->type,
                 GTK_SIGNAL_OFFSET (GtkButtonClass, leave),
                 gtk_marshal_NONE__NONE,
                 GTK_TYPE_NONE, 0);

gtk_object_class_add_signals (object_class, button_signals,
LAST_SIGNAL);
```

Earlier in `gtkbutton.c`, an enumeration and an array were declared as shown here:

```
enum {
  PRESSED,
  RELEASED,
  CLICKED,
  ENTER,
  LEAVE,
  LAST_SIGNAL
};
```

```
static guint button_signals[LAST_SIGNAL] = { 0 };
```

`gtk_signal_new()` has the following effects:

- It registers the name of the signal.
- It associates the signal with a particular `GtkType`.
- It tells GTK+ where to find the default handler in the class struct (if any).
- It tells GTK+ what signature the signal's callbacks will have.
- It registers a *marshaller*, a function that invokes the signal's callbacks in an appropriate way.
- It generates an integer identifier that can be used to refer to the signal. (If you refer to the symbol by name, GTK+ will find the ID associated with the name and then use the ID.)

`gtk_object_class_add_signals()` attaches signal identifiers to the object's class struct so that the signals for a given class can be located quickly. Conventionally, the argument to this function is an enumeration-indexed static array, like that shown for `GtkButton`. The static array is also useful when implementing the functionality of the class (the signal identifiers are used to emit the signals).

The first argument to `gtk_signal_new()` is a name for the signal; you refer to the signal by name when you call `gtk_signal_connect()`, for example. The third argument is the `GtkType` of the object type emitting the signal, and the fourth is the location of the associated class function in the type's class struct. A macro is provided to compute the offset. If you specify an offset of `0`, no class function will be associated with the signal. Note that giving a zero offset is distinct from giving a valid offset but setting the function member in the struct to `NULL`; in the latter case, subclasses of the object can fill in a value for the default handler.

The second argument is a bitfield. Here are the associated flags:

- `GTK_RUN_FIRST` means that the default handler in the class struct, if any, will run before user-connected callbacks. If this flag is set, signal handlers should not return a value.

- `GTK_RUN_LAST` means the opposite: The default handler will run last. (Caveat: User callbacks connected with `gtk_signal_connect_after()` run after a `GTK_RUN_LAST` default handler. There is no way to ensure a default handler is *always* run last. However, `GTK_RUN_FIRST` handlers are always first.)

- `GTK_RUN_BOTH` is an alias for (`GTK_RUN_FIRST | GTK_RUN_LAST`). So, the default handler will run twice (on either side of user-connected callbacks).

- `GTK_RUN_NO_RECURSE` means that the signal should not be called recursively. If a handler for a signal emits the same signal again, normally the second emission is performed as usual (calling all handlers), and then the first emission continues, invoking its remaining handlers. With `GTK_RUN_NO_RECURSE` in effect, a second emission aborts the first emission (ignoring any handlers that remain) and restarts the emission process. So only one emission is in progress at a time. (Right now this is used only for `GtkAdjustment`'s `"changed"` and `"value_changed"` signals. Usually you don't care about how many times a value changed, only whether it changed and its most recent value. `GTK_RUN_NO_RECURSE` "compresses" multiple emissions into a single emission.)

- `GTK_RUN_ACTION` means the signal can be "bound" and invoked by the user. In other words, no special setup or shutdown is required in order to emit it. Among other things, GTK+ will allow users to bind keyboard accelerators to these signals using statements in the `.gtkrc` configuration file.

- `GTK_RUN_NO_HOOKS` means that emission hooks are not allowed (you can't monitor this signal for an entire object type, only for particular object instances). It is used for `GtkObject`'s `"destroy"` signal because hooks are not invoked on objects with the `GTK_DESTROYED` flag set and that flag is set before emitting `"destroy"`. It's probably not good for anything else.

The last few arguments to gtk_signal_new() provide a *marshaller* and tell GTK+ the marshaller's type. A marshaller invokes a callback function based on an array of GtkArg it receives from GTK+. Marshallers are needed because C function argument lists can't be constructed at runtime. GTK+ comes with a number of prewritten marshallers. Here is the one used for all GtkButton signals:

```
typedef void (*GtkSignal_NONE__NONE) (GtkObject* object,
                                      gpointer user_data);
void
gtk_marshal_NONE__NONE (GtkObject * object,
                        GtkSignalFunc func,
                        gpointer func_data,
                        GtkArg * args)
{
  GtkSignal_NONE__NONE rfunc;
  rfunc = (GtkSignal_NONE__NONE) func;
  (*rfunc) (object,
            func_data);
}
```

As you can see, the NONE__NONE refers to the fact that the expected callback type returns no value and has no "special" arguments. GTK+ automatically passes the object emitting the signal and a user_data field to all callbacks. Special signal arguments are inserted in between these two. Because there are no signal-specific arguments in this case, the array of GtkArg is ignored.

The naming convention for marshallers places a double underscore between the return value and the special arguments (if any). Here's a more complex example:

```
typedef gint (*GtkSignal_INT__POINTER) (GtkObject * object,
                                        gpointer arg1,
                                        gpointer user_data);
void
gtk_marshal_INT__POINTER (GtkObject * object,
                          GtkSignalFunc func,
                          gpointer func_data,
                          GtkArg * args)
{
  GtkSignal_INT__POINTER rfunc;
  gint *return_val;
  return_val = GTK_RETLOC_INT (args[1]);
  rfunc = (GtkSignal_INT__POINTER) func;
  *return_val = (*rfunc) (object,
                          GTK_VALUE_POINTER (args[0]),
                          func_data);
}
```

Notice that the last element of the array of GtkArg is a space for the return value. If there is no return value, this element will have type GTK_TYPE_NONE and can be ignored. GTK+ provides macros such as GTK_RETLOC_INT() to extract a "return location" from a GtkArg. Similar GTK_RETLOC_ macros exist for all the fundamental types.

The function pointer signatures in the class structure for an object will correspond to the type of the signal. This is a convenient way to find out what signature the callbacks connected to a signal should have, if the GTK+ header files are readily available on your system.

The last arguments to gtk_signal_new() give the type of the signal's marshaller. First a return value type is given, followed by the number of special arguments, and then a variable argument list containing that many GtkType values in the appropriate order. Because GtkButton has no examples of signals with arguments, here is one from GtkWidget:

```
widget_signals[BUTTON_PRESS_EVENT] =
  gtk_signal_new("button_press_event",
                GTK_RUN_LAST,
                object_class->type,
                GTK_SIGNAL_OFFSET (GtkWidgetClass, button_press_event),
                gtk_marshal_BOOL__POINTER,
                GTK_TYPE_BOOL, 1,
                GTK_TYPE_GDK_EVENT);
```

"button_press_event" returns a boolean value and has a GdkEvent* argument. Notice that the marshaller works with any GTK_TYPE_POINTER, but the signal requires the more specific boxed type GTK_TYPE_GDK_EVENT, allowing language bindings to query the correct *kind* of pointer.

Signals can have many arguments. Here is one from GtkCList:

```
clist_signals[SELECT_ROW] =
  gtk_signal_new ("select_row",
                GTK_RUN_FIRST,
                object_class->type,
                GTK_SIGNAL_OFFSET (GtkCListClass, select_row),
                gtk_marshal_NONE__INT_INT_POINTER,
                GTK_TYPE_NONE, 3,
                GTK_TYPE_INT,
                GTK_TYPE_INT,
                GTK_TYPE_GDK_EVENT);
```

The "select_row" signal returns no value but has three arguments (the selected row, column number, and the event that caused the selection).

9.6.2 Using Existing Signals

Function Listing 9.2 shows the wide array of functions available for manipulating signals.

Function Listing 9.2 **Using Signals** *#include <gtk/gtksignal.h>*

```
guint
gtk_signal_lookup(const gchar* name,
                  GtkType object_type)

gchar*
gtk_signal_name(guint signal_id)

void
gtk_signal_emit_stop(GtkObject* object,
                     guint signal_id)

void
gtk_signal_emit_stop_by_name(GtkObject* object,
                             const gchar* name)

guint
gtk_signal_connect(GtkObject* object,
                   const gchar* name,
                   GtkSignalFunc func,
                   gpointer func_data)

guint
gtk_signal_connect_after(GtkObject* object,
                         const gchar* name,
                         GtkSignalFunc func,
                         gpointer func_data)

guint
gtk_signal_connect_object(GtkObject* object,
                          const gchar* name,
                          GtkSignalFunc func,
                          GtkObject* slot_object)

guint
gtk_signal_connect_object_after(GtkObject* object,
                                const gchar* name,
                                GtkSignalFunc func,
                                GtkObject* slot_object)

guint
gtk_signal_connect_full(GtkObject* object,
                        const gchar* name,
                        GtkSignalFunc func,
                        GtkCallbackMarshal marshal,
                        gpointer data,
                        GtkDestroyNotify destroy_func,
                        gint object_signal,
                        gint after)
```

```
void
gtk_signal_connect_object_while_alive(GtkObject* object,
                                      const gchar* signal,
                                      GtkSignalFunc func,
                                      GtkObject* alive_object)
void
gtk_signal_connect_while_alive(GtkObject* object,
                               const gchar* signal,
                               GtkSignalFunc func,
                               gpointer func_data,
                               GtkObject  * alive_object)
void
gtk_signal_disconnect(GtkObject* object,
                      guint handler_id)
void
gtk_signal_disconnect_by_func(GtkObject* object,
                              GtkSignalFunc func,
                              gpointer func_data)
void
gtk_signal_disconnect_by_data(GtkObject  * object,
                              gpointer func_data)
void
gtk_signal_handler_block(GtkObject* object,
                         guint handler_id)
void
gtk_signal_handler_block_by_func(GtkObject* object,
                                 GtkSignalFunc func,
                                 gpointer func_data)
void
gtk_signal_handler_block_by_data(GtkObject* object,
                                 gpointer func_data)
void
gtk_signal_handler_unblock(GtkObject* object,
                           guint handler_id)
void
gtk_signal_handler_unblock_by_func(GtkObject* object,
                                   GtkSignalFunc func,
                                   gpointer func_data)
void
gtk_signal_handler_unblock_by_data(GtkObject* object,
                                   gpointer func_data)
guint
gtk_signal_add_emission_hook(guint signal_id,
                             GtkEmissionHook hook_func,
                             gpointer data)
guint
gtk_signal_add_emission_hook_full(guint signal_id,
                                  GtkEmissionHook hook_func,
```

continues

Function Listing 9.2 **Continued**

```
                                gpointer data,
                                GDestroyNotify destroy)
void
gtk_signal_remove_emission_hook(guint signal_id,
                                guint hook_id)

GtkSignalQuery*
gtk_signal_query(guint signal_id)
```

You should already be familiar with the most fundamental signal operation: connecting a signal handler to be invoked when the signal is emitted. It looks like this:

```
gtk_signal_connect(GTK_OBJECT(window),
                   "delete_event",
                   GTK_SIGNAL_FUNC(delete_event_cb),
                   NULL);

gtk_signal_connect(GTK_OBJECT(button),
                   "clicked",
                   GTK_SIGNAL_FUNC(button_click_cb),
                   label);
```

You may not be aware that `gtk_signal_connect()` returns a "handler ID," which can be used to refer to the connection it creates. Using the handler ID, you can unregister the callback with `gtk_signal_disconnect()`. You can also temporarily "block" the callback by calling `gtk_signal_handler_block()`. This increments a "block count," and the callback will not be invoked until the block count returns to 0. `gtk_signal_handler_unblock()` decrements the block count. Both `gtk_signal_disconnect()` and `gtk_signal_handler_unblock()` have variants that search for the handler ID given a callback function or user data pointer. These are possibly more convenient, but they decrease efficiency somewhat.

It can be useful to block signal handlers if you'll be changing some aspect of an object yourself and, therefore, don't need to run the callbacks you use to respond to user actions. For example, you normally change some boolean variable if the user clicks a toggle button, in a callback connected to the `"toggled"` signal. If you update the toggle button programmatically because the flag was changed via some mechanism other than the button, `"toggled"` will still be emitted; but you want to block your callback because the flag is already correct.

`gtk_signal_connect()` is not the only way to connect to a signal. You can also use `gtk_signal_connect_object()`, which simply swaps the signal-emitting object pointer and the user data pointer in the arguments passed to the callback. Normally, the object comes first, followed by any arguments unique to the signal and then the user data pointer. With `gtk_signal_connect_object()` however the object is last, and user data is first. This function is useful when you want to use an existing function as a callback without writing a wrapper to move its arguments, as in this example:

```
gtk_signal_connect_object(GTK_OBJECT(button),
                          "clicked",
                          GTK_SIGNAL_FUNC(gtk_widget_destroy),
                          GTK_OBJECT(dialog));
```

Because the user data and the button are swapped, the first argument to `gtk_widget _destroy()` will be the dialog box rather than the button, closing the dialog box. When you use `gtk_signal_connect_object()`, your callback data must be a `GtkObject` to avoid confusing marshallers that expect an object as their first argument.

`gtk_signal_connect_after()` asks GTK+ to run the callback after the object's default signal handler instead of before it. However, this works only with certain signals: those with the `GTK_RUN_LAST` flag set. Section 9.6.1 explains this flag. `gtk_ signal_connect_object_after()` combines the effects of `gtk_signal_connect_object()` and `gtk_signal_connect_after()`.

`gtk_signal_connect_full()` gives you complete control over the connection and is mostly useful in language bindings. The `object_signal` and `after` arguments can be `TRUE` or `FALSE`, toggling argument order and time of callback invocation. The functions just mentioned also let you change this. So, `gtk_signal_connect_full()` doesn't add much. Its unique features are the ability to specify a callback marshaller and the ability to specify a `GtkDestroyNotify` function. Notice that `gtk_signal_connect_full()` does not expect the same kind of marshaller described in Section 9.6.1; it expects a more general marshaller appropriate for marshalling functions written in languages other than C. If you give a non-`NULL` `GtkDestroyNotify` function, it will be invoked on the user data pointer when this handler is disconnected or the `GtkObject` is destroyed. Here is the proper signature for the function:

```
typedef void (*GtkDestroyNotify)  (gpointer  data);
```

Conveniently, you can use `g_free()` or `gtk_object_destroy()` as a `GtkDestroyNotify`. Of course, if neither of these is appropriate, you can write a custom function.

`gtk_signal_connect_while_alive()` is a variant on `gtk_signal_connect()`. Its additional argument is an object to monitor. When the monitored object is destroyed (emits the `"destroy"` signal), the handler will be disconnected. That is, handlers connected with this function are automatically disconnected when a specified object no longer exists.

There's rarely a need to do so, but you can look up a signal's ID number if you know the signal name and the object type that emits it. The function to use is `gtk_signal_lookup()`. Note that names are not globally unique, but they are unique with respect to a particular object type. On the other hand, signal IDs *are* globally unique.

During the emission of a signal (that is, during the process of invoking its handlers), you can call gtk_signal_emit_stop() (or its by_name() variant) to halt the emission. These functions are only useful from within signal handlers because they must be called during the emission process or they won't have anything to stop. They do not take effect immediately; instead, they set a variable that GTK+ checks at key points during emission. Section 9.6.4 describes this in detail.

Emission hooks can be used to monitor all emissions of a given signal (regardless of the object instance doing the emitting). Emission hooks have the following signature:

```
typedef gboolean (*GtkEmissionHook) (GtkObject    *object,
                                      guint        signal_id,
                                      guint        n_params,
                                      GtkArg       *params,
                                      gpointer     data);
```

They are passed the same parameters GTK+ would normally pass to callback marshallers (see Section 9.6.1). You can connect an emission hook with a destroy notify function to be invoked on the user data pointer when the hook is removed. When you add an emission hook, an integer identify is returned. You can remove emission hooks with this ID number.

Emission hooks are rarely useful, but sometimes they are the only way to do something. For example, Gnome optionally plays sound effects when certain signals are emitted (such as button clicks).

Finally, you can ask everything you ever wanted to know about a signal by using gtk_signal_query(). This function is intended for GUI builders and language bindings; it is probably not useful in application code. It returns a GtkSignalQuery structure filled with information about the signal. The return value should be freed with g_free() but not modified in any way (it contains pointers to internal data that isn't copied). Here is the definition of GtkSignalQuery:

```
typedef struct _GtkSignalQuery GtkSignalQuery;

struct _GtkSignalQuery
{
  GtkType          object_type;
  guint            signal_id;
  const gchar      *signal_name;
  guint            is_user_signal : 1;
  GtkSignalRunType signal_flags;
  GtkType          return_val;
  guint            nparams;
  const GtkType    *params;
};
```

9.6.3 Emitting a Signal

It's your object's responsibility to emit its signals at appropriate times. This is very simple. If you've saved the return value from gtk_signal_new(), that identifier can be used to emit the signal. Otherwise, you can emit the signal by name (with some cost in execution speed because GTK+ will have to look up the identifier in a hash table).

Here is code from gtk/gtkbutton.c that is used to emit the "button_pressed" signal:

```
void
gtk_button_pressed (GtkButton *button)
{
  g_return_if_fail (button != NULL);
  g_return_if_fail (GTK_IS_BUTTON (button));

  gtk_signal_emit (GTK_OBJECT (button), button_signals[PRESSED]);
}
```

If a signal has arguments (other than the standard two), you must specify those in a variable argument list:

```
gtk_signal_emit (GTK_OBJECT (widget), widget_signals[SIZE_REQUEST],
                 &widget->requisition);
```

If a signal returns a value, you must pass a location for the returned value as the final argument:

```
gint return_val;

return_val = FALSE;

gtk_signal_emit (GTK_OBJECT (widget), widget_signals[EVENT], event,
                 &return_val);
```

Notice that return_val is initialized to something sane. If there are no signal handlers, none of them will assign a value to return_val. Therefore, you must initialize the variable. Each signal handler's return value will be assigned to the same location. So, the final value of return_val is determined by the last signal handler to run. Note that certain return values (such as strings) must be freed by the signal emitter.

gtk_signal_emit_by_name() is the same as gtk_signal_emit(), except that the second argument is a signal name rather than a signal ID number. There are also variants of both emission functions that take a vector of GtkArg instead of a variable argument list. These variants expect arrays of $n+1$ GtkArg structs, where n is the number of signal arguments and there is an additional GtkArg for the return value. The GtkArg structs should be initialized with sane values. If the function returns no value, the return value GtkArg will have GTK_TYPE_NONE.

All four signal emission functions are summarized in Function Listing 9.3.

Function Listing 9.3 **Signal Emission** *#include <gtk/gtksignal.h>*

```
void
gtk_signal_emit(GtkObject* object,
                guint signal_id,
                ...)
void
gtk_signal_emit_by_name(GtkObject* object,
                        const gchar* name,
                        ...)
void
gtk_signal_emitv(GtkObject* object,
                 guint signal_id,
                 GtkArg* params)
void
gtk_signal_emitv_by_name(GtkObject* object,
                         const gchar* name,
                         GtkArg* params)
```

Keep in mind that it is usually inappropriate to simply emit a signal outside of an object's implementation. Only GTK_RUN_ACTION signals are guaranteed to work properly without special setup or shutdown. Objects often export functions that you can use to emit signals properly. For example, to emit the "size_request" signal, GtkWidget provides this function:

```
void
gtk_widget_size_request (GtkWidget      *widget,
                         GtkRequisition *requisition)
{
  g_return_if_fail (widget != NULL);
  g_return_if_fail (GTK_IS_WIDGET (widget));

  gtk_widget_ref (widget);
  gtk_widget_ensure_style (widget);
  gtk_signal_emit (GTK_OBJECT (widget), widget_signals[SIZE_REQUEST],
                   &widget->requisition);

  if (requisition)
    gtk_widget_get_child_requisition (widget, requisition);

  gtk_widget_unref (widget);
}
```

As you can see, particular actions are required before and after emitting the signal; thus it should be emitted only via the gtk_widget_size_request() function.

9.6.4 What Happens When a Signal Is Emitted

Given the many different options available when creating signals and connecting callbacks, you may be thoroughly confused about what happens when a signal is emitted. Here's a summary of the sequence of events:

1. If you are emitting the signal by name, the signal ID is looked up.

2. If another emission of the same signal is in progress and the signal has the `GTK_RUN_NO_RECURSE` flag set, GTK+ signals the previous emission to restart, and this emission ends.

3. If the signal is `GTK_RUN_FIRST`, the default signal handler is called using the signal's marshaller. If the emission is stopped from within the handler (using `gtk_emit_stop_by_name()` or one of its cousins), this emission ends. If the signal is re-emitted from within the handler and is `GTK_RUN_NO_RECURSE`, this emission restarts.

4. If there are any emission hooks installed for this signal, they are invoked. GTK+ does *not* check whether the emission has been stopped or re-emitted at this point; it will not check until the next step. Emission hooks should not re-emit the signal they are watching or try to stop the emission.

5. Any normally connected callbacks are invoked using the signal's marshaller. Callbacks connected with `gtk_signal_connect_after()` are not invoked at this point. After invoking each callback, GTK+ checks whether it stopped the signal, and if it did, the emission ends. GTK+ also checks whether the signal was re-emitted, and if so, it restarts the emission process for `GTK_RUN_NO_RECURSE` signals.

6. If the signal is `GTK_RUN_LAST`, the default handler is invoked. Afterward GTK+ again checks whether the emission has been stopped or should be restarted.

7. Any callbacks connected with `gtk_signal_connect_after()` are invoked. After invoking each one, GTK+ checks whether the emission should be stopped or restarted.

Within each step the handlers are invoked in the order they were connected. The order of the steps is fixed: `GTK_RUN_FIRST` default handler, emission hooks, normal connections, `GTK_RUN_LAST` default handler, "after" connections.

9.7 Object Finalization

To write a `GtkObject`, you must implement the methods provided by the `GtkObject` interface—or at least be sure you are happy with the default implementations. There are only five `GtkObject` methods. Two of them are `get_arg` and `set_arg`, described in Section 9.5.3. The other three implement object destruction. Here are the finalization functions in `GtkObjectClass`:

```
void (* shutdown) (GtkObject *object);
void (* destroy)  (GtkObject *object);

void (* finalize) (GtkObject *object);
```

As you might guess from this, objects are destroyed in a three-stage process, and each method represents one stage in the process. If your object subclass overrides any of them, it must "chain up" to the corresponding method in the parent class (see Section 9.7.1). The three methods do the following:

- The shutdown method allows objects to perform actions before destruction begins. Most subclasses do not override this method; the default shutdown method emits the "destroy" signal to start the next phase. (The default implementation will *always* be invoked, even if it's overridden, because subclasses are required to "chain up.")

- The destroy method marks the object "useless" and cleans up associated resources, but it does not free the object itself. Typically a destroy method would free data, strings, and so on, stored in the instance struct and set the struct members to NULL. This is the method most subclasses override.

- The finalize method is invoked *only when the object's reference count reaches 0.* The default implementation frees the object instance struct so that further attempts to use the object result in a segmentation fault. The finalize method must also consider that user code could have been invoked after the destroy method and must free any data that user code could have allocated.

Note

Objects can be destroyed regardless of their reference count. This means that the shutdown method is invoked and the destroy signal is emitted. However, as long as the reference count is greater than 0, the object will not be *finalized.*

The shutdown method has no defined role; its purpose depends on the particular object. For example, the GtkWidget shutdown implementation removes the widget from its parent container and unrealizes the widget. This is especially important for containers: Their destroy method destroys all children of the container. If the container was not unrealized before destruction, it would still be visible, and the user would see each child disappear, followed by the container. With the shutdown method, everything disappears at once.

The destroy method frees as many resources as possible without rendering the object "unsafe." If your object has invariants describing its integrity, a destroy method will not violate them. All public functions exported by an object implementation should gracefully handle destroyed objects (they should not crash; remember that an object can be destroyed while references to it persist). The finalize method actually frees the object, meaning that attempts to use the object become dangerous bugs.

The statement, "All public functions exported by an object implementation should gracefully handle destroyed objects," requires some qualification. This is the intended behavior; otherwise, code could not ensure the sanity of an object by increasing its reference count. However, the implementation does not yet live up to the guarantee in all cases. Some public functions in GTK+ and Gnome still assume data structures freed in the destroy method exist, and some reallocate data structures the destroy method already freed. Unless the finalize method re-frees those data structures, they will be leaked. To avoid these bugs, it is best to avoid calling functions on destroyed objects (in practice, it would be uncommon to do so).

You *can* count on being able to check the type and object flags of a destroyed object, however; and it is certainly safe to call gtk_object_unref() on a destroyed object. In your own object implementations, be sure you implement each public function correctly. Check whether the object is destroyed with GTK_OBJECT_DESTROYED(), and keep in mind that user code can run between the destroy method and the finalize method.

Notice that the destroy method is the default handler for a "destroy" signal, but the shutdown and finalize methods are class functions only. This reduces the complexity and increases the speed of the finalization process. Also, because finalize destroys the integrity of an object, it would be unsafe to emit as a signal. (GTK+ does have a facility called "weak references" that allows you to invoke a callback when an object is finalized; weak references do not assume that the GtkObject is in a sane state.)

To make things more concrete, let's look at the functions that you would use to destroy an object. First, here's gtk_object_destroy():

```
void
gtk_object_destroy (GtkObject *object)
{
  g_return_if_fail (object != NULL);
  g_return_if_fail (GTK_IS_OBJECT (object));
  g_return_if_fail (GTK_OBJECT_CONSTRUCTED (object));

  if (!GTK_OBJECT_DESTROYED (object))
    {
      gtk_object_ref (object);
      object->klass->shutdown (object);
      gtk_object_unref (object);
    }
}
```

Notice that destroyed-but-not-finalized objects are flagged, and the flag can be checked with the `GTK_OBJECT_DESTROYED()` macro. `gtk_object_destroy()` ensures that objects are not destroyed twice by ignoring any already-destroyed objects. If an object has not been destroyed, `gtk_object_destroy()` references it to prevent finalization during the destroy process and invokes the `shutdown` method. By default, that method looks like this:

```
static void
gtk_object_shutdown (GtkObject *object)
{
  GTK_OBJECT_SET_FLAGS (object, GTK_DESTROYED);
  gtk_signal_emit (object, object_signals[DESTROY]);
}
```

This method sets the destroyed flag in order to ensure that any recursive `gtk_object_destroy()` calls have no effect. Then it emits the `"destroy"` signal. `gtk_object_shutdown()` seems pointless by itself; however, subclasses may override this method with something more substantial chaining up to the `GtkObject` default method (see Section 9.7.1).

It may be unclear that `gtk_object_shutdown()` is a method implementation, and `gtk_object_destroy()` is a public function. Note that `gtk_object_shutdown()` is the internal function that implements the `shutdown` method for the `GtkObject` class, whereas `gtk_object_destroy()` is part of the public API. The `GtkObject` implementation of the `destroy` method is called `gtk_object_real_destroy()`:

```
static void
gtk_object_real_destroy (GtkObject *object)
{
  if (GTK_OBJECT_CONNECTED (object))
    gtk_signal_handlers_destroy (object);
}
```

This code simply cleans up any signal handlers associated with the object. `gtk_object_real_destroy()` is the default handler invoked when the `"destroy"` signal is emitted. `gtk_object_destroy()` invokes the (possibly overridden) class function `shutdown`, and the default `shutdown` method emits the `"destroy"` signal.

Finalization is initiated by `gtk_object_unref()` if—and only if—the reference count has reached zero. `gtk_object_unref()` can be invoked directly by a user, but often `gtk_object_destroy()` invokes it. Here it is:

```
void
gtk_object_unref (GtkObject *object)
{
  g_return_if_fail (object != NULL);
  g_return_if_fail (GTK_IS_OBJECT (object));
  g_return_if_fail (object->ref_count > 0);
```

```
    if (object->ref_count == 1)
      {
        gtk_object_destroy (object);

        g_return_if_fail (object->ref_count > 0);
      }

    object->ref_count -= 1;

    if (object->ref_count == 0)
      {
        object->klass->finalize (object);
      }
  }
```

If an object has a reference count of one, calling gtk_object_unref() invokes the shutdown and destroy methods (via gtk_object_destroy()) and then finalizes the object (unless the reference count was incremented sometime during the shutdown/destroy process, which is allowed and will prevent finalization). If an object's reference count is greater than one at the start of gtk_object_unref(), the reference count is simply decremented.

Again, notice that an object can be *destroyed* while the reference count is greater than one if the user calls gtk_object_destroy(). If this happens, finalization does not take place until the holders of the remaining references call gtk_object_unref(). In the most common case, the gtk_object_destroy() implementation holds the last reference count. Take another look at the gtk_object_destroy() code with this in mind.

For completeness, here is GtkObject's default finalize method:

```
static void
gtk_object_finalize (GtkObject *object)
{
  gtk_object_notify_weaks (object);

  g_datalist_clear (&object->object_data);

  gtk_type_free (GTK_OBJECT_TYPE (object), object);
}
```

The three function calls in this method do the following things:

- Invoke "weak references," which are callbacks invoked on object finalization. This is a little-used GtkObject feature not described in this book (usually connecting to the "destroy" signal is more appropriate).

- Clear any object data (described in Section 9.8).

- Free the instance struct.

Section 3.3.1 has more to say about reference counting and destruction with respect to widgets.

9.7.1   Chaining Up

If an object overrides a `shutdown`, `destroy`, or `finalize` method, it should chain up to the default implementation to ensure that each parent class has a chance to clean up. Here is an example of chaining up:

```
static void
gtk_widget_real_destroy (GtkObject *object)
{

  /* ... */

  if (parent_class->destroy)
    parent_class->destroy (object);

};
```

`gtk_widget_real_destroy()` is installed in the widget's class struct in the class initialization function, overwriting the `GtkObject` default. `parent_class` is a pointer to the parent's class struct; usually you will want to store this pointer in your class initialization function, as `GtkWidget` does:

```
static GtkObjectClass *parent_class = NULL;

/* ... code omitted ... */

static void
gtk_widget_class_init (GtkWidgetClass *klass)
{
  GtkObjectClass *object_class;

  object_class = (GtkObjectClass*) klass;

  parent_class = gtk_type_class (gtk_object_get_type ());

  /* ... code omitted ... */

  object_class->set_arg = gtk_widget_set_arg;
  object_class->get_arg = gtk_widget_get_arg;
  object_class->shutdown = gtk_widget_shutdown;
  object_class->destroy = gtk_widget_real_destroy;
  object_class->finalize = gtk_widget_finalize;
}
```

Of course, if `parent_class` is not a `GtkObjectClass*`, you will need to cast it with the `GTK_OBJECT_CLASS()` macro.

Notice that you should *not* chain up when implementing `get_arg` and `set_arg`; GTK+ special-cases these methods in `gtk_object_set()` and `gtk_object_get()`. Recall that the `GtkObject` base class initializer zeroes these two methods instead of leaving the default implementation. When setting or getting an argument value, GTK+ uses the information provided on argument registration to jump directly to the correct class struct and invoke only the correct `get_arg` or `set_arg` method. Chaining up would be a much slower way to implement the same thing (and would require unique argument IDs within the same class ancestry).

9.8   Attaching Data to Objects

You can "attach" arbitrary string-pointer pairs to a `GtkObject` instance, in effect adding a new data member. GTK+ uses this some internally, but it can also be a convenient way to pass data around in your application. In particular, it's a nice way to pass information to callbacks.[1]

Here's a simple example:

```
GtkWidget* button = gtk_button_new();
GtkWidget* label  = gtk_label_new(_("Foo"));

gtk_object_set_data(GTK_OBJECT(button), "my_label_key", label);
```

Later, when you have a pointer to the button but not the label (perhaps in a callback connected to the button's `"clicked"` signal), you can do the following:

```
GtkWidget* label = gtk_object_get_data(GTK_OBJECT(button),
                                        "my_label_key");

/* If no data is found for the key, NULL is returned. */

if (label == NULL)
  {
    g_warning("No data was associated with 'my_label_key'!");
  }
```

A pair of convenience functions use a predetermined key and prevent you from having to type (and remember) the object data key. These are `gtk_object_set_user_data()` and `gtk_object_get_user_data()`. You can also register a function to free the data when the data is removed or replaced or the `GtkObject` is destroyed; this function should be of type `GtkDestroyNotify` as follows:

```
typedef void (*GtkDestroyNotify) (gpointer data);
```

Conveniently, `g_free()` and `gtk_object_unref()` will work here. You register a "destroy notification" function when you set the data, by using `gtk_object_set_data_full()`. You can remove data before the object is destroyed by using `gtk_object_remove_data()`, or you can remove it without calling the `destroy` function by using `gtk_object_remove_no_notify()`. Setting the data to `NULL` is equivalent to removing it with `gtk_object_remove_data()` and will also call the `destroy` function if you registered one. Function Listing 9.4 summarizes the object data functions.

---

1. Be careful though; object data can be used to create incredibly difficult-to-read code. If you have a lot of data, creating a sensible struct or object is likely to be nicer. In many cases, a nice design involves subclassing an object and adding additional members to its instance struct.

Function Listing 9.4 **Attaching Key-Value Pairs to a** *GtkObject*
#include <gtk/gtkobject.h>

```
void
gtk_object_set_data(GtkObject* object,
                    const gchar* key,
                    gpointer data)

void
gtk_object_set_data_full(GtkObject* object,
                         const gchar* key,
                         gpointer data,
                         GtkDestroyNotify destroy)

void
gtk_object_remove_data(GtkObject* object,
                       const gchar* key)

gpointer
gtk_object_get_data(GtkObject* object,
                    const gchar* key)

void
gtk_object_remove_no_notify(GtkObject* object,
                            const gchar* key)

void
gtk_object_set_user_data(GtkObject* object,
                         gpointer data)

gpointer
gtk_object_get_user_data(GtkObject* object)
```

It's worth pointing out that the object data system is a thin wrapper around the GData facility in glib, which can be used on a stand-alone basis.

10

Gdk Basics

THIS CHAPTER WILL DISCUSS GDK, THE UNDERPINNING OF GTK+, and some of the occasions you might have to use it. To write custom widgets and canvas items, you will need to understand a few of these low-level details. Like chapters two and three, this chapter is a quick summary that doesn't hold your hand; there is no way to cover all of Gdk in a single chapter. However, this chapter will try to cover the important concepts and data types of Gdk, and it should be a useful reference on certain topics. As details come up in later chapters, you can use this background to understand them. This chapter does not attempt to exhaustively catalog Gdk's API.

10.1 Gdk and Xlib

The X Window System comes with a low-level and thoroughly unpleasant library called Xlib. Almost every function in Gdk is a very thin wrapper around a corresponding Xlib function. But some of the complexity (and functionality) of Xlib is hidden to simplify programming and to make Gdk easier to port to other windowing systems. (There is a port of Gdk to Windows available.) The concealed Xlib functionality will rarely be of interest to application programmers. For example, many features used only by window managers are not exposed in Gdk. If necessary, you can use Xlib directly in your application by including the special `gdk/gdkx.h` header file. (Check out the Gdk source code to see how to extract the low-level Xlib data structures from their Gdk wrappers.)

If you need excruciating details on a Gdk function, you can usually glance at the source to determine the Xlib function it wraps and then read the `man` page for the Xlib function. For example, here is the implementation of `gdk_draw_point()`:

```
void
gdk_draw_point (GdkDrawable *drawable,
                GdkGC        *gc,
                gint         x,
                gint         y)
{
  GdkWindowPrivate *drawable_private;
  GdkGCPrivate *gc_private;

  g_return_if_fail (drawable != NULL);
  g_return_if_fail (gc != NULL);

  drawable_private = (GdkWindowPrivate*) drawable;
  if (drawable_private->destroyed)
    return;
  gc_private = (GdkGCPrivate*) gc;

  XDrawPoint (drawable_private->xdisplay, drawable_private->xwindow,
              gc_private->xgc, x, y);
}
```

Each data structure is cast to its "private" version, which contains information relating to the particular window system Gdk is being used on. This is to keep window-system-specific declarations out of the `gdk/gdk.h` header file. The private version of each data structure contains a wrapped Xlib data structure, which is passed to `XDrawPoint()`. So the `XDrawPoint()` documentation will also apply to `gdk_draw_point()`.

10.2   *GdkWindow*

`GdkWindow` is a wrapper around Xlib's `Window` object. (This was discussed briefly in Section 3.3.2.) A `GdkWindow` represents a region on the screen. It can be shown or hidden (called *mapping* and *unmapping* the window in Xlib). You can capture events received by a `GdkWindow`, draw graphics inside it, and move or resize it. `GdkWindows` are arranged in a tree structure; that is, each window can have child windows. Child windows are positioned relative to their parent window and move when the parent moves. Child windows don't draw outside of their parent's bounds. (In other words, they are clipped by the parent window.)

The tree of GdkWindows is not specific to each application; there is a global tree of windows controlled by the X server and the window manager. The *root window* has no parent; all windows derive from it. All or part of it is visible as your desktop background. Each window can be owned by a different UNIX process. Some windows are created by the window manager, and some come from user applications.

GdkWindow and GtkWindow are very different things; GtkWindow is a GTK+ widget used to represent toplevel windows (toplevel windows are the highest application-controlled windows in the window hierarchy). Window managers typically create *decorations* for toplevel windows. Decorations include title bars, close buttons, and the like.

It's important for you to understand that an X window is primarily an object on the X server. X clients receive a unique integer ID for each window and refer to windows by their IDs. Thus, all window operations take place on the server, and all functions that deal with X windows go across the network.

GdkWindow is a wrapper around the integer ID returned by X. It does keep local copies of some information (such as the window's dimensions), so some Gdk operations are more efficient than the corresponding Xlib operations. Still, GdkWindow is essentially a handle for a server-side object. Many Gdk objects are similar; fonts, pixmaps, cursors, and so on are also handles for server-side objects.

10.2.1   *GdkWindow* and *GtkWidget*

Many GtkWidget subclasses have an associated GdkWindow. In theory, GTK+ applications could create only toplevel windows and have all widgets draw into them. However, it would make little sense to do so because GdkWindow allows the X Window System to automatically handle many details. For example, events received from Gdk are marked with the window that they occurred in. GTK+ can rapidly determine which widget each event corresponds to.

Some widgets have no associated GdkWindow. These are called "no window" widgets, an allusion to the GTK_NO_WINDOW flag that marks them. (You can test this flag with the macro GTK_WIDGET_NO_WINDOW().) Widgets without a window render themselves into their parent container's GdkWindow. Windowless widgets are relatively small and lightweight; GtkLabel is the most common example. Because events are always received on a GdkWindow, windowless widgets do not receive events.[1] (You can use the GtkEventBox container to capture events on a windowless widget.)

---

1. This is not quite true. GTK+ will synthesize expose events for windowless widgets. Also, they may receive events that occur on a child widget and are propagated upward. However, they do not receive events directly.

10.2.2 *GdkWindow* **Attributes**

gdk_window_new() (shown in Function Listing 10.1) allows you to specify most of a window's attributes when you create it. Many of these attributes can be changed later as well.

Function Listing 10.1 **GdkWindow** *#include <gdk/gdk.h>*

```
GdkWindow*
gdk_window_new(GdkWindow* parent,
               GdkWindowAttr* attributes,
               gint attributes_mask)

void
gdk_window_destroy(GdkWindow* window)
```

To specify a block of attributes, you pass in a GdkWindowAttr object. Its contents will give you an idea what attributes a GdkWindow can have:

```
typedef struct _GdkWindowAttr GdkWindowAttr;

struct _GdkWindowAttr
{
  gchar *title;
  gint event_mask;
  gint16 x, y;
  gint16 width;
  gint16 height;
  GdkWindowClass wclass;
  GdkVisual *visual;
  GdkColormap *colormap;
  GdkWindowType window_type;
  GdkCursor *cursor;
  gchar *wmclass_name;
  gchar *wmclass_class;
  gboolean override_redirect;
};
```

Because some of the fields in GdkWindowAttr are optional, gdk_window_new() is used with an attributes_mask to specify which optional fields contain valid information (bit flags are available representing each optional field). Gdk will examine only the optional fields given in the mask, so you can leave the default values for fields you aren't interested in. Table 10.1 summarizes the GdkWindowAttr fields. Fields with no attributes_mask flag are required and have no default value.

Table 10.1 *GdkWindowAttr* Fields

Field	Type	Flag	Default Value	Purpose
title	gchar*	GDK_WA_TITLE	Program Name	The window's title
event_mask	gint	none	none	Events to receive on this window
x	gint16	GDK_WA_X	0	X position relative to parent window
y	gint16	GDK_WA_Y	0	Y position relative to parent window
width	gint16	none	none	Width of window
height	gint16	none	none	Height of window
wclass	GdkWindowClass	none	none	GDK_INPUT_ONLY vs. GDK_INPUT_OUTPUT
visual	GdkVisual*	GDK_WA_VISUAL	X's "default visual"	Visual for this window
colormap	GdkColormap*	GDK_WA_COLORMAP	X's "default colormap"[1]	Colormap for this window
window_type	GdkWindowType	none	none	Window type (see text)
cursor	GdkCursor*	GDK_WA_CURSOR	Parent window's cursor	Mouse pointer for this window
wmclass_name	gchar*	GDK_WA_WMCLASS	none (doesn't set hint)	Set the "name" part of the class hint (see text)
wmclass_class	gchar*	GDK_WA_WMCLASS	none (doesn't set hint)	Set the "class" part of the class hint (see text)

continues

Table 10.1   **Continued**

Field	Type	Flag	Default Value	Purpose
override_ redirect	gboolean	GDK_WA_NOREDIR	FALSE[2]	Make the window "override redirect" (see text)

1.   Colormaps are specific to visuals, so the default colormap is used with the default visual only. A new colormap will be created if you are using a non-default visual and do not specify a colormap.

2.   The default is TRUE and cannot be changed if the window's type is GDK_ WINDOW_TEMP.

gdk_window_new() is typically used in widget implementations to create the widget's GdkWindow; you will rarely use it in any other context. gdk_window_destroy() destroys a window when you are done with it. Windows are also reference counted; be sure to read Section 10.10 for more details on this.

A GdkWindow's title is important for toplevel windows only. Most window managers will place it in the title bar. Usually, you should not specify it when creating a GdkWindow; instead, let your widget's users call gtk_window_set_title().

The window's event mask determines which events will be received on this window. Section 10.5 goes into more detail about events.

The X and Y coordinates for a window are specified in pixels, relative to the parent window's origin. The origin of each window is its top left ("northwest") corner. Notice that a 16-bit signed integer is used. X windows have a maximum size of 32,767 pixels. Negative values are allowed, but the window will be clipped by its parent window (only the portion inside the parent window will be visible).

The width and height of a window are given in pixels and are also 16-bit signed integers.

A window's GdkWindowClass can have one of two values:

- GDK_INPUT_OUTPUT is a normal window.
- GDK_INPUT_ONLY is a window that has a position and receives events but has no visual representation. Its children must also be input-only. You can set the cursor and other attributes for an input-only window, but there is no way to draw to it (it's invisible). Input-only windows are occasionally useful for capturing events or changing the cursor in a region that overlaps two normal windows.

A *visual* describes the color-handling characteristics of a display; a *colormap* contains the colors you can use to draw. Section 10.3 gives details on visuals and colormaps.

Windows can be of several different types, as specified by the GdkWindowType enumeration:

- GDK_WINDOW_ROOT is the type of the Gdk wrapper for the root window, created at initialization time.

- GDK_WINDOW_TOPLEVEL is a toplevel window. The parent argument to gdk_window_new() should be NULL in this case. Gdk automatically uses the root window as the window's parent.

- GDK_WINDOW_CHILD is a subwindow within a toplevel window.

- GDK_WINDOW_DIALOG is essentially the same as a toplevel window. Its parent should be NULL, and Gdk will substitute the root window. A hint will be set to tell the window manager the window is a dialog box. Some window managers take this into account.

- GDK_WINDOW_TEMP is used for pop-up menus and the like; it's a window that will exist only briefly. This is a toplevel window, so its parent should be NULL. These windows are always override redirect, and their cursor is always the same as their parent's. They will ignore those elements of the attribute struct.

- GDK_WINDOW_PIXMAP is not a window at all; GdkPixmap and GdkWindow are almost always treated the same, so Gdk uses the same struct to represent them. They can both be considered kinds of GdkDrawables. (See Section 10.4.)

- GDK_WINDOW_FOREIGN identifies a wrapper around a window not created by Gdk.

Only GDK_WINDOW_TOPLEVEL, GDK_WINDOW_CHILD, GDK_WINDOW_TEMP, and GDK_WINDOW_DIALOG are valid for gdk_window_new(). Library users cannot create a GDK_WINDOW_ROOT. Pixmaps (GDK_WINDOW_PIXMAP) are created with gdk_pixmap_new(). Foreign windows (GDK_WINDOW_FOREIGN) are X windows created outside of Gdk and wrapped using gdk_window_foreign_new() (declared in gdk/gdkx.h, because you will need this function only if you are using Xlib directly).

The cursor field specifies the mouse pointer (cursor) to use in this window; see Section 10.6 for information about cursors.

The "class hint" is described in Section 6.5.2. When writing widgets, you will not usually set the class hint. It is only relevant for toplevel windows. GTK+ provides gtk_window_set_wmclass() so that application authors can set it to something sensible.

The last field in GdkWindowAttr determines whether the window is "override redirect." Normally, window managers intercept all requests to show, hide, move, or resize a toplevel window. They can then redirect or cancel these requests in order to force windows to behave according to the window manager's layout policy. You can override this behavior by setting `override_redirect` to `TRUE`. Because window managers cannot move windows with this flag set, they will normally not put a title bar or other decoration on them. Note that all `GDK_WINDOW_TEMP` windows use `TRUE` for this field, and recall that `GDK_WINDOW_TEMP` is often used for pop-up menus, which are not controlled by the window manager.

Typically you should not change the `override_redirect` field; the default is almost always right if you specify the correct `GdkWindowType`. However, there are some exceptions.

10.3   Visuals and Colormaps

Unfortunately, not all hardware is created equal. The most primitive X servers support only two colors; each pixel is either on or off. This is referred to as a "one bit per pixel (bpp)" display. A display with one bit per pixel is said to have a *depth* of one. More advanced X servers support 24 or 32 bits per pixel and allow you to specify a different depth on a window-by-window basis. 24 bits per pixel allows 2^{24} different pixels, which includes more colors than the human eye can differentiate.

Conceptually, a bitmap display consists of a rectangular grid of pixels. Each pixel consists of some fixed number of bits. Pixels are mapped to visible colors in a hardware-dependent way. One way to think about a bitmap display is to imagine a two-dimensional array of integers, where the integer size is chosen to hold the required number of bits. Alternatively, you can think of a bitmap display as a stack of *bit planes*, or two-dimensional arrays of bits. If all the planes are parallel to one another, a pixel is a perpendicular line passing through the same coordinates on each plane, taking a single bit from each one. This is the origin of the term *depth* because the number of bits per pixel is equal to the depth of the stack of bit planes.

In the X Window System, pixels represent entries in a color lookup table. A *color* is a red, green, blue (RGB) value (that is, monitors mix red, green, and blue light in some ratio to display each pixel). Take an eight-bit display, for example. Eight bits are not enough to encode a color in-place; only a few arbitrary RGB values would be possible. Instead, the bits are interpreted as an integer and used to index an array of RGB color values. This table of colors is called the *colormap*. It can sometimes be modified to contain the colors you plan to use. However, this is hardware-dependent because some colormaps are read-only.

A *visual* is required to determine how a pixel's bit pattern is converted into a visible color. Thus, a visual also defines how colormaps work. On an 8-bit display, the X server might interpret each pixel as an index into a single colormap containing the 256 possible colors. 24-bit visuals typically have three colormaps: one for shades of red, one for shades of green, and one for shades of blue. Each colormap is indexed with an eight-bit value, and the three eight-bit values are packed into a 24-bit pixel. The visual defines the meaning of the pixel contents. Visuals also define whether the colormap is read-only or modifiable.

In short, a visual is a description of the color capabilities of a particular X server. In Xlib, you have to do a lot of fooling around with visuals. Gdk and GTK+ shield you from most of the mess, though.

10.3.1 *GdkVisual*

Xlib can report a list of all available visuals and information about each one. Gdk keeps a client-side copy of this information in a struct called `GdkVisual`. Gdk can report the available visuals and rank them in different ways. Most of the time, you will only use `gdk_visual_get_system()`, which returns a pointer to the default visual (see Function Listing 10.2). (If you're writing a `GtkWidget`, `gtk_widget_get_visual()` returns the visual you should use; more on this in Chapter 11, "Writing a `GtkWidget`.") The returned visual is not a copy, so there is no need to free it. Gdk keeps visuals around permanently.

Function Listing 10.2   **Default Visual**   *#include <gdk/gdk.h>*

```
GdkVisual*
gdk_visual_get_system()
```

For reference, here are the contents of `GdkVisual`. Most of the members are used to calculate pixel values from colors. Because this is fairly involved and rarely used, this book glosses over the topic. The `depth` member is convenient sometimes. Section 10.3.1 has more to say about the `type` member.

```
typedef struct _GdkVisual GdkVisual;

struct _GdkVisual
{
  GdkVisualType type;
  gint depth;
  GdkByteOrder byte_order;
  gint colormap_size;
  gint bits_per_rgb;

  guint32 red_mask;
  gint red_shift;
  gint red_prec;

  guint32 green_mask;
  gint green_shift;
  gint green_prec;

  guint32 blue_mask;
  gint blue_shift;
  gint blue_prec;
};
```

10.3.1.1 Types of Visuals

Visuals differ along several dimensions. They can be grayscale or RGB, colormaps can be modifiable or fixed, and the pixel value can either index a single colormap, or contain packed red, green, and blue indexes. Here are the possible values for GdkVisualType:

- GDK_VISUAL_STATIC_GRAY means the display is either monochrome or grayscale, and the colormap cannot be modified. A pixel value is simply a level of gray. Each pixel is "hard coded" to represent a certain on-screen color.

- GDK_VISUAL_GRAYSCALE means the display has a modifiable colormap, but only levels of gray are possible. The pixel represents an entry in the colormap, so a given pixel can represent a different level of gray at different times.

- GDK_VISUAL_STATIC_COLOR represents a color display that uses a single read-only colormap instead of a separate colormap for each of red, green, and blue. The display is almost certainly 12-bit or less. (A 24-bit display using a single colormap would need a colormap with 2^{24} entries, occupying close to half a gigabyte—not very practical!) This is an annoying visual, because relatively few colors are available, and you can't change which colors they are.

- GDK_VISUAL_PSEUDO_COLOR is the most common visual on low-end PC hardware from several years ago. If you have a one-megabyte 256-color video card, this is most likely your X server's visual. It represents a color display with a read/write colormap. Pixels index a single colormap.

- GDK_VISUAL_TRUE_COLOR is a color display with three read-only colormaps, one for each of red, green, and blue. A pixel contains three indexes, one per colormap. There is a fixed mathematical relationship between pixels and RGB triplets. You can get a pixel from red, green, and blue values in [0, 255] using the formula: `gulong pixel = (gulong)(red*65536 + green*256 + blue)`.

- GDK_VISUAL_DIRECT_COLOR is a color display with three read-write colormaps. If you use the Gdk color handling routines, they simply fill up all three colormaps to emulate a true color display and then pretend the direct color display is true color.

10.3.2 Color and *GdkColormap*

A GdkColor stores an RGB value and a pixel. Red, green, and blue are given as 16-bit unsigned integers, so they are in the range [0, 65535]. The contents of the pixel depend on the visual. Here is GdkColor:

```
typedef struct _GdkColor GdkColor;

struct _GdkColor
{
  gulong  pixel;
```

```
    gushort red;
    gushort green;
    gushort blue;
  };
```

Before you can use a color to draw, you must do two things:

- Ensure that the `pixel` field contains an appropriate value.

- Ensure that the color exists in the colormap of the drawable you intend to draw to. (A *drawable* is a window or pixmap you can draw to; see Section 10.4.)

In Xlib, this is an enormously complicated process because it has to be done differently for every kind of visual. Gdk conceals things fairly well. You simply call `gdk_colormap_alloc_color()` to fill in the pixel value and add the color to the colormap (see Function Listing 10.3).

Function Listing 10.3   **Color Allocation**   *#include <gdk/gdk.h>*

```
gboolean
gdk_colormap_alloc_color(GdkColormap* colormap,
                         GdkColor* color,
                         gboolean writeable,
                         gboolean best_match)

void
gdk_colormap_free_colors(GdkColormap* colormap,
                         GdkColor* colors,
                         gint ncolors)

gint
gdk_color_parse(gchar* spec,
                GdkColor* color)
```

The following example assumes a preexisting `GdkColormap* colormap`, which should be the colormap of the drawable you are targeting:

```
    GdkColor color;

    /* Describe a pure red */
    color.red   = 65535;
    color.green = 0;
    color.blue  = 0;

    if (gdk_colormap_alloc_color(colormap, &color, FALSE, TRUE))
      {
        /* Success! */
      }
```

If `gdk_colormap_alloc_color()` returns TRUE, the color was allocated, and `color.pixel` contains a valid value. The color can then be used to draw. The two boolean arguments to `gdk_colormap_alloc_color()` specify whether the color should be *writeable* and whether to try to find a "best match" if the color can't be allocated. If a best match is used instead of allocating a new color, the color's RGB values will be changed to the best match. If you request a best match for a non-writeable entry, allocation really should not fail because even on a black and white display either black or white will be the best match. Only an empty colormap could cause failure. The only way to get an empty colormap is to create a custom colormap yourself. If you don't ask for the best match, failure is quite possible on displays with a limited number of colors. Failure is always possible with writeable colormap entries (where using a best match makes no sense because the entry can be modified).

A *writeable* colormap entry is one that you can change at any time; some visuals support this, and some don't. The purpose of a writeable colormap entry is to change an on-screen color without redrawing the graphics. Some hardware stores pixels as indices into a color lookup table. So, changing the lookup table changes how the pixels are displayed. The disadvantages of writeable colormap entries are numerous. Most notably: not all visuals support them, and writeable colormap entries can't be used by other applications (read-only entries can be shared because other applications know the color will remain constant). Thus, it is a good idea to avoid allocating writeable colors. On modern hardware, they are more trouble than they are worth. The speed gain compared to simply redrawing your graphics will not be noticeable.

When you're finished with a color, you can remove it from the colormap with `gdk_colormap_free_colors()`. This is only really important for pseudo color and grayscale visuals, where colors are in short supply, and the colormap can be modified by clients. Gdk will automatically do the right thing for each visual type, so always call this function.

A convenient way to obtain RGB values is with the `gdk_color_parse()` function. This takes an X color specification and fills in the `red`, `green`, and `blue` fields of a `GdkColor`. An X color specification can have many forms; one possibility is an RGB string:

```
RGB:FF/FF/FF
```

This specifies white (red, green, and blue are all at full intensity). The `RGB:` specifies a "color space" and determines the meaning of the numbers after it. X also understands several more obscure color spaces. If the color specification string doesn't begin with a recognized color space, X assumes it's a color name and looks it up in a database of names. So you can write code like this:

```
GdkColor color;

if (gdk_color_parse("orange", &color))
  {
    if (gdk_colormap_alloc_color(colormap, &color, FALSE, TRUE))
```

```
    {
      /* We have orange! */
    }
  }
```

As you can see, `gdk_color_parse()` returns `TRUE` if it figures out the string that you pass it. There is no way to know exactly what will be in the color database, so always check this return value.

10.3.2.1   Obtaining a Colormap

If you're writing a `GtkWidget` subclass, the correct way to obtain a colormap is with `gtk_widget_get_colormap()` (see Chapter 11). Otherwise, the system (default) colormap is usually what you want. In that case, call `gdk_colormap_get_system()`, which takes no arguments and returns the default colormap.

The GdkRGB module (described in Section 10.9.8) offers another way to deal with colors. Among other capabilities, it can set the foreground and background colors of a graphics context from an RGB value. The relevant functions are `gdk_rgb_gc_set_foreground()` and `gdk_rgb_gc_set_background()`. GdkRGB has a pre-allocated colormap that it uses to pick a best-match color. If you use it, your application can share limited colormap resources with other applications using GdkRGB (such as the Gimp). You can also obtain GdkRGB's colormap and use it directly (see Section 10.9.8).

10.4   Drawables and Pixmaps

A *pixmap* is an off-screen buffer you can draw graphics into. After drawing into a pixmap, you can copy it to a window, causing it to appear on the screen (when the window is visible). (You can also draw into a window directly, of course. Using a pixmap as a buffer allows you to rapidly update the screen without repeating a series of primitive drawing operations.) Pixmaps are also good for storing image data loaded from disk, such as icons and logos. You can then copy the image to a window. In Gdk, the pixmap type is called `GdkPixmap`. A pixmap with a single bit representing each pixel is called a `bitmap`. Gdk's bitmap type is `GdkBitmap`. "Bitmap" is not really a separate type; from X's point of view, it is simply a pixmap with a depth of one. Like windows, pixmaps are server-side resources.

In X terminology, a *drawable* is anything you can draw graphics on. Gdk has a corresponding type, called `GdkDrawable`. Drawables include windows, pixmaps, and bitmaps. Here is how the types are defined in Gdk:

```
typedef struct _GdkWindow GdkWindow;
typedef struct _GdkWindow GdkPixmap;
typedef struct _GdkWindow GdkBitmap;
typedef struct _GdkWindow GdkDrawable;
```

On the client side, pixmaps and bitmaps are just GdkWindows with type GDK_WINDOW_PIXMAP. GdkDrawable is used in function declarations when either a window or a pixmap is an acceptable argument. Functions that draw graphics take either type; functions that move windows around or set window manager hints accept only windows. Only windows can receive events. GDK_INPUT_ONLY windows are a special case, however. They are not drawables, and you can't draw on them.

Three of the four logical combinations of "window features" and drawability actually exist:

	Drawable	Not Drawable
Window Features	Normal Window	Input Only Window
No Window Features	Pixmap/Bitmap	—

Unfortunately, all three of these logically distinct cases appear the same to the C compiler. So be careful not to use the wrong one. Also keep in mind that a normal window is not drawable until it actually appears on the screen; you should wait until you receive an expose event before you draw. (Expose events are covered in Section 10.5.8.)

Like GdkWindow, a GdkPixmap is merely a client-side handle for an object located on the X server. Because of this, some things are entirely infeasible from a performance point of view. Notably, if you are doing anything that requires significant manipulation of individual pixels, drawables will be far too slow. On the other hand, copying a pixmap to a window is not as slow as you might think because both objects are on the same machine.

Creating a pixmap is much easier than creating a window because most of the window attributes are not relevant to pixmaps. The function is gdk_pixmap_new() (see Function Listing 10.4). It accepts an initial size and a bit depth. If a depth of −1 is given, the depth is copied from its GdkWindow argument. You can't choose an arbitrary number for the depth; the server will not support all depths, and the pixmap's depth must match the depth of any windows you plan to copy it to. To destroy a pixmap, call gdk_pixmap_unref().

Function Listing 10.4 *GdkPixmap* **Constructor**   *#include <gdk/gdk.h>*

```
GdkPixmap*
gdk_pixmap_new(GdkWindow* window,
               gint width,
               gint height,
               gint depth)

void
gdk_pixmap_unref(GdkPixmap* pixmap)
```

The GdkWindow argument to gdk_pixmap_new() may not seem strictly necessary. However, the function wraps XCreatePixmap(), which takes an X window as an argument. It uses this argument to determine which *screen* to create the window on; some X servers have multiple displays. Screens are an Xlib concept totally concealed by Gdk. Gdk supports only one screen at a time. Thus the window argument to gdk_pixmap_new() seems mysterious from a Gdk point of view.

10.5 Events

Events are sent to your application to indicate changes in a GdkWindow or user actions you might be interested in. All events are associated with a GdkWindow. They also come to be associated with a GtkWidget because the GTK+ main loop passes events from Gdk to the GTK+ widget tree.

10.5.1 Types of Events

There are many kinds of events, and the GdkEvent union can represent any of them. A special event type, GdkEventAny, contains the three fields common to all events. Any event can be cast to GdkEventAny. The first field in GdkEventAny is a type marker, GdkEventType. GdkEventType is also included in the GdkEvent union. Confused yet? Seeing the code should help. Here is GdkEventAny:

```
struct _GdkEventAny
{
  GdkEventType type;
  GdkWindow *window;
  gint8 send_event;
};
```

and here is GdkEvent:

```
union _GdkEvent
{
  GdkEventType        type;
  GdkEventAny         any;
  GdkEventExpose      expose;
  GdkEventNoExpose    no_expose;
  GdkEventVisibility  visibility;
  GdkEventMotion      motion;
  GdkEventButton      button;
  GdkEventKey         key;
  GdkEventCrossing    crossing;
  GdkEventFocus       focus_change;
  GdkEventConfigure   configure;
  GdkEventProperty    property;
  GdkEventSelection   selection;
  GdkEventProximity   proximity;
  GdkEventClient      client;
  GdkEventDND         dnd;
};
```

Every event type has the three members of GdkEventAny as its first three members. Thus, the type of an event can be referred to in many ways (assume a GdkEvent* called event):

- event->type
- event->any.type
- event->button.type
- ((GdkEventAny*)event)->type
- ((GdkEventButton*)event)->type

You'll probably see all these in GTK+ source code. Of course, each event subtype has its own unique members; the type field tells you which subtype is valid.

The window field of GdkEventAny is the GdkWindow the event was sent to. If the send_event flag is TRUE, the event was synthesized by another (or your own) application; if FALSE, it originated with the X server. Gdk does not export the X interface for sending events (XSendEvent()). However, GTK+ often "makes up" an event by declaring a static event struct, filling it in, and then emitting the event's corresponding widget signal. These synthesized events will have send_event set to TRUE. Section 10.5.3 explains how GTK+ associates events with widget signals.

There are more possible values for GdkEventType than there are members in the GdkEvent union. Many event types share the same data. For example, GDK_BUTTON_PRESS and GDK_BUTTON_RELEASE both use the button member of GdkEvent because the same information is conveyed when mouse buttons are pressed and released. Table 10.2 shows all possible values of the GdkEventType enumeration and the corresponding GdkEvent members. The meaning of each event type is described later in this section.

Table 10.2 *GdkEventType* **Values**

Value	GdkEvent **Member**
GDK_NOTHING	none[1]
GDK_DELETE	GdkEventAny
GDK_DESTROY	GdkEventAny
GDK_EXPOSE	GdkEventExpose
GDK_MOTION_NOTIFY	GdkEventMotion
GDK_BUTTON_PRESS	GdkEventButton
GDK_2BUTTON_PRESS	GdkEventButton
GDK_3BUTTON_PRESS	GdkEventButton
GDK_BUTTON_RELEASE	GdkEventButton
GDK_KEY_PRESS	GdkEventKey
GDK_KEY_RELEASE	GdkEventKey
GDK_ENTER_NOTIFY	GdkEventCrossing
GDK_LEAVE_NOTIFY	GdkEventCrossing

Value	GdkEvent Member
GDK_FOCUS_CHANGE	GdkEventFocus
GDK_CONFIGURE	GdkEventConfigure
GDK_MAP	GdkEventAny
GDK_UNMAP	GdkEventAny
GDK_PROPERTY_NOTIFY	GdkEventProperty
GDK_SELECTION_CLEAR	GdkEventSelection
GDK_SELECTION_REQUEST	GdkEventSelection
GDK_SELECTION_NOTIFY	GdkEventSelection
GDK_PROXIMITY_IN	GdkEventProximity
GDK_PROXIMITY_OUT	GdkEventProximity
GDK_DRAG_LEAVE	GdkEventDND
GDK_DRAG_MOTION	GdkEventDND
GDK_DROP_START	GdkEventDND
GDK_DROP_FINISHED	GdkEventDND
GDK_CLIENT_EVENT	GdkEventClient
GDK_VISIBILITY_NOTIFY	GdkEventNoExpose

1. *GDK_NOTHING is an "invalid" value. Gdk uses this internally.*

10.5.2 The Event Mask

Each GdkWindow has an associated *event mask* that determines which events on that window the X server will forward to your application. You specify the event mask when a GdkWindow is created, as part of the GdkWindowAttr struct (see Section 10.2.2). You can access and change the event mask later using gdk_window_set_events() and gdk_window_get_events(). If the GdkWindow in question belongs to a widget, you should not change the event mask directly; rather, call gtk_widget_set_events() or gtk_widget_add_events(). gtk_widget_set_events() should be used after a widget is realized, and gtk_widget_add_events() can be used to add events to the existing mask at any time. Function Listing 10.5 and Function Listing 10.6 show these functions.

Function Listing 10.5   *GdkWindow* Event Mask   *#include <gdk/gdk.h>*

```
GdkEventMask
gdk_window_get_events(GdkWindow* window)

void
gdk_window_set_events(GdkWindow* window,
                      GdkEventMask event_mask)
```

Function Listing 10.6 **Widget Event Mask** *#include <gtk/gtkwidget.h>*

```
gint
gdk_widget_get_events(GtkWidget* widget)

void
gtk_widget_add_events(GtkWidget* widget,
                      gint event_mask)

void
gtk_widget_set_events(GtkWidget* widget,
                      gint event_mask)
```

Table 10.3 outlines which event masks request which events. Some events, however, do not have to be selected to be received:

- `Map`, `unmap`, `destroy`, and `configure` events are selected with `GDK_STRUCTURE_MASK`, but Gdk automatically selects them on any new window. (Xlib programmers beware; Xlib does not do this.)

- `Selection`, `client`, `drag-and-drop`, and `delete` events have no masks because they are automatically selected (Xlib selects them for all windows).

Table 10.3 **Event Masks**

Mask	Event Type
GDK_EXPOSURE_MASK	GDK_EXPOSE
GDK_POINTER_MOTION_MASK	GDK_MOTION_NOTIFY
GDK_POINTER_MOTION_HINT_MASK	N/A (see Section 10.5.6)
GDK_BUTTON_MOTION_MASK	GDK_MOTION_NOTIFY (while a button is pressed)
GDK_BUTTON1_MOTION_MASK	GDK_MOTION_NOTIFY (while button 1 is pressed)
GDK_BUTTON2_MOTION_MASK	GDK_MOTION_NOTIFY (while button 2 is pressed)
GDK_BUTTON3_MOTION_MASK	GDK_MOTION_NOTIFY (while button 3 is pressed)
GDK_BUTTON_PRESS_MASK	GDK_BUTTON_PRESS, GDK_2BUTTON_PRESS, GDK_3BUTTON_PRESS
GDK_BUTTON_RELEASE_MASK	GDK_BUTTON_RELEASE
GDK_KEY_PRESS_MASK	GDK_KEY_PRESS
GDK_KEY_RELEASE_MASK	GDK_KEY_RELEASE
GDK_ENTER_NOTIFY_MASK	GDK_ENTER_NOTIFY
GDK_LEAVE_NOTIFY_MASK	GDK_LEAVE_NOTIFY
GDK_FOCUS_CHANGE_MASK	GDK_FOCUS_IN, GDK_FOCUS_OUT
GDK_STRUCTURE_MASK	GDK_CONFIGURE, GDK_DESTROY, GDK_MAP, GDK_UNMAP
GDK_PROPERTY_CHANGE_MASK	GDK_PROPERTY_NOTIFY
GDK_VISIBILITY_NOTIFY_MASK	GDK_VISIBILITY_NOTIFY
GDK_PROXIMITY_IN_MASK	GDK_PROXIMITY_IN

Mask	Event Type
GDK_PROXIMITY_OUT_MASK	GDK_PROXIMITY_OUT
GDK_SUBSTRUCTURE_MASK	Receive GDK_STRUCTURE_MASK events for *child windows*
GDK_ALL_EVENTS_MASK	All events

10.5.3 Receiving Gdk Events in GTK+

In a GTK+ program, you will never receive Gdk events directly. Instead, all events are passed to a GtkWidget, which emits a corresponding signal. You handle events by connecting handlers to GtkWidget signals.

The X server sends each X client a stream of events. Events are sent and received in the order of their occurrence. Gdk converts each XEvent it receives into a GdkEvent and then places events in a queue. GTK+ monitors Gdk's event queue; for each event received, it decides which widget (if any) should receive the event. The GtkWidget base class defines signals for most event types (such as "button_press_event"). It also defines a generic "event" signal. The GTK+ main loop calls gtk_widget_event() to deliver an event to a widget. This function first emits the "event" signal and then emits a signal for the specific event type (if appropriate). Some events are handled in special ways; notably, drag-and-drop events do not directly correspond to drag-and-drop signals.

In general, events go to the widget owning the GdkWindow that the event occurred on. However, there are certain special cases. If a widget has the grab (if, for example, gtk_grab_add() was called; see Section 3.3.3), certain events will be forwarded to only the widget with the grab or the children of that widget. Events that occur on other widgets are ignored. Only certain user-initiated events such as button events and key events are affected by a grab. Widget sensitivity (discussed in Section 3.3.3) also affects where events are sent. Events representing user interaction are not forwarded to insensitive widgets. As you might expect, widgets with no associated GdkWindow do not originate events; X only sends events to windows. There is one exception: Containers synthesize expose events for their windowless children.

The GTK+ main loop *propagates* certain events from child widgets to their parent containers. That is, for each event, a signal is emitted first from a child widget, then from its immediate parent, then from the parent's parent, and so on. For example, if you click a GtkMenuItem, it ignores the button press and lets the menu it is a part of handle it. Some events are not propagated; Table 10.4 gives details.

Event propagation ends after a widget "handles" the event. This ensures that only one user-visible change results from any user action. Handlers for GtkWidget's event signals must return a gint value. Recall that the last signal handler to run determines the return value of a signal emission (see Section 9.6.3). All event signals are GTK_RUN_LAST, so the return value will come from one of the following sources:

- The last handler connected with gtk_signal_connect_after() if any.
- The widget's default signal handler if any.
- The last handler connected with gtk_signal_connect() if any.
- The default return value is FALSE.

If the emission of an event signal returns TRUE, the GTK+ main loop stops propagating the current event. If it returns FALSE, the main loop propagates the event to the widget's parent. Recall that each event results in two signal emissions: a generic "event" signal and a specific signal (such as "button_press_event" or "key_press_event"). If *either* emission returns TRUE, event propagation ends. The return value from the generic "event" signal has one additional effect: If TRUE, the second, more specific, signal will not be emitted.

Table 10.4 summarizes how GtkWidget signals correspond to event types, which events are affected by an active grab, and which events are propagated from parent to child. Signal handlers for all event signals should return a gint and take three arguments: the widget emitting the signal, the event that triggered the signal, and a user data pointer.

Table 10.4 *GtkWidget* **Events**

Event Type	GtkWidget **Signal**	**Propagated?**	**Grabbed?**
GDK_DELETE	"delete_event"	No	No
GDK_DESTROY	"destroy_event"	No	No
GDK_EXPOSE	"expose_event"	No	No
GDK_MOTION_NOTIFY	"motion_notify_event"	Yes	Yes
GDK_BUTTON_PRESS	"button_press_event"	Yes	Yes
GDK_2BUTTON_PRESS	"button_press_event"	Yes	Yes
GDK_3BUTTON_PRESS	"button_press_event"	Yes	Yes
GDK_BUTTON_RELEASE	"button_release_event"	Yes	Yes
GDK_KEY_PRESS	"key_press_event"	Yes	Yes
GDK_KEY_RELEASE	"key_release_event"	Yes	Yes
GDK_ENTER_NOTIFY	"enter_notify_event"	No	Yes
GDK_LEAVE_NOTIFY	"leave_notify_event"	No	Yes[1]
GDK_FOCUS_CHANGE	"focus_in_event", "focus_out_event"	No	No
GDK_CONFIGURE	"configure_event"	No	No
GDK_MAP	"map_event"	No	No

Event Type	GtkWidget Signal	Propagated?	Grabbed?
GDK_UNMAP	"unmap_event"	No	No
GDK_PROPERTY_NOTIFY	"property_notify_event"	No	No
GDK_SELECTION_CLEAR	"selection_clear_event"	No	No
GDK_SELECTION_REQUEST	"selection_request_event"	No	No
GDK_SELECTION_NOTIFY	"selection_notify_event"	No	No
GDK_PROXIMITY_IN	"proximity_in_event"	Yes	Yes
GDK_PROXIMITY_OUT	"proximity_out_event"	Yes	Yes
GDK_CLIENT_EVENT	"client_event"	No	No
GDK_VISIBILITY_NOTIFY	"visibility_notify_event"	No	No
GDK_NO_EXPOSE	"no_expose_event"	No	No

1. *GDK_LEAVE_NOTIFY goes to the grabbing widget, if the grabbing widget also received the corresponding GDK_ENTER_NOTIFY. Otherwise, the leave notification goes to the widget that received the enter notification. This ensures that enter and leave events are received in pairs.*

10.5.4   Button Events

Four different event types result in a GdkEventButton:

- GDK_BUTTON_PRESS means a mouse button was pressed.
- GDK_BUTTON_RELEASE means a button was released after being pressed. This will not necessarily be received after a button press event: If the user moves the mouse to a different GdkWindow, that window will receive it instead.
- GDK_2BUTTON_PRESS means a mouse button was pressed down twice in a short interval—a "double-click." This is always preceded by a GDK_BUTTON_PRESS/GDK_BUTTON_RELEASE pair for the first click.
- GDK_3BUTTON_PRESS means a mouse button was pressed three times in a short interval—a "triple-click." This will be preceded by two GDK_BUTTON_PRESS/GDK_BUTTON_RELEASE pairs and GDK_2BUTTON_PRESS.

If you click three times quickly on the same GdkWindow, the following events are received in this order:

1. GDK_BUTTON_PRESS
2. GDK_BUTTON_RELEASE
3. GDK_BUTTON_PRESS
4. GDK_2BUTTON_PRESS
5. GDK_BUTTON_RELEASE
6. GDK_BUTTON_PRESS
7. GDK_3BUTTON_PRESS
8. GDK_BUTTON_RELEASE

The X server automatically causes a pointer grab when a button is pressed and then releases it when the button is released. This means the button release event always goes to the same window that received the button press event. Xlib allows you to change this behavior, but Gdk does not. (In the Xlib documentation, this automatic grab is referred to as a "passive" grab. It's distinct from an "active" grab, which is initiated with gdk_pointer_grab(), described in Section 10.6.2.) A button event is defined as shown in the following code:

```
typedef struct _GdkEventButton GdkEventButton;

struct _GdkEventButton
{
  GdkEventType type;
  GdkWindow *window;
  gint8 send_event;
  guint32 time;
  gdouble x;
  gdouble y;
  gdouble pressure;
  gdouble xtilt;
  gdouble ytilt;
  guint state;
  guint button;
  GdkInputSource source;
  guint32 deviceid;
  gdouble x_root, y_root;
};
```

Button events are marked with a timestamp (time) by the X server. The time is given in milliseconds of "server time." Every few weeks, the integer overflows, and timestamps begin again at zero. Thus, you should not rely on the value as an absolute measure of time; it is intended only to determine relative time between events.

The mouse pointer's X and Y coordinates (relative to the window the event occurred in) are included in GdkEventButton. Keep in mind that the pointer may be outside the window (if a pointer grab is in effect; see Section 10.6). If the pointer is outside the window, its coordinates could be negative or larger than the window's size. Coordinates are given as doubles rather than integers because some input devices such as graphics tablets have sub-pixel resolution. For most purposes, you will want to cast the doubles to integers. pressure, xtilt, and ytilt are also special features of some input devices; they can be ignored almost all the time.

The state member of GdkEventButton indicates which modifier keys or mouse buttons were held down an instant before the button was pressed. It is a bitfield that has one or more of the flags in Table 10.5 set. Because the modifiers are read just before the button press, it follows that button press events do not have the pressed button in state, but button release events do have it.

Be careful to check for the presence of certain bit masks and not the exact value of state. In other words, prefer this:

```
if ( (state & GDK_SHIFT_MASK) == GDK_SHIFT_MASK )
```

and avoid this:

```
if ( state == GDK_SHIFT_MASK )
```

If you check the exact value of state, your application will mysteriously stop working if the user has Num Lock or some other obscure modifier turned on.

Table 10.5 **Modifier Masks for Key and Button Events**

Modifier Mask	Meaning
GDK_SHIFT_MASK	Shift
GDK_LOCK_MASK	Caps Lock
GDK_CONTROL_MASK	Control
GDK_MOD1_MASK	Mod1 (often Meta or Alt)
GDK_MOD2_MASK	Mod2
GDK_MOD3_MASK	Mod3
GDK_MOD4_MASK	Mod4
GDK_MOD5_MASK	Mod5
GDK_BUTTON1_MASK	Button 1
GDK_BUTTON2_MASK	Button 2
GDK_BUTTON3_MASK	Button 3
GDK_BUTTON4_MASK	Button 4
GDK_BUTTON5_MASK	Button 5
GDK_RELEASE_MASK[1]	Key releases

1. GDK_RELEASE_MASK is not used by Gdk. GTK+ uses it to allow keyboard accelerators to be bound to key releases. Normal events will never have GDK_RELEASE_MASK in their state field.

The button member of GdkEventButton indicates which button triggered the event (that is, the button that was pressed or released). Buttons are numbered from one to five. Most of the time, button one is the left button, button two is the middle button, and button three is the right button. Left-handed users might reverse these, however. Button four and five events are generated by some scroll wheel mice when you spin the scroll wheel; GTK+ attempts to capture these events and move nearby scroll bars. You should probably ignore any events you receive for buttons four and five.

The three standard mouse buttons have conventional meanings in Gnome. Button one is used for selection, drag-and-drop, and operating widgets (the most common tasks). Button three typically activates a pop-up menu. Button two is traditionally used to move objects, such as the panel. Sometimes button one moves objects also; for example, desktop icons can be moved with either button one or button two. It is a good idea to be consistent with other applications whenever possible.

The source and deviceid members are used to determine which device triggered the event; the user may have a graphics tablet and a mouse connected simultaneously, for example. You can ignore these fields unless you are writing an application that can take advantage of non-mouse devices.

The last two members of GdkEventButton, x_root and y_root, are the x and y coordinates translated to be relative to the root window rather than the window receiving the event. You can use these as "absolute" coordinates to compare events from two different windows.

10.5.5 Keyboard Events

There are only two types of key events: GDK_KEY_PRESS and GDK_KEY_RELEASE. Some hardware does not generate key release events. You should not write code that depends on GDK_KEY_RELEASE events, though your code should respond sanely if one is received. Here are the contents of a key event:

```
typedef struct _GdkEventKey GdkEventKey;

struct _GdkEventKey
{
  GdkEventType type;
  GdkWindow *window;
  gint8 send_event;
  guint32 time;
  guint state;
  guint keyval;
  gint length;
  gchar *string;
};
```

The first three members are the standard members from GdkEventAny. The time and state members are identical to those found in GdkEventButton.

keyval contains a *keysym*. The X server keeps a global translation table that converts combinations of physical keys and modifiers to keysyms. For example, the key marked "A" on the keyboard typically generates the keysym GDK_a with no modifiers and GDK_A with Shift held down. Users can change the physical-key-to-keysym mapping. For example, you might rearrange your keys to create a Dvorak keyboard. (More commonly, you might swap Control and Caps Lock, or use the Alt key as a Meta key.) Keysyms are defined in gdk/gdkkeysyms.h. You will need to include this file to use the keyval field.

Keysyms are matched with a string representation. For example, the GDK_a keysym typically maps to the string "a". (However, X allows the keysym-to-string mapping to be modified.) The string member of GdkEventKey contains a keysym's string representation, and the length member contains the string's length. Keep in mind that the length may be zero (many non-alphanumeric keys have no string representation by default). (If you're familiar with Xlib, note that the string field is simply the result of XLookupString() or XmbLookupString(). If you aren't familiar with Xlib, the man pages for these functions may be helpful.)

In general, if you are reading key events in order to create a textual representation of what the user is typing, you should use the string field of GdkEventKey. GtkEntry and GtkText use the string field, for example. A word processor would also read this field. If you're reading key events for some other reason (such as keyboard shortcuts), or if you are interested in keys with no string representation by default (such as function keys or arrow keys), you will need to use the keyval field and the keysyms defined in gdk/gdkkeysyms.h.

Here is a sample key event callback that demonstrates how to extract information from a key event. It would be suitable for connection to the "key_press_event" signal of any GtkWidget:

```
static gint
key_press_cb(GtkWidget* widget, GdkEventKey* event, gpointer data)
{
  if (event->length > 0)
    printf("The key event's string is `%s'\n", event->string);

  printf("The name of this keysym is `%s'\n",
         gdk_keyval_name(event->keyval));

  switch (event->keyval)
    {
    case GDK_Home:
      printf("The Home key was pressed.\n");
      break;
    case GDK_Up:
      printf("The Up arrow key was pressed.\n");
      break;
    default:
      break;
    }

  if (gdk_keyval_is_lower(event->keyval))
    {
      printf("A non-uppercase key was pressed.\n");
    }
  else if (gdk_keyval_is_upper(event->keyval))
    {
      printf("An uppercase letter was pressed.\n");
    }
}
```

`gdk_keyval_name()` is useful for debugging; it returns the name of the keysym without the `GDK_` prefix. For example, it returns `"Home"` if it's passed the value `GDK_Home`. The string is statically allocated. `gdk_keyval_is_lower()` returns `FALSE` if the keysym has an uppercase equivalent. Thus it returns `TRUE` for lowercase letters, numbers, and all non-alphanumeric characters. It returns `FALSE` only for uppercase letters. `gdk_keyval_is_upper()` returns the opposite values.

Note that all widgets do not receive key events; a widget must have the `gtk_can_focus` flag set to indicate that it can be focused, and then it must actually have the keyboard focus. See Section 10.5.6.1 for more information.

10.5.6   Mouse Movement Events

Events are emitted to let you track the mouse as it moves around the screen. *Motion events* are emitted as the pointer moves inside a window; *crossing events* are emitted when the pointer enters or leaves a GdkWindow. The `type` field for motion events is `GDK_MOTION_NOTIFY`. There are two kinds of crossing events: `GDK_ENTER_NOTIFY` and `GDK_LEAVE_NOTIFY`.

There are two ways to track motion events. If you specify `GDK_POINTER_MOTION_MASK` in the event mask for a window, you will receive as many motion events as the X server can generate. If the user moves the pointer rapidly, you will be deluged in motion events; you must handle them quickly, or your application may become unresponsive while it processes the backlog. If you *also* specify `GDK_POINTER_MOTION_HINT_MASK`, motion events are sent one at a time. At most, one event will be sent until you call `gdk_window_get_pointer()`, or the pointer leaves and re-enters the window, or a button or key event occurs. Thus, each time you receive a motion event, you must call `gdk_window_get_pointer()` to get the current pointer position and signal the server that you are ready for another event. See Section 10.6 for details on `gdk_window_get_pointer()`.

Which mode you choose depends on the application. If you need to trace the exact trajectory of the pointer, you will want to get all motion events. If you only care about the most recent pointer position, you will want to include `GDK_POINTER_MOTION_HINT_MASK` in your window's event mask to minimize network traffic and maximize responsiveness. One caveat: `gdk_window_get_pointer()` requires a server round-trip to obtain the pointer position. So, it does place some maximum limit on your application's responsiveness. If you can handle motion events quickly enough to keep them from backlogging, your application will probably seem faster without `GDK_POINTER_MOTION_HINT_MASK`. Motion events are unlikely to come more often than a couple hundred per second—so if you can handle them in less than 5 milliseconds, you should be okay.

You can ask to receive motion events only while one or more mouse buttons are held down. To receive motion events while any button is down, use `GDK_BUTTON_MOTION_MASK` in place of `GDK_POINTER_MOTION_MASK`. You can use `GDK_POINTER_MOTION_HINT_MASK` with `GDK_BUTTON_MOTION_MASK` to limit the number of events received, just as you can use it with `GDK_POINTER_MOTION_MASK`. If you are only interested in motion events while a certain button is pressed, you can use the more specific `GDK_BUTTON1_MOTION_MASK`, `GDK_BUTTON2_MOTION_MASK`, or `GDK_BUTTON3_MOTION_MASK`.

Any combination of these three is allowed. They can also be combined with GDK_POINTER_MOTION_HINT_MASK to limit the number of events. In sum, you can select which motion events to receive along the "button state" dimension using these five masks:

- GDK_POINTER_MOTION_MASK: all motion events that occur, regardless of button state.

- GDK_BUTTON_MOTION_MASK: all motion events that occur while any button is held.

- GDK_BUTTON1_MOTION_MASK: all motion events that occur while button 1 is held.

- GDK_BUTTON2_MOTION_MASK: all motion events that occur while button 2 is held.

- GDK_BUTTON3_MOTION_MASK: all motion events that occur while button 3 is held.

By default, you are deluged with events as quickly as the X server can generate them. Adding GDK_POINTER_MOTION_HINT_MASK to the event mask enables one-at-a-time behavior. Motion events are represented by GdkEventMotion:

```
typedef struct _GdkEventMotion GdkEventMotion;

struct _GdkEventMotion
{
  GdkEventType type;
  GdkWindow *window;
  gint8 send_event;
  guint32 time;
  gdouble x;
  gdouble y;
  gdouble pressure;
  gdouble xtilt;
  gdouble ytilt;
  guint state;
  gint16 is_hint;
  GdkInputSource source;
  guint32 deviceid;
  gdouble x_root, y_root;
};
```

Most of these fields should be familiar to you from GdkEventButton. In fact, the only field unique to GdkEventMotion is the is_hint flag. If this field is TRUE, GDK_POINTER_MOTION_HINT_MASK was selected. You might use this flag if you are writing a widget for other people to use and you want to let them choose how to receive motion events. In your motion event handler, you could do this:

```
double x, y;

x = event->motion.x;
y = event->motion.y;

if (event->motion.is_hint)
  gdk_window_get_pointer(event->window, &x, &y, NULL);
```

That is, you call `gdk_window_get_pointer()` only if necessary. If you are using `GDK_POINTER_MOTION_HINT_MASK`, you should prefer the results from `gdk_window_get_pointer()` to the coordinates given in the event, because they are more recent. (If you are receiving every event, it makes no sense to call `gdk_window_get_pointer()` because it is relatively slow and will worsen the backlog—you're getting every event eventually anyway.)

Crossing events occur when the mouse pointer enters or leaves a window. If you move the mouse pointer rapidly across your application, Gdk generates these events for every window you pass through. However, GTK+ will try to remove the events "in the middle" and forward only the first `leave` event and the last `enter` event to widgets. If you feel you should be getting `enter`/`leave` events when you aren't, this optimization is a likely cause. Here is `GdkEventCrossing`:

```
typedef struct _GdkEventCrossing GdkEventCrossing;

struct _GdkEventCrossing
{
  GdkEventType type;
  GdkWindow *window;
  gint8 send_event;
  GdkWindow *subwindow;
  guint32 time;
  gdouble x;
  gdouble y;
  gdouble x_root;
  gdouble y_root;
  GdkCrossingMode mode;
  GdkNotifyType detail;
  gboolean focus;
  guint state;
};
```

Again, many of the fields should be familiar: coordinates relative to the event window and the root window, a timestamp, a `state` bitfield indicating which buttons and modifiers are active, and the standard three fields from `GdkEventAny`. However, there are several new fields.

The standard `window` field contains a pointer to the window the pointer is entering or leaving. `x` and `y` are relative to this window. However, the pointer may have been in a child of the window receiving the event before a `leave` event occurred, or the pointer may end up in a child window when an `enter` event occurs. In these cases, `subwindow` is set to the child window. Otherwise `subwindow` is `NULL`. Note that the child window will receive its own `enter` and `leave` events if either `GDK_ENTER_NOTIFY_MASK` or `GDK_LEAVE_NOTIFY_MASK` is in its event mask.

The `mode` field indicates whether the event occurred normally or as part of a pointer grab. When the pointer is grabbed or ungrabbed (see Section 10.6), the pointer may be moved. Crossing events caused by a grab have the `GDK_CROSSING_GRAB` mode; those caused by an ungrab have `GDK_CROSSING_UNGRAB`; and all others have `GDK_CROSSING_NORMAL`. This field appears to be completely useless. Some quick greps through GTK+ and Gnome reveal no examples of its use.

The `detail` field is rarely used. It gives information about the relative tree positions of the window being left and the window being entered. It has two simple and useful values:

- `GDK_NOTIFY_INFERIOR` marks a crossing event received by a parent window when the pointer moves into or out of a child window.

- `GDK_NOTIFY_ANCESTOR` marks a crossing event received by a child window when the pointer moves into or out of its parent window.

Several other values are also possible: `GDK_NOTIFY_VIRTUAL`, `GDK_NOTIFY_INFERIOR`, `GDK_NOTIFY_NONLINEAR`, `GDK_NOTIFY_NONLINEAR_VIRTUAL`, and `GDK_NOTIFY_UNKNOWN`. However, they are never used and are too complicated to explain here.

10.5.6.1 Keyboard Focus

The `focus` field in `GdkEventCrossing` indicates whether the event window or one of its ancestors has the keyboard input focus. Keyboard focus is an X concept that's used to determine which window should receive key events. The window manager decides which toplevel window has the focus (usually the focused window is highlighted and brought to the top; most window managers let you choose between "focus follows mouse" and "click to focus" modes). When an application has the focus, it is free to move the focus among its subwindows—perhaps different text entry fields. However, GTK+ does not use the X focus mechanism for subwindows. Toplevel `GtkWindow` widgets are the only ones that receive the X focus. Thus, they receive all raw key events from X (by way of Gdk). GTK+ implements its own concept of *widget focus*, which is analogous to X's window focus, but in reality is entirely distinct. When a toplevel `GtkWindow` widget receives key events, it forwards them to the widget with GTK+'s focus.

In short, this means the `focus` flag will be `TRUE` if the toplevel `GtkWindow` containing the event window currently has the X focus. The `focus` flag is unrelated to GTK+'s widget focus concept.

10.5.7 Focus Change Events

The previous section explained the difference between GTK+'s concept of keyboard focus and the X/Gdk concept. This makes focus events a little bit confusing. There is only one type of focus event, GDK_FOCUS_CHANGE, which is received whenever a window gains or loses the keyboard focus. As we just said, only toplevel GtkWindow widgets ever gain or lose the focus from Gdk's point of view; so this event may not seem useful. However, each GtkWindow maintains a current "focus widget" and forwards key events to that widget. It also synthesizes Gdk-style focus events as the focus widget changes. Thus, even though Gdk-style focus is not being used, widgets receive events in the same way that they would if it were being used. There are subtle differences: For example, widgets receive focus events whether or not their GdkWindow's event mask includes GDK_FOCUS_CHANGE_MASK. Only toplevel widgets need to specify this mask.

Focus events themselves are very simple. When a widget gains the keyboard focus, it receives a focus event with its in member set to TRUE (a "focus in event"); likewise, when a widget loses the focus, it receives a focus event with the in member set to FALSE (a "focus out event"). Otherwise, focus events contain only the three standard fields from GdkEventAny:

```
typedef struct _GdkEventFocus GdkEventFocus;

struct _GdkEventFocus
{
  GdkEventType type;
  GdkWindow *window;
  gint8 send_event;
  gint16 in;
};
```

10.5.8 Expose Events

Expose events are received when a previously obscured region of a window becomes visible. GdkWindow contents are not recorded; that is, if you draw to a GdkWindow, and the X server places another window on top of it, the graphics in the bottom window will be lost. When the top window is moved away, the bottom window will receive an expose event, indicating that the region needs to be redrawn. Expose events are also sent when a window first appears on-screen. (Incidentally, you should not draw into a GdkWindow until you receive the first expose event. The first expose event is your signal that the window is actually on-screen.)

Expose events have a unique feature: GTK+ synthesizes them for windowless widgets. This is the only kind of event GTK_NO_WINDOW widgets will receive. Expose events are very simple:

```
typedef struct _GdkEventExpose GdkEventExpose;

struct _GdkEventExpose
{
```

```
    GdkEventType type;
    GdkWindow *window;
    gint8 send_event;
    GdkRectangle area;
    gint count;
};
```

area is the area that has been exposed and should be redrawn. count is the number of expose events that follow this one. Conceivably you might want to compress successive events into a single redraw. However, Gdk already makes a reasonable effort to do this, so adding another pass is not likely to gain much. GdkRectangle is defined as follows:

```
typedef struct _GdkRectangle GdkRectangle;

struct _GdkRectangle
{
  gint16 x;
  gint16 y;
  guint16 width;
  guint16 height;
};
```

There is one other time you will receive expose events. If you call gdk_window_copy_area() to copy part of one window into another, the source window region may be partially or completely obscured. If it is, X will be unable to copy something sensible from the obscured region. By default, expose events will be generated for the areas of the *destination* window that X was unable to copy something to. Your program's standard redraw routine can then refresh these areas of the destination window by hand. You can turn this behavior off by calling gdk_gc_set_exposures() on the *graphics context* passed to gdk_window_copy_area(). (Graphics contexts are discussed in Section 10.8.)

If the source window region is *not* obscured, gdk_window_copy_area() can successfully draw the entire destination region. In this case, no expose events are generated; a single "no expose" event is generated instead. This event contains no information beyond the standard event fields:

```
typedef struct _GdkEventNoExpose GdkEventNoExpose;

struct _GdkEventNoExpose
{
  GdkEventType type;
  GdkWindow *window;
  gint8 send_event;
};
```

10.5.9 Window Change Events

As a GdkWindow is shown, hidden, resized, or destroyed, events are emitted. Configure events indicate that the size or position of the event window has changed. They include the new size and position of the window, as shown here:

```
typedef struct _GdkEventConfigure GdkEventConfigure;

struct _GdkEventConfigure
{
  GdkEventType type;
  GdkWindow *window;
  gint8 send_event;
  gint16 x, y;
  gint16 width;
  gint16 height;
};
```

All widgets receive this event (because GDK_STRUCTURE_MASK is automatically in the event mask), but the widget size allocation system already conveys the necessary information. That is, most widgets resize their GdkWindows themselves in response to a size allocation; configure events just report back the resize—which is not very useful. There are two notable exceptions. First, the toplevel GtkWindow widget is in charge of initiating the size allocation process and has no parent to get an allocation from, so it monitors configure events to determine its size allocation. When you resize a GtkWindow using its window manager decorations, it receives configure events and act accordingly. The second exception is GtkDrawingArea. GtkDrawingArea sends itself a configure event when it receives its size allocation. This is convenient because you will usually want to repaint the contents of the drawing area if it is resized. Like all "fake" events GTK+ creates, send_event will be TRUE for this configure event.

Other changes in a GdkWindow are signaled with GdkEventAny. These events contain no special information, they just tell you that something has occurred. They are distinguished by their type field:

- GDK_DELETE means that the window manager has asked the application to destroy this window. If a widget receives the signal corresponding to this event and the signal emission returns FALSE, the widget is automatically destroyed by the GTK+ main loop. Because FALSE is the default return value, you must connect a signal handler that returns TRUE to prevent users from destroying GtkWindow widgets.

- GDK_DESTROY means the window has been destroyed. Widgets normally destroy their own windows when they are unrealized. If a widget is not destroyed after a destroy event on its window, the GTK+ main loop destroys it.

- GDK_MAP means the window has been shown on the screen. However, you should wait for the first expose event before you draw to the window.

- GDK_UNMAP means the window has been hidden; perhaps it was iconified, or perhaps you called gtk_widget_hide().

10.5.10   Little-Used Events

There are a few other event types that aren't very useful, so this book does not cover them in detail. However, this section gives a brief description of each one, for completeness. You can safely skip this section if you want.

10.5.10.1   Visibility Events

Visibility events occur when a window is obscured or unobscured. They are not very useful because other events already give you the information you need. In particular, when a window is unobscured you receive expose events indicating which newly visible areas should be redrawn. Here is the event:

```
typedef struct _GdkEventVisibility GdkEventVisibility;

struct _GdkEventVisibility
{
  GdkEventType type;
  GdkWindow *window;
  gint8 send_event;
  GdkVisibilityState state;
};
```

state is an enumeration value indicating whether the window was obscured or unobscured.

10.5.10.2   Property Events

X associates *properties* with windows. These are basically key-value pairs used for inter-client communication. Most commonly, they relay some information about a toplevel window to the window manager. GTK+ provides a high-level interface for all the important properties, so you should not need to deal with them directly. Property events are sent when a property's value changes.

```
typedef struct _GdkEventProperty GdkEventProperty;

struct _GdkEventProperty
{
  GdkEventType type;
  GdkWindow *window;
  gint8 send_event;
  GdkAtom atom;
  guint32 time;
  guint state;
};
```

10.5.10.3   Selection Events

X has a simple cut-and-paste mechanism (typically, you select some text with button 1 and paste with button 2). The current contents of the "Clipboard" are called the *selection*. You need to know about this only if you are writing a widget like GtkText or GtkEntry that allows you to cut and paste text. Selection events indicate that the current selection has changed; they look like this:

```
typedef struct _GdkEventSelection GdkEventSelection;

struct _GdkEventSelection
{
  GdkEventType type;
  GdkWindow *window;
  gint8 send_event;
  GdkAtom selection;
  GdkAtom target;
  GdkAtom property;
  guint32 requestor;
  guint32 time;
};
```

Most GTK+ widgets deal with the selection using a higher-level interface, found in gtk/gtkselection.h. If you're interested in writing selection-handling code, be sure to look at that header.

10.5.10.4   Client Events

A client event is an arbitrary chunk of data sent from one application to another. However, some conventional "messages" can be sent, most of which are defined in the Inter-Client Communication Conventions Manual (ICCCM). The ICCCM is free with the X Window System distribution from the Open Group. Client events are mostly used for communication between applications and the window manager. (The Xlib event being wrapped is called ClientMessage, so look for ClientMessage in the ICCCM.) An important ClientMessage event is sent from the window manager to applications, asking for windows to be deleted. However, Gdk converts these events to a GdkEventAny with type GDK_DELETE. So, a GdkEventClient will not be received. Some events involved in drag-and-drop are also ClientMessage events. However, Gdk translates these to GdkEventDND. So, a GdkEventClient will not be received for them either. GdkEventClient will be received only if some other client sends your application an unconventional message that Gdk and GTK+ are not prepared to understand. Most common messages are nicely wrapped in a high-level interface.

Just for reference, here is the event:

```
typedef struct _GdkEventClient GdkEventClient;

struct _GdkEventClient
{
  GdkEventType type;
  GdkWindow *window;
  gint8 send_event;
  GdkAtom message_type;
  gushort data_format;
  union {
    char b[20];
    short s[10];
    long l[5];
  } data;
};
```

The union at the end is used to hold the contents of the message. send_event is always
TRUE because this event is always sent from one client to another and does not come
from the X server.

10.5.10.5   Drag-and-Drop Events

Drag-and-drop events are actually pretty useful if you're implementing a drag-and-
drop feature in your application. However, because few applications need to do this
and the topic is fairly involved, this book glosses over the topic. GTK+ comes with
some documentation on drag-and-drop and several examples. Here is the event struct:

```
typedef struct _GdkEventDND GdkEventDND;

struct _GdkEventDND {
  GdkEventType type;
  GdkWindow *window;
  gint8 send_event;
  GdkDragContext *context;

  guint32 time;
  gshort x_root, y_root;
};
```

10.5.10.6   Proximity Events

Proximity events are generated when Gdk's wrapper for the XInput extension is used.
The XInput extension is an add-on for standard X that allows you to use nonstandard
devices such as graphics tablets. A proximity event indicates that the stylus has moved
in or out of contact with the tablet, or perhaps that the user's finger has moved in or

out of contact with a touch screen. The X distribution comes with some documentation for the XInput extension, and Owen Taylor's gsumi application contains example
Gdk code.

```
typedef struct _GdkEventProximity GdkEventProximity;

struct _GdkEventProximity
{
  GdkEventType type;
  GdkWindow *window;
  gint8 send_event;
  guint32 time;
  GdkInputSource source;
  guint32 deviceid;
};
```

10.6   The Mouse Pointer

The mouse pointer is represented on the screen by a small bitmap called the *cursor*.
The cursor is normally an arrow shape, but it can be changed on a window-by-
window basis. As the pointer moves, it generates motion events and moves the cursor
on the screen to give the user feedback.

10.6.1   Pointer Location

You can query the pointer's location with gdk_window_get_pointer() (see Function
Listing 10.7). This function requests the X and Y coordinates of the pointer relative to
the window passed as its first argument. It also requests the currently active modifiers
(including modifier keys and buttons; this field is identical to the state field in several
events, such as button events). If NULL is passed for the x, y, or state argument, that
argument will be ignored.

Function Listing 10.7   **Querying Pointer Location**   *#include <gdk/gdk.h>*

```
GdkWindow*
gdk_window_get_pointer(GdkWindow* window,
                       gint* x,
                       gint* y,
                       GdkModifierMask* state)
```

10.6.2   Grabbing the Pointer

It is possible to *grab* the pointer, which means that all pointer events will go to the *grab window* for the duration of the grab. Normally, pointer events go to the window the pointer is inside. You should grab the pointer, for example, if the user is using click-and-drag selection to select a rectangular area. If the user clicks and then inadvertently drags the pointer outside the window, you should continue to track the pointer's location and change the selection accordingly. The grab also ensures that pointer events won't be sent to other applications.

To grab the pointer, call `gdk_pointer_grab()`, shown in Function Listing 10.8. The first argument to this function is the grab window, which will receive events during the grab. The next argument should be `TRUE` or `FALSE` to specify whether events will go to the grab window only or to its child windows as well. The `confine_to` argument specifies a window to confine the pointer to or it can be `NULL` to allow free pointer motion. The user will not be able to move the pointer outside this window. You can specify a different `cursor` for the duration of the grab; see the next section for details on creating a cursor. If you don't want to change the cursor, give `NULL` as the `cursor` argument. (Side note: it is safe to destroy the cursor immediately after calling `gdk_pointer_grab()` because it is a server-side resource, and X will not deallocate it until the grab is over.)

The final argument, `time`, specifies when the grab should take effect (in server time). This is intended to resolve conflicts if two clients try to grab the pointer simultaneously; the time must be after the last grab time, and it must not be in the future. Usually, you will want to use either the `time` field from the event you're processing or the `GDK_CURRENT_TIME` macro. `GDK_CURRENT_TIME` is a magic constant that tells the X server to substitute the current time.

Function Listing 10.8   **Grabbing the Pointer**   *#include <gdk/gdk.h>*

```
gint
gdk_pointer_grab(GdkWindow* window,
                 gint owner_events,
                 GdkWindow* confine_to,
                 GdkCursor* cursor,
                 guint32 time)
void
gdk_pointer_ungrab(guint32 time)
gint
gdk_pointer_is_grabbed()
```

`gdk_pointer_grab()` returns `TRUE` if it succeeds. It is possible for it to fail if the grab window or `confine_to` window is hidden, or another client has the grab already, or any of the arguments are invalid. Regrettably, few applications check this return value, which is a bug (although it's difficult-to-trigger).

To ungrab the pointer, call `gdk_pointer_ungrab()`. The `time` argument is identical to the one in `gdk_pointer_grab()`. You can find out if the pointer is grabbed by using `gdk_pointer_is_grabbed()`. You *must* ungrab the pointer when you're finished with it because the user will be unable to use other applications while the pointer is grabbed.

Note that the Gdk-level concept of grabbing the pointer is distinct from the GTK+-level grab concept. A GTK+ grab redirects certain events to a grabbing *widget*, creating a "modal" widget such as a dialog box (see Section 3.3.3). GTK+'s grab affects only the current application; only events that occur on one of the current application's widgets are redirected. The scope of a Gdk grab is wider, encompassing the entire X server and not just your application.

10.6.3 Changing the Cursor

You can change the cursor shape at any time. Cursor shapes are set on a window-by-window basis with `gdk_window_set_cursor()` (shown in Function Listing 10.9). By default, windows use their parent's cursor. You can restore the default cursor by setting a window's cursor to `NULL`.

Function Listing 10.9 *GdkCursor*   *#include <gdk/gdk.h>*

```
GdkCursor*
gdk_cursor_new(GdkCursorType cursor_type)

GdkCursor*
gdk_cursor_new_from_pixmap(GdkPixmap* source,
                           GdkPixmap* mask,
                           GdkColor* fg,
                           GdkColor* bg,
                           gint x,
                           gint y)
void
gdk_cursor_destroy(GdkCursor* cursor)
void
gdk_window_set_cursor(GdkWindow* window,
                      GdkCursor* cursor)
```

Two ways are provided to create a cursor. The simplest way is to choose a cursor from the cursor font that comes with X. The cursor font contains cursors instead of characters; you can view it with the command `xfd -fn cursor`. You can also browse the available cursors using the `testgtk` program that comes with GTK+. Each cursor shape has a constant defined in `gdk/gdkcursors.h`. `gdk_cursor_new()` accepts one of these constants as its only argument:

```
GdkCursor* cursor;
cursor = gdk_cursor_new(GDK_CLOCK);
gdk_window_set_cursor(window, cursor);
gdk_cursor_destroy(cursor);
```

Notice that you can destroy the cursor as soon as you attach it to a window; GdkCursor is a client-side handle for a server-side resource, and X will keep the server-side resource around as long as it's in use.

If none of the cursors in the cursor font is appropriate, you can create a custom cursor from a bitmap—two bitmaps, actually: the source pixmap and the mask. Because these are bitmaps, every pixel is either on or off (0 or 1). If a pixel is 0 in the mask, that pixel will be transparent. If a pixel is 1 in both pixmaps, it will be displayed in the fg (foreground) color passed to gdk_cursor_new_from_pixmap(). If a pixel is 1 in the mask but 0 in the source pixmap, it will be displayed in the bg (background) color. The source and mask pixmaps must be the same size, and they must have a depth of one.

The foreground and background colors should be contrasting so that the cursor will be visible against any background. Most cursors are drawn in the foreground color and outlined in the background color. (To see this, move an X cursor over a dark background; you will notice a white outline around its edges.) To achieve this, mask should be slightly larger than source, but the same shape.

The final two arguments to gdk_cursor_new_from_pixmap() are the coordinates of the cursor's *hot spot*. This is the point drawn at the mouse pointer's location—the tip of an arrow cursor, or the center of a crosshair cursor. gdk_cursor_new_from_pixmap() will fail if the hot spot is not within the bitmap.

10.7 Fonts

An X font is (yet another) server-side resource. In essence, a font is a collection of bitmaps representing characters. The bitmaps in a single font will have a similar size and style. Gdk allows you to manipulate fonts with a client-side handle called GdkFont.

To obtain a GdkFont, call gdk_font_load() (or use the font from a preexisting GtkStyle; more on this in Section 10.11). Fonts are loaded by name, and font names are a fairly involved topic. Names follow a convention called the "X Logical Font Description," or XLFD. The best way to get a feel for XLFD is to play with the xfontsel program that comes with X. You can also get a list of font names on your X server with the xlsfonts program. The standard X distribution includes a 30-page XLFD manual, but the basics aren't too complicated.

A font name is a string made up of hyphen-separated fields. Each field describes some aspect of the font, as in this example:

```
misc-fixed-medium-r-normal—0-0-75-75-c-0-iso8859-1
```

or this one:

```
-adobe-new century schoolbook-bold-i-normal—11-80-100-100-p-66-iso8859-1
```

The fourteen fields are listed here:

- **Foundry**: The vendor who created the font, such as Adobe or Sony. misc is used for some generic fonts that come with X.

- **Family**: The typeface or style of the font—Courier, Times, Helvetica, and so on.

- **Weight**: Bold, demibold, medium, and so forth.

- **Slant**: Italic, Roman, or Oblique (abbreviated as i, r, or o).

- **Set Width**: The "proportionate width" of the font; possible values include normal, condensed, semicondensed, and so on.

- **"Add Style"**: Any additional information about the font can go in this field. It is used to distinguish two fonts that otherwise have the same name. There are no constraints on the string.

- **Pixels**: The pixel size of the font.

- **Points**: The point size of the font, in tenths of a point. A point is 1/72 of an inch. The relationship of point size to pixel size is determined by the resolution (dots per inch) the X server thinks the display has. Typically, people do not configure their X servers to match their monitors, so the X server's idea of the current resolution may be wildly inaccurate.

- **Horizontal Resolution**: Horizontal display resolution in dots per inch (dpi) that the font is designed for.

- **Vertical Resolution**: Vertical display resolution the font is designed for.

- **Spacing**: Monospace (abbreviated m) or proportional (abbreviated p). Indicates whether all characters have the same width or whether different characters may have different widths.

- **Average Width**: The mean width of all characters in the font, in tenths of a pixel.

- **Character Set Registry**: The organization or standard defining the character set.

- **Character Set Encoding**: Specifies the specific character set encoding. These last two fields in combination specify the character set. For European languages iso8859-1 will almost always be used. This is the "Latin-1" character set, which is an 8-bit encoding set that includes ASCII as a subset.

It is not necessary to specify all 14 fields when requesting a font. "Wild cards" are allowed. The asterisk (*) matches any number of characters, and the question mark (?) matches any single character. For example, a 160-point Bold Roman Helvetica font can be requested like this:

```
-*-helvetica-bold-r-*-*-*-160-*-*-*-*-*-*
```

When you pass a font name to `gdk_font_load()`, you should consider it a default choice only. Users in other countries will certainly want to use a font appropriate to their language; U.S. and European users might want to customize fonts, too. Also, no fonts are guaranteed to exist on all servers. Thus you should provide a way to customize any font you use. The easiest way is to use fonts from a widget's `GtkStyle` (again, see Section 10.11).

   `gdk_font_load()` returns `NULL` if it fails to find a font matching the supplied name. When you are done with a font, you should release it by calling `gdk_font_unref()`. Function Listing 10.10 summarizes these functions.

Function Listing 10.10 **GdkFont**   *#include <gdk/gdk.h>*

```
GdkFont*
gdk_font_load(const gchar* font_name)

void
gdk_font_unref(GdkFont* font)
```

When loading fonts, you will need to specify at least the font name, the weight, the slant, and a size—otherwise the * wildcard would probably load a random bold italic font, which is unlikely to be what you want. The *Xlib Programming Manual* suggests that you always specify the font size in points, so that users with different monitors will get the right effect; however, X servers do not reliably know the display resolution, so this is more theory than reality. Perhaps it's better to specify pixels because you do know the pixel size of other elements of your display. Neither method is perfect. Just be sure you make your application's fonts configurable.

10.7.1 Font Metrics

To use a font, you typically need detailed information about its *metrics*. Font metrics are used to position characters with respect to one another and to determine the size of strings rendered in the font. The most fundamental metrics are the *ascent* and *descent* of the font. Text is placed on a *baseline*, which is like a rule on a sheet of notebook paper. The bottom of each character touches the baseline. Some characters (such as lowercase "p" and "y") extend below the baseline. A font's *descent* is the maximum distance below the baseline its characters reach. Its *ascent* is the maximum distance above the baseline. The *height* of a font is the sum of the ascent and the descent. When rendering multiple lines of text, you should leave at least the font's height between baselines. Figure 10.1 depicts the various font metrics.

Figure 10.1　Font metrics.

Ascent and descent are available as members of the `GdkFont` struct:

```
typedef struct _GdkFont GdkFont;

struct _GdkFont
{
  GdkFontType type;
  gint ascent;
  gint descent;
};
```

The `type` field distinguishes fonts from fontsets; fontsets are used to display non-European languages.[1]

Individual characters in a font have their own ascent and descent. A character's ascent and descent will always be less than or equal to the font's ascent and descent. Gdk can calculate the maximum ascent and descent for a particular string, rather than an entire font, and this height will be less than or equal to the font's height. The relevant functions are `gdk_string_height()`, `gdk_text_height()`, and `gdk_char_height()`. `gdk_text_height()` is different from `gdk_string_height()` because it accepts the length of the string as an argument. `gdk_string_height()` calls `strlen()` for you. Thus `gdk_text_height()` is preferred if you already know a string's length.

---

1. If you're wondering where the reference to the server-side resource is hidden, here's the answer. The `GdkFont*` returned from `gdk_font_load()` actually points to a `GdkFontPrivate` defined in `gdk/gdkprivate.h`; `GdkFont` contains only the public fields of `GdkFontPrivate`. Nearly all the Gdk types work this way.

In addition to its vertical metrics, each character in a font has three metrics describing its horizontal dimensions. The *width* of a character is the distance from the left origin of the character to the start of the next character. Note: The width is *not* the distance to the furthest-right pixel in a character. In some fonts, especially italic fonts, characters may lean over past the start of the next character. The *left-side-bearing,* or *lbearing,* is the distance from the left origin to the leftmost pixel in the character; the *right-side-bearing,* or *rbearing,* is the distance from the origin to the rightmost pixel in the character. Thus the rbearing can be larger than the width, as it is in the case of italic fonts that lean over past the start of the next character.

Gdk functions that return a character or string width return the width of the character, or the sum of the character widths in the string. If the rbearing of the rightmost character is greater than its width, a string may require more space than `gdk_string_width()`, `gdk_text_width()`, or `gdk_char_width()` will return. Like the height-measurement functions, the `_string_` variant computes the length of the string for you, and the `_text_` variant accepts a precomputed length as an argument.

The functions ending in `_measure` are more often what you want. For a string with N characters, these return the sum of the widths of the first *N-1* characters, plus the rbearing of the final character. That is, they take into account the fact that rbearing may be greater than width. If you're trying to decide how much space to leave for rendering a string, you probably want the `gdk_string_measure()`, `gdk_text_measure()`, or `gdk_char_measure()` functions. Sometimes you don't want to consider the rbearing, however. For example, if you're centering a string, it may look nicer to use the width (because a small italic flourish extending past the width won't "fill" the space, and the string will look slightly left of center).

`gdk_text_extents()` and `gdk_string_extents()` return all the metrics for a string, including both bearings, the width, ascent, and descent. The returned left-side-bearing is the leftmost pixel in the string; the right-side-bearing is the rightmost pixel as returned by `gdk_text_measure()`. The width is the sum of character widths, as returned by `gdk_text_width()`.

Function Listing 10.11 summarizes the API for querying font metrics. All font metrics are computed on the client side, so these functions are not expensive compared to most of the drawing API.

Function Listing 10.11   **Font Metrics**   *#include <gdk/gdk.h>*

```
gint
gdk_string_width(GdkFont* font,
                 const gchar* string)

gint
gdk_text_width(GdkFont* font,
               const gchar* string,
               gint string_length)

gint
gdk_char_width(GdkFont* font,
               gchar character)
```

continues

Function Listing 10.11   **Continued**

```
gint
gdk_string_measure(GdkFont* font,
                   const gchar* string)
gint
gdk_text_measure(GdkFont* font,
                 const gchar* string,
                 gint string_length)
gint
gdk_char_measure(GdkFont* font,
                 gchar character)
gint
gdk_string_height(GdkFont* font,
                  const gchar* string)
gint
gdk_text_height(GdkFont* font,
                const gchar* string,
                gint string_length)
gint
gdk_char_height(GdkFont* font,
                gchar character)
void
gdk_string_extents(GdkFont* font,
                   const gchar* string,
                   gint* lbearing,
                   gint* rbearing,
                   gint* width,
                   gint* ascent,
                   gint* descent)
void
gdk_text_extents(GdkFont* font,
                 const gchar* string,
                 gint string_length,
                 gint* lbearing,
                 gint* rbearing,
                 gint* width,
                 gint* ascent,
                 gint* descent)
```

10.8   Graphics Contexts

A *graphics context*, or *GC*, is simply a set of parameters to be used when drawing (such as color, clip mask, font, and so on). It is a server-side resource, just as pixmaps and windows are. GCs reduce the number of arguments to the Gdk drawing functions and also reduce the number of parameters passed from client to server with each drawing request.

A graphics context can be created with a `GdkGCValues` struct, analogous to `GdkWindowAttr`; the struct contains all the interesting features of a graphics context, and you pass `gdk_gc_new_with_values()` flags, indicating which fields are valid. The other fields retain their default values. You can also create an all-default GC with `gdk_gc_new()` (this is usually easier). Functions are provided to change GC settings after the GC is created as well—but remember that each change requires a message to the X server. These functions are summarized in Function Listing 10.12. Table 10.6 outlines the attributes of a GC and the flags used as the final argument to `gdk_gc_new_with_values()`.

Function Listing 10.12   *GdkGC*   *#include <gdk/gdk.h>*

```
GdkGC*
gdk_gc_new(GdkWindow* window)

GdkGC*
gdk_gc_new_with_values(GdkWindow* window,
                GdkGCValues* values,
                GdkGCValuesMask values_mask)

void
gdk_gc_set_dashes(GdkGC* gc,
                gint dash_offset,
                gchar dash_list,
                gint n)

void
gdk_gc_unref(GdkGC* gc)
```

Table 10.6   **GC Attributes**

Attribute	GdkGCValuesMask	Modifying Function	Default Value
GdkColor foreground	GDK_GC_FOREGROUND	gdk_gc_set_ foreground()	Black
GdkColor background	GDK_GC_BACKGROUND	gdk_gc_set_ background()	White
GdkFont *font	GDK_GC_FONT	gdk_gc_set_font	Depends on X server
GdkFunction function	GDK_GC_FUNCTION	gdk_gc_set_ function()	GDK_COPY
GdkFill fill	GDK_GC_FILL	gdk_gc_set_fill()	GDK_SOLID
GdkPixmap *tile	GDK_GC_TILE	gdk_gc_set_tile()	Pixmap filled with foreground color (that is, effectively none)

continues

Table 10.6 **Continued**

Attribute	GdkGCValuesMask	Modifying Function	Default Value
GdkPixmap *stipple	GDK_GC_STIPPLE	gdk_gc_set_ stipple()	All-bits-on bitmap (that is, effectively none)
GdkPixmap *clip_mask	GDK_GC_CLIP_MASK	gdk_gc_set_ clip_mask()	None
GdkSubwindowMode subwindow_mode	GDK_GC_SUBWINDOW	gdk_gc_set_ subwindow()	GDK CLIP_BY _CHILDREN
gint ts_x_origin	GDK_GC_TS_X_ ORIGIN	gdk_gc_set_ts_ origin()	0
gint ts_y_origin	GDK_GC_TS_Y_ ORIGIN	gdk_gc_set_ts_ origin()	0
gint clip_ x_origin	GDK_GC_CLIP_X_ ORIGIN	gdk_gc_set_clip_ origin()	0
gint clip_ y_origin	GDK_GC_CLIP_Y_ ORIGIN	gdk_gc_set_clip_ origin()	0
gint graphics_ exposures	GDK_GC_EXPOSURES	gdk_gc_set_ exposures()	TRUE
gint line_width	GDK_GC_LINE_WIDTH	gdk_gc_set_line_ attributes()	0
GdkLineStyle line_style	GDK_GC_LINE_STYLE	gdk_gc_set_line_ attributes()	GDK_ LINE_ SOLID
GdkCapStyle cap_style	GDK_GC_CAP_STYLE	gdk_gc_set_line_ attributes()	GDK_CAP_ BUTT
GdkJoinStyle join_style	GDK_GC_JOIN_STYLE	gdk_gc_set_line_ attributes()	GDK_JOIN_ MITER
gchar dash_list[]	None	gdk_gc_set_ dashes()	{4, 4}
gint dash_offset	None	gdk_gc_set_ dashes()	0

All GCs are not interchangeable; they are tied to particular depths and visuals. The
GC's depth and visual must match the depth and visual of the drawable you are drawing to. A GC's depth and visual are taken from the GdkWindow* argument to
gdk_gc_new(), so the easiest way to handle this issue is to create the GC with the
window you plan to draw on. GdkGCValues is a nice summary of a GC's attributes:

```
typedef struct _GdkGCValues GdkGCValues;

struct _GdkGCValues
{
  GdkColor          foreground;
  GdkColor          background;
  GdkFont           *font;
  GdkFunction       function;
  GdkFill           fill;
  GdkPixmap         *tile;
  GdkPixmap         *stipple;
  GdkPixmap         *clip_mask;
  GdkSubwindowMode  subwindow_mode;
  gint              ts_x_origin;
  gint              ts_y_origin;
  gint              clip_x_origin;
  gint              clip_y_origin;
  gint              graphics_exposures;
  gint              line_width;
  GdkLineStyle      line_style;
  GdkCapStyle       cap_style;
  GdkJoinStyle      join_style;
};
```

The foreground color is the "pen color" used to draw lines, circles, and other
shapes. The purpose of the background color depends on the particular drawing operation. These colors must be allocated in the current colormap with gdk_color_alloc().

The font field is unused. In Xlib, it specifies the font to use when drawing text.
In Gdk, it used to have the same purpose, but now the Gdk routines for drawing text
all require a GdkFont* argument instead. An Xlib graphics context can store only plain
fonts, but a GdkFont can also represent a fontset (used to render some foreign languages). Gdk should probably store a font field in its GdkGC instead of requiring a font
argument to the text-drawing functions, but it doesn't.

The function field specifies how each pixel being drawn is combined with the pixel that already exists in the drawable. There are many possible values, but only two are ever used:

- GDK_COPY is the default. It ignores the existing pixel (and just writes the new pixel over it).
- GDK_XOR combines the old and new pixels in an invertable way. That is, if you perform exactly the same GDK_XOR operation twice, the first draw is undone by the second. GDK_XOR is often used for "rubberbanding" because it makes it easy to restore the original contents of the drawable after rubberbanding is complete.

The fill field determines how the tile and stipple fields are used. A tile is a pixmap with the same depth as the destination drawable; it is copied over and over into the destination drawable—the origin of the first tile is (ts_x_origin, ts_y_origin). A stipple is a bitmap (pixmap with depth 1); stipples are also tiled starting at (ts_x_origin, ts_y_origin). Possible fill values include the following:

- GDK_SOLID means to ignore the tile and stipple. Shapes are drawn in the fore-ground and background colors.
- GDK_TILED means that shapes are drawn with the tile instead of with the foreground and background colors. Imagine a tiled surface under your drawable; when you draw in GDK_TILED mode, the contents of the drawable are scratched away, revealing the tiled surface underneath.
- GDK_STIPPLED is like GDK_SOLID with a bitmask defined by the stipple. That is, bits not set in the stipple are not drawn.
- GDK_OPAQUE_STIPPLED draws bits set in the stipple with the foreground color and bits not set in the stipple with the background color.

Some X servers do not implement the more obscure function and fill modes very effi-ciently. Don't be surprised if using them noticeably slows down drawing.

The optional clip_mask is a bitmap; only bits set in this bitmap will be drawn. The mapping from the clip mask to the drawable is determined by clip_x_origin and clip_y_origin. These define the drawable coordinates corresponding to (0,0) in the clip mask. It is also possible to set a clip rectangle (the most common and useful form of clipping) or a clip region (a region is an arbitrary area on the screen, typically a polygon or list of rectangles). To set a clip rectangle, use gdk_gc_set_clip_rectangle() as shown here:

```
GdkRectangle clip_rect;
clip_rect.x = 10;
clip_rect.y = 20;
clip_rect.width = 200;
clip_rect.height = 100;
gdk_gc_set_clip_rectangle(gc, &clip_rect);
```

To turn off clipping, set the clip rectangle, clip region, or clip mask to NULL.

The subwindow_mode of a GC matters only if the drawable is a window. The default setting is GDK_CLIP_BY_CHILDREN. This means that child windows are not affected by drawing on parent windows. This preserves the illusion that child windows are "on top" of parents and child windows are opaque. GDK_INCLUDE_INFERIORS will draw right over the top of any child windows, overwriting any graphics the child windows may contain. Normally, this mode is not used. If you do use GDK_INCLUDE_INFERIORS, you will probably use GDK_XOR as your drawing function because it allows you to restore the child windows' previous contents.

graphics_exposures is a boolean value that defaults to TRUE. It determines whether gdk_window_copy_area() sometimes generates expose events. Section 10.5.8 explained this in more detail.

The final four GC values determine how lines are drawn. These values are used for drawing lines, including the borders of unfilled polygons and arcs. The line_width field specifies the width of a line, in pixels. A line width of 0 specifies a "thin line"; thin lines are one-pixel lines that can be drawn very quickly (usually with hardware acceleration), but the exact pixels drawn depend on the X server in use. For consistent results, use a width of 1 instead.

The line_style field can have one of three values:

- GDK_LINE_SOLID is the default. It draws a solid line.

- GDK_LINE_ON_OFF_DASH draws a dashed line with the foreground color, leaving the "off" parts of the dash blank.

- GDK_LINE_DOUBLE_DASH draws a dashed line in the foreground color, but the "off" parts of the dash are drawn in the background color.

Dashes are specified with gdk_gc_set_dashes(). GdkGCValues does not include a field for this. gdk_gc_set_dashes() accepts three arguments:

- dash_list is an array of dash lengths. Even-indexed lengths are "on" dashes, which are drawn in the foreground color. Odd-indexed lengths are "off" dashes, which are not drawn or are drawn in the background color, depending on line_style. 0 is not a permitted value; all lengths must be positive.

- dash_offset is the index of the first pixel to use in the dash list. That is, if the dash list specifies 5 pixels "on" and 5 "off" and the offset is 3, the line will begin in the middle of the "on" dash.

- n is simply the number of elements in dash_list.

You might set a whimsical dash pattern this way, for example:

```
gchar dash_list[] = { 5, 5, 3, 3, 1, 1, 3, 3 };
gdk_gc_set_dashes(gc, 0, dash_list, sizeof(dash_list));
```

The default dash list is {4, 4} with an offset of 0.

Figure 10.2 shows some dashed lines drawn with GDK_LINE_DOUBLE_DASH. The graphics context's foreground color is black, and its background color is a light gray. The first five lines are the default {4, 4} dash pattern with offsets of 0, 1, 2, 3, and 4. Remember that 0 is the default. Figure 10.3 shows a magnified view of these five lines. The last line is the whimsical dash pattern mentioned above; it's shown magnified in Figure 10.4.

Figure 10.2   Five dashed lines with GDK LINE DOUBLE DASH.

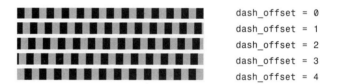

Figure 10.3   Default dash pattern with varied offsets.

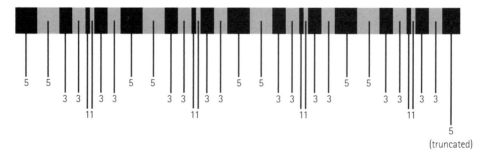

Figure 10.4   A complex dash pattern.

cap_style determines how X draws line endpoints (or dash endpoints if a line is dashed). It has four possible values:

- GDK_CAP_BUTT is the default; it means that lines have square ends (as you might expect).

- GDK_CAP_NOT_LAST specifies that the last pixel is skipped for one-pixel lines. It is otherwise the same as GDK_CAP_BUTT.

- GDK_CAP_ROUND draws a small arc on the end of the line, extending beyond the line's endpoint. The center of the arc is on the endpoint, and the radius of the arc is one-half the width of the line. For one-pixel lines, it has no effect (because there is no way to draw a one-pixel-wide arc).

- GDK_CAP_PROJECTING extends the line past its endpoint by one-half its width. It has no effect on one-pixel lines.

The join_style parameter affects how lines are connected to one another when a polygon or multiple lines are being drawn in one function call. If you think of lines as long thin rectangles, it is clear that they do not connect smoothly; there is a "notch" where the two endpoints come together. The following three join styles fill in this notch:

- GDK_JOIN_MITER is the default; it draws a sharp angle where the lines intersect.

- GDK_JOIN_ROUND creates rounded corners by drawing an arc in the notch.

- GDK_JOIN_BEVEL creates a flat corner, filling the notch with the smallest possible shape.

10.9   Drawing

If you understand drawables, colors, visuals, graphics contexts, and fonts, the actual drawing is very simple. This section is a quick summary of the Gdk drawing routines. Remember that drawing is a server-side operation; for example, if you ask to draw a line, Xlib will send the line's endpoints to the server, and the server will do the actual drawing using the specified GC (the GC is also a server-side resource). Often this is an important performance consideration.[1]

---

1. That is, it is much faster to pass the server two line endpoints, rather than all the points in the line. But if your image consists of arbitrary pixels and is not easy to represent as a series of Gdk calls, using the Gdk functions can be much slower than rendering on the client side and then passing the server a finished raster image with GdkRGB.

10.9.1   Points

You can draw a single point with `gdk_draw_point()` or multiple points with
`gdk_draw_points()` (see Function Listing 10.13). The point is drawn in the current
foreground color. Multiple points are given as an array. A `GdkPoint` looks like this:

```
typedef struct _GdkPoint GdkPoint;

struct _GdkPoint
{
  gint16 x;
  gint16 y;
};
```

Remember that X coordinates start in the upper-left corner, are relative to the drawable, and may not overflow a signed sixteen-bit integer.

Function Listing 10.13   **Drawing Points**   *#include <gdk/gdk.h>*

```
void
gdk_draw_point(GdkDrawable* drawable,
               GdkGC* gc,
               gint x,
               gint y)
void
gdk_draw_points(GdkDrawable* drawable,
                GdkGC* gc,
                GdkPoint* points,
                gint npoints)
```

10.9.2   Lines

To draw a single line, pass its endpoints as arguments to `gdk_draw_line()` (as shown in
Function Listing 10.14). To draw connected lines, you pass a list of points to
`gdk_draw_lines()`, and Gdk will "connect the dots." To draw multiple lines that aren't
necessarily connected, pass a list of segments to `gdk_draw_segments()`. A `GdkSegment` is
shown here:

```
typedef struct _GdkSegment GdkSegment;

struct _GdkSegment
{
  gint16 x1;
  gint16 y1;
  gint16 x2;
  gint16 y2;
};
```

If lines or segments drawn in the same request meet at their endpoints, they are joined with the join style from the GC.

Function Listing 10.14 **Drawing Lines** *#include <gdk/gdk.h>*

```
void
gdk_draw_line(GdkDrawable* drawable,
            GdkGC* gc,
            gint x1,
            gint y1,
            gint x2,
            gint y2)
void
gdk_draw_lines(GdkDrawable* drawable,
            GdkGC* gc,
            GdkPoint* points,
            gint npoints)
void
gdk_draw_segments(GdkDrawable* drawable,
            GdkGC* gc,
            GdkSegment* segments,
            gint nsegments)
```

10.9.3 Rectangles

To draw a rectangle, you use gdk_draw_rectangle(), as shown in Function Listing 10.15. The **filled** argument indicates whether to fill the rectangle; TRUE means to fill it.

Function Listing 10.15 **Drawing Rectangles** *#include <gdk/gdk.h>*

```
void
gdk_draw_rectangle(GdkDrawable* drawable,
            GdkGC* gc,
            gint filled,
            gint x,
            gint y,
            gint width,
            gint height)
```

10.9.4 Arcs

gdk_draw_arc() draws an ellipse or a portion of one (see Function Listing 10.16). The arc can be filled or unfilled; the third argument to the function toggles the fill setting. The fourth through seventh arguments describe a rectangle. The ellipse is inscribed in this rectangle. angle1 is the angle at which to start drawing. It is relative to the

3 o'clock position (that is, 0 radians). `angle2` is the distance to travel around the arc; if positive, travel is counterclockwise, otherwise travel is clockwise. Both `angle1` and `angle2` are specified in sixty-fourths of a degree. So, 360 degrees is given as `360*64`. This allows more precise specification of the arc's size and shape without the need for floating point numbers. `angle2` should not exceed 360 degrees because it is nonsensical to move more than 360 degrees around the ellipse. To draw a circle, draw from 0 to `360*64` inside a square:

```
gdk_draw_arc(drawable, gc, TRUE,
             0, 0,
             50, 50,
             0, 360*64);
```

To draw half an ellipse, change the aspect ratio and half the span of the arc:

```
gdk_draw_arc(drawable, gc, TRUE,
             0, 0,
             100, 50,
             0, 180*64);
```

Many X servers draw the edges of filled arcs in an aesthetically unpleasing way. In particular, very small circles may not look very circular. You can work around this by also drawing the circle's outline.

Function Listing 10.16 **Drawing Arcs**   *#include <gdk/gdk.h>*

```
void
gdk_draw_arc(GdkDrawable* drawable,
             GdkGC* gc,
             gint filled,
             gint x,
             gint y,
             gint width,
             gint height,
             gint angle1,
             gint angle2)
```

10.9.5 Polygons

`gdk_draw_polygon()` draws a filled or unfilled polygon (Function Listing 10.17). Notice that `gdk_draw_lines()` can also be used to draw an unfilled polygon. (There is no reason to prefer one or the other.) The arguments to `gdk_draw_polygon()` are the same as those to `gdk_draw_lines()`. The polygon does not have to be convex. It may also be self-intersecting. Self-intersecting polygons are filled with an "Even-Odd Rule," which means regions with an odd number of polygon areas overlapping them are not filled. That is, if the polygon does not overlap itself, it is entirely filled; if a region is overlapped once, it is not filled; if it's overlapped twice, it is filled; and so on.

Function Listing 10.17   **Drawing Polygons**   *#include <gdk/gdk.h>*

```
void
gdk_draw_polygon(GdkDrawable* drawable,
                 GdkGC* gc,
                 gint filled,
                 GdkPoint* points,
                 gint npoints)
```

10.9.6   Text

There are two functions for drawing strings (see Function Listing 10.18). As an optimization, gdk_draw_text() takes the length of the string to draw as an argument. gdk_draw_string() uses strlen() to compute the string length for you. Otherwise, the two are identical. The x and y coordinates specify the location of the left side of the text's baseline. See Section 10.7 for more information on fonts and font metrics. Text is drawn in the foreground color.

There is no way to draw scaled or rotated text with Gdk. GnomeCanvasText offers a slow and low-quality way to render scaled and rotated text (see Section 12.4). If you need high-quality scaling and rotating, you will need to use additional libraries, such as t1lib for Type 1 fonts or FreeType for True Type fonts. Another possibility is the Display Postscript extension to X (XDPS); the GNU Project is working on a free implementation of XDPS. The Gnome project also has a text solution in development, as part of the gnome-print library.

Function Listing 10.18   **Drawing Text**   *#include <gdk/gdk.h>*

```
void
gdk_draw_string(GdkDrawable* drawable,
                GdkFont* font,
                GdkGC* gc,
                gint x,
                gint y,
                const gchar* text)
void
gdk_draw_text(GdkDrawable* drawable,
              GdkFont* font,
              GdkGC* gc,
              gint x,
              gint y,
              const gchar* text,
              gint text_length)
```

10.9.7 Pixmaps

gdk_draw_pixmap() copies a region from a pixmap to another drawable (pixmap or window). The source and destination drawables must have the same depth and visual. If you pass −1 for the width or height, the full size of the source pixmap is substituted. The source can actually be any drawable, including a window, but gdk_window_copy_ area() will make your code clearer if the source is a window. Function Listing 10.19 shows gdk_draw_pixmap().

Function Listing 10.19   **Drawing Pixmaps**   *#include <gdk/gdk.h>*

```
void
gdk_draw_pixmap(GdkDrawable* drawable,
                GdkGC* gc,
                GdkDrawable* src,
                gint xsrc,
                gint ysrc,
                gint xdest,
                gint ydest,
                gint width,
                gint height)
```

10.9.8 RGB Buffers

Gdk's GdkRGB module allows you to copy a client-side buffer of image data to a drawable. If you need to manipulate images extensively or copy image data to the server, this is the correct way to do it. You can't directly manipulate a GdkPixmap because a pixmap is a server-side object. Copying image data to the server with gdk_draw_point() would be unbelievably slow because each point would require a server request (probably more than one because you would need to change the GC for each point).

Internally, GdkRGB uses an object called GdkImage to rapidly copy image data to the server in a single request. This is still somewhat slow—sizeable data does have to be copied—but GdkRGB is highly tuned and uses shared memory if the client and server happen to be on the same machine. So it's the fastest way to perform this task given the X architecture. It will also handle some tricky issues for you (such as adapting to the colormaps and visuals available on a given X server).

The GdkRGB functions are in a separate header, gdk/gdkrgb.h. Before using any GdkRGB functions, you must initialize the module with gdk_rgb_init() (see Function Listing 10.20). This sets up the visual and colormap GdkRGB will use, as well as some internal data structures.

Function Listing 10.20　**GdkRGB**　　*#include <gdk/gdkrgb.h>*

```
void
gdk_rgb_init()

GdkColormap*
gdk_rgb_get_cmap()

GdkVisual*
gdk_rgb_get_visual()

void
gdk_draw_rgb_image(GdkDrawable* drawable,
                   GdkGC* gc,
                   gint x,
                   gint y,
                   gint width,
                   gint height,
                   GdkRGBDither dither,
                   guchar* rgb_buf,
                   gint rowstride)
```

The drawable you intend to copy the RGB buffer to must use GdkRGB's visual and colormap. If the drawable is a part of a widget, the easiest way to ensure this is to push the GdkRGB visual and colormap when you create the widget:

```
GtkWidget* widget;
gtk_widget_push_visual(gdk_rgb_get_visual());
gtk_widget_push_colormap(gdk_rgb_get_cmap());
widget = gtk_whatever_new();
gtk_widget_pop_visual();
gtk_widget_pop_colormap();
```

The current version of GTK+ will behave better if you do this when creating the toplevel window containing the drawable, instead of when you create the drawable itself. However, in principle you can do it for only the drawable.

GdkRGB understands several kinds of image data, including 24- and 32-bit RGB data, 8-bit grayscale, and 8-bit indexes into an array of RGB values (a client-side GdkRgbCmap). This section describes only the simplest: 24-bit RGB data. This kind of buffer is rendered with `gdk_draw_rgb_image()`. There are separate functions for rendering the other buffer types, but all of them work in essentially the same way.

A 24-bit RGB buffer is a one-dimensional array of bytes. Every byte triplet makes up a pixel (byte 0 is red, byte 1 is green, and byte 2 is blue). Three numbers describe the size of the array and the location of bytes within it:

- The *width* is the number of pixels (byte triplets) per row of the image.
- The *height* is the number of rows in the image.
- The *rowstride* is the number of bytes between rows. That is, for a buffer with rowstride *r*, if row *n* starts at array index *i*, row *n+1* starts at array index *i+r*. The rowstride is not necessarily three times the buffer's width. GdkRGB is faster if both the source pointer and the rowstride are aligned to a 4-byte boundary. Specifying a rowstride allows you to use padding to achieve this.

The x, y, width, and height arguments to gdk_rgb_draw_image() define a region of the target drawable to copy the RGB buffer to. The RGB buffer must have at least width columns and height rows. Row 0, column 0 of the RGB buffer will be copied to point (x, y) on the drawable.

Dithering simulates a larger number of colors on displays that have a limited palette. Dithering only matters on 8- and 16-bit displays; 24-bit displays do not have a limited palette. The dither argument is an enumerated type that has three possible values:

- GDK_RGB_DITHER_NONE specifies that no dithering will be done. It's appropriate for text or line drawings with few colors, but it's inappropriate for photographic images.

- GDK_RGB_DITHER_NORMAL specifies dithering on 8-bit displays, but not 16-bit displays. This is usually the best quality/performance tradeoff.

- GDK_RGB_DITHER_MAX specifies that dithering will always be done on 8- and 16-bit displays. The quality gain on 16-bit displays is probably not worth the speed penalty.

The gc argument to gdk_draw_rgb_image() is simply passed through to gdk_draw_image() (recall that GdkRGB uses GdkImage internally). The gc components that make sense are used (such as the clip mask, drawing function, and subwindow mode).

10.10   Gdk Resource Management

Gdk objects have either reference counting or destruction, but not both. Pixmaps, fonts, graphics contexts, and colormaps are purely reference counted. (gdk_gc_destroy() exists but is deprecated; it's just a wrapper for gdk_gc_unref().) In general, reference counting is analogous to GtkObject reference counting. That is, objects start with a reference count of one, and when the reference count reaches 0, the object is destroyed.

Cursors and images are not reference counted; they simply have a destroy function. Some types represent static objects that are never destroyed; GdkVisual is the main example of those.

GdkWindow is the strange case. It is reference counted, but gdk_window_destroy() *must* be called at some point. The reference counting applies to the client-side GdkWindow handle; gdk_window_destroy() applies to the actual server-side object. See Section 10.2 for an explanation of the distinction. gdk_window_destroy() unreferences the client-side handle after it destroys the server-side object. It's safe to call any of the GdkWindow functions on a destroyed window that still has a reference count greater than zero. They will all return immediately without taking any action.

In practice, this means that one section of code should "own" the GdkWindow; it will create the window and hold the initial reference. (Remember that objects are created with a reference count of one.) It will also call gdk_window_destroy() eventually, destroying the server-side object and removing the initial reference count. If no other code increases the count, the client-side handle will be freed. If some other code has increased the reference count with gdk_window_ref(), the client-side handle will remain safe to use but attempts to use it will have no effect. When the reference count is eventually decremented to zero, the client-side handle will be freed.

In GTK+, windows are generally created and destroyed by the same widget; if other widgets want to draw on the window, they increase the window's reference count.

10.11   *GtkStyle* **and Themes**

GtkStyle is not part of Gdk, but it is an important abstraction layer between GTK+ and Gdk that allows users to customize how widgets are rendered. Instead of drawing with Gdk directly, widgets should prefer Gdk resources from a GtkStyle and special drawing functions provided in gtk/gtkstyle.h. Often there is no appropriate function, but when there is, it should be used.

A GtkStyle stores Gdk resources to be used when drawing widgets. Styles allow widgets to share these resources, reducing overhead. They also permit users to customize GTK+'s appearance. Here is the GtkStyle struct:

```
typedef struct _GtkStyle GtkStyle;

struct _GtkStyle
{
  GtkStyleClass *klass;

  GdkColor fg[5];
  GdkColor bg[5];
  GdkColor light[5];
  GdkColor dark[5];
  GdkColor mid[5];
  GdkColor text[5];
  GdkColor base[5];

  GdkColor black;
  GdkColor white;
  GdkFont *font;

  GdkGC *fg_gc[5];
  GdkGC *bg_gc[5];
  GdkGC *light_gc[5];
  GdkGC *dark_gc[5];
  GdkGC *mid_gc[5];
  GdkGC *text_gc[5];
```

```
    GdkGC *base_gc[5];
    GdkGC *black_gc;
    GdkGC *white_gc;

    GdkPixmap *bg_pixmap[5];

    /* private */

    gint ref_count;
    gint attach_count;

    gint depth;
    GdkColormap *colormap;

    GtkThemeEngine *engine;

    gpointer       engine_data;

    GtkRcStyle     *rc_style;

    GSList         *styles;
};
```

The private fields should be ignored. The public fields contain Gdk resources for widget rendering. The first group of fields contains arrays of colors; these arrays are indexed by the widget state enumeration (GTK_STATE_ACTIVE and so on). A widget might use widget->style->fg[GTK_STATE_NORMAL] to render text, for example. Each widget has an associated style, stored in the style field of GtkWidget.

Widgets should use the font stored in their associated GtkStyle. They should use the style's graphics contexts when drawing in the style's colors.

GtkStyle also contains a virtual table, GtkStyleClass, which can be implemented by a dynamically loaded theme engine. The virtual table is quite large, so it isn't reproduced here. Instead, take a look at gtk/gtkstyle.h.

gtk/gtkstyle.h contains drawing functions that use a style's virtual table to draw various GUI elements. There are two variants of each drawing function. One variant, prefixed with gtk_draw_, renders to any drawable; the other variant, prefixed with gtk_paint_, renders part of a widget. For example, gtk_draw_shadow() looks like this:

```
    void gtk_draw_shadow   (GtkStyle       *style,
                            GdkWindow      *window,
                            GtkStateType   state_type,
                            GtkShadowType  shadow_type,
                            gint           x,
                            gint           y,
                            gint           width,
                            gint           height);
```

gtk_paint_shadow() adds area, widget, and detail arguments:

```
    void gtk_paint_shadow  (GtkStyle       *style,
                            GdkWindow      *window,
```

```
              GtkStateType  state_type,
              GtkShadowType shadow_type,
              GdkRectangle  *area,
              GtkWidget     *widget,
              gchar         *detail,
              gint          x,
              gint          y,
              gint          width,
              gint          height);
```

Each of these corresponds to the draw_shadow member in GtkStyleClass.

All gtk_paint_ functions add the same three arguments to their gtk_draw_ counterparts. The area argument is a clipping rectangle, the widget argument is the widget being drawn to, and the detail argument is a hint used by theme engines. Here's a call to gtk_paint_shadow() from the GtkEntry source code, for example:

```
gtk_paint_shadow (widget->style, widget->window,
                  GTK_STATE_NORMAL, GTK_SHADOW_IN,
                  NULL, widget, "entry",
                  x, y, width, height);
```

Here the area argument is NULL, specifying that no clipping should be used.

Because there are a couple dozen functions in GtkStyleClass, and there are numerous examples in the GTK+ source code, this book won't describe them in detail. When writing your own widgets, simply locate a GTK+ widget that draws a similar graphical element, and then use the same gtk_paint_ function it uses.

11

Writing a *GtkWidget*

THIS CHAPTER DESCRIBES HOW TO WRITE A NEW `GtkWidget`. A widget is any
`GtkObject` that derives from `GtkWidget`. Before reading this chapter, you should be
familiar with Chapter 9, "The GTK+ Object and Type System." This chapter discusses
the details of `GtkWidget`, but it does not re-explain `GtkObject` in general. You will also
need to know something about Gdk to write a widget, so be sure to skim Chapter 10,
"Gdk Basics," if you haven't already.

Creating a widget is easy. You only need to cut and paste the usual `GtkObject` boilerplate (instance and class initializers, a `get_type()` function, and so on), and then
implement your widget's functionality. Writing new widgets is an important application development technique.

After a brief overview, this chapter jumps straight to the implementation of a very
simple widget called `GtkEv`. Then it takes a step back, describing widget implementation more systematically. It ends with more examples, taken from GTK+ itself. (It pays
to become familiar with the GTK+ source code: Often the easiest way to implement
a widget is to subclass or slightly modify the most similar stock GTK+ widget. Of
course, you must comply with the terms of GTK+'s license if you want to cut and
paste code from the library.)

11.1 Overview

This section gives a brief overview of widgets, including the different kinds of widgets you might encounter and the general functionality required of a `GtkWidget`.

11.1.1 Kinds of Widgets

The term "widget" is really very broad because it encompasses any object that implements the `GtkWidget` interface. There are many ways to classify widgets:

- *Containers* are widgets that store other widgets, such as the boxes and tables described in Chapter 3, "GTK+ Basics." As Chapter 3 discussed, containers can be subdivided into those that add functionality to a single child (`GtkButton`, `GtkFrame`, `GtkEventBox`, and so forth) and those that manage layout for multiple children (`GtkBox`, `GtkTable`, and so on). Container widgets are harder to implement than "plain" widgets because the `GtkContainer` interface must be implemented in addition to the `GtkWidget` interface.

- *Composite* widgets are containers that already contain a useful collection of child widgets in a nice package. For example, the `GtkFileSelection` widget is a subclass of `GtkWindow` that already contains a list widget to show files, dialog box buttons, and so on. Widgets like this are easy to write and offer a convenient way to code applications. You could write a "MainWindow" widget for your main application window, for example, and then create a new instance of the widget whenever the user opens a new document. `GnomeApp` and `GnomeDialog` are two important composite widgets in Gnome.

- Non-container widgets can be actual controls (buttons, scroll bars, and so on), information displays (`GtkLabel`), or decorative flourishes (`GtkSeparator`, for example). As Chapter 3 briefly mentioned, there are two primary ways to implement widgets: Most widgets (those that need to receive events or draw their own backgrounds) have an associated `GdkWindow`; "no window" widgets draw on their parent container. Widgets without windows are implemented slightly differently.

This chapter presents several widgets as examples, including a `GtkEv` widget written especially for this book, `GtkVBox` from GTK+, and `GnomeAppBar` from `libgnomeui`.

11.1.2   What a Widget Does

A minimal widget implements the following (although `GtkWidget`'s default implementation may be sufficient in many cases):

- *Creation and destruction.* This means the usual `GtkObject` boilerplate (instance and class initializers, `shutdown`, `destroy`, and `finalize` methods). See Chapter 9, especially Section 9.1 and Section 9.7. Also see Section 3.3.1.

- *The realize/map/unmap/unrealize cycle discussed in Section 3.3.2.* Widgets must be able to create and uncreate their associated X resources any number of times, and they must be able to show and hide themselves any number of times.

- *Geometry negotiation, discussed in Section 3.2.1.* Your widget must respond to size requests and honor size allocations.

- *Drawing.* Widgets must be able to draw themselves on the screen. For container widgets, the widget itself may be invisible but it must ensure child widgets are drawn.

- *The widget's unique functionality.* Typically this means implementing handlers for some of the widget's event signals.

11.2   The *GtkWidget* Base Class

Obviously, to subclass `GtkWidget`, you will have to be familiar with the base class. This section offers a brief tour of the `GtkWidget` class and instance structs and some important GTK+ routines that aren't very common in everyday programming.

11.2.1   The *GtkWidget* Instance Struct

A `GtkWidget` instance looks like this:

```
typedef struct _GtkWidget GtkWidget;

struct _GtkWidget
{
  GtkObject object;

  guint16 private_flags;

  guint8 state;

  guint8 saved_state;

  gchar *name;

  GtkStyle *style;

  GtkRequisition requisition;
```

```
    GtkAllocation allocation;

    GdkWindow *window;

    GtkWidget *parent;
};
```

The `private_flags`, `state`, and `saved_state` fields should all be accessed with macros, if at all. Some of these macros will come up as the chapter discusses widget implementations. The `state` field stores the widget's state as described in Section 3.3.3. `saved_state` is used to save the widget's previous state when the current state is `GTK_STATE_INSENSITIVE`; when the widget is re-sensitized, its original state is restored. As Section 3.3.3 explains, the current state can be accessed with the `GTK_WIDGET_STATE()` macro.

The `name` of a widget is used in a `gtkrc` file to group widgets for customization purposes. By default, the name of a widget is the type name registered with the object system (in GTK+, this type name is always the name of the instance struct, such as `"GtkLabel"`). Particular widgets can be given a different name with `gtk_widget_set_name()`. For example, if you want a particular label to appear in a different font, you can give it a name like "FunkyFontLabel" and then specify a different font for that name in a `gtkrc` shipped with your application.

The `requisition` and `allocation` fields store the last requested and allocated size of the widget, respectively. Section 11.4.5 will have more to say about this.

The `window` field stores the widget's `GdkWindow` or the widget's parent's `GdkWindow` if the widget doesn't have one of its own. The `parent` field is a pointer to the widget's parent container. It will be `NULL` if the widget is not inside a container.

11.2.2   The *GtkWidget* Class Struct

There are a truly huge number of class functions in `GtkWidgetClass`. Thankfully, in most cases, you have to override only a few of them. Here is the code:

```
    typedef struct _GtkWidgetClass GtkWidgetClass;

    struct _GtkWidgetClass
    {
      GtkObjectClass parent_class;

      guint activate_signal;

      guint set_scroll_adjustments_signal;

      /* Basics */
      void (* show)          (GtkWidget      *widget);
      void (* show_all)      (GtkWidget      *widget);
      void (* hide)          (GtkWidget      *widget);
      void (* hide_all)      (GtkWidget      *widget);
      void (* map)           (GtkWidget      *widget);
```

```
void (* unmap)                (GtkWidget      *widget);
void (* realize)              (GtkWidget      *widget);
void (* unrealize)            (GtkWidget      *widget);
void (* draw)                 (GtkWidget      *widget,
                               GdkRectangle   *area);
void (* draw_focus)           (GtkWidget      *widget);
void (* draw_default)         (GtkWidget      *widget);
void (* size_request)         (GtkWidget      *widget,
                               GtkRequisition *requisition);
void (* size_allocate)        (GtkWidget      *widget,
                               GtkAllocation  *allocation);
void (* state_changed)        (GtkWidget      *widget,
                               GtkStateType   previous_state);
void (* parent_set)           (GtkWidget      *widget,
                               GtkWidget      *previous_parent);
void (* style_set)            (GtkWidget      *widget,
                               GtkStyle       *previous_style);


/* Accelerators */
gint (* add_accelerator)      (GtkWidget      *widget,
                               guint          accel_signal_id,
                               GtkAccelGroup  *accel_group,
                               guint          accel_key,
                               GdkModifierType accel_mods,
                               GtkAccelFlags  accel_flags);
void (* remove_accelerator)   (GtkWidget      *widget,
                               GtkAccelGroup  *accel_group,
                               guint          accel_key,
                               GdkModifierType accel_mods);


/* Explicit focus */
void (* grab_focus)           (GtkWidget      *widget);


/* Events */
gint (* event)                (GtkWidget       *widget,
                               GdkEvent        *event);
gint (* button_press_event)   (GtkWidget       *widget,
                               GdkEventButton  *event);
gint (* button_release_event) (GtkWidget       *widget,
                               GdkEventButton  *event);
gint (* motion_notify_event)  (GtkWidget       *widget,
                               GdkEventMotion  *event);
gint (* delete_event)         (GtkWidget       *widget,
                               GdkEventAny     *event);
gint (* destroy_event)        (GtkWidget       *widget,
                               GdkEventAny     *event);
gint (* expose_event)         (GtkWidget       *widget,
                               GdkEventExpose  *event);
gint (* key_press_event)      (GtkWidget       *widget,
                               GdkEventKey     *event);
```

```
gint (* key_release_event)       (GtkWidget          *widget,
                                  GdkEventKey         *event);
gint (* enter_notify_event)      (GtkWidget          *widget,
                                  GdkEventCrossing    *event);
gint (* leave_notify_event)      (GtkWidget          *widget,
                                  GdkEventCrossing    *event);
gint (* configure_event)         (GtkWidget          *widget,
                                  GdkEventConfigure   *event);
gint (* focus_in_event)          (GtkWidget          *widget,
                                  GdkEventFocus       *event);
gint (* focus_out_event)         (GtkWidget          *widget,
                                  GdkEventFocus       *event);
gint (* map_event)               (GtkWidget          *widget,
                                  GdkEventAny         *event);
gint (* unmap_event)             (GtkWidget          *widget,
                                  GdkEventAny         *event);
gint (* property_notify_event)   (GtkWidget          *widget,
                                  GdkEventProperty    *event);
gint (* selection_clear_event)   (GtkWidget          *widget,
                                  GdkEventSelection   *event);
gint (* selection_request_event) (GtkWidget          *widget,
                                  GdkEventSelection   *event);
gint (* selection_notify_event)  (GtkWidget          *widget,
                                  GdkEventSelection   *event);
gint (* proximity_in_event)      (GtkWidget          *widget,
                                  GdkEventProximity   *event);
gint (* proximity_out_event)     (GtkWidget          *widget,
                                  GdkEventProximity   *event);
gint (* visibility_notify_event) (GtkWidget          *widget,
                                  GdkEventVisibility *event);
gint (* client_event)            (GtkWidget          *widget,
                                  GdkEventClient      *event);
gint (* no_expose_event)         (GtkWidget          *widget,
                                  GdkEventAny         *event);

/* Selection */
void (* selection_get)           (GtkWidget          *widget,
                                  GtkSelectionData   *selection_data,
                                  guint               info,
                                  guint               time);
void (* selection_received)      (GtkWidget          *widget,
                                  GtkSelectionData   *selection_data,
                                  guint               time);

/* Source side drag signals */
void (* drag_begin)              (GtkWidget          *widget,
                                  GdkDragContext      *context);
void (* drag_end)                (GtkWidget          *widget,
                                  GdkDragContext      *context);
```

```
    void (* drag_data_get)          (GtkWidget        *widget,
                                     GdkDragContext   *context,
                                     GtkSelectionData *selection_data,
                                     guint             info,
                                     guint             time);
    void (* drag_data_delete)       (GtkWidget        *widget,
                                     GdkDragContext   *context);

    /* Target side drag signals */
    void (* drag_leave)             (GtkWidget        *widget,
                                     GdkDragContext   *context,
                                     guint             time);
    gboolean (* drag_motion)        (GtkWidget        *widget,
                                     GdkDragContext   *context,
                                     gint              x,
                                     gint              y,
                                     guint             time);
    gboolean (* drag_drop)          (GtkWidget        *widget,
                                     GdkDragContext   *context,
                                     gint              x,
                                     gint              y,
                                     guint             time);
    void (* drag_data_received)     (GtkWidget        *widget,
                                     GdkDragContext   *context,
                                     gint              x,
                                     gint              y,
                                     GtkSelectionData *selection_data,
                                     guint             info,
                                     guint             time);

    /* Action signals */
    void (* debug_msg)              (GtkWidget        *widget,
                                     const gchar      *string);

    /* Padding for future expansion */
    GtkFunction pad1;
    GtkFunction pad2;
    GtkFunction pad3;
    GtkFunction pad4;
};
```

Most of the functions in `GtkWidgetClass` are registered as default handlers for signals. The exceptions are `show_all` and `hide_all`, which are class functions only. Of course, `GtkWidgetClass` inherits the five class functions and single signal ("`destroy`") from `GtkObjectClass`. This chapter will describe the important methods in more detail; also, Section 10.5 is important for understanding the event methods. Section 11.4 describes the default implementation of each method in some detail.

11.2.2.1   Overridable Signals

You may notice that `GtkWidgetClass` contains two signal identifiers in addition to function pointers. These are 0 by default; otherwise, they indicate the signal to emit to "activate" the widget or to set its scroll adjustments.

The `activate_signal` is emitted when the user presses the spacebar or Enter key while the widget is focused. For buttons, it will be the `"clicked"` signal; for menu items, it will be the `"activate"` signal.

The `set_scroll_adjustments_signal` is used by `GtkScrolledWindow` to set the scroll adjustments used by the widget. `GtkLayout`, `GtkCList`, and others have a signal to set the scroll adjustments.

These two hacks are necessary because GTK+ 1.2 does not support interfaces or multiple inheritance. (A future version of GTK+ may support interfaces similar in spirit to Java's interfaces.) Ideally, there would be "GtkActivatable" and "GtkScrollable" base classes or interfaces, and all widgets supporting these actions would derive from them. Including the two signal IDs in `GtkWidgetClass` is a short-term workaround.

11.3   An Example: The *GtkEv* Widget

This section describes a very simple widget called `GtkEv`, which is inspired by the `xev` client and comes with X. `GtkEv` has two components: a small subwindow that receives events and a larger window where information about each event is reported. Figure 11.1 shows `GtkEv` in action. The complete `GtkEv` source code is given in Appendix E, "Code Listings." `GtkEv` would be a lovely way to implement a `xev`-style application for Gnome; it packages the core application functionality in a nice module.

Figure 11.1   The `GtkEv` widget. Events are reported for the white subwindow.

11.3.1   Overview

GtkEv uses two GdkWindows. The larger one, GtkEv's widget->window, has a gray background and is used to render text describing each event. The smaller one is a child of
the primary window and is the window the widget reports events for. Here are the
class and instance structs for GtkEv:

```
typedef struct _GtkEv       GtkEv;
typedef struct _GtkEvClass  GtkEvClass;

struct _GtkEv
{
  GtkWidget widget;

  GdkWindow*    event_window;

  GdkRectangle  event_window_rect;

  GdkRectangle  description_rect;

  GList*        buffer;
  GList*        buffer_end;
  gint          buffer_size;
};

struct _GtkEvClass
{
  GtkWidgetClass parent_class;


};
```

As you can see, GtkEv has no class functions or signals of its own. Each instance stores
a pointer to the small event window in event_window. Two rectangles cache the area
covered by the event window and the area covered by the event description text. The
widget's allocation is divided between these two areas. Finally, GtkEv stores a list of
string vectors describing events. It caches the end of the list and the length of the list.
As events are received, text describing them is pushed on to the front of the buffer.
When the list becomes too long to fit on the screen, GtkEv removes an event from the
back of the buffer each time it adds a new event to the front, keeping the buffer size
constant.

11.3.2 *GtkObject* Features

Like all GtkObjects, GtkEv provides for its creation and destruction.

11.3.2.1 Creation

GtkEv's init, class init, and constructor functions are pure boilerplate and should require no explanation. Here they are, to help you get oriented:

```
static GtkWidgetClass *parent_class = NULL;

guint
gtk_ev_get_type (void)
{
  static guint ev_type = 0;

  if (!ev_type)
    {
      static const GtkTypeInfo ev_info =
      {
        "GtkEv",
        sizeof (GtkEv),
        sizeof (GtkEvClass),
        (GtkClassInitFunc) gtk_ev_class_init,
        (GtkObjectInitFunc) gtk_ev_init,
        /* reserved_1 */ NULL,
        /* reserved_2 */ NULL,
        (GtkClassInitFunc) NULL,
      };

      ev_type = gtk_type_unique (gtk_widget_get_type (), &ev_info);
    }

  return ev_type;
}

static void
gtk_ev_class_init (GtkEvClass *klass)
{
  GtkObjectClass *object_class;
  GtkWidgetClass *widget_class;

  object_class = (GtkObjectClass*) klass;
  widget_class = (GtkWidgetClass*) klass;

  parent_class = gtk_type_class (gtk_widget_get_type ());

  object_class->destroy = gtk_ev_destroy;

  widget_class->realize = gtk_ev_realize;
  widget_class->unrealize = gtk_ev_unrealize;
```

```
  widget_class->size_request = gtk_ev_size_request;

  widget_class->size_allocate = gtk_ev_size_allocate;

  widget_class->draw = gtk_ev_draw;

  widget_class->event = gtk_ev_event;

  widget_class->draw_focus = gtk_ev_draw_focus;

  widget_class->expose_event = gtk_ev_expose;

  widget_class->focus_in_event = gtk_ev_focus_in;
  widget_class->focus_out_event = gtk_ev_focus_out;
}

static void
gtk_ev_init (GtkEv *ev)
{
  GTK_WIDGET_SET_FLAGS (GTK_WIDGET(ev), GTK_CAN_FOCUS);

  ev->event_window = NULL;
  ev->buffer       = NULL;
  ev->buffer_end   = NULL;
  ev->buffer_size  = 0;

  ev->event_window_rect.x = ev->event_window_rect.y = 0;
  ev->event_window_rect.width = ev->event_window_rect.height = 0;

  ev->description_rect.x = ev->description_rect.y = 0;
  ev->description_rect.width = ev->description_rect.height = 0;
}

GtkWidget*
gtk_ev_new (void)
{
  GtkEv *ev;

  ev = gtk_type_new (gtk_ev_get_type ());

  return GTK_WIDGET (ev);
}
```

11.3.2.2   Destruction

GtkEv overrides only the destroy method from GtkObject, to clean up the event description buffer. The widget's windows will be destroyed in GtkWidget's shutdown method, which unrealizes the widget. GtkWidget's finalize method cleans up some GtkWidget resources and then chains to the GtkObject method, which frees the instance struct. (Refer to Section 9.7 for more details on these methods.)

Because `GtkEv` has no object arguments, it does not need to implement `get_arg` or `set_arg` methods.

Here is its `destroy` method implementation:

```
static void
gtk_ev_destroy        (GtkObject   *object)
{
  GtkEv* ev;
  GList* tmp;

  g_return_if_fail(object != NULL);
  g_return_if_fail(GTK_IS_EV(object));

  ev = GTK_EV(object);

  tmp = ev->buffer;
  while (tmp != NULL)
    {
      g_strfreev((gchar**)tmp->data);

      tmp = g_list_next(tmp);
    }

  g_list_free(ev->buffer);

  ev->buffer = NULL;
  ev->buffer_end = NULL;
  ev->buffer_size = 0;

  /* Chain up */
  if (GTK_OBJECT_CLASS(parent_class)->destroy)
    (* GTK_OBJECT_CLASS(parent_class)->destroy) (object);
}
```

The only detail worthy of note is that freed pointers are set to `NULL` because a destroyed object should remain "sane," unlike a finalized object. The `GtkEv` code depends on the fact that destroyed widgets are always unrealized; otherwise, text could be re-added to the buffer after destruction but before finalization, and a `finalize` method would be required.

11.3.3 Realization and Mapping

If you aren't familiar with the concept of *realizing* and *mapping* a widget, go back and read Section 3.3.2 before reading this section.

`GtkEv` does not override the `map` or `unmap` method; the default `GtkWidget` methods suffice. The defaults set and unset the `GTK_WIDGET_MAPPED` flag and show or hide `widget->window`.

Any widget with a GdkWindow that has GtkWidget as its immediate parent will need to override the realize method. The default is suitable only for windowless widgets. GtkEv is no exception. GtkEv also overrides the unrealize method, in order to destroy the event window.

Here is GtkEv's realize method:

```
static void
gtk_ev_realize          (GtkWidget        *widget)
{
  GdkWindowAttr attributes;
  gint attributes_mask;
  GtkEv* ev;
  GdkCursor* cursor;

  g_return_if_fail(widget != NULL);
  g_return_if_fail(GTK_IS_EV(widget));

  ev = GTK_EV(widget);

  /* Set realized flag */

  GTK_WIDGET_SET_FLAGS (widget, GTK_REALIZED);

  /* Main widget window */

  attributes.window_type = GDK_WINDOW_CHILD;
  attributes.x = widget->allocation.x;
  attributes.y = widget->allocation.y;
  attributes.width = widget->allocation.width;
  attributes.height = widget->allocation.height;
  attributes.wclass = GDK_INPUT_OUTPUT;
  attributes.visual = gtk_widget_get_visual (widget);
  attributes.colormap = gtk_widget_get_colormap (widget);
  attributes.event_mask = gtk_widget_get_events (widget) | GDK_EXPOSURE_MASK;

  attributes_mask = GDK_WA_X | GDK_WA_Y | GDK_WA_VISUAL | GDK_WA_COLORMAP;

  widget->window = gdk_window_new (gtk_widget_get_parent_window (widget),
                                   &attributes, attributes_mask);
  gdk_window_set_user_data (widget->window, widget);

  /* Event window */

  cursor = gdk_cursor_new(GDK_CROSSHAIR);

  attributes.window_type = GDK_WINDOW_CHILD;
  attributes.x = ev->event_window_rect.x;
  attributes.y = ev->event_window_rect.y;
  attributes.width = ev->event_window_rect.width;
  attributes.height = ev->event_window_rect.height;
  attributes.wclass = GDK_INPUT_OUTPUT;
```

```
        attributes.visual = gtk_widget_get_visual (widget);
        attributes.colormap = gtk_widget_get_colormap (widget);
        attributes.event_mask = GDK_ALL_EVENTS_MASK;
        attributes.cursor = cursor;

        attributes_mask = GDK_WA_X | GDK_WA_Y | GDK_WA_VISUAL |
          GDK_WA_COLORMAP | GDK_WA_CURSOR;

        ev->event_window = gdk_window_new (widget->window,
                                           &attributes, attributes_mask);
        gdk_window_set_user_data (ev->event_window, widget);

        gdk_window_show(ev->event_window);

        gdk_cursor_destroy(cursor);

        /* Style */

        widget->style = gtk_style_attach (widget->style, widget->window);

        gtk_style_set_background (widget->style, widget->window, GTK_STATE_NORMAL);

        gdk_window_set_background (ev->event_window,
                                  &widget->style->base[GTK_STATE_NORMAL]);
    }
```

The first step in any `realize` method is to set the `GTK_REALIZED` flag. This is a small but important detail. After that, most of the `realize` method is concerned with creating the two `GdkWindows`, as described in Section 10.2. `widget->window` should be created as a subwindow of the widget's parent's `GdkWindow`; the parent window is obtained with `gtk_widget_get_parent_window()`.

Notice that *all* events are requested on the event window, for obvious reasons. Also, the event window has a special cursor that gives the user visual feedback when the pointer moves into it. The client-side cursor handle is destroyed immediately after you attach the cursor to the window. The X server will keep it around as long as it's in use.

After each `GdkWindow` is created, a pointer to the `GtkEv` is stored in the `GdkWindow`'s "user data" field. GTK+ uses the contents of this field to determine which widget should receive events that occur on the window. Recall that GTK+ receives a stream of events from Gdk, and that each `GdkEvent` has a `window` field indicating the `GdkWindow` that received it. GTK+ forwards each event to the widget owning the event's `GdkWindow`. (Section 10.5 details this process if you don't remember.)

The code calls `gdk_window_show()` on the event window but not `widget->window`. `widget->window` should not be shown until the widget is mapped. Because the event window is a child of `widget->window`, it will remain offscreen until its parent is shown. Alternatively, `GtkEv` could implement a `map` method to show the child, but this way seems simpler.

Every widget must create its associated `GtkStyle` in its `realize` method because a style contains X resources. (See Section 10.11 for more information about `GtkStyle`.) Recall from Section 3.3.2 that widgets allocate all X resources in their `realize` method. GTK+ provides the following simple function to create a widget's style:

```
widget->style = gtk_style_attach (widget->style, widget->window);
```

After filling in `widget->style`, `GtkEv` uses colors from the style to set window backgrounds. It sets the main window's background using `gtk_style_set_background()`, which could do almost anything (it might invoke a routine from a dynamically loaded theme module). If the default theme is running, it simply sets the window's background to an appropriate color or pixmap tile. There is no special style function to set the background of the event window, so we set it to the "base" color (the base color is white by default; it's the background color for lists and text entries). If you select a color from the style, users will be able to customize the widget's color. It also makes it convenient to program, because you can avoid allocating and deallocating a custom color.

Notice that the `realize` method does not chain up to the default `realize` method because the default isn't appropriate for `GtkEv`.

Unrealizing `GtkEv` is relatively simple:

```
static void
gtk_ev_unrealize (GtkWidget         *widget)
{
  GtkEv* ev;

  g_return_if_fail(widget != NULL);
  g_return_if_fail(GTK_IS_EV(widget));

  ev = GTK_EV(widget);

  /* Hide all windows */

  if (GTK_WIDGET_MAPPED (widget))
    gtk_widget_unmap (widget);

  GTK_WIDGET_UNSET_FLAGS (widget, GTK_MAPPED);

  /* Destroy our child window */

  if (ev->event_window)
    {
      gdk_window_set_user_data(ev->event_window, NULL);
      gdk_window_destroy(ev->event_window);
      ev->event_window = NULL;
    }
```

```
/* This destroys widget->window and unsets the realized flag
 */
if (GTK_WIDGET_CLASS(parent_class)->unrealize)
  (* GTK_WIDGET_CLASS(parent_class)->unrealize) (widget);
}
```

First, the `unrealize` method ensures that the widget is unmapped. This is essential: GTK+ maintains the invariant that mapped widgets are also realized. Next, the `unrealize` method destroys the event window. It sets the window's user data to `NULL` before destroying it. Otherwise, `GtkEv` would receive a useless `destroy` event signal. Finally, `GtkEv` chains up to the default `unrealize` method, which unsets the `GTK_WIDGET_REALIZED` flag and destroys `widget->window`. `unrealize` implementations are *required* to chain up to their base class's implementation.

When you're writing `realize` and `unrealize` methods, keep in mind that they can be called multiple times, but they are always paired. That is, a widget can be unrealized and re-realized over and over, but it will never be realized twice without an intervening `unrealize`. The pairing is guaranteed; that is, if a widget is realized, it will definitely be unrealized sooner or later, unless the program exits.

11.3.4 Size Negotiation

Section 3.2.1 describes the size negotiation process; be sure you're familiar with it before reading this section.

There's no obvious "right" size for `GtkEv`, so the `size_request` method requests an arbitrary size that looks nice:

```
static void
gtk_ev_size_request    (GtkWidget       *widget,
                        GtkRequisition  *requisition)
{
  g_return_if_fail(widget != NULL);
  g_return_if_fail(GTK_IS_EV(widget));

  /*
   * GtkEv always wants to be the same fixed size.
   */

  requisition->width  = 450;
  requisition->height = 300;
}
```

GTK+ takes care of storing a widget's last size request in `widget->requisition`.

If `GtkEv` were a real-life widget rather than an illustrative example, it would be unnecessary to implement a `size request` method. The default `GtkWidget` method simply returns the current value of `widget->requisition`, so `GtkEv` could initialize `widget->requisition` in `gtk_ev_init()` and use the default method.

Alternatively, the `size request` method could be implemented more elaborately. GtkEv could attempt to predict the maximum width of the text to be displayed, for example.

Once a widget's parent container decides how much space is actually available, the widget receives a size allocation. The `size allocation` method should do the following:

- Assign the new allocation to `widget->allocation`. (This does *not* happen automatically, as it does for `widget->requisition`.)
- Divide the allocation among any child widgets.
- Resize any GdkWindows, if the widget is realized.
- Perform any widget-specific tasks. For example, GtkEv updates the two GdkRectangles representing its internal layout.

Here is the GtkEv `size allocation` method, which should be self-explanatory:

```
static void
gtk_ev_size_allocate  (GtkWidget      *widget,
                       GtkAllocation  *allocation)
{
  static const gint spacing = 10;
  GtkEv* ev;

  g_return_if_fail(widget != NULL);
  g_return_if_fail(GTK_IS_EV(widget));

  ev = GTK_EV(widget);

  widget->allocation = *allocation;

  ev->event_window_rect.width =
    MAX(allocation->width - spacing*2, 0);
  ev->event_window_rect.height =
    MAX(allocation->height / 5 - spacing / 2, 0);

  ev->event_window_rect.x =
    (allocation->width - ev->event_window_rect.width)/2;
  ev->event_window_rect.y =
    MIN(spacing, allocation->height);

  ev->description_rect.x = ev->event_window_rect.x;
  ev->description_rect.y =
    ev->event_window_rect.y + ev->event_window_rect.height + spacing;
  ev->description_rect.width =
    ev->event_window_rect.width;
  ev->description_rect.height =
```

```
          MAX((allocation->height - ev->event_window_rect.height - spacing*3), 0);

  if (GTK_WIDGET_REALIZED (widget))
    {
      gdk_window_move_resize (widget->window,
                              allocation->x,
                              allocation->y,
                              allocation->width,
                              allocation->height);

      gdk_window_move_resize (ev->event_window,
                              ev->event_window_rect.x,
                              ev->event_window_rect.y,
                              ev->event_window_rect.width,
                              ev->event_window_rect.height);
    }
}
```

11.3.5   Drawing

Three common situations require a widget to redraw all or part of itself:

- Expose events signal that all or part of a widget's `GdkWindow` has just become visible on the screen and needs repainting (see Section 10.5.8). A widget's `expose_event` method performs these redraws.

- GTK+ sometimes determines that a widget should be redrawn. This might happen when a widget receives a new size allocation different from its previous size allocation or when a new theme is loaded. A widget's `draw` method, usually invoked via `gtk_widget_queue_draw()` or `gtk_widget_queue_clear()`, handles this case.

- Widgets sometimes decide to redraw themselves. For example, if you change the text of a `GtkLabel`, the label will redraw itself to reflect the new text. Widget implementations are free to handle this case however they like, but most will use the `draw` method.

There are two special cases of the second situation. The first occurs when a widget receives or loses the keyboard focus; the second occurs when the widget becomes (or unbecomes) the "default" widget. Widgets should indicate these states visually, but they can often do so without a complete redraw. For that reason, there are special `draw_focus` and `draw_default` signals to handle them. These signals have to be implemented only if a widget can meaningfully receive the focus or default.

Because there is typically little difference between a widget's `draw` and `expose` methods, a common convention is to write a static function to handle both of them. This function is typically called `gtk_whatever_paint()`. It's also possible to avoid implementing the `draw` method, because the default `draw` method synthesizes an `expose` event covering the widget's entire allocation and invokes the `expose` method. (Remember that a synthetic `expose` event will have its `send_event` flag set to `TRUE`;

you can use this to distinguish synthetic events.)

The primary reason for distinguishing expose events from other draws is that expose events are marked with the window they occurred on. For widgets with multiple windows such as GtkEv, this can increase efficiency. GtkEv implements two private functions, gtk_ev_paint() and gtk_ev_paint_event_window(), which it uses to implement the expose and draw methods.

Here is the draw method:

```
static void
gtk_ev_draw            (GtkWidget        *widget,
                        GdkRectangle     *area)
{
  GdkRectangle event_window_area;
  GdkRectangle intersection;
  GtkEv* ev;

  g_return_if_fail(widget != NULL);
  g_return_if_fail(GTK_IS_EV(widget));

  ev = GTK_EV(widget);

  gtk_ev_paint(ev, area);

  event_window_area = *area;

  if (gdk_rectangle_intersect(area, &ev->event_window_rect, &intersection))
    {
      /* Make the intersection relative to the event window */
      intersection.x -= ev->event_window_rect.x;
      intersection.y -= ev->event_window_rect.y;

      gtk_ev_paint_event_window(ev, &intersection);
    }
}
```

And this is the expose method:

```
static gint
gtk_ev_expose          (GtkWidget        *widget,
                        GdkEventExpose   *event)
{
  if (event->window == widget->window)
    gtk_ev_paint(GTK_EV(widget), &event->area);
  else if (event->window == GTK_EV(widget)->event_window)
    gtk_ev_paint_event_window(GTK_EV(widget), &event->area);
  else
    g_assert_not_reached();

  return TRUE;
```

```
}
```

Both the `draw` and `expose` methods should be self-explanatory. All the work is done in the two paint functions. Here is `gtk_ev_paint()`, which renders the main widget window:

```
static void
gtk_ev_paint            (GtkEv             *ev,
                         GdkRectangle      *area)
{
  GtkWidget* widget;

  g_return_if_fail(ev != NULL);
  g_return_if_fail(GTK_IS_EV(ev));

  widget = GTK_WIDGET(ev);

  if (!GTK_WIDGET_DRAWABLE (widget))
    return;

  gdk_window_clear_area (widget->window,
                         area->x,
                         area->y,
                         area->width,
                         area->height);

  gdk_gc_set_clip_rectangle(widget->style->black_gc, area);

  /* Draw a black rectangle around the event window */

  gdk_draw_rectangle(widget->window,
                     widget->style->black_gc,
                     FALSE,
                     ev->event_window_rect.x - 1,
                     ev->event_window_rect.y - 1,
                     ev->event_window_rect.width + 2,
                     ev->event_window_rect.height + 2);

  gdk_gc_set_clip_rectangle(widget->style->black_gc, NULL);

  /* Draw text in the description area, if applicable */

  if (ev->buffer)
    {
      GdkRectangle intersection;

      if (gdk_rectangle_intersect(area,
                                  &ev->description_rect,
                                  &intersection))
        {
          static const gint space = 2;
          gint line;
          gint step;
          gint first_baseline;
          GList* tmp;
```

```
      step  = widget->style->font->ascent +
        widget->style->font->descent + space;

      first_baseline = ev->description_rect.y +
        widget->style->font->ascent + space;

      line = 0;

      tmp = ev->buffer;

      while (tmp != NULL)
        {
          gchar** this_event = tmp->data;
          gint i = 0;
          while (this_event[i])
            {
              gtk_paint_string (widget->style,
                                widget->window,
                                widget->state,
                                &intersection, widget, "ev",
                                ev->description_rect.x,
                                first_baseline + line*step,
                                this_event[i]);
              ++i;
              ++line;
            }

          /* Bail out if we're off the bottom; the "- 2*step" is
           *  needed because the next baseline may be outside the
           *  redraw area but we are interested in the whole row of
           *  text, not the baseline. The 2* is because line is one
           *  larger than we've actually drawn.
           */
          if ((first_baseline + line*step - 2*step) >
              (intersection.y + intersection.height))
            break;

          tmp = g_list_next(tmp);
        }
    }
  }

  if (GTK_WIDGET_HAS_FOCUS (widget))
    {
      gtk_paint_focus (widget->style, widget->window,
                       area, widget, "ev",
                       widget->allocation.x, widget->allocation.y,
                       widget->allocation.width-1, widget->allocation.height-1);
    }
}
```

Most of gtk_ev_paint() is GtkEv-specific: It simply draws the contents of the window. Notice that it checks GTK_WIDGET_DRAWABLE() at the beginning. This is required because the draw method may invoke the function. Unsynthesized expose events guarantee that a widget's X window is on-screen, so this check is not really necessary is response to expose events.

gtk_ev_paint_event_window() paints the small subwindow. It's a very simple function:

```
static void
gtk_ev_paint_event_window  (GtkEv          *ev,
                            GdkRectangle   *area)
{
  GtkWidget* widget;
  gint width;
  gint x, y;
  const char* title;

  g_return_if_fail(ev != NULL);
  g_return_if_fail(GTK_IS_EV(ev));

  widget = GTK_WIDGET(ev);

  if (!GTK_WIDGET_DRAWABLE (widget))
    return;

  title = _("Event Window");

  gdk_window_clear_area (ev->event_window,
                         area->x,
                         area->y,
                         area->width,
                         area->height);

  gdk_gc_set_clip_rectangle(widget->style->black_gc, area);

  /* Clearly it would be better to cache this */

  width = gdk_string_width(widget->style->font,
                           title);

  x = (ev->event_window_rect.width - width)/2;
  y = widget->style->font->ascent + 2;

  gdk_draw_string(ev->event_window,
                  widget->style->font,
                  widget->style->black_gc,
                  x, y,
                  title);

  gdk_gc_set_clip_rectangle(widget->style->black_gc, NULL);
}
```

11.3.6   Handling Focus

GtkEv wants to receive key press events so it can report information about them. As Section 3.3.3 and Section 10.5.6 discussed, only top-level windows receive key events from Gdk. GtkWindow keeps track of a current *focus widget* and forwards key events to it.

If a widget wants to receive key events, it must do the following:

- Set its GTK_CAN_FOCUS flag so GTK+ will consider it as a possible focus widget.

- Respond to "focus_in" and "focus_out" signals by drawing and erasing a visual indication that it has the focus.

GtkEv set the GTK_CAN_FOCUS flag in gtk_ev_init(). It implements focus in and focus out methods as shown here:

```
static gint
gtk_ev_focus_in         (GtkWidget          *widget,
                         GdkEventFocus      *event)
{
  g_return_val_if_fail(widget != NULL, FALSE);
  g_return_val_if_fail(GTK_IS_EV(widget), FALSE);

  GTK_WIDGET_SET_FLAGS (widget, GTK_HAS_FOCUS);
  gtk_widget_draw_focus (widget);

  return FALSE;
}

static gint
gtk_ev_focus_out        (GtkWidget          *widget,
                         GdkEventFocus      *event)
{
  g_return_val_if_fail(widget != NULL, FALSE);
  g_return_val_if_fail(GTK_IS_EV(widget), FALSE);

  GTK_WIDGET_UNSET_FLAGS (widget, GTK_HAS_FOCUS);
  gtk_widget_draw_focus (widget);

  return FALSE;
}
```

These implementations are the minimal ones; all focusable widgets must set or unset the GTK_HAS_FOCUS flag when they gain or lose the focus, and they must emit the "draw_focus" signal.

GtkEv has a lazy implementation of the "draw_focus" signal. It just calls the same
gtk_ev_paint() used to respond to expose events and redraw requests. Recall that
gtk_ev_paint() checks to see whether the GtkEv has the focus, and if so, it draws a
focus frame. Here is the code for that:

```
static void
gtk_ev_draw_focus     (GtkWidget        *widget)
{
  GdkRectangle rect;
  GtkEv* ev;

  g_return_if_fail(widget != NULL);
  g_return_if_fail(GTK_IS_EV(widget));

  ev = GTK_EV(widget);

  rect.x = 0;
  rect.y = 0;
  rect.width = widget->allocation.width;
  rect.height = widget->allocation.height;

  if (GTK_WIDGET_DRAWABLE (ev))
    gtk_ev_paint(ev, &rect);
}
```

Notice that widget implementations are responsible for emitting the "draw_focus" signal themselves; GTK+ does not emit it as the focus moves. Contrast this with the
"draw_default" signal, which GTK+ automatically emits whenever a widget gains or
loses the default. GtkEv cannot be the default widget, so it does not implement this
signal.

11.3.7   *GtkEv's* Functionality

All the code presented so far implements the GtkWidget and GtkObject interfaces.
GtkEv does have some unique functionality. Namely, it responds to events on its event
window by adding text describing the event to its buffer and then queuing a redraw.
To do this, it overrides the default "event" signal handler.

Here is GtkEv's event method:

```
static gint
gtk_ev_event (GtkWidget        *widget,
              GdkEvent         *event)
{
  GtkEv* ev;

  g_return_val_if_fail(widget != NULL, FALSE);
  g_return_val_if_fail(GTK_IS_EV(widget), FALSE);

  ev = GTK_EV(widget);
```

```
    if (event->any.window == widget->window)
      {
        if (GTK_WIDGET_CLASS(parent_class)->event)
          return (* GTK_WIDGET_CLASS(parent_class)->event) (widget, event);
        else
          return FALSE;
      }
    else
      {
        gchar* text;

        /* The event is either on ev->event_window, or it is a key event
         * passed down to us from the toplevel GtkWindow
         */

        text = event_to_text(event);

        gtk_ev_push_text(ev, text);

        g_free(text);

        /* If it was a motion event, make sure we get more */
        if (event->type == GDK_MOTION_NOTIFY)
          {
            gdk_window_get_pointer(ev->event_window, NULL, NULL, NULL);
          }

        /* We didn't "handle" the event, just listened in on it. */
        return FALSE;
      }
  }
```

Notice that the window method of the event is used to distinguish events that occur on widget->window from events that occur on the event subwindow. Some events will be received from a different window entirely; for example, key events actually occur on a top-level window and are passed to GtkEv if GtkEv has the focus.

event_to_text() is a lengthy but trivial function that creates a string describing the event. gtk_ev_push_text() pushes the text onto the front of the buffer and queues a redraw. The implementation of these functions is part of the complete GtkEv code listing, shown in Appendix E.

11.4 *GtkWidget* In Detail

This section catalogs the functions in `GtkWidgetClass` more rigorously and describes the default implementation of each.

11.4.1 Destruction

Widget destruction is not significantly different from object destruction in general, as described in Section 9.7. As always, there are three phases: shutdown, destroy, and finalize. Only the `destroy` method is a signal; the others are class functions only. If you override any of the three, you must "chain up" to the parent class implementation.

`GtkWidget` has default implementations of all three. You should know what they do:

- In its `shutdown` method, a `GtkWidget` removes itself from its parent container (if any) and then unrealizes itself. This implies that widgets are always unrealized inside their `destroy` methods. It chains up to the `GtkObject` `shutdown` method, which emits the `"destroy"` signal.

- In its `destroy` method, a `GtkWidget` releases the grab if it has it, unreferences its style and sets `widget->style` to `NULL`, and gives up any connections it had to the current selection. (`GtkEntry` and other editable-text widgets allow you to select and paste text.) It chains up to the `GtkObject` `destroy` method, which disconnects any signal handlers for the object.

- In its `finalize` method, a `GtkWidget` frees a number of private data structures (stored as object data, see Section 9.8), and frees `widget->name`. It chains up to the `GtkObject` `finalize` method, which frees the instance struct.

11.4.2 Showing, Hiding, and Mapping

Four methods are provided to show and hide widgets. `show` and `hide` are rarely overridden; the default implementations almost always suffice. `show_all` and `hide_all` are overridden by container widgets; they show or hide the container and all its children. Their default implementation simply shows the widget itself. No non-container should need to change this. `"show"` and `"hide"` are registered as signals, but the `_all` variants are not.

The default implementation of `show` sets the `GTK_VISIBLE` flag and maps the widget if its parent is mapped. When containers are mapped, they map any children with the `GTK_VISIBLE` flag set. Thus, the `show` implementation ensures that a widget will be mapped eventually. (When a widget is finally mapped, the `GTK_MAPPED` flag is set in addition to `GTK_VISIBLE`.)

The default `hide` implementation does the opposite: It unsets the `GTK_VISIBLE` flag and unmaps the widget if `GTK_MAPPED` is set.

The default `map` and `unmap` implementations are much more frequently overridden. The default implementations should suffice for windowless widgets and widgets with a single window (`widget->window`). Widgets with additional subwindows or other special needs may need to override the defaults.

The map method is responsible for putting a widget on the screen. The default implementation sets the `GTK_MAPPED` flag and calls `gdk_window_show()` on `widget->window` for widgets that have a window. If a widget has subwindows or needs to take any special action when it appears on the screen, it must override the `map` method. (It may optionally chain up to the default method, however.) Container widgets are required to override the `map` method because they must iterate over their children and map each child widget with the `GTK_VISIBLE` flag set (i.e., each child widget that's been shown).

The `unmap` method is simply the reverse of the `map` method: It undoes anything the `map` method did. By default, it unsets the `GTK_MAPPED` flag and calls `gdk_window_hide()` to hide `widget->window`. Container widgets must override the method to unmap their child windows.

Keep in mind that none of these methods are invoked directly. They are invoked by calling `gtk_widget_show()`, `gtk_widget_map()`, and so on. These functions may perform special actions before and after invocation. Here is a summary:

- `gtk_widget_show()` "queues a resize" on the widget before emitting the show signal. This means it notifies the widget's parent container that it should rearrange its layout.

- `gtk_widget_hide()` does the same because a newly invisible widget implies recalculating the layout just as a newly visible one does.

- `gtk_widget_show_all()` and `gtk_widget_hide_all()` don't do anything special; they simply invoke the corresponding class function.

- `gtk_widget_map()` realizes the widget before emitting the `"map"` signal (if the widget is not realized). This maintains an important invariant (all mapped widgets are also realized). After emitting the signal, `gtk_widget_map()` queues a draw for windowless widgets. Widgets with windows receive an `expose` event when the window appears on the screen, so queuing a draw is not necessary.

- `gtk_widget_unmap()` redraws part of the parent widget if a windowless child is unmapped (remember that windowless widgets draw on their parent's `widget->window`).

11.4.3 Realization

The `realize` and `unrealize` class functions are registered as signals. *Realization* is the process of creating Gdk resources associated with the widget, including but not limited to `widget->window` and `widget->style`.

A `realize` method should do the following things:

- Set the `GTK_REALIZED` flag.

- Create the widget's windows, especially `widget->window`, which should be a child of the widget's parent's `widget->window` (obtained with `gtk_widget_get_parent_window()`).

- Place a pointer to the widget in the user data field of each window.

- For windowless widgets, `widget->window` should be set to the parent widget's window (obtained with `gtk_widget_get_parent_window()`). These widgets should also increase the reference count on `widget->window` by calling `gdk_window_ref()`.

- Set `widget->style` using `gtk_style_attach()`.

- Set the background of each window by using `gtk_style_set_background()` if possible or, if that's not possible, by using some color from the style. A windowless widget should not do this because its parent already has.

The default implementation of `realize` is appropriate only for windowless widgets. It sets the `GTK_REALIZED` flag, sets `widget->window` to the parent widget's window, increases the reference count on the parent's window, and sets `widget->style`. Widgets with their own `GdkWindow` must override the `realize` method.

The `"realize"` signal invokes the `realize` method as its default handler. This signal should never be emitted directly because substantial pre- and post-conditions must be enforced. `gtk_widget_realize()` takes care of the details. Among other things, it ensures that the widget's parent is realized. GTK+ maintains the invariant that widgets cannot be realized unless their parents are also realized.

As you might expect, the `unrealize` method reverses a widget's realization, freeing the resources created in `realize`. The default `unrealize` method is appropriate for all widgets. It performs the following tasks:

- Unmaps the widget if the widget is mapped (remember the GTK+ invariant that all mapped widgets are realized).

- Unrealizes all child widgets if the widget is a container. This maintains the invariant that widgets cannot be realized unless their parents are also realized.

- Unreferences `widget->style`.

- Destroys `widget->window` (windowless widgets only unreference it).

- Unsets the `GTK_REALIZED` flag.

Widgets are required to chain up if they override their base class's `unrealize` method. This ensures that all resources are freed. Overriding the default method may be necessary if a widget has more than one `GdkWindow` or other special needs. All windows should be destroyed just as `GtkEv` destroys its `event_window`, that is, the window's user data field should be set to `NULL` before destruction, as shown here:

```
gdk_window_set_user_data(ev->event_window, NULL);
gdk_window_destroy(ev->event_window);
ev->event_window = NULL;
```

This keeps GTK+ from seeing a useless `GDK_DESTROY` event for the window.

The `"unrealize"` signal is emitted via `gtk_widget_unrealize()`. `gtk_widget_unrealize()` does some internal bookkeeping that is important but not very interesting. Just be careful to use this function instead of emitting the signal directly.

11.4.4   Drawing

The relationships between `draw`, `draw_focus`, `draw_default`, and `expose_event` were discussed in Section 11.3.5. All four class functions are registered as default handlers for a signal of the same name. The `"draw"` signal redraws a portion of the widget; it is emitted by GTK+ or by widget implementations.

Widget implementations should emit the `"draw_focus"` signal themselves, generally in response to focus events. The signal draws or undraws a frame indicating that the widget is focused. `gtk_window_set_default()` emits the `"draw_default"` signal for both the widget losing default status and the widget gaining it. (`gtk_widget_grab_default()` calls `gtk_window_set_default()`.) Only widgets with the `GTK_CAN_FOCUS` or `GTK_CAN_DEFAULT` flag set need to worry about the `draw_focus` and `draw_default` methods. These flags should be set in a widget's instance initialization function.

Only the draw method has a default implementation in `GtkWidget`. The default implementation synthesizes an `expose` event covering the widget's entire allocation. This allows you to write an expose event handler that also handles the `"draw"` signal.

GTK+ normally emits the `"draw"` signal in an idle function. That is, it keeps a list of widgets (and regions of them) that need to be redrawn; when no events are pending, the GTK+ main loop runs an idle function that traverses the list and emits the `"draw"` signal for each widget. Redraw areas are merged as much as possible to avoid multiple redraws, and the idle function is removed after it runs once. This arrangement minimizes the number of redraws and reduces flicker.

11.4.5   Size Negotiation

The size negotiation process has already been described in Section 3.2.1 and Section 11.3.4. The two signals/methods involved are `size_request` and `size_allocate`. `GtkWidget` provides default implementations of each.

Here is the default `size_request` method:

```
static void
gtk_widget_real_size_request (GtkWidget        *widget,
                              GtkRequisition   *requisition)
{
  g_return_if_fail (widget != NULL);
  g_return_if_fail (GTK_IS_WIDGET (widget));

  requisition->width = widget->requisition.width;
  requisition->height = widget->requisition.height;
}
```

This implementation is appropriate for widgets that always request the same size; `GtkArrow` and `GtkDrawingArea`, for example, use this default. Widgets using the default must initialize `widget->requisition` with their fixed request; `GtkArrow` does this in `gtk_arrow_init()`. `GtkDrawingArea` begins with a default size, but allows users to change the request with `gtk_drawing_area_set_size()`.

Widgets whose request depends on their children, or the amount of text they contain, or some other factor, should override the default `size_request` method with a method that calculates the size they want.

Size allocation is slightly more complicated; here is its default implementation:

```
static void
gtk_widget_real_size_allocate (GtkWidget     *widget,
                               GtkAllocation *allocation)
{
  g_return_if_fail (widget != NULL);
  g_return_if_fail (GTK_IS_WIDGET (widget));

  widget->allocation = *allocation;

  if (GTK_WIDGET_REALIZED (widget) &&
      !GTK_WIDGET_NO_WINDOW (widget))
    {
      gdk_window_move_resize (widget->window,
                              allocation->x, allocation->y,
                              allocation->width, allocation->height);
    }
}
```

This should suffice for most simple widgets. Widgets like `GtkEv`, or any container, need to update internal data structures or distribute the allocation they receive among child widgets; these widgets will override `size_allocate`. It is possible but not required to chain up to the default implementation.

The wrapper function, which emits the `"size_allocate"` signal, is significantly more involved than the signal handler. `gtk_widget_size_allocate()` takes into account `gtk_widget_set_usize()` and ensures that widgets are redrawn if their size changes. (Not surprisingly, `gtk_widget_size_request()` also exists and should be used instead of emitting `"size_request"` directly.)

11.4.6   *GtkContainer*

GtkContainer is the base class for all widgets that contain one or more other widgets. GtkBin is a subclass of GtkContainer and is the base class for widgets with a single child.

11.4.6.1   The *GtkContainer* Instance Struct

Here is GtkContainer:

```
typedef struct _GtkContainer        GtkContainer;

struct _GtkContainer
{
  GtkWidget widget;

  GtkWidget *focus_child;

  guint border_width : 16;
  guint need_resize : 1;
  guint resize_mode : 2;

  GSList *resize_widgets;
};
```

The focus_child member is the child in the container with the keyboard focus. It can be NULL if no child has the focus. The GtkContainer implementation handles setting and unsetting this field. The border_width member is a width in pixels to add to the container's size request on all sides; the container will also subtract this value from its allocation. (In other words, the border_width is a blank space around the container.) Library users set the border_width field with gtk_container_set_border_width(); GtkContainer subclasses must honor its value in their size_request and size_allocate implementations.

The need_resize, resize_mode, and resize_widgets fields are implementation details that subclasses should not have to read or modify. These fields are used to implement gtk_widget_queue_resize(); when a resize is queued for a widget, the GtkContainer implementation ensures that the size negotiation process (requisition/allocation) will take place in a one-shot idle handler. Subclasses of GtkContainer simply implement size_request and size_allocate, and everything works.

11.4.6.2   The *GtkContainer* Class Struct

```
typedef struct _GtkContainerClass  GtkContainerClass;

struct _GtkContainerClass
{
  GtkWidgetClass parent_class;

  guint   n_child_args;

  void (* add)              (GtkContainer    *container,
                             GtkWidget       *widget);
  void (* remove)           (GtkContainer    *container,
                             GtkWidget       *widget);
  void (* check_resize)     (GtkContainer    *container);
  void (* forall)           (GtkContainer    *container,
                             gboolean          include_internals,
                             GtkCallback       callback,
                             gpointer          callbabck_data);
  gint (* focus)            (GtkContainer    *container,
                             GtkDirectionType  direction);
  void (* set_focus_child)  (GtkContainer    *container,
                             GtkWidget       *widget);
  GtkType (*child_type)     (GtkContainer    *container);
  void    (*set_child_arg)  (GtkContainer    *container,
                             GtkWidget       *child,
                             GtkArg          *arg,
                             guint            arg_id);
  void    (*get_child_arg)  (GtkContainer    *container,
                             GtkWidget       *child,
                             GtkArg          *arg,
                             guint            arg_id);
  gchar*  (*composite_name) (GtkContainer    *container,
                             GtkWidget       *child);

  /* Padding for future expansion */
  GtkFunction pad1;
  GtkFunction pad2;
};
```

Many of these class functions do not have corresponding signals. add, remove, check_resize, focus, and set_focus_child methods are default handlers for signals with the same name. The others are just methods.

The check_resize method recalculates layout if necessary; it is invoked by the idle handler installed by gtk_widget_queue_resize(). As the previous section mentioned, subclasses should not have to concern themselves with this process.

The focus and set_focus_child methods handle moving focus around a GtkWindow. Users can move the focus with the arrow keys and the Tab key. This results in emissions of the "focus" signal, with the direction argument indicating which way the focus should move. The possible directions are: GTK_DIR_TAB_FORWARD,

GTK_DIR_TAB_BACKWARD, GTK_DIR_UP, GTK_DIR_DOWN, GTK_DIR_LEFT, and GTK_DIR_RIGHT.
GtkContainer provides a default implementation based on the geometric location of
child widgets. It works fine for most standard layout containers, such as GtkBox and
GtkTable. It should also work for GtkBin subclasses. More elaborate or unusual containers, such as the tree and list widgets, or GtkNotebook, override this method. The
focus method should return TRUE if an appropriate child was found and the focus was
moved (using gtk_widget_grab_focus()).

The set_focus_child method is used by gtk_widget_grab_focus() to set the focus
child of a container. gtk_widget_grab_focus() can be invoked by the focus method
of a container or by a widget implementation (for example, GtkEntry grabs the focus
if the user clicks on it). The default implementation simply sets the focus_child field
of the container and increments the child's reference count.

composite_name returns a special name for a child when it's a part of a particular
container. For example, the composite names of the two GtkScrollbar widgets in a
GtkScrolledWindow are "hscrollbar" and "vscrollbar." These names allow themes to
specify widget attributes precisely. The default implementation of this method should
always work fine; it returns the name set with gtk_widget_set_composite_name().

n_child_args, set_child_arg, and get_child_arg are exactly the same as the
n_args, get_arg, and set_arg fields of GtkObjectClass. Section 9.5.3 mentions this
briefly. Child arguments are used to get and set attributes of the container-child unit,
such as the packing parameters for GtkBox or the attachment parameters for GtkTable.
In contrast, normal object arguments set the characteristics of a single object in isola-
tion. Though the implementation differs, child arguments work almost exactly like the
object arguments described in Chapter 9. The only visible difference is that the get
and set functions take a container and a widget as arguments instead of a single object.

The following section introduces the remaining functions in GtkContainer by
describing their implementation in GtkBin.

11.4.7 *GtkBin*: Containers with One Child

GtkBin doesn't introduce any new interfaces; it simply adds a data member to each
container instance for storing a single child and provides default implementations for
the container methods that operate on this one child. GtkBin implements the add,
remove, forall, and child_type methods from GtkContainer. Combined with
GtkContainer's default implementations, simple subclasses of GtkBin (such as
GtkEventBox, GtkAlignment, and GtkFrame) do not need to override any GtkContainer
methods. Here's the instance struct:

```
typedef struct _GtkBin      GtkBin;

struct _GtkBin
{
  GtkContainer container;

  GtkWidget *child;
};
```

And here's the class struct:

```
typedef struct _GtkBinClass  GtkBinClass;

struct _GtkBinClass
{
  GtkContainerClass parent_class;
};
```

No rocket science here.

11.4.7.1 Adding and Removing Children

The add and remove functions do not have a default implementation (well, technically
they do; the default implementation prints a warning that they aren't implemented).
All containers should override these functions. Their corresponding signals are emitted
when library users call gtk_container_add() and gtk_container_remove(). For containers that normally require parameters when adding children (such as GtkBox and
GtkTable), the add method should simply use reasonable defaults.

GtkBin implements an add method as shown here:

```
static void
gtk_bin_add (GtkContainer *container,
             GtkWidget    *child)
{
  GtkBin *bin;

  g_return_if_fail (container != NULL);
  g_return_if_fail (GTK_IS_BIN (container));
  g_return_if_fail (child != NULL);
  g_return_if_fail (GTK_IS_WIDGET (child));

  bin = GTK_BIN (container);
  g_return_if_fail (bin->child == NULL);

  gtk_widget_set_parent (child, GTK_WIDGET (bin));
  bin->child = child;

  if (GTK_WIDGET_VISIBLE (child->parent))
    {
      if (GTK_WIDGET_REALIZED (child->parent) &&
          !GTK_WIDGET_REALIZED (child))
        gtk_widget_realize (child);

      if (GTK_WIDGET_MAPPED (child->parent) &&
          !GTK_WIDGET_MAPPED (child))
        gtk_widget_map (child);
    }

  if (GTK_WIDGET_VISIBLE (child) && GTK_WIDGET_VISIBLE (container))
    gtk_widget_queue_resize (child);
}
```

The following are required parts of the add method:

- gtk_widget_set_parent() is called to set the widget's parent; this fills in widget->parent and handles reference counting and some other internal details.

- The container saves a pointer to the child; this is easy for GtkBin because there is only one child and it goes in bin->child.

- If the container has been shown (for example, if its GTK_VISIBLE flag is set), parent and child's GTK_REALIZED and GTK_MAPPED states are synchronized. That is, the child is realized and mapped if the parent is realized and mapped.

- If both parent and child have been shown, a resize is queued. That is, layout will be recalculated in light of the new child.

The remove method reverses the process. Here is its implementation:

```
static void
gtk_bin_remove (GtkContainer *container,
                GtkWidget     *child)
{
  GtkBin *bin;
  gboolean widget_was_visible;

  g_return_if_fail (container != NULL);
  g_return_if_fail (GTK_IS_BIN (container));
  g_return_if_fail (child != NULL);
  g_return_if_fail (GTK_IS_WIDGET (child));

  bin = GTK_BIN (container);
  g_return_if_fail (bin->child == child);

  widget_was_visible = GTK_WIDGET_VISIBLE (child);

  gtk_widget_unparent (child);
  bin->child = NULL;

  if (widget_was_visible)
    gtk_widget_queue_resize (GTK_WIDGET (container));
}
```

A remove method is little more than a wrapper for gtk_widget_unparent(), which queues a resize if necessary. Most remove methods would check the container's GTK_VISIBLE flag before queuing a resize, just as gtk_bin_add() does. GtkBin does not, however, because top-level widgets like GtkWindow derive from it, and those widgets always queue a resize regardless of visibility.

11.4.7.2 Iterating over Children

Containers have a `forall` method for iterating over their children. `GtkContainer`'s default methods use `forall` because they know nothing about the data members in subclasses' instance structs. The `forall` method invokes a callback on each child, and the provided callback data is the second argument. Obviously, it's going to be trivial for `GtkBin`:

```
static void
gtk_bin_forall (GtkContainer *container,
                gboolean     include_internals,
                GtkCallback  callback,
                gpointer     callback_data)
{
  GtkBin *bin;

  g_return_if_fail (container != NULL);
  g_return_if_fail (GTK_IS_BIN (container));
  g_return_if_fail (callback != NULL);

  bin = GTK_BIN (container);

  if (bin->child)
    (* callback) (bin->child, callback_data);
}
```

You may notice that `GtkBin` ignores the `include_internals` argument. Some containers have "incidental" child widgets in addition to the user-provided children they are primarily designed to hold. For example, `GtkNotebook` has a widget labeling each of its tabs, and `GtkCList` uses buttons to title each column in the list. These internal widgets must be included in the iteration in many cases, for example, when they're used for drawing or destroying each child in a container. However, some operations operate on only the "primary" children, such as the pages in `GtkNotebook`. The `include_internals` flag indicates whether to invoke the callback on incidental widgets.

Convenience functions are provided that invoke the `forall` method. These are used by application authors as well as GtkContainer internals. `gtk_container_foreach()` iterates over only the primary children of a container, whereas `gtk_container_forall()` iterates over all the children.

11.4.7.3 Child Type

The `child_type` method returns the type of children a container can hold. For example, a `GtkMenuShell` (parent class of `GtkMenu` and `GtkMenuBar`) can hold children of type `GTK_TYPE_MENU_ITEM` only. The `child_type` method allows GUI builders and scripting languages to determine at runtime what sort of children a container will accept. `GTK_TYPE_NONE` indicates that a container will not accept children at this time, for whatever reason.

The GtkBin implementation accepts GTK_TYPE_WIDGET if the bin is empty and GTK_TYPE_NONE if the bin already contains a child:

```
static GtkType
gtk_bin_child_type (GtkContainer *container)
{
  if (!GTK_BIN (container)->child)
    return GTK_TYPE_WIDGET;
  else
    return GTK_TYPE_NONE;
}
```

11.4.7.4 Other *GtkBin* Functionality

GtkBin also provides default implementations of expose, map, unmap, and draw from GtkWidgetClass. Most GtkBin subclasses will override these methods to handle the unique features of the subclass but will chain up to the GtkBin method to deal with their child widget.

The GtkBin map and unmap implementations are mostly the usual boilerplate (set GTK_MAPPED, show widget->window), but they add an important step unique to containers: mapping the child if it has been shown (remember that GTK_VISIBLE signals a widget has been shown) and unmapping the child when the bin is unmapped. Here's the code:

```
static void
gtk_bin_map (GtkWidget *widget)
{
  GtkBin *bin;

  g_return_if_fail (widget != NULL);
  g_return_if_fail (GTK_IS_BIN (widget));

  GTK_WIDGET_SET_FLAGS (widget, GTK_MAPPED);
  bin = GTK_BIN (widget);

  if (bin->child &&
      GTK_WIDGET_VISIBLE (bin->child) &&
      !GTK_WIDGET_MAPPED (bin->child))
    gtk_widget_map (bin->child);

  if (!GTK_WIDGET_NO_WINDOW (widget))
    gdk_window_show (widget->window);
}

static void
gtk_bin_unmap (GtkWidget *widget)
{
  GtkBin *bin;

  g_return_if_fail (widget != NULL);
  g_return_if_fail (GTK_IS_BIN (widget));
```

```
    GTK_WIDGET_UNSET_FLAGS (widget, GTK_MAPPED);
    bin = GTK_BIN (widget);

    if (GTK_WIDGET_NO_WINDOW (widget))
      gtk_widget_queue_clear (widget);
    else
      gdk_window_hide (widget->window);

    if (bin->child && GTK_WIDGET_MAPPED (bin->child))
      gtk_widget_unmap (bin->child);
}
```

GtkBin's draw and expose implementations simply redraw the child widget. Most subclasses will need to override these methods in order to draw themselves and will then chain up to draw the child. The code is shown here:

```
static void
gtk_bin_draw (GtkWidget    *widget,
              GdkRectangle *area)
{
  GtkBin *bin;
  GdkRectangle child_area;

  g_return_if_fail (widget != NULL);
  g_return_if_fail (GTK_IS_BIN (widget));

  bin = GTK_BIN (widget);

  if (GTK_WIDGET_DRAWABLE (bin))
    {
      if (bin->child && GTK_WIDGET_DRAWABLE (bin->child) &&
          gtk_widget_intersect (bin->child, area, &child_area))
        gtk_widget_draw (bin->child, &child_area);
    }
}

static gint
gtk_bin_expose (GtkWidget     *widget,
                GdkEventExpose *event)
{
  GtkBin *bin;
  GdkEventExpose child_event;

  g_return_val_if_fail (widget != NULL, FALSE);
  g_return_val_if_fail (GTK_IS_BIN (widget), FALSE);
  g_return_val_if_fail (event != NULL, FALSE);

  if (GTK_WIDGET_DRAWABLE (widget))
    {
      bin = GTK_BIN (widget);

      child_event = *event;
```

```
    if (bin->child && GTK_WIDGET_DRAWABLE (bin->child) &&
        GTK_WIDGET_NO_WINDOW (bin->child) &&
        gtk_widget_intersect (bin->child, &event->area, &child_event.area))
      gtk_widget_event (bin->child, (GdkEvent*) &child_event);
  }

  return FALSE;
}
```

Notice that `expose` events are generated for windowless widgets only. Widgets with windows will receive their own `expose` events. Containers are required to generate `expose` events for windowless children.

You can probably guess that `gtk_widget_intersect()` determines the intersection of a rectangle and a child widget.

11.5   *GtkVBox*: A Windowless Container

This section describes some aspects of the `GtkVBox` widget, which differs substantially from the `GtkEv` widget presented earlier in the chapter. To understand this section, you must first understand how `GtkBox` works from a user's point of view (see Section 3.2.2). You might want to look through the files `gtkvbox.h` and `gtkvbox.c` from your GTK+ distribution as you read.

Most of `GtkVBox` is implemented in the `GtkBox` base class. `GtkVBox` itself implements only `size_request` and `size_allocate`. The `GtkBox` instance struct looks like this:

```
typedef struct _GtkBox        GtkBox;

struct _GtkBox
{
  GtkContainer container;

  GList *children;
  gint16 spacing;
  guint homogeneous : 1;
};
```

`GtkBoxClass` adds nothing to `GtkContainerClass`, and `GtkVBox` adds nothing to `GtkBox`.

11.5.1 Coding a *GTK_NO_WINDOW* Widget

The implementation of windowless widgets is slightly different from the implementation of "normal" widgets.

Windowless widgets must set the `GTK_NO_WINDOW` flag, so GTK+ can treat them appropriately. This should be done in the `init` function:

```
static void
gtk_box_init (GtkBox *box)
{
  GTK_WIDGET_SET_FLAGS (box, GTK_NO_WINDOW);

  box->children = NULL;
  box->spacing = 0;
  box->homogeneous = FALSE;
}
```

GtkBox uses the default `realize` method described in Section 11.4.3. Because no GdkWindow needs to be created, a `GTK_NO_WINDOW` widget rarely needs a `realize` method. Recall that the default `realize` implementation sets the windowless widget's window field to the parent widget's `window` field.

Because boxes are invisible layout containers, the `GtkBox` draw and `expose` implementations simply pass the `draw` or `expose` request on to the box's children. This is identical to GtkBin's draw and `expose` implementations, except that there's a list of children to iterate over.

A `GTK_NO_WINDOW` widget that *isn't* invisible, such as `GtkLabel`, should be careful not to draw a background; instead, the parent widget's background is used.

11.5.2 Size Negotiation

GtkVBox's purpose in life is size negotiation: It passes size requests up from its children and then divides a size allocation among them. This leads to the layout behavior described in Section 3.2.2.

Here is the `size request` implementation:

```
static void
gtk_vbox_size_request (GtkWidget      *widget,
                       GtkRequisition *requisition)
{
  GtkBox *box;
  GtkBoxChild *child;
  GtkRequisition child_requisition;
  GList *children;
  gint nvis_children;
  gint height;

  g_return_if_fail (widget != NULL);
  g_return_if_fail (GTK_IS_VBOX (widget));
  g_return_if_fail (requisition != NULL);
```

```
box = GTK_BOX (widget);
requisition->width = 0;
requisition->height = 0;
nvis_children = 0;

children = box->children;
while (children)
  {
    child = children->data;
    children = children->next;

    if (GTK_WIDGET_VISIBLE (child->widget))
      {
        gtk_widget_size_request (child->widget, &child_requisition);

        if (box->homogeneous)
          {
            height = child_requisition.height + child->padding * 2;
            requisition->height = MAX (requisition->height, height);
          }
        else
          {
            requisition->height += child_requisition.height + child->padding * 2;
          }

        requisition->width = MAX (requisition->width, child_requisition.width);

        nvis_children += 1;
      }
  }

if (nvis_children > 0)
  {
    if (box->homogeneous)
      requisition->height *= nvis_children;
    requisition->height += (nvis_children - 1) * box->spacing;
  }

requisition->width += GTK_CONTAINER (box)->border_width * 2;
requisition->height += GTK_CONTAINER (box)->border_width * 2;
}
```

If the box is homogeneous, it multiplies the maximum child requisition times the number of children; otherwise, it sums the child requisitions. Then it adds padding, spacing, and border width as appropriate. Recall that all containers must honor their border width, which is set with gtk_container_set_border_width() and is available as the border_width field in the GtkContainer instance struct.

When you're reading this code, it may help you to know that `GtkBox` stores a small struct for each child widget in its `children` field. The struct looks like this:

```
typedef struct _GtkBoxChild   GtkBoxChild;

struct _GtkBoxChild
{
  GtkWidget *widget;
  guint16 padding;
  guint expand : 1;
  guint fill : 1;
  guint pack : 1;
};
```

Size allocation is more complex. Here, all the box-packing flags come into play. It will probably take you a while to fully understand this function, but there is no need to. The important thing is to see how layout takes place via size allocation.

```
static void
gtk_vbox_size_allocate (GtkWidget     *widget,
                        GtkAllocation *allocation)
{
  GtkBox *box;
  GtkBoxChild *child;
  GList *children;
  GtkAllocation child_allocation;
  gint nvis_children;
  gint nexpand_children;
  gint child_height;
  gint height;
  gint extra;
  gint y;

  g_return_if_fail (widget != NULL);
  g_return_if_fail (GTK_IS_VBOX (widget));
  g_return_if_fail (allocation != NULL);

  box = GTK_BOX (widget);
  widget->allocation = *allocation;

  nvis_children = 0;
  nexpand_children = 0;
  children = box->children;

  while (children)
    {
      child = children->data;
      children = children->next;
```

```
      if (GTK_WIDGET_VISIBLE (child->widget))
        {
          nvis_children += 1;
          if (child->expand)
            nexpand_children += 1;
        }
    }

  if (nvis_children > 0)
    {
      if (box->homogeneous)
        {
          height = (allocation->height -
                    GTK_CONTAINER (box)->border_width * 2 -
                    (nvis_children - 1) * box->spacing);
          extra = height / nvis_children;
        }
      else if (nexpand_children > 0)
        {
          height = (gint) allocation->height - (gint) widget->requisition.height;
          extra = height / nexpand_children;
        }
      else
        {
          height = 0;
          extra = 0;
        }

      y = allocation->y + GTK_CONTAINER (box)->border_width;
      child_allocation.x = allocation->x + GTK_CONTAINER (box)->border_width;
      child_allocation.width = MAX (1, (gint) allocation->width - (gint)
➥GTK_CONTAINER (box)->border_width * 2);

      children = box->children;
      while (children)
        {
          child = children->data;
          children = children->next;

          if ((child->pack == GTK_PACK_START) && GTK_WIDGET_VISIBLE
➥(child->widget))
            {
              if (box->homogeneous)
                {
                  if (nvis_children == 1)
                    child_height = height;
                  else
                    child_height = extra;

                  nvis_children -= 1;
                  height -= extra;
```

```
                     }
                  else
                    {
                      GtkRequisition child_requisition;

                      gtk_widget_get_child_requisition (child->widget,
➡&child_requisition);
                      child_height = child_requisition.height + child->padding * 2;

                      if (child->expand)
                        {
                          if (nexpand_children == 1)
                            child_height += height;
                          else
                            child_height += extra;

                          nexpand_children -= 1;
                          height -= extra;
                        }
                    }

                  if (child->fill)
                    {
                      child_allocation.height = MAX (1, child_height -
➡(gint)child->padding * 2);
                      child_allocation.y = y + child->padding;
                    }
                  else
                    {
                      GtkRequisition child_requisition;

                      gtk_widget_get_child_requisition (child->widget,
➡&child_requisition);
                      child_allocation.height = child_requisition.height;
                      child_allocation.y = y + (child_height -
➡child_allocation.height) / 2;
                    }

                  gtk_widget_size_allocate (child->widget, &child_allocation);

                  y += child_height + box->spacing;
                }
            }

      y = allocation->y + allocation->height - GTK_CONTAINER (box)->border_width;

      children = box->children;
      while (children)
        {
          child = children->data;
          children = children->next;
```

```
            if ((child->pack == GTK_PACK_END) && GTK_WIDGET_VISIBLE (child->widget))
          {
            GtkRequisition child_requisition;
            gtk_widget_get_child_requisition (child->widget,
➥&child_requisition);

            if (box->homogeneous)
              {
                if (nvis_children == 1)
                  child_height = height;
                else
                  child_height = extra;

                nvis_children -= 1;
                height -= extra;
              }
            else
              {
                child_height = child_requisition.height + child->padding * 2;

                if (child->expand)
                  {
                    if (nexpand_children == 1)
                      child_height += height;
                    else
                      child_height += extra;

                    nexpand_children -= 1;
                    height -= extra;
                  }
              }

            if (child->fill)
              {
                child_allocation.height = MAX (1, child_height -
➥(gint)child->padding * 2);
                child_allocation.y = y + child->padding - child_height;
              }
            else
              {
                child_allocation.height = child_requisition.height;
                child_allocation.y = y + (child_height -
➥child_allocation.height) / 2 - child_height;
              }

            gtk_widget_size_allocate (child->widget, &child_allocation);

            y -= (child_height + box->spacing);
          }
        }
    }
}
```

11.5.3 Child Arguments

GtkBox implements *child arguments*, which were briefly described in Section 9.5.3. Child arguments represent a property of a pair of objects. In this case, the box-packing flags for each child can be read and written using the object argument system.

Here's how `GtkBox` registers its child arguments in `gtk_box_class_init()`:

```
gtk_container_add_child_arg_type ("GtkBox::expand", GTK_TYPE_BOOL,
                                  GTK_ARG_READWRITE, CHILD_ARG_EXPAND);
gtk_container_add_child_arg_type ("GtkBox::fill", GTK_TYPE_BOOL,
                                  GTK_ARG_READWRITE, CHILD_ARG_FILL);
gtk_container_add_child_arg_type ("GtkBox::padding", GTK_TYPE_ULONG,
                                  GTK_ARG_READWRITE, CHILD_ARG_PADDING);
gtk_container_add_child_arg_type ("GtkBox::pack_type", GTK_TYPE_PACK_TYPE,
                                  GTK_ARG_READWRITE, CHILD_ARG_PACK_TYPE);
gtk_container_add_child_arg_type ("GtkBox::position", GTK_TYPE_LONG,
                                  GTK_ARG_READWRITE, CHILD_ARG_POSITION);
```

GtkBox then implements the `get_child_arg` and `set_child_arg` methods from GtkContainerClass. Here's `gtk_box_get_child_arg()`; the `gtk_box_set_child_arg()` is the same.

```
static void
gtk_box_get_child_arg (GtkContainer   *container,
                       GtkWidget      *child,
                       GtkArg         *arg,
                       guint           arg_id)
{
  gboolean expand = 0;
  gboolean fill = 0;
  guint padding = 0;
  GtkPackType pack_type = 0;
  GList *list;

  if (arg_id != CHILD_ARG_POSITION)
    gtk_box_query_child_packing (GTK_BOX (container),
                                 child,
                                 &expand,
                                 &fill,
                                 &padding,
                                 &pack_type);

  switch (arg_id)
    {
    case CHILD_ARG_EXPAND:
      GTK_VALUE_BOOL (*arg) = expand;
      break;
    case CHILD_ARG_FILL:
      GTK_VALUE_BOOL (*arg) = fill;
      break;
```

```
    case CHILD_ARG_PADDING:
      GTK_VALUE_ULONG (*arg) = padding;
      break;
    case CHILD_ARG_PACK_TYPE:
      GTK_VALUE_ENUM (*arg) = pack_type;
      break;
    case CHILD_ARG_POSITION:
      GTK_VALUE_LONG (*arg) = 0;
      for (list = GTK_BOX (container)->children; list; list = list->next)
        {
          GtkBoxChild *child_entry;

          child_entry = list->data;
          if (child_entry->widget == child)
            break;
          GTK_VALUE_LONG (*arg)++;
        }
      if (!list)
        GTK_VALUE_LONG (*arg) = -1;
      break;
    default:
      arg->type = GTK_TYPE_INVALID;
      break;
    }
}
```

11.6   *GnomeAppBar*: A Trivial Composite Widget

This section quickly describes the GnomeAppBar widget. GnomeAppBar demonstrates how to bundle a pre-packed container and some special functionality into a single new object. Section 6.3.1 describes GnomeAppBar from a user's point of view.

A composite widget derives from some kind of container and then adds child widgets and sets up callbacks to implement some sort of functionality. GnomeAppBar derives from GtkHBox, and the box is packed with a progress bar and/or a status line. GnomeAppBar has members in its instance struct to store a stack of status messages, and it adds some signals to the class struct for use with its "interactive" mode.

As an aside, GnomeAppBar does not follow the GTK+/Gnome naming conventions. Because Bar is capitalized, the functions and macros should have an underscore, as in app_bar rather than appbar. Don't copy this aspect of the widget.

Here's the implementation of gnome_appbar_new():

```
GtkWidget*
gnome_appbar_new (gboolean has_progress,
                  gboolean has_status,
                  GnomePreferencesType interactivity)
```

```
{
  GnomeAppBar * ab = gtk_type_new (gnome_appbar_get_type ());

  gnome_appbar_construct(ab, has_progress, has_status, interactivity);

  return GTK_WIDGET(ab);
}

void
gnome_appbar_construct(GnomeAppBar * ab,
                       gboolean has_progress,
                       gboolean has_status,
                       GnomePreferencesType interactivity)
{
  GtkBox *box;


  g_return_if_fail( ((has_status == FALSE) &&
                     (interactivity == GNOME_PREFERENCES_NEVER)) ||
                    (has_status == TRUE));

  box = GTK_BOX (ab);

  box->spacing = GNOME_PAD_SMALL;
  box->homogeneous = FALSE;

  if (has_progress)
    ab->progress = gtk_progress_bar_new();
  else
    ab->progress = NULL;

  /*
   * If the progress meter goes on the right then we place it after we
   * create the status line.
   */
  if (has_progress && !gnome_preferences_get_statusbar_meter_on_right ())
    gtk_box_pack_start (box, ab->progress, FALSE, FALSE, 0);

  if ( has_status ) {
    if ( (interactivity == GNOME_PREFERENCES_ALWAYS) ||
         ( (interactivity == GNOME_PREFERENCES_USER) &&
           gnome_preferences_get_statusbar_interactive()) ) {
      ab->interactive = TRUE;

      ab->status = gtk_entry_new();

      gtk_signal_connect (GTK_OBJECT(ab->status), "delete_text",
                          GTK_SIGNAL_FUNC(entry_delete_text_cb),
                          ab);
      gtk_signal_connect (GTK_OBJECT(ab->status), "insert_text",
                          GTK_SIGNAL_FUNC(entry_insert_text_cb),
                          ab);
```

```
        gtk_signal_connect_after(GTK_OBJECT(ab->status), "key_press_event",
                                 GTK_SIGNAL_FUNC(entry_key_press_cb),
                                 ab);
        gtk_signal_connect(GTK_OBJECT(ab->status), "activate",
                           GTK_SIGNAL_FUNC(entry_activate_cb),
                           ab);

        /* no prompt now */
        gtk_entry_set_editable(GTK_ENTRY(ab->status), FALSE);

        gtk_box_pack_start (box, ab->status, TRUE, TRUE, 0);
      }
      else {
        GtkWidget * frame;

        ab->interactive = FALSE;

        frame = gtk_frame_new (NULL);
        gtk_frame_set_shadow_type (GTK_FRAME(frame), GTK_SHADOW_IN);

        ab->status = gtk_label_new ("");
        gtk_misc_set_alignment (GTK_MISC (ab->status), 0.0, 0.0);

        gtk_box_pack_start (box, frame, TRUE, TRUE, 0);
        gtk_container_add (GTK_CONTAINER(frame), ab->status);

        gtk_widget_show (frame);
      }
    }
    else {
      ab->status = NULL;
      ab->interactive = FALSE;
    }

  if (has_progress && gnome_preferences_get_statusbar_meter_on_right ())
    gtk_box_pack_start (box, ab->progress, FALSE, FALSE, 0);

  if (ab->status) gtk_widget_show (ab->status);
  if (ab->progress) gtk_widget_show(ab->progress);
}
```

Most of this code could be in the instance initializer. It's in the constructor instead
because it depends on the arguments passed to gnome_appbar_new(). There's not much
to explain here; the code is straightforward. Do note that gtk_widget_show() is called
for each child widget. This ensures that the right thing happens when the user calls
gtk_widget_show() on GnomeAppBar. Another approach would be to override the map
method and map all children (normally, containers such as GtkBox map only children
that have been shown). When you're writing a composite container, keep the
gtk_widget_show_all() function in mind. Never rely on hiding child widgets,
because the user might accidentally show them.

A composite widget is just a special case of extending a base widget with additional functionality. You can extend widgets without adding new children to them; for example, `GtkClock` extends `GtkLabel` by constantly changing the label to reflect the time.

11.7   Other Examples

Here are some other widgets you might look at for inspiration and code. Of course, these are only a few of the many widgets in GTK+ and Gnome. Appendix A, "GTK+/Gnome Object Hierarchy," gives a more comprehensive list of the available widgets and a brief description of each one.

- Bins: `GtkEventBox, GtkFrame, GtkButton`
- Containers: `GtkBox, GtkTable`
- Composites: `GtkFileSelection, GnomeAppBar`
- Windowless: `GtkLabel, GtkBox`
- Set scroll adjustments: `GtkCList, GtkLayout`
- Activatable: `GtkButton, GtkMenuItem`
- Toplevel: `GtkWindow`
- Multiple GdkWindows: `GtkCList, GtkCalendar, GtkRange`
- Extended functionality for existing widgets: `GtkClock, GnomeEntry`
- Floating windows: `GnomeDock, GtkHandleBox`

12

GnomeCanvas

THIS CHAPTER DESCRIBES THE GnomeCanvas WIDGET AND the standard canvas items that come with Gnome. Chapter 13, "Writing a GnomeCanvasItem," offers more detail on how to write a custom canvas item.

12.1 Introduction to the Canvas

The canvas widget is a powerful and extensible object-oriented display engine that's useful in a variety of Gnome applications. The widget itself is simply a blank area, but you can place GnomeCanvasItems on it. A GnomeCanvasItem is a GtkObject representing some element of the display, such as an image, a rectangle, an ellipse, or some text. You can refer to this architecture as *structured graphics*. The canvas lets you deal with graphics in terms of items rather than as an undifferentiated grid of pixels. Because a GnomeCanvasItem is a GtkObject, you can create your own subclasses to supplement those that come with Gnome. This gives you quite a bit of flexibility. When you use custom canvas items, the canvas can render almost anything. At the same time, you can use stock canvas items to save time and effort. The canvas puts you in control.

GnomeCanvas has two modes, which represent a quality/speed tradeoff. In *Gdk mode*, canvas items render directly to a GdkPixmap buffer using the Gdk drawing primitives. The canvas copies the buffer to the screen after all items are rendered. In *antialiased*, or *AA mode*, the canvas items write RGB pixels to a vector of bytes. After all the items have drawn on the RGB buffer, the canvas copies it to the screen. This RGB buffer mode is called "antialiased" mode because all the standard canvas items draw to the RGB buffer using the high-quality antialiased routines in libart_lgpl. This results in smooth lines and very high display quality but with some cost to speed.

12.2   Basic Canvas Architecture

This section introduces the architecture of the canvas, including the arrangement of items into hierarchical groups and the many coordinate systems involved in using the canvas.

12.2.1   *GnomeCanvasGroup*

Canvas items are arranged in a tree structure. You can group items together to be moved as a unit. Canvas architect Federico Mena Quintero likes to use a circuit diagram editor as an example. You might group together the shapes representing each logic gate so that you could manipulate the logic gate as a unit. You could also collect several logic gates into a single component; that is, groups can contain subgroups. Within each group, the canvas maintains a stacking order; objects higher in the stacking order obscure objects lower in the stacking order.

To implement this, the canvas comes with a special kind of canvas item called GnomeCanvasGroup. As the name suggests, a canvas group groups a number canvas items together so you can manipulate the child items as a single item. A GnomeCanvasGroup is invisible; to render itself, it simply recurses its children, rendering each of them in turn. When you create a new GnomeCanvas, a default group called the "root" is created for you. All canvas items are added somewhere below the root group. The canvas widget deals with only the root canvas item directly; all other canvas items are managed by their parent groups.

An accessory function is provided to access the root canvas group, as shown in Function Listing 12.1.

Function Listing 12.1   Root Group Accessor
#include <libgnomeui/gnome-canvas.h>

```
GnomeCanvasGroup*
gnome_canvas_root(GnomeCanvas* canvas)
```

Items must always be part of a group; there is no such thing as an "orphan" canvas item. When you create an item, you must specify its canvas group. It is also possible to reparent items after creation. However, items are permanently bound to the `GnomeCanvas` they were created on. Therefore, you cannot re-parent an item to a group on a different canvas.

12.2.2 Coordinates

Many of the features of the canvas are implemented via translations between different coordinate systems. Canvas items can be moved, rotated, or scaled via *affine transformations*, described in more detail shortly. (Short version: An affine transformation is a way to convert from one coordinate system to another.) Here are the important coordinate systems that come up when you're using the canvas and writing custom canvas items:

- *World coordinates* are an absolute coordinate system. For example, the same world coordinate refers to the same place on the canvas in all cases. World coordinates are conceptually infinite and are represented by a `double`. World coordinates are the real, toplevel, untransformed, canonical coordinate system. Consistent with the X Window System and Gdk, Y coordinates increase as they move *downward*, so lower Y coordinates are located toward the top of the canvas.

- *Item coordinates* are the coordinates used by a particular canvas item. Item coordinates exist because each canvas item has an affine transformation associated with it. In the case of `GnomeCanvasGroup`, this transformation is applied to the group's children. To convert from world coordinates to item coordinates for some particular item, you apply the transform for each canvas group in the item's ancestry, starting with the root canvas group; then you apply the item's own transform. (Don't worry, Gnome comes with a function to do this for you.) Like world coordinates, item coordinates are conceptually infinite.

- *Canvas coordinates* are pixel coordinates. Whereas item and world coordinates are floating-point numbers, canvas pixel coordinates are integers. To use the canvas, you must specify a "scroll region," which is the rectangle in world coordinate space you want the user to be able to see. Canvas pixel coordinates are relative to this rectangle. Canvas pixel coordinates also take into account a scaling factor representing the number of pixels per world coordinate unit. To convert from world coordinates to canvas coordinates, the canvas subtracts the X and Y coordinates of the scroll region, multiplies by the scaling factor, and then rounds to an integer. Thus, (`0,0`) in canvas coordinates will be the upper-left corner of the scroll region.

- *Buffer coordinates* are canvas coordinates modified by some offset. Item implementations use these during rendering. The canvas passes the item implementation a buffer (which is either a GdkDrawable or an RGB buffer, depending on the canvas mode). The canvas tells the item implementation which region of the screen the buffer represents—the buffer region is defined by an X offset, Y offset, width, and height. The X and Y offsets are in canvas coordinates and are equivalent to (0,0) in buffer coordinates. To convert from canvas coordinates to buffer coordinates, simply subtract the offset. Buffer coordinates are only valid from (0,0) to the maximum width and height of the buffer.

- *Window coordinates* are rarely used. The canvas eventually copies each temporary buffer to a GdkWindow (to be precise, it copies them to GTK_LAYOUT(canvas)->bin_window). Window coordinates are relative to this GdkWindow. In some rare cases, you might want to draw to the window directly instead of using a canvas item, or you might want to respond to an event on the window (such as a drag-and-drop procedure). Then you need to convert from window coordinates to one of the other coordinate systems.

When using preexisting canvas items, you will mostly be interested in world and item coordinates. When writing your own items, you will also need to use canvas and buffer coordinates.

There are two ways to convert between the various coordinate systems. One way is to obtain and use affines directly—this is described in the next section. The easy way is to use one of the convenience functions provided for the purpose and shown in Function Listing 12.2. Converting between canvas and item coordinates requires you to convert to world coordinates first as an intermediate step. There is no function to convert to or from buffer coordinates because that is a simple matter of subtracting the buffer offsets from the canvas coordinates (canvas to buffer) or adding the buffer offsets to the buffer coordinates (buffer to canvas).

Function Listing 12.2   Coordinate Conversions
#include <libgnomeui/gnome-canvas.h>

```
void
gnome_canvas_w2c(GnomeCanvas* canvas,
                 double wx,
                 double wy,
                 int* cx,
                 int* cy)
void
gnome_canvas_w2c_d(GnomeCanvas* canvas,
                   double wx,
                   double wy,
                   double* cx,
                   double* cy)
```

```
void
gnome_canvas_c2w(GnomeCanvas* canvas,
                 int cx,
                 int cy,
                 double* wx,
                 double* wy)
void
gnome_canvas_item_w2i(GnomeCanvasItem* item,
                      double* x,
                      double* y)
void
gnome_canvas_item_i2w(GnomeCanvasItem* item,
                      double* x,
                      double* y)
void
gnome_canvas_window_to_world(GnomeCanvas* canvas,
                             double winx,
                             double winy,
                             double* worldx,
                             double* worldy)
void
gnome_canvas_world_to_window(GnomeCanvas* canvas,
                             double worldx,
                             double worldy,
                             double* winx,
                             double* winy)]
```

12.2.3   Affine Transformations

An *affine* is a transformation matrix made up of six real numbers that can be *applied* to an ordered pair. Depending on the contents of the affine, the point it is applied to can be affected in one of the following ways:

- *Translated*—shifted by an arbitrary distance in either dimension
- *Rotated* some number of degrees
- *Scaled* by some factor.

Conceptually, an affine defines a relationship between points on a plane. For any point (A, B), the affine defines a single corresponding transformed point. The mapping is one-to-one. So, given the transformed point, you can determine the original point.

Affines have interesting properties that make them useful in computer graphics. Most importantly, they can be *composed*, *concatenated*, or *multiplied* (the three terms are synonymous). You can compose any number of affines to create a single affine; applying the single affine then has the same effect as applying each of the original affines in order. Note that the order of composition is important! Unlike multiplication, affine composition is not commutative (which is a reason to avoid the term "multiply" in this context).

libart_lgpl contains a module for affine manipulation. It represents affines as an array of six doubles. Its affine functions are shown in Function Listing 12.3.

Function Listing 12.3   Affine Manipulation   *#include <libart_lgpl/art_affine.h>*

```
void
art_affine_point(ArtPoint* dst,
                 const ArtPoint* src,
                 const double affine[6])

void
art_affine_invert(double dst_affine[6],
                  const double src_affine[6])

void
art_affine_multiply(double dst[6],
                    const double src1[6],
                    const double src2[6])

void
art_affine_identity(double dst[6])

void
art_affine_scale(double dst[6],
                 double sx,
                 double sy)

void
art_affine_rotate(double dst[6],
                  double theta)

void
art_affine_translate(double dst[6],
                     double tx,
                     double ty)

int
art_affine_rectilinear(const double src[6])
```

art_affine_point() applies an affine to a point. The affine is then applied to the second argument (src), and the result is copied into the first argument (dst). An ArtPoint is shown here:

```
typedef struct _ArtPoint ArtPoint;

struct _ArtPoint {
  double x, y;
};
```

Affines can be *inverted*. If an affine converts points in coordinate system A into points in coordinate system B, its inverse converts points in coordinate system B to points in coordinate system A. art_affine_invert() fills its first argument with the inverse of its second. art_affine_multiply() composes two affines as described earlier in this section, placing the result in its first argument.

Four functions are provided to create affines with particular properties.

- `art_affine_identity()` creates the identity affine. Applying the identity affine to a point has no effect.
- `art_affine_rotate()` gives an affine that rotates points by `theta` degrees.
- `art_affine_translate()` gives an affine that translates points `tx` in the X dimension and `ty` in the Y dimension.
- `art_affine_scale()` gives an affine that scales the plane by the given factors (a factor of 1.0 does no scaling, less than 1.0 shrinks, greater than 1.0 expands).

`art_affine_rectilinear()` returns `TRUE` if the affine rotates rectangles aligned to the axes in such a way that they remain aligned to the axes. That is, it returns `TRUE` if the rotation is 0, 90, 180, or 270 degrees.

You can ask the canvas widget to compute affines that convert between its various coordinate systems. These functions are shown in Function Listing 12.4. Each of them fills an array you pass in with the affine being requested.

Function Listing 12.4   Canvas Affines   *#include <libgnomeui/gnome-canvas.h>*

```
void
gnome_canvas_item_i2w_affine(GnomeCanvasItem* item,
                             double affine[6])

void
gnome_canvas_item_i2c_affine(GnomeCanvasItem* item,
                             double affine[6])

void
gnome_canvas_w2c_affine(GnomeCanvas* canvas,
                        double affine[6])
```

12.3   Using the Canvas

`GnomeCanvas` is easy to use; this is its virtue compared to `GtkDrawingArea` or some other low-level approach. This section describes how to create a canvas and work with canvas items. It ends with a programming example.

12.3.1   Preparing the *GnomeCanvas* Widget

The first decision you have to make is whether to use the canvas in Gdk mode or antialiased mode. When you create a canvas widget, you must specify the mode you want, and there is no way to change it later. `gnome_canvas_new()` creates a Gdk canvas. `gnome_canvas_new_aa()` creates an antialiased canvas. These are shown in Function Listing 12.5.

Function Listing 12.5   Canvas Constructors
#include <libgnomeui/gnome-canvas.h>

```
GtkWidget*
gnome_canvas_new()

GtkWidget*
gnome_canvas_new_aa()
```

Sometimes it matters which visual and colormap the canvas will use. In particular, follow these guidelines:

- In Gdk mode, if you want to use the `GnomeCanvasImage` item to display images, you must use Imlib's visual and colormap. `GnomeCanvasImage` uses Imlib to render images.

- In antialiased mode, Gdk's RGB buffer-rendering facilities (see Section 10.9.8) are used to copy the RGB buffer to the screen. You must use the visual and colormap from the Gdk RGB module.

To create a widget with a non-default visual and colormap, you use `gtk_widget_push_visual()` and `gtk_widget_push_colormap()`. Here is the code to create a Gdk canvas that supports the image item:

```
GtkWidget* canvas;
gtk_widget_push_visual(gdk_imlib_get_visual());
gtk_widget_push_colormap(gdk_imlib_get_colormap());
canvas = gnome_canvas_new();
gtk_widget_pop_visual();
gtk_widget_pop_colormap();
```

To create an antialiased canvas, do this:

```
GtkWidget* canvas;
gtk_widget_push_visual(gdk_rgb_get_visual());
gtk_widget_push_colormap(gdk_rgb_get_cmap());
canvas = gnome_canvas_new_aa();
gtk_widget_pop_colormap();
gtk_widget_pop_visual();
```

12.3.1.1   Scroll Region

The canvas is practically infinite from a programmer's standpoint; however, in reality your application probably uses only a small area. When using the canvas, you must specify which region is interesting to the user with `gnome_canvas_set_scroll_region()` (see Function Listing 12.6). The scroll region is given in world coordinates. You can query the scroll region with `gnome_canvas_get_scroll_region()`.

Function Listing 12.6   Canvas Scrolling   *#include <libgnomeui/gnome-canvas.h>*

```
void
gnome_canvas_set_scroll_region(GnomeCanvas* canvas,
                               double x1,
                               double y1,
                               double x2,
                               double y2)

void
gnome_canvas_get_scroll_region(GnomeCanvas* canvas,
                               double* x1,
                               double* y1,
                               double* x2,
                               double* y2)

void
gnome_canvas_scroll_to(GnomeCanvas* canvas,
                       gint cx,
                       gint cy)

void
gnome_canvas_get_scroll_offsets(GnomeCanvas* canvas,
                                gint* cx,
                                gint* cy)
```

To add scrollbars to the canvas, simply create a `GtkScrolledWindow` and add the canvas to it:

```
GtkWidget* sw;
sw = gtk_scrolled_window_new(NULL, NULL);
gtk_container_add(GTK_CONTAINER(sw), canvas);
```

If you want to implement scrolling via some mechanism other than the scrollbars, you can get and set the "scroll offsets." The scroll offsets are in canvas pixel coordinates; they specify the top-left visible pixel. Remember that canvas pixel coordinates are relative to the scroll region.

12.3.1.2   Zooming

The canvas gives you zooming "for free"; it is included in the world-to-canvas and canvas-to-world coordinate system conversions. You can set the zoom factor with `gnome_canvas_set_pixels_per_unit()` as shown in Function Listing 12.7. By default, the ratio of pixels to canvas units is 1.0, which means no zoom. Specifying a value less than 1.0 reduces the size; a value greater than 1.0 increases the size.

In antialiased mode, you could achieve the same visual effect by applying a scaling affine transformation to the root canvas group. The `pixels_per_unit` member of the `GnomeCanvas` struct predates the canvas's use of affines. Still, `gnome_canvas_set_pixels_per_unit()` is a bit more convenient than the affine transform method, and it does work in Gdk mode. (Because Gdk mode uses Xlib primitives, it's nontrivial to implement arbitrary affine transformations; a future version of Gnome may do so, however.)

Function Listing 12.7 **Canvas Zooming** *#include <libgnomeui/gnome-canvas.h>*

```
void
gnome_canvas_set_pixels_per_unit(GnomeCanvas* canvas,
                                 double ppu)
```

12.3.2 Canvas Items

Most of the time you will be interested in canvas items more than you are in the canvas itself. Canvas items are typically very easy to use compared to widgets. None of the standard items have any unique signals because they are not interactive. (Because GnomeCanvasItem is a subclass of GtkObject, however, you could certainly have an item with signals if you wanted to.) The GnomeCanvasItem base class has a single signal, "event", which is used to convey all types of events. The "event" signal has no default handler; canvas items do not respond to events unless you connect handlers of your own. Function Listing 12.8 lists all the useful functions for working with the GnomeCanvasItem base class.

Function Listing 12.8 **Using GnomeCanvasItem** **#include <libgnomeui/gnome-canvas.h>**

```
GnomeCanvasItem*
gnome_canvas_item_new(GnomeCanvasGroup* parent,
                      GtkType type,
                      const gchar* first_arg_name,
                      ...)
GnomeCanvasItem*
gnome_canvas_item_newv(GnomeCanvasGroup* parent,
                       GtkType type,
                       guint nargs,
                       GtkArg* args)
void
gnome_canvas_item_set(GnomeCanvasItem* item,
                      const gchar* first_arg_name,
                      ...)
void
gnome_canvas_item_setv(GnomeCanvasItem* item,
                       guint nargs,
                       GtkArg* args)
void
gnome_canvas_item_affine_relative(GnomeCanvasItem* item,
                                  const double affine[6])
void
gnome_canvas_item_affine_absolute(GnomeCanvasItem* item,
                                  const double affine[6])
```

```
void
gnome_canvas_item_raise(GnomeCanvasItem* item,
                        int positions)

void
gnome_canvas_item_lower(GnomeCanvasItem* item,
                        int positions)

void
gnome_canvas_item_raise_to_top(GnomeCanvasItem* item)

void
gnome_canvas_item_lower_to_bottom(GnomeCanvasItem* item)

void
gnome_canvas_item_show(GnomeCanvasItem* item)

void
gnome_canvas_item_hide(GnomeCanvasItem* item)

void
gnome_canvas_item_reparent(GnomeCanvasItem* item,
                           GnomeCanvasGroup* new_group)

void
gnome_canvas_item_grab_focus(GnomeCanvasItem* item)

int
gnome_canvas_item_grab(GnomeCanvasItem* item,
                       unsigned int event_mask,
                       GdkCursor* cursor,
                       guint32 etime)

void
gnome_canvas_item_ungrab(GnomeCanvasItem* item,
                         guint32 etime)

void
gnome_canvas_item_get_bounds(GnomeCanvasItem* item,
                             double* x1,
                             double* y1,
                             double* x2,
                             double* y2)

void
gnome_canvas_item_request_update(GnomeCanvasItem* item)
```

To create a canvas item, you use the generic gnome_canvas_item_new() (or gnome_canvas_item_newv()). This function accepts the group the item is to be placed in, the GtkType of the GnomeCanvasItem subclass to be created, and finally a NULL-terminated list of arguments to be set. The argument list is purely for convenience, so you don't have to call gnome_canvas_item_set() immediately. gnome_canvas_item_new() creates a new instance of the type with gtk_type_new(), adds the item to its GnomeCanvasGroup, and schedules it to be redrawn.

To destroy an item and remove it from the canvas, call `gtk_object_destroy()`. You can also use the standard reference counting mechanism with canvas items.

You can set an item's affine using `gnome_canvas_item_affine_absolute()`, or you can compose a new affine with the item's existing affine using `gnome_canvas_item _affine_relative()`. These functions can be used to translate, scale, or rotate a canvas item (however, scaling and rotation only work in antialiased mode).

Items in a group are normally stacked in the order you add them, with the most recently added item "on top" and the oldest item on the bottom. You can manipulate the stacking order with `gnome_canvas_item_raise()` and `gnome_canvas_item_lower()`. These move an item up or down by the given number of positions. It is safe to pass in a too-large value for `positions`; the item will be moved as far as possible and no more. You can also request that an item be moved to one extreme or the other by using `gnome_canvas_item_raise_to_top()` and `gnome_canvas_item_lower_to_bottom()`.

Items can be shown and hidden. Hidden items are not rendered by the canvas and do not receive events. All items are visible by default. The routines are `gnome_canvas _item_show()` and `gnome_canvas_item_hide()`.

Reparenting a canvas item is straightforward. The only rule is that the new group must be on the same canvas as the old group.

`gnome_canvas_item_grab_focus()` functions the same as `gtk_widget_grab _focus()`: It sends all key events to the item with the grab. It also sends focus change events to the item (when the item gains or loses the focus).

Canvas items can grab and ungrab the mouse pointer just as a `GdkWindow` can. The arguments to `gnome_canvas_item_grab()` are exactly the same as those of `gdk_pointer _grab()` (see Chapter 10). While a canvas item has the pointer grabbed, no other item receives events. Behind the scenes, `GnomeCanvas` uses `gdk_pointer_grab()` to implement `gnome_canvas_item_grab()` so that when an item grabs the mouse away from other items, it seems as if the canvas is grabbing the mouse away from other widgets.

The visual properties of canvas items are manipulated almost entirely via object arguments. If you skipped Chapter 9, go back and read the section on object arguments now. Two functions are used to set canvas item properties: `gnome_canvas _item_set()` and `gnome_canvas_item_setv()`. These are almost—but not quite— equivalent to `gtk_object_set()` and `gtk_object_setv()`. They set object arguments in the same way, but they also mark the canvas item to be redrawn, so you should prefer them to the `GtkObject` variants. (This is something of a design bug, and future canvas versions will most likely allow you to use `gtk_object_set()`.)

`gnome_canvas_item_request_update()` marks the canvas item as "dirty" and queues it to be redrawn. Internally, the canvas uses a one-shot idle function to perform redraws; that is, it waits until no more GTK+ events are pending, and then it redraws itself one time. It does this by installing an idle function with `gtk_idle_add()` and removing it after it runs once. Thus, `gnome_canvas_item_request_update()` can be called many times without creating an efficiency problem; it pretty much does nothing at all if an update is already pending.

12.3.3 Canvas Items and Events

The standard Gnome canvas items have only one signal, "event", which is emitted for *all* types of events. The canvas widget preprocesses all Gdk events that it receives, and it forwards some of them to canvas items. It also synthesizes certain events. Remember that X sends events only to X windows (GdkWindows), and canvas items do not have an associated GdkWindow. Thus, the canvas widget must act as intermediary. Here are some of the actions it takes:

- Coordinates are automatically converted to canvas world coordinates. For example, if a canvas item receives an event of type GDK_BUTTON_PRESS, the x and y fields of the event will be in world coordinates. (The raw event was received on the canvas's GdkWindow and thus had window coordinates.)

- Enter/leave events are synthesized for canvas items as the mouse pointer moves across the canvas.

- Events are propagated up the canvas item hierarchy until some item's "event" signal handler returns TRUE. This works just as it does with GtkWidget: Events are first sent to the bottommost or leaf canvas item and eventually make it up to the root item.

- Only user-generated events are sent to canvas items. Many events you might expect to receive on a GdkWindow, such as expose and configure events, are not forwarded to canvas items.

The canvas does this work behind the scenes, so item events work intuitively and in much the same way as normal Gdk events.

A canvas item event callback looks like this:

```
static gint
item_event_callback(GnomeCanvasItem* item,
                    GdkEvent* event,
                    gpointer data)
{
  switch (event->type) {
    case GDK_BUTTON_PRESS:
      break;

    case GDK_MOTION_NOTIFY:
      break;

    case GDK_BUTTON_RELEASE:
      break;

    default:
      break;
  }

  /* Returning FALSE propagates the event to parent items;
   * returning TRUE ends event propagation.
```

```
    */
    return FALSE;
}
```

Of course, a real callback would probably examine the contents of the event and take action in response to some of them.

12.3.4 A Canvas Example

This section gives a brief example program that demonstrates the use of the canvas. It does not explain the particulars of the canvas items that are created, however; see Section 12.4 for that. Figure 12.1 shows the example program in action. You can drag canvas items around the screen with the left mouse button. Clicking an item with the Shift key held down destroys it.

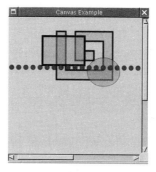

Figure 12.1 Simple **GnomeCanvas** program.

Here is the code for creating an antialiased canvas. You should note three things in particular: the call to **gdk_rgb_init()**, that the canvas's scroll region is set, and that the GdkRGB colormap and visual are pushed when creating the canvas.

```
#include <gnome.h>

static gint delete_event_cb(GtkWidget* window, GdkEventAny* e, gpointer data);
static void create_canvas_items(GtkWidget* canvas);

int
main(int argc, char* argv[])
{
  GtkWidget* window;
  GtkWidget* sw;
  GtkWidget* canvas;

  gnome_init("canvas-example", "0.0", argc, argv);

  gdk_rgb_init();
```

```
  window = gtk_window_new(GTK_WINDOW_TOPLEVEL);

  gtk_window_set_title(GTK_WINDOW(window), "Canvas Example");

  gtk_window_set_policy(GTK_WINDOW(window), TRUE, TRUE, TRUE);

  gtk_signal_connect(GTK_OBJECT(window),
                     "delete_event",
                     GTK_SIGNAL_FUNC(delete_event_cb),
                     NULL);

  sw = gtk_scrolled_window_new(NULL, NULL);

  gtk_scrolled_window_set_policy(GTK_SCROLLED_WINDOW(sw),
                                 GTK_POLICY_AUTOMATIC,
                                 GTK_POLICY_AUTOMATIC);


  gtk_widget_push_visual(gdk_rgb_get_visual());
  gtk_widget_push_colormap(gdk_rgb_get_cmap());
  canvas = gnome_canvas_new_aa();
  gtk_widget_pop_colormap();
  gtk_widget_pop_visual();

  gnome_canvas_set_scroll_region(GNOME_CANVAS(canvas), 0, 0, 600, 450);

  create_canvas_items(canvas);

  gtk_container_add(GTK_CONTAINER(sw), canvas);
  gtk_container_add(GTK_CONTAINER(window), sw);

  gtk_window_set_default_size(GTK_WINDOW(window), 300, 300);

  gtk_widget_show_all(window);

  gtk_main();

  return 0;
}

static gint
delete_event_cb(GtkWidget* window, GdkEventAny* e, gpointer data)
{
  gtk_main_quit();
  return FALSE;
}
```

After the canvas has been created, the program adds some items to it and connects a simple callback to the item's "event" signal. Here's the code:

```
static gint
item_event(GnomeCanvasItem *item, GdkEvent *event, gpointer data)
{
  static double x, y;
  double new_x, new_y;
  GdkCursor *fleur;
  static int dragging;
  double item_x, item_y;

  item_x = event->button.x;
  item_y = event->button.y;
  gnome_canvas_item_w2i(item->parent, &item_x, &item_y);

  switch (event->type)
    {
    case GDK_BUTTON_PRESS:
      switch(event->button.button)
        {
        case 1:
          if (event->button.state & GDK_SHIFT_MASK)
            {
              gtk_object_destroy(GTK_OBJECT(item));
            }
          else
            {
              x = item_x;
              y = item_y;

              fleur = gdk_cursor_new(GDK_FLEUR);
              gnome_canvas_item_grab(item,
                                     GDK_POINTER_MOTION_MASK |
                                     GDK_BUTTON_RELEASE_MASK,
                                     fleur,
                                     event->button.time);
              gdk_cursor_destroy(fleur);
              dragging = TRUE;
            }
          break;

        default:
          break;
        }
      break;

    case GDK_MOTION_NOTIFY:
      if (dragging && (event->motion.state & GDK_BUTTON1_MASK))
        {
          new_x = item_x;
          new_y = item_y;
```

```
        gnome_canvas_item_move(item, new_x - x, new_y - y);
        x = new_x;
        y = new_y;
      }
    break;

  case GDK_BUTTON_RELEASE:
    gnome_canvas_item_ungrab(item, event->button.time);
    dragging = FALSE;
    break;

  default:
    break;
  }

  return FALSE;
}

static void
setup_item(GnomeCanvasItem *item)
{
  gtk_signal_connect(GTK_OBJECT(item), "event",
                     (GtkSignalFunc) item_event,
                     NULL);
}

static void
create_canvas_items(GtkWidget* canvas)
{
  GnomeCanvasPoints* points;
  GnomeCanvasGroup* group;
  GnomeCanvasItem* item;
  double affine[6];

  group = gnome_canvas_root(GNOME_CANVAS(canvas));

  /* A polygon */
  points = gnome_canvas_points_new(14);

  points->coords[0] = 270.0;
  points->coords[1] = 330.0;
  points->coords[2] = 270.0;
  points->coords[3] = 430.0;
  points->coords[4] = 390.0;
  points->coords[5] = 430.0;
  points->coords[6] = 390.0;
  points->coords[7] = 330.0;
  points->coords[8] = 310.0;
  points->coords[9] = 330.0;
  points->coords[10] = 310.0;
  points->coords[11] = 390.0;
```

```
        points->coords[12] = 350.0;
        points->coords[13] = 390.0;
        points->coords[14] = 350.0;
        points->coords[15] = 370.0;
        points->coords[16] = 330.0;
        points->coords[17] = 370.0;
        points->coords[18] = 330.0;
        points->coords[19] = 350.0;
        points->coords[20] = 370.0;
        points->coords[21] = 350.0;
        points->coords[22] = 370.0;
        points->coords[23] = 410.0;
        points->coords[24] = 290.0;
        points->coords[25] = 410.0;
        points->coords[26] = 290.0;
        points->coords[27] = 330.0;

        item = gnome_canvas_item_new(group,
                                     gnome_canvas_polygon_get_type (),
                                     "points", points,
                                     "fill_color", "tan",
                                     "outline_color", "black",
                                     "width_units", 3.0,
                                     NULL);

        setup_item(item);

        gnome_canvas_points_unref(points);

        /* Translate the polygon */

        art_affine_translate(affine, -150.0, -300.0);

        gnome_canvas_item_affine_relative(item, affine);

        /* A translucent rectangle */
        setup_item (gnome_canvas_item_new (group,
                                           gnome_canvas_rect_get_type(),
                                           "x1", 90.0,
                                           "y1", 40.0,
                                           "x2", 180.0,
                                           "y2", 100.0,
                                           "fill_color_rgba", 0x3cb37180,
                                           "outline_color", "black",
                                           "width_units", 4.0,
                                           NULL));

        /* A translucent ellipse */
        setup_item (gnome_canvas_item_new (group,
                                           gnome_canvas_ellipse_get_type(),
                                           "x1", 210.0,
```

```
                                        "y1", 80.0,
                                        "x2", 280.0,
                                        "y2", 140.0,
                                        "fill_color_rgba", 0x5f9ea080,
                                        "outline_color", "black",
                                        "width_pixels", 0,
                                        NULL));

   /* Create ellipses arranged in a line; they're manipulated as a
      single item. */

   group =
     GNOME_CANVAS_GROUP (gnome_canvas_item_new (group,
                                        gnome_canvas_group_get_type(),
                                        "x", 0.0,
                                        "y", 0.0,
                                        NULL));
   setup_item(GNOME_CANVAS_ITEM(group));

   {
      double xpos = 20.0;
      while (xpos < 300.0)
        {
           gnome_canvas_item_new(group,
                                 gnome_canvas_ellipse_get_type(),
                                 "x1", xpos,
                                 "y1", 100.0,
                                 "x2", xpos + 10.0,
                                 "y2", 110.0,
                                 "fill_color_rgba", 0x0000FFFF,
                                 "outline_color_rgba", 0xFF,
                                 NULL);
           xpos += 15.0;
        }
   }
}
```

12.4 Standard Canvas Item Reference

This section describes the canvas items that come with Gnome, gives a table of arguments, and describes any non-obvious arguments.

12.4.1 Rectangle and Ellipse Items

The GnomeCanvasRect and GnomeCanvasEllipse canvas items share exactly the same interface, via a GnomeCanvasRE base class (see Table 12.1). Their shape is given as a bounding box: a top left coordinate (x1, y1) and a bottom right coordinate (x2, y2). The rectangle item matches the shape of the bounding box; the ellipse is inscribed in the bounding box, touching the center of each side. Rectangles and ellipses can be filled or simply outlined. If they are only outlines, they are considered to be "hollow"; that is, the transparent area inside the shape is not part of the canvas item, and events that occur in that area will not be relayed to the item.

GnomeCanvasRE does not behave gracefully if you give the coordinates in the wrong order. That is, x2 must be greater than x1, and y2 must be greater than y1. Otherwise GnomeCanvasRE gets confused.

Table 12.1   *GnomeCanvasRE* Arguments

Name	Type	Read/Write	Description
x1	double	Both	Leftmost coordinate
y1	double	Both	Topmost coordinate
x2	double	Both	Rightmost coordinate
y2	double	Both	Bottommost coordinate
fill_color	gchar*	Write-only	Fill color; string for gdk_color_parse(), or NULL for transparent
fill_color_gdk	GdkColor*	Both	Fill color; specified as already allocated GdkColor
fill_color_rgba	guint32	Both	Fill color; specified as 32-bit value packing red, green, blue, and alpha into bytes 1, 2, 3, and 4; alpha of 255 is opaque, 0 is invisible
outline_color	gchar*	Write-only	Outline color; string for gdk_color_parse, or NULL for transparent
outline_color_gdk	GdkColor*	Both	Outline color; specified as already allocated GdkColor
outline_color_rgba	guint32	Both	Outline color; specified as 32-bit value packing red, green, blue, and alpha into bytes 1, 2, 3, and 4; alpha of 255 is opaque, 0 is invisible
fill_stipple	GdkBitmap*	Both	Stipple to use when drawing fill; Gdk mode only
outline_stipple	GdkBitmap*	Both	Stipple to use when drawing outline; Gdk mode only

Name	Type	Read/Write	Description
width_pixels	guint	Write-only	Width of the outline, in pixels (independent of zoom)
width_units	double	Write-only	Width of the outline, in canvas units; pixel width changes with zoom factor (pixels per unit)

12.4.2 Line Item

GnomeCanvasLine (see Table 12.2) represents one or more line segments joined at their endpoints. You can use it to represent an unfilled polygon as well. GnomeCanvasPolygon is used for filled polygons. A line is specified using a GnomeCanvasPoints structure, which looks like this:

```
typedef struct {
        int num_points;
        double *coords;
        int ref_count;
} GnomeCanvasPoints;
```

The coords field contains an array of points, alternating X and Y coordinates. You fill the coords array directly after creating a GnomeCanvasPoints with gnome_canvas _points_new(). The structure should be destroyed with gnome_canvas_points _unref().

Lines can have arrowheads on either end. The arrowhead shape is specified via three parameters arbitrarily named A, B, and C. Parameter A (specified with the arrow_shape_a argument) specifies the distance from the base of the arrowhead to the tip. B specifies the distance from the tip of the arrowhead to one of the trailing points. C specifies the distance of a trailing point from the outer edge of the line.

Table 12.2 *GnomeCanvasLine* **Arguments**

Name	Type	Read/Write	Description
points	GnomeCanvas Points*	Both	Points in the line
fill_color	gchar*	Write-only	Fill color; string for gdk_color_parse()
fill_color_gdk	GdkColor*	Both	Fill color; specified as already allocated GdkColor

continues

Table 12.2 **Continued**

Name	Type	Read/Write	Description
fill_color_rgba	guint32	Both	Fill color; specified as 32-bit value packing red, green, blue, and alpha into bytes 1, 2, 3, and 4; alpha of 255 is opaque, 0 is invisible
fill_stipple	GdkBitmap*	Both	Stipple to use when drawing line; Gdk mode only
width_pixels	guint	Write-only	Width of the line, in pixels (independent of zoom)
width_units	double	Write-only	Width of the line, in canvas units; pixel width changes with zoom factor (pixels per unit)
cap_style	GdkCapStyle	Both	Cap style (Gdk mode only)
join_style	GdkJoinStyle	Both	Join style (Gdk mode only)
line_style	GdkLineStyle	Both	Line style (Gdk mode only)
first_arrowhead	gboolean	Both	Whether to put an arrowhead at the start of the line
last_arrowhead	gboolean	Both	Whether to put an arrowhead at the end of the line
smooth	gboolean	Both	Whether to smooth the line using parabolic splines
spline_steps	guint	Both	Number of steps to use when rendering curves
arrow_shape_a	double	Both	Length of arrowhead
arrow_shape_b	double	Both	Length of arrowhead edges (tip to trailing points)
arrow_shape_c	double	Both	Width of arrowhead

12.4.3 Polygon Item

GnomeCanvasPolygon (see Table 12.3) represents a filled polygon; it can be filled or only an outline. Unlike GnomeCanvasRE, an unfilled GnomeCanvasPolygon is not "hollow." The transparent portion in the center is part of the canvas item. GnomeCanvasLine is used for "hollow" polygons.

Table 12.3   *GnomeCanvasPolygon* **Arguments**

Name	Type	Read/ Write	Description
points	GnomeCanvas Points*	Both	Points in the polygon
fill_color	gchar*	Write-only	Fill color; string for gdk_color_parse() or NULL for transparent
fill_color_gdk	GdkColor*	Both	Fill color; specified as already allocated GdkColor
fill_color_rgba	guint32	Both	Fill color; specified as 32-bit value packing red, green, blue, and alpha into bytes 1, 2, 3, and 4; alpha of 255 is opaque, 0 is invisible
outline_color	gchar*	Write-only	Outline color; string for gdk_color_parse, or NULL for transparent
outline_color_gdk	GdkColor*	Both	Outline color; specified as already allocated GdkColor
outline_color_rgba	guint32	Both	Outline color; specified as 32-bit value packing red, green, blue, and alpha into bytes 1, 2, 3, and 4; alpha of 255 is opaque, 0 is invisible
fill_stipple	GdkBitmap*	Both	Stipple to use when drawing fill; Gdk mode only
outline_stipple	GdkBitmap*	Both	Stipple to use when drawing outline; Gdk mode only
width_pixels	guint	Write-only	Width of the outline, in pixels (independent of zoom)
width_units	double	Write-only	Width of the outline, in canvas units; pixel width changes with zoom factor (pixels per unit)

12.4.4   Image Item

GnomeCanvasImage (see Table 12.4) places an image on the canvas. You pass it a GdkImlibImage that's loaded using one of the Imlib routines. If the image has transparent areas, they will be properly handled (they won't be considered part of the item and will not receive events). To use GnomeCanvasImage with a Gdk canvas, you must push the Imlib visual and colormap before creating the canvas (see Section 12.3.1).

Table 12.4   *GnomeCanvasImage* **Arguments**

Name	Type	Read/Write	Description
image	GdkImlibImage*	Both	GdkImlibImage to display
x	double	Both	X coordinate of the anchor point
y	double	Both	Y coordinate of the anchor point
anchor	GtkAnchorType	Both	Location of anchor point
width	double	Both	Width in canvas units (image will be scaled)
height	double	Both	Height in canvas units (image will be scaled)

12.4.5   Text Item

GnomeCanvasText (see Table 12.5) displays a text string. You can specify the coordinates of the string as an ordered pair; these coordinates will represent the location of the text's *anchor*. For example, if the "anchor" argument is set to GTK_ANCHOR_NORTH, the text item's coordinates will represent the location of the top-center of the item. That is, the text will be centered around the X position and begin just below the Y position. The following are possible anchor values:

- GTK_ANCHOR_CENTER
- GTK_ANCHOR_NORTH
- GTK_ANCHOR_NORTH_WEST
- GTK_ANCHOR_NORTH_EAST
- GTK_ANCHOR_SOUTH
- GTK_ANCHOR_SOUTH_WEST
- GTK_ANCHOR_SOUTH_EAST
- GTK_ANCHOR_WEST
- GTK_ANCHOR_EAST

The affine transformation of `GnomeCanvasText` is not implemented very well. Because the X font model is inflexible and limited, there is no good way to rotate and otherwise transform rendered text. In antialiased mode, the canvas item implements this in the only way it can. It draws the entire font to a `GdkPixmap`, copies the pixmap to a `GdkImage`, reads individual pixels out of the image into a client-side bitmap, copies the characters to be displayed from the entire-font bitmap into a temporary buffer, uses `libart_lgpl` to apply any affine transformations to this buffer, and then copies the transformed buffer to the canvas RGB buffer. Finally, the canvas copies the RGB buffer to the screen. Needless to say, this is slower than molasses. An entire bitmap goes over the network more than once. Moreover, scaling and rotating fonts as bitmaps produces a low-quality image. If you try to use `GnomeCanvasText` with antialiased mode, you will probably notice this; if your canvas is slow to update, suspect the text item.

There are plans to fix the text item using a new font abstraction called `GnomeFont`. However, Gnome 1.0 lacks this feature.

There is not a good solution to the problem. If your application allows it, you can get dramatic speed increases by creating your own text item that caches the entire-font bitmaps. However, if you don't reuse the same fonts often, caching will be useless. Another possibility is to abandon X fonts and use Type 1 fonts with a rasterization library like `t1lib`, but this limits the fonts available to you and adds a library dependency. You could also use True Type fonts with the FreeType library, or you could use the Display PostScript extension to X (XDPS).

Unfortunately, your best bet is probably to wait for the `GnomeFont` feature in a future version of the Gnome libraries.

Table 12.5   *GnomeCanvasText* **Arguments**

Name	Type	Read/Write	Description
text	gchar*	Both	String to display
x	double	Both	X coordinate of the anchor point
y	double	Both	Y coordinate of the anchor point
anchor	GtkAnchorType	Both	Location of the anchor point
font	gchar*	Write-only	Font name for gdk_font_load()
fontset	gchar*	Write-only	Fontset name for gdk_fontset_load()
font_gdk	GdkFont*	Both	Font for rendering the text
justification	GtkJustification	Both	Justification (multiline text only)

continues

Table 12.5   **Continued**

Name	Type	Read/Write	Description
fill_color	gchar*	Write-only	Fill color; string for gdk_color_parse() or NULL for transparent
fill_color_gdk	GdkColor*	Both	Fill color; specified as already allocated GdkColor
fill_color_rgba	guint32	Both	Fill color; specified as 32-bit value packing red, green, blue, and alpha into bytes 1, 2, 3, and 4; alpha of 255 is opaque, 0 is invisible
fill_stipple	GdkBitmap*	Both	Stipple to use when drawing text; Gdk mode only
clip_width	double	Both	Width of clip rectangle in canvas units
clip_height	double	Both	Height of clip rectangle in canvas units
clip	gboolean	Both	Enables or disables clipping
x_offset	double	Both	Horizontal offset to add to X position
y_offset	double	Both	Vertical offset to add to Y position
text_width	double	Read-only	Width of rendered text
text_height	double	Read-only	Height of rendered text

12.4.6   Widget Item

The GnomeCanvasWidget item (see Table 12.6) places a widget on the canvas. The canvas item emulates a container widget, passing a size allocation to the widget it holds. You can specify an anchor point for the widget item just as you can for GnomeCanvasText.

Table 12.6 *GnomeCanvasWidget* **Arguments**

Name	Type	Read/Write	Description
Widget	GtkWidget*	Both	Widget to display
X	double	Both	X coordinate of the anchor point
Y	double	Both	Y coordinate of the anchor point
anchor	GtkAnchorType	Both	Location of the anchor point
width	double	Both	Width of widget
height	double	Both	Height of widget
size_pixels	gboolean	Both	Specifies how to interpret the width and height arguments; if TRUE, they are in pixels; if FALSE, they are in canvas units

13

Writing a *GnomeCanvasItem*

THIS CHAPTER EXPLAINS HOW TO WRITE A GnomeCanvasItem. Custom canvas items enable you to extend the canvas. You might consider writing a canvas item if the stock items (or some combination of them placed in a GnomeCanvasGroup) do not meet your needs. As an example, the chapter describes the implementation of GnomeCanvasRect.

13.1 Overview

To write a GnomeCanvasItem, you create a concrete implementation of the GnomeCanvasItem abstract base class. This chapter assumes you've read Chapter 9, "The GTK+ Object and Type System," and understand how a GtkObject works. You must understand objects to write your own.

Canvas items can support Gdk mode, antialiased mode, or both. The canvas has a flag indicating which kind of canvas it is. Items can check this flag at runtime:

```
if (item->canvas->aa)
  {
    /* antialiased mode */
  }
else
```

```
{
  /* Gdk mode */
}
```

However, most code will be the same for both canvas types. The only real difference is in the drawing process: Gdk mode draws to a pixmap, whereas antialiased mode draws to an RGB buffer. You do not have to support both kinds of canvas, just be careful not to use your item with the unsupported canvas type.

Here is the GnomeCanvasItem type you will be subclassing:

```
typedef struct _GnomeCanvasItem      GnomeCanvasItem;
typedef struct _GnomeCanvasItemClass GnomeCanvasItemClass;

struct _GnomeCanvasItem {
  GtkObject object;

  /* Canvas we are on */
  GnomeCanvas *canvas;

  /* Parent group */
  GnomeCanvasItem *parent;

  /* Bounding box for this item */
  double x1, y1, x2, y2;

  /* If NULL, the identity transform */
  double *xform;
};

struct _GnomeCanvasItemClass {
  GtkObjectClass parent_class;

  void (* update) (GnomeCanvasItem *item, double *affine,
                   ArtSVP *clip_path, int flags);

  void (* realize) (GnomeCanvasItem *item);

  void (* unrealize) (GnomeCanvasItem *item);

  void (* map) (GnomeCanvasItem *item);

  void (* unmap) (GnomeCanvasItem *item);

  /* Unused in Gnome 1.0 */
  ArtUta *(* coverage) (GnomeCanvasItem *item);

  /* Used only in Gdk mode */
  void (* draw) (GnomeCanvasItem *item, GdkDrawable *drawable,
                 int x, int y, int width, int height);

  /* Used only in RGB mode */
  void (* render) (GnomeCanvasItem *item, GnomeCanvasBuf *buf);
```

```
double (* point) (GnomeCanvasItem *item, double x, double y,
                  int cx, int cy,
                  GnomeCanvasItem **actual_item);

/* Obsolete; not used in Gnome 1.0 */
void (* translate) (GnomeCanvasItem *item, double dx, double dy);

/* Deprecated, but occasionally used in Gnome 1.0 */
void (* bounds) (GnomeCanvasItem *item,
                 double *x1, double *y1,
                 double *x2, double *y2);

/* The only canvas item class function that is also a signal */
gint (* event) (GnomeCanvasItem *item, GdkEvent *event);
};
```

This chapter explains everything in more detail; keep reading.

13.1.1   GnomeCanvasRect

GnomeCanvasRect and GnomeCanvasEllipse have almost identical implementations; in fact, the GnomeCanvasRE base class implements all but three of GnomeCanvasItem's methods. GnomeCanvasRE handles their user-visible interface, as discussed in the previous chapter.

To understand the implementation of GnomeCanvasRect presented in this chapter, you should first read the previous chapter's discussion of the object arguments it supports. You'll also want to see the object itself:

```
typedef struct _GnomeCanvasRE GnomeCanvasRE;

struct _GnomeCanvasRE {
  GnomeCanvasItem item;

  double x1, y1, x2, y2;       /* Corners of item, item coordinates */
  double width;                /* Outline width, item coordinates */

  guint fill_color;            /* Fill color, RGBA */
  guint outline_color;         /* Outline color, RGBA */

  gulong fill_pixel;           /* Fill color */
  gulong outline_pixel;        /* Outline color */

  GdkBitmap *fill_stipple;     /* Stipple for fill */
  GdkBitmap *outline_stipple;  /* Stipple for outline */

  GdkGC *fill_gc;              /* GC for filling */
  GdkGC *outline_gc;           /* GC for outline */

  /* Antialiased specific stuff follows */
```

```
ArtSVP *fill_svp;          /* The SVP for the filled shape */
ArtSVP *outline_svp;       /* The SVP for the outline shape */

/* Configuration flags */

unsigned int fill_set : 1;      /* Is fill color set? */
unsigned int outline_set : 1;   /* Is outline color set? */
unsigned int width_pixels : 1;/* Is outline width specified in pixels or units?
*/
};
```

`GnomeCanvasRect` adds no new members found in `GnomeCanvasRE`. The method implementations discussed in this chapter should make clear the purpose of the various
struct members.

This chapter discusses all the interesting parts of `GnomeCanvasRect`. Complete source
code comes with the Gnome libraries.

13.2   Drawing Methods

The most important task of any canvas item is rendering itself onto the canvas.
Rendering is a two-stage process for efficiency reasons. The first stage, implemented in
a `GnomeCanvasItem`'s update method, is guaranteed to happen only once per item per
rendering cycle; the idea is to do any expensive affine transformations or other calculations in the update method. In the second stage, the canvas item renders itself to
some region on the screen. The render method implements stage two for antialiased
items, whereas the draw method implements stage two for Gdk items. An item's render
or draw method may be invoked multiple times during a canvas repaint.

Rendering occurs in a one-shot idle function. That is, whenever the canvas receives
an expose event or otherwise determines that a redraw is needed, it adds an idle function, which removes itself after a single invocation. (An idle function runs when no
GTK+ events are pending and the flow of execution is in the GTK+ main loop—see
Section 3.4 for details.) The canvas maintains a list of redraw regions and adds to it
whenever a redraw request is received so that it knows which areas to repaint when
the idle handler is finally invoked.

Canvas items carry a flag indicating whether they need to be updated. Whenever a
canvas item "changes" (for example, if you set a new fill color for `GnomeCanvasRect`), it
will call `gnome_canvas_item_request_update()` to set the "update needed" flag for
itself and the groups that contain it, up to and including the root canvas group. (The
`GnomeCanvas` widget is only aware of a single canvas item: the root group. All other
items are handled recursively when methods are invoked on the root group.) In its
one-shot idle function, the canvas invokes the update method of the root canvas item
if its update flag is set, and then it clears the flag so that the update method will not be
run the next time. The `GnomeCanvasGroup` update method does the same for each child
item.

After all canvas items have been updated, the rendering process begins. The canvas creates an RGB or GdkPixmap buffer, converts its list of redraw regions into a list of buffer-sized rectangles, and then invokes the render or draw method of the root canvas group once per rectangle. After each rectangle is rendered, the buffer is copied to the screen.

13.2.1 The Update Method

The update method is primarily used by antialiased canvas items. libart_lgpl can prebuild a vector path to be rendered, performing clipping and affine transformation in advance. The render method stamps the pre-assembled path into the RGB buffer.

The update method is one of the two that GnomeCanvasRect and GnomeCanvasEllipse have to implement differently. Here is the GnomeCanvasRect implementation:

```
static void
gnome_canvas_rect_update (GnomeCanvasItem *item, double affine[6],
                          ArtSVP *clip_path, gint flags)
{
  GnomeCanvasRE *re;
  ArtVpath vpath[11];
  ArtVpath *vpath2;
  double x0, y0, x1, y1;
  double dx, dy;
  double halfwidth;
  int i;

  gnome_canvas_re_update_shared (item, affine, clip_path, flags);

  re = GNOME_CANVAS_RE (item);

  if (item->canvas->aa) {
    x0 = re->x1;
    y0 = re->y1;
    x1 = re->x2;
    y1 = re->y2;

    gnome_canvas_item_reset_bounds (item);

    if (re->fill_set) {
      vpath[0].code = ART_MOVETO;
      vpath[0].x = x0;
      vpath[0].y = y0;
      vpath[1].code = ART_LINETO;
      vpath[1].x = x0;
      vpath[1].y = y1;
      vpath[2].code = ART_LINETO;
      vpath[2].x = x1;
      vpath[2].y = y1;
```

```
          vpath[3].code = ART_LINETO;
          vpath[3].x = x1;
          vpath[3].y = y0;
          vpath[4].code = ART_LINETO;
          vpath[4].x = x0;
          vpath[4].y = y0;
          vpath[5].code = ART_END;
          vpath[5].x = 0;
          vpath[5].y = 0;

          vpath2 = art_vpath_affine_transform (vpath, affine);

          gnome_canvas_item_update_svp_clip (item, &re->fill_svp, art_svp_from_vpath
➥(vpath2), clip_path);
          art_free (vpath2);
       } else
          gnome_canvas_item_update_svp (item, &re->fill_svp, NULL);

       if (re->outline_set) {
         if (re->width_pixels)
           halfwidth = re->width * 0.5;
         else
           halfwidth = re->width * item->canvas->pixels_per_unit * 0.5;

         if (halfwidth < 0.25)
           halfwidth = 0.25;

         i = 0;
         vpath[i].code = ART_MOVETO;
         vpath[i].x = x0 - halfwidth;
         vpath[i].y = y0 - halfwidth;
         i++;
         vpath[i].code = ART_LINETO;
         vpath[i].x = x0 - halfwidth;
         vpath[i].y = y1 + halfwidth;
         i++;
         vpath[i].code = ART_LINETO;
         vpath[i].x = x1 + halfwidth;
         vpath[i].y = y1 + halfwidth;
         i++;
         vpath[i].code = ART_LINETO;
         vpath[i].x = x1 + halfwidth;
         vpath[i].y = y0 - halfwidth;
         i++;
         vpath[i].code = ART_LINETO;
         vpath[i].x = x0 - halfwidth;
         vpath[i].y = y0 - halfwidth;
         i++;

         if (x1 - halfwidth > x0 + halfwidth &&
             y1 - halfwidth > y0 + halfwidth) {
```

```
              vpath[i].code = ART_MOVETO;
              vpath[i].x = x0 + halfwidth;
              vpath[i].y = y0 + halfwidth;
              i++;
              vpath[i].code = ART_LINETO;
              vpath[i].x = x1 - halfwidth;
              vpath[i].y = y0 + halfwidth;
              i++;
              vpath[i].code = ART_LINETO;
              vpath[i].x = x1 - halfwidth;
              vpath[i].y = y1 - halfwidth;
              i++;
              vpath[i].code = ART_LINETO;
              vpath[i].x = x0 + halfwidth;
              vpath[i].y = y1 - halfwidth;
              i++;
              vpath[i].code = ART_LINETO;
              vpath[i].x = x0 + halfwidth;
              vpath[i].y = y0 + halfwidth;
              i++;
          }
          vpath[i].code = ART_END;
          vpath[i].x = 0;
          vpath[i].y = 0;

          vpath2 = art_vpath_affine_transform (vpath, affine);

          gnome_canvas_item_update_svp_clip (item, &re->outline_svp,
    ➥art_svp_from_vpath (vpath2), clip_path);
          art_free (vpath2);
        } else
          gnome_canvas_item_update_svp (item, &re->outline_svp, NULL);
    } else {
      get_bounds (re, &x0, &y0, &x1, &y1);
      gnome_canvas_update_bbox (item, x0, y0, x1, y1);
    }
}
```

As you can see, the first thing this function does is invoke an update function shared
by GnomeCanvasRect and GnomeCanvasEllipse. Here is that function:

```
static void
gnome_canvas_re_update_shared (GnomeCanvasItem *item, double *affine,
                               ArtSVP *clip_path, int flags)
{
  GnomeCanvasRE *re;

  re = GNOME_CANVAS_RE (item);

  if (re_parent_class->update)
    (* re_parent_class->update) (item, affine, clip_path, flags);
```

```
if (!item->canvas->aa) {
    set_gc_foreground (re->fill_gc, re->fill_pixel);
    set_gc_foreground (re->outline_gc, re->outline_pixel);
    set_stipple (re->fill_gc, &re->fill_stipple,
                re->fill_stipple, TRUE);
    set_stipple (re->outline_gc, &re->outline_stipple,
                re->outline_stipple, TRUE);
    set_outline_gc_width (re);
}
}
```

A lot of code is involved here. The update method is almost always the most complicated one because it does all the work of preparing to render a canvas item. Also, the
update method is different for Gdk and antialiased mode; notice the code that depends
on the item->canvas->aa flag.

The first thing GnomeCanvasRE does during an update is invoke the update method
of its parent class. The GnomeCanvasItem default update method does nothing whatsoever in Gnome 1.0, but it is good practice to chain up for future robustness. Then
GnomeCanvasRE calls a series of utility routines to fill in its graphics contexts with their
correct values. These are straightforward functions, so their implementations are omitted here.

Next gnome_canvas_rect_update() continues with GnomeCanvasRect-specific
details. Several tasks are accomplished:

- The bounding box of the canvas item is updated. Every canvas item has an associated bounding box. The GnomeCanvasGroup draw and render methods use this
  box to determine which items are in the redraw region. The bounding box must
  be updated in both Gdk and antialiased mode.

- In antialiased mode, a *sorted vector path* is created. A sorted vector path is simply a
  series of drawing instructions, similar to primitive PostScript operations, that
  libart_lgpl can render to an RGB buffer.

- In antialiased mode, the affine and clip_path arguments to the update method
  are used to transform the sorted vector path; thus the affine and clip path are
  implicitly stored for use in the render method. If you do not use libart_lgpl's
  sorted vector paths in your own canvas items, you must arrange some other way
  to ensure that the affine and clip are taken into account when you render.

- In both modes, a redraw is requested for both the region the item used to
  occupy *and* the region the item will now occupy.

Much of this work takes place behind the scenes in utility functions from libgnomeui/
gnome-canvas-util.h. gnome_canvas_update_bbox() sets the item's new bounding box
and requests a redraw on both the old and new bounding boxes; it is used in Gdk
mode. (gnome_canvas_update_bbox() expects canvas pixel coordinates; get_bounds() is
a trivial function that computes the rectangle's bounds in canvas pixel coordinates.)

So you know what's happening behind the scenes, here is the implementation of

```
gnome_canvas_update_bbox():
    void
    gnome_canvas_update_bbox (GnomeCanvasItem *item,
                              int x1, int y1,
                              int x2, int y2)
    {
      gnome_canvas_request_redraw (item->canvas,
                                   item->x1, item->y1,
                                   item->x2, item->y2);
      item->x1 = x1;
      item->y1 = y1;
      item->x2 = x2;
      item->y2 = y2;
      gnome_canvas_request_redraw (item->canvas,
                                   item->x1, item->y1,
                                   item->x2, item->y2);
    }
```

Of course you're free to do the equivalent yourself—this is merely a convenience function.

In Gdk mode, that's about all that happens; the bounds are updated and then the function returned. Antialiased mode is a bit more complex, but essentially the same tasks are performed. First, gnome_canvas_item_reset_bounds() sets the item's bounds back to an empty rectangle. Then two sorted vector paths are prepared: one for the solid part of the rectangle (if any) and one for the rectangle's outline (if any). The same procedure is followed each time. First, a vector path for libart_lgpl is prepared. Then the path is affine transformed. Then gnome_canvas_item_update_svp_clip() is used to request a redraw on the old path, free the old path, clip the new path, request a redraw on the new one, and save the new one for use in rendering. If the rectangle's fill or outline has been turned off, a redraw is requested on the old vector path, but no new path is created.

To give you a clearer idea what is happening, here is the implementation of gnome_canvas_item_update_svp_clip():

```
    void
    gnome_canvas_item_update_svp_clip (GnomeCanvasItem *item,
                                       ArtSVP **p_svp, ArtSVP *new_svp,
                                       ArtSVP *clip_svp)
    {
      ArtSVP *clipped_svp;

      if (clip_svp != NULL)
        {
          clipped_svp = art_svp_intersect (new_svp, clip_svp);
          art_svp_free (new_svp);
        }
      else
        {
          clipped_svp = new_svp;
```

```
          }

        gnome_canvas_item_update_svp (item, p_svp, clipped_svp);
      }
```

and gnome_canvas_item_update_svp():

```
    void
    gnome_canvas_item_update_svp (GnomeCanvasItem *item,
                                  ArtSVP **p_svp, ArtSVP *new_svp)
    {
      ArtDRect bbox;

      gnome_canvas_update_svp (item->canvas, p_svp, new_svp);
      if (new_svp)
        {
          bbox.x0 = item->x1;
          bbox.y0 = item->y1;
          bbox.x1 = item->x2;
          bbox.y1 = item->y2;
          art_drect_svp_union (&bbox, new_svp);
          item->x1 = bbox.x0;
          item->y1 = bbox.y0;
          item->x2 = bbox.x1;
          item->y2 = bbox.y1;
        }
    }
```

And here's the implementation of gnome_canvas_update_svp():

```
    void
    gnome_canvas_update_svp (GnomeCanvas *canvas,
                             ArtSVP **p_svp, ArtSVP *new_svp)
    {
      ArtSVP *old_svp;
      ArtSVP *diff;
      ArtUta *repaint_uta;

      old_svp = *p_svp;
      if (old_svp != NULL && new_svp != NULL)
        {
          repaint_uta = art_uta_from_svp (old_svp);
          gnome_canvas_request_redraw_uta (canvas, repaint_uta);
          repaint_uta = art_uta_from_svp (new_svp);
          gnome_canvas_request_redraw_uta (canvas, repaint_uta);
        }
      else if (old_svp != NULL)
        {
          repaint_uta = art_uta_from_svp (old_svp);
          art_svp_free (old_svp);
          gnome_canvas_request_redraw_uta (canvas, repaint_uta);
```

```
      }
    *p_svp = new_svp;
  }
```

Again, all these are in `libgnomeui/gnome-canvas-util.h` for any canvas item to use. Ignore the implementation details; the idea is simply to see what work is being done. You might understand the code better if you know that an `ArtDRect` is a "rectangle defined with doubles," from `libart_lgpl`, and that an `ArtUta` is a "microtile array," basically a list of small regions. (The antialiased canvas tracks the redraw region in a fairly sophisticated way. Note that the "U" in "`Uta`" is supposed to suggest the Greek letter symbolizing "micro" (μ); it does not stand for a word beginning with "U".)

13.2.1.1 Requesting Updates

It is the canvas item's responsibility to request an update or redraw when the properties of the item are changed and the screen should be refreshed. This is straightforward. For example, here is a snippet of code from `gnome_canvas_re_set_arg()`, which sets the `"y2"` argument:

```
    case ARG_Y2:
      re->y2 = GTK_VALUE_DOUBLE (*arg);

      gnome_canvas_item_request_update (item);
      break;
```

Because `"y2"` modifies the shape of the rectangle, the path must be recreated, and an update is necessary. Note that `gnome_canvas_item_request_update()` simply sets a flag and installs an idle handler if none is pending, so it can be called many times without a performance penalty.

Not all changes require an update. A redraw may be sufficient, or perhaps the argument is unrelated to the display. It depends on the canvas item and what exactly is being changed.

13.2.2 The Render Method (Antialiased Mode)

The render method is shared between `GnomeCanvasRect` and `GnomeCanvasEllipse`. All it does is stamp the two paths created in the update method into the RGB buffer:

```
    static void
    gnome_canvas_re_render (GnomeCanvasItem *item,
                            GnomeCanvasBuf *buf)
    {
      GnomeCanvasRE *re;
      guint32 fg_color, bg_color;

      re = GNOME_CANVAS_RE (item);

      if (re->fill_svp != NULL) {
        gnome_canvas_render_svp (buf, re->fill_svp, re->fill_color);
      }

      if (re->outline_svp != NULL) {
```

```
        gnome_canvas_render_svp (buf, re->outline_svp, re->outline_color);
    }
}
```

As you can see, most of the work takes place in gnome_canvas_render_svp(), another
function from libgnomeui/gnome-canvas-util.h. Here is its implementation:

```
void
gnome_canvas_render_svp (GnomeCanvasBuf *buf, ArtSVP *svp, guint32 rgba)
{
    guint32 fg_color, bg_color;

    if (buf->is_bg) {
        bg_color = buf->bg_color;
        fg_color = rgba >> 8;
        art_rgb_svp_aa (svp,
                        buf->rect.x0, buf->rect.y0, buf->rect.x1, buf->rect.y1,
                        fg_color, bg_color,
                        buf->buf, buf->buf_rowstride,
                        NULL);
        buf->is_bg = 0;
        buf->is_buf = 1;
    } else {
        art_rgb_svp_alpha (svp,
                           buf->rect.x0, buf->rect.y0, buf->rect.x1, buf->rect.y1,
                           rgba,
                           buf->buf, buf->buf_rowstride,
                           NULL);
    }
}
```

To understand gnome_canvas_render_svp() or to do your own RGB buffer drawing
(without using libart_lgpl), you must know what a GnomeCanvasBuf is. See the
following example:

```
typedef struct {
    guchar *buf;

    int buf_rowstride;

    ArtIRect rect;

    guint32 bg_color;

    unsigned int is_bg : 1;
    unsigned int is_buf : 1;
} GnomeCanvasBuf;
```

The buf member is an RGB buffer (explained in detail in Section 10.9.8). The
buf_rowstride is the buffer's rowstride, also explained in Section 10.9.8. An ArtIRect
is an integer rectangle. rect defines the redraw region in canvas pixel coordinates that
this buffer represents. rect.x0 and rect.y0 are the buffer offsets and correspond to

row 0, column 0 in the RGB buffer. You can convert from canvas pixel coordinates to RGB buffer coordinates by subtracting these values.

As an optimization, the canvas does not initialize the RGB buffer with the background color because the first canvas item might cover the entire background anyway. Thus, if your canvas item is the first one to render, you must put some pixel value in every pixel of the redraw region defined by the buffer's rect. If your item does not cover a pixel, you should fill that pixel with the bg_color; bg_color is a packed RGB value (no alpha). If you do this manually, unpack an RGB value rgb like this:

```
guchar r, g, b;

r = (rgb >> 16) & 0xff;
g = (rgb >> 8) & 0xff;
b = rgb & 0xff;
```

However, a convenience function is provided to fill a GnomeCanvasBuf with its bg_color:

```
void
gnome_canvas_buf_ensure_buf (GnomeCanvasBuf *buf)
{
  guchar *bufptr;
  int y;

  if (!buf->is_buf) {
    bufptr = buf->buf;
    for (y = buf->rect.y0; y < buf->rect.y1; y++) {
      art_rgb_fill_run (bufptr,
                        buf->bg_color >> 16,
                        (buf->bg_color >> 8) & 0xff,
                        buf->bg_color & 0xff,
                        buf->rect.x1 - buf->rect.x0);
      bufptr += buf->buf_rowstride;
    }
    buf->is_buf = 1;
  }
}
```

As you can see from the implementation of gnome_canvas_buf_ensure_buf(), is_bg is a flag indicating that the RGB buffer still contains random memory garbage; it has not been initialized with RGB pixels. is_buf indicates that the buffer *has* been initialized, and subsequent items should only draw themselves, ignoring background pixels. These two flags are mutually exclusive; if your item receives a buffer with is_bg set, it should take steps to fill the buffer, unset is_bg, and set is_buf, as shown here:

```
if (buf->is_bg)
  {
    gnome_canvas_buf_ensure_buf(buf);
    buf->is_bg = FALSE;
  }
```

13.2.2.1 Speed and RGB Rendering

If you have a large number of objects, RGB mode can be faster than Gdk mode. Drawing to an RGB buffer is a simple matter of assigning to an array, which is much, much faster than making a Gdk call (because Gdk has to contact the X server and ask it to do the actual drawing). The expensive part is copying the RGB buffer to the X server when you're done. However, the copy takes the same amount of time no matter how many canvas items you have because it is done only once, when all the items have been rendered.

This is a big win in an application called "Guppi" that I'm in the process of writing. Guppi is a plot program. One of the things it has to do is render a scatter plot with tens of thousands of points. Each point is a small colored shape; if I called Gdk to render each one, it would take tens of thousands of trips to the X server, possibly across a network. Instead, I use the canvas in RGB mode, with a custom canvas item representing the scatter plot. This allows me to do all the rendering on the client side, and then the canvas copies the RGB buffer to the server in a single burst. It's quite fast and responsive. For less speed-intensive elements of the plot, such as the legend, I can save time and use the built-in canvas items.

The one difficulty with direct-to-RGB rendering is that you need a rasterization library comparable to the Gdk drawing primitives if you want to draw anything interesting. `libart_lgpl` is a very high-quality antialiased rasterization library used by the default canvas items. You can use it in your custom items as well, and it is the best choice if you will be drawing only hundreds of shapes. If you'll be drawing thousands of shapes, however, you'll quickly see the need for something faster. Fortunately, something is available. The maintainers of a package called GNU Plotutils extracted the rasterization library from the X distribution, and during the development of Guppi, I extracted it from Plotutils and hacked it to work with the canvas's RGB buffers. I also added alpha transparency support. The resulting library allows you to draw on an RGB buffer much as you would draw using Gdk. The library is distributed under the same license as the X Window System and is free for anyone to include with his application.

Raph Levien, author of `libart_lgpl` and the GdkRGB module, tells me that still faster routines could be written. If you need more speed, consider that a challenge.

13.2.3 The Draw Method (Gdk Mode)

Drawing with Gdk is much less complicated than drawing with `libart_lgpl`, but it is also less flexible and produces lower-quality results. Here is the `GnomeCanvasRect` implementation of the draw method:

```
static void
gnome_canvas_rect_draw (GnomeCanvasItem *item, GdkDrawable *drawable,
                        int x, int y, int width, int height)
{
  GnomeCanvasRE *re;
```

```
double i2w[6], w2c[6], i2c[6];
int x1, y1, x2, y2;
ArtPoint i1, i2;
ArtPoint c1, c2;

re = GNOME_CANVAS_RE (item);

/* Get canvas pixel coordinates */

gnome_canvas_item_i2w_affine (item, i2w);
gnome_canvas_w2c_affine (item->canvas, w2c);
art_affine_multiply (i2c, i2w, w2c);

i1.x = re->x1;
i1.y = re->y1;
i2.x = re->x2;
i2.y = re->y2;
art_affine_point (&c1, &i1, i2c);
art_affine_point (&c2, &i2, i2c);
x1 = c1.x;
y1 = c1.y;
x2 = c2.x;
y2 = c2.y;

if (re->fill_set) {
  if (re->fill_stipple)
    gnome_canvas_set_stipple_origin (item->canvas, re->fill_gc);

  gdk_draw_rectangle (drawable,
                      re->fill_gc,
                      TRUE,
                      x1 - x,
                      y1 - y,
                      x2 - x1 + 1,
                      y2 - y1 + 1);
}

if (re->outline_set) {
  if (re->outline_stipple)
    gnome_canvas_set_stipple_origin (item->canvas, re->outline_gc);

  gdk_draw_rectangle (drawable,
                      re->outline_gc,
                      FALSE,
                      x1 - x,
                      y1 - y,
                      x2 - x1,
                      y2 - y1);
}
}
```

The draw method receives a drawable (the buffer), the buffer offsets (x and y—the canvas pixel coordinates of the buffer), and the buffer's size (width and height). GnomeCanvasRect's draw method obtains the item-to-world and world-to-canvas affines and then composes (multiplies) them to create an item-to-canvas affine. (See Section 12.2.3 for more on affines.) Using this affine, it converts the rectangle's corner points to canvas pixel coordinates; then it draws the rectangle, converting the canvas coordinates to buffer coordinates by subtracting the buffer offsets.

13.3   Other Methods

This section describes the remaining GnomeCanvasItem methods, including event, point, bounds, realize, unrealize, map, and unmap.

13.3.1   Events

The GnomeCanvasItem class has a slot in its vtable called event. This is the only GnomeCanvasItem class function associated with a signal. None of the stock canvas items implement a default handler for event, but of course your own canvas item could.

The return value of event works just like the GtkWidget "event" signal: If the last signal handler returns FALSE, the event is propagated to the item's parent item (by emitting the event signal on the parent). If the last signal handler returns TRUE, propagation ends.

13.3.2   Point

The point method is used to determine which canvas item is located at a given point. The canvas uses this information to decide which item should receive events. A point method calculates the distance from some point to the canvas item. Canvas items *must* correctly report a distance of 0 if the point is on the canvas item, or they will not receive events; they *must* report non-zero if the point is not on the item or they will receive too many events. The exact value returned is not nearly as important as the zero/non-zero distinction.

For convenience, the point method receives the same point pre-translated into both item and canvas pixel coordinates.

The point method also receives a pointer to a pointer to a GnomeCanvasItem. Non-group canvas items should store a pointer to themselves in this space. Groups store the *actual_item received from the topmost child that returns 0 from its point method. If you think about it for a while, you will see the implication: The root canvas group's point method stores a pointer to the deepest child in the item tree at the point in question. The canvas sends events occurring at that point to this most-junior child. Note that the canvas item tree corresponds to the item stacking order (i.e. the root group is on the bottom), so events go to the topmost items, as you might expect. Remember that events are then propagated up the item tree hierarchy.

Here is the point method for `GnomeCanvasRect`:

```
static double
gnome_canvas_rect_point (GnomeCanvasItem *item,
                         double x, double y, int cx, int cy,
                         GnomeCanvasItem **actual_item)
{
  GnomeCanvasRE *re;
  double x1, y1, x2, y2;
  double hwidth;
  double dx, dy;
  double tmp;

  re = GNOME_CANVAS_RE (item);

  *actual_item = item;

  /* Find the bounds for the rectangle plus its outline width */

  x1 = re->x1;
  y1 = re->y1;
  x2 = re->x2;
  y2 = re->y2;

  if (re->outline_set) {
    if (re->width_pixels)
      hwidth = (re->width / item->canvas->pixels_per_unit) / 2.0;
    else
      hwidth = re->width / 2.0;

    x1 -= hwidth;
    y1 -= hwidth;
    x2 += hwidth;
    y2 += hwidth;
  } else
    hwidth = 0.0;

  /* Is point inside rectangle (which can be hollow if it has no fill set)? */

  if ((x >= x1) && (y >= y1) && (x <= x2) && (y <= y2)) {
    if (re->fill_set || !re->outline_set)
      return 0.0;

    dx = x - x1;
    tmp = x2 - x;
    if (tmp < dx)
      dx = tmp;

    dy = y - y1;
    tmp = y2 - y;
    if (tmp < dy)
```

```
      dy = tmp;

   if (dy < dx)
      dx = dy;

   dx -= 2.0 * hwidth;

   if (dx < 0.0)
      return 0.0;
   else
      return dx;
}

/* Point is outside rectangle */

if (x < x1)
   dx = x1 - x;
else if (x > x2)
   dx = x - x2;
else
   dx = 0.0;

if (y < y1)
   dy = y1 - y;
else if (y > y2)
   dy = y - y2;
else
   dy = 0.0;

   return sqrt (dx * dx + dy * dy);
}
```

It should be obvious how this function works; it is simple geometry. Again, notice the following line:

```
*actual_item = item;
```

If your item isn't receiving any events, make sure you included a similar statement.

13.3.3 Bounds

The `bounds` method computes the approximate bounding box of a canvas item. In Gnome 1.0, this method is used only in `gnome_canvas_item_get_bounds()`, a user-visible function to return the bounds of a canvas item. The canvas does not use it at all internally, and most likely you could get away without implementing it, though all the stock items do.

The function should return an item's bounding box in item coordinates. Here is the `GnomeCanvasRE` version:

```
static void
gnome_canvas_re_bounds (GnomeCanvasItem *item,
```

```
                        double *x1, double *y1,
                        double *x2, double *y2)
{
  GnomeCanvasRE *re;
  double hwidth;

  re = GNOME_CANVAS_RE (item);

  if (re->width_pixels)
    hwidth = (re->width / item->canvas->pixels_per_unit) / 2.0;
  else
    hwidth = re->width / 2.0;

  *x1 = re->x1 - hwidth;
  *y1 = re->y1 - hwidth;
  *x2 = re->x2 + hwidth;
  *y2 = re->y2 + hwidth;
}
```

13.3.4 Realizing and Mapping

Canvas items are realized and mapped just as widgets are. These methods play the same role they do for widgets: Realizing a canvas item allocates any Gdk resources it plans to use, and unrealizing it deallocates the same resources. Likewise, mapping a canvas item shows its GdkWindow, and unmapping it hides the GdkWindow. Very few canvas items have a GdkWindow (GnomeCanvasWidget is the exception), so most canvas items will not even implement map and unmap methods. GnomeCanvasRect does not. It does have realize and unrealize methods, however.

Here is the GnomeCanvasRect realize method:

```
static void
gnome_canvas_re_realize (GnomeCanvasItem *item)
{
  GnomeCanvasRE *re;

  re = GNOME_CANVAS_RE (item);

  if (re_parent_class->realize)
    (* re_parent_class->realize) (item);

  if (!item->canvas->aa) {
    re->fill_gc = gdk_gc_new (item->canvas->layout.bin_window);
    re->outline_gc = gdk_gc_new (item->canvas->layout.bin_window);
  }
}
```

And this is the unrealize method:

```
static void
gnome_canvas_re_unrealize (GnomeCanvasItem *item)
{
  GnomeCanvasRE *re;

  re = GNOME_CANVAS_RE (item);

  if (!item->canvas->aa) {
    gdk_gc_unref (re->fill_gc);
    gdk_gc_unref (re->outline_gc);
  }

  if (re_parent_class->unrealize)
    (* re_parent_class->unrealize) (item);
}
```

Note that your realize and unrealize methods are not likely to have anything to do in antialiased mode because there will not be any Gdk resources to worry about.

13.3.5 *GtkObject* **Methods**

Of course, any canvas item subclass must implement the usual `GtkObject` methods, including `destroy` if the object allocates resources that need to be cleaned up, and a `get_arg`/`set_arg` pair if the object defines any arguments. The only canvas-item-specific concern is that you must schedule an update or redraw as needed if `set_arg` changes the properties of the canvas item. These functions are quite long due to the number of arguments, but they're not very interesting, so they are omitted here. See the full `GnomeCanvasRect` source code if you're curious.

IV

Appendices

A   GTK+/Gnome Object Hierarchy

B   Table of Header Files

C   Frequently Asked Questions

D   Online Resources

E   Code Listings

F   Open Publication License Version 1.0

GTK+/Gnome Object Hierarchy

THIS APPENDIX IS A QUICK TOUR OF THE GTK+ and Gnome object hierarchy. It includes GtkObject and all subclasses from both libraries, a brief description of each, and the header files that the objects are found in. It also includes screen shots of widgets to help you find the correct widget for a given task. The testgtk and test-gnome programs that come with the GTK+ and Gnome libraries are also a good way to find widgets; many of the screen shots in this appendix are from those programs.

The specific header file containing each object is listed; however, all GTK+ header files can be included with the gtk/gtk.h convenience header. All GTK+ and Gnome headers can be included with the gnome.h header.

Some objects are described as "abstract base classes." This means that only the subclasses of the object can be instantiated, but all of the subclasses can be manipulated through the base class's interface.

As a general rule, you should try to use *the most specific object possible*. In other words, you could use GtkWindow for your main application window, but GnomeApp is a better choice. You could roll your own About dialog from GnomeDialog, but GnomeAbout is a better choice. This maximizes UI consistency and minimizes your effort.

Both GTK+ and Gnome come with "test" programs, called testgtk and test-gnome, respectively. These programs are used to test the widgets and other features in each library. They're also an excellent source of sample code and a good way to browse the available widgets and find the one you need.

A.1 Hierarchy Summary

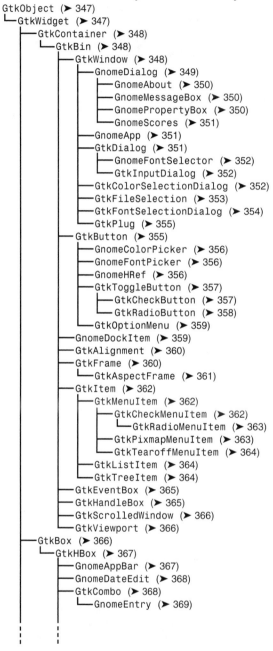

```
GtkObject (➤ 347)
└─GtkWidget (➤ 347)
   ├─GtkContainer (➤ 348)
   │  └─GtkBin (➤ 348)
   │     ├─GtkWindow (➤ 348)
   │     │  ├─GnomeDialog (➤ 349)
   │     │  │  ├─GnomeAbout (➤ 350)
   │     │  │  ├─GnomeMessageBox (➤ 350)
   │     │  │  ├─GnomePropertyBox (➤ 350)
   │     │  │  └─GnomeScores (➤ 351)
   │     │  ├─GnomeApp (➤ 351)
   │     │  ├─GtkDialog (➤ 351)
   │     │  │  ├─GnomeFontSelector (➤ 352)
   │     │  │  └─GtkInputDialog (➤ 352)
   │     │  ├─GtkColorSelectionDialog (➤ 352)
   │     │  ├─GtkFileSelection (➤ 353)
   │     │  ├─GtkFontSelectionDialog (➤ 354)
   │     │  └─GtkPlug (➤ 355)
   │     ├─GtkButton (➤ 355)
   │     │  ├─GnomeColorPicker (➤ 356)
   │     │  ├─GnomeFontPicker (➤ 356)
   │     │  ├─GnomeHRef (➤ 356)
   │     │  ├─GtkToggleButton (➤ 357)
   │     │  │  ├─GtkCheckButton (➤ 357)
   │     │  │  └─GtkRadioButton (➤ 358)
   │     │  └─GtkOptionMenu (➤ 359)
   │     ├─GnomeDockItem (➤ 359)
   │     ├─GtkAlignment (➤ 360)
   │     ├─GtkFrame (➤ 360)
   │     │  └─GtkAspectFrame (➤ 361)
   │     ├─GtkItem (➤ 362)
   │     │  ├─GtkMenuItem (➤ 362)
   │     │  │  ├─GtkCheckMenuItem (➤ 362)
   │     │  │  │  └─GtkRadioMenuItem (➤ 363)
   │     │  │  ├─GtkPixmapMenuItem (➤ 363)
   │     │  │  └─GtkTearoffMenuItem (➤ 364)
   │     │  ├─GtkListItem (➤ 364)
   │     │  └─GtkTreeItem (➤ 364)
   │     ├─GtkEventBox (➤ 365)
   │     ├─GtkHandleBox (➤ 365)
   │     ├─GtkScrolledWindow (➤ 366)
   │     └─GtkViewport (➤ 366)
   ├─GtkBox (➤ 366)
   │  └─GtkHBox (➤ 367)
   │     ├─GnomeAppBar (➤ 367)
   │     ├─GnomeDateEdit (➤ 368)
   │     ├─GtkCombo (➤ 368)
   │     │  └─GnomeEntry (➤ 369)
```

```
                  ┌──GnomeFileEntry (➤ 369)
                  ├──GnomeNumberEntry (➤ 369)
                  ├──GnomeProcBar (➤ 370)
                  └──GtkStatusbar (➤ 370)
              ├──GtkVBox (➤ 370)
                  ├──GnomeCalculator (➤ 371)
                  ├──GnomeGuru (➤ 371)
                  ├──GnomeIconEntry (➤ 372)
                  ├──GnomeIconSelection (➤ 372)
                  ├──GnomeLess (➤ 373)
                  ├──GnomePaperSelector (➤ 373)
                  ├──GnomePixmapEntry (➤ 373)
                  ├──GnomeSpell (➤ 374)
                  ├──GtkColorSelection (➤ 374)
                  └──GtkGammaCurve (➤ 374)
              └──GtkButtonBox (➤ 375)
                  ├──GtkHButtonBox (➤ 375)
                  └──gtk/gtkvbbox.h (➤ 376)
         ├──GtkLayout (➤ 376)
              └──GnomeCanvas (➤ 376)
                  └──GnomeIconList (➤ 377)
         ├──GnomeDockBand (➤ 378)
         ├──GnomeDock (➤ 379)
         ├──GtkCList (➤ 379)
              └──GtkCTree (➤ 380)
         ├──GtkFixed (➤ 381)
         ├──GtkNotebook (➤ 381)
              └──GtkFontSelection (➤ 382)
         ├──GtkPaned (➤ 382)
              ├──GtkHPaned (➤ 383)
              └──GtkVPaned (➤ 383)
         ├──GtkList (➤ 383)
         ├──GtkMenuShell (➤ 384)
              ├──GtkMenuBar (➤ 384)
              └──GtkMenu (➤ 384)
         ├──GtkPacker (➤ 385)
         ├──GtkSocket (➤ 385)
         ├──GtkTable (➤ 385)
              └──GtkTed (➤ 386)
         ├──GtkToolbar (➤ 386)
         └──GtkTree (➤ 386)
    ├──GnomeAnimator (➤ 387)
    ├──GnomePixmap (➤ 388)
         └──GnomeStock (➤ 388)
    ├──GtkMisc (➤ 388)
         └──GtkLabel (➤ 389)
              ├──GtkAccelLabel (➤ 390)
              ├──GtkClock (➤ 390)
              └──GtkTipsQuery (➤ 390)
```

```
    ┌   ┌
    │   │
    │   ├─GtkArrow (➤ 391)
    │   ├─GtkImage (➤ 391)
    │   └─GtkPixmap (➤ 391)
    ├─GtkCalendar (➤ 392)
    ├─GtkDrawingArea (➤ 392)
    │   └─GtkCurve (➤ 393)
    ├─GtkDial (➤ 393)
    ├─GtkEditable (➤ 394)
    │   ├─GtkEntry (➤ 394)
    │   │   └─GtkSpinButton (➤ 394)
    │   └─GtkText (➤ 395)
    ├─GtkRuler (➤ 396)
    │   ├─GtkHRuler (➤ 396)
    │   └─GtkVRuler (➤ 397)
    ├─GtkRange (➤ 397)
    │   └─GtkScale (➤ 397)
    │       ├─GtkHScale (➤ 398)
    │       └─GtkVScale (➤ 398)
    │       GtkScrollbar (➤ 398)
    │           ├─GtkHScrollbar (➤ 399)
    │           └─GtkVScrollbar (➤ 399)
    ├─GtkSeparator (➤ 399)
    │   ├─GtkHSeparator (➤ 400)
    │   └─GtkVSeparator (➤ 400)
    ├─GtkPreview (➤ 400)
    ├─GtkProgress (➤ 401)
    │   └─GtkProgressBar (➤ 401)
    └─ZvtTerm (➤ 402)
GnomeCanvasItem (➤ 403)
    ├─GnomeCanvasRE (➤ 403)
    │   ├─GnomeCanvasEllipse (➤ 403)
    │   └─GnomeCanvasRect (➤ 404)
    ├─GnomeCanvasGroup (➤ 404)
    ├─GnomeCanvasImage (➤ 404)
    ├─GnomeCanvasLine (➤ 405)
    ├─GnomeCanvasPolygon (➤ 405)
    ├─GnomeCanvasText (➤ 405)
    ├─GnomeCanvasWidget (➤ 406)
    └─GnomeIconTextItem (➤ 406)
GnomeClient (➤ 406)
GnomeDEntryEdit (➤ 407)
GnomeDockLayout (➤ 407)
GnomeMDIChild (➤ 408)
    └─GnomeMDIGenericChild (➤ 408)
GnomeMDI (➤ 408)
GtkData (➤ 409)
    ├─GtkAdjustment (➤ 409)
    └─GtkTooltips (➤ 410)
GtkItemFactory (➤ 410)
```

A.2   *GtkObject*

Library

GTK+

Header File

gtk/gtkobject.h

Description

GtkObject is the base of GTK+'s object hierarchy. It is not a graphical component; it implements interfaces for reference counting, attaching key-value pairs to objects, and object destruction ("virtual destructors" in C++ terms). GtkObject itself makes heavy use of the GTK+ type system. The signal/callback infrastructure of GTK+ works in terms of GtkObject. In other words, signals are emitted from a particular GtkObject, and callbacks are connected to a particular object and signal.

Chapter 9, "The GTK+ Object and Type System," covers GtkObject in detail.

A.3   Widgets

Widgets are the reason for GTK+'s existence. Widgets are subclasses of GtkWidget, which is in turn a subclass of GtkObject. A widget represents a rectangular region on the screen. It may be purely decorative, an interactive control, or a container controlling the arrangement of child widgets. Chapter 3, "GTK+ Basics," introduces GTK+ and thus widgets. Chapter 11, "Writing a GtkWidget," covers widget implementation and concepts in more detail.

A.3.1   *GtkWidget*

Library

GTK+

Header File

gtk/gtkwidget.h

Description

GtkWidget is the parent class of all widgets. Chapters 3 and 11 describe widgets in general terms.

GtkWidget is an abstract base class.

A.3.2 *GtkContainer*

Library

GTK+

Header File

gtk/gtkcontainer.h

Description

GtkContainer is the abstract base class for widgets that can contain other widgets. Section 3.2 describes containers in some detail. Chapter 11 includes information on container widget implementation.

A.3.3 *GtkBin*

Library

GTK+

Header File

gtk/gtkbin.h

Description

GtkBin is an abstract base class for containers with one child. It provides default implementations of the GtkContainer interface. So, it is very easy to subclass. Chapter 11 describes how to implement a GtkBin subclass.

A.3.4 *GtkWindow*

Library

GTK+

Header File

gtk/gtkwindow.h

Description

GtkWindow represents a top-level dialog or application window. As the primary top-level widget in GTK+, it has many special responsibilities. For example, it maintains the current keyboard focus and determines its own size allocation (rather than receiving one from a parent widget).

Gnome applications typically use GnomeApp for main application windows to take advantage of its added features. For dialogs, you should use GnomeDialog with Gnome and GtkDialog with GTK+. Of course, several specialized dialog subclasses are available as well. If none of GtkWindow's subclasses seem appropriate to your application, GtkWindow can also be used directly.

Here's a danger worthy of note: GtkWindow is automatically destroyed if it receives a "delete_event" signal. To prevent this, you must install the *last* "delete_event" signal handler to run, and your signal handler must return TRUE. This is a very common GTK+ programming mistake; see Section 10.5.9 for details. GnomeDialog will help you handle this situation; see Chapter 7, "User Communication: Dialogs."

It's a good idea to make GtkWindow the last container you call gtk_widget_show() on. Most widgets are not actually mapped (placed onscreen) until their parent container is, but GtkWindow has no parent, so it appears immediately. Therefore, if you show its children after you've shown the window, you will see some flicker.

A.3.5   *GnomeDialog*

Library

Gnome

Header File

libgnomeui/gnome-dialog.h

Description

GnomeDialog (or a subclass) should be used for all dialogs in a Gnome program. Chapter 7 describes the GnomeDialog interface.

If you aren't using Gnome, GnomeDialog is still useful because it implements all the basic features that a dialog really must have. Studying the GnomeDialog source is highly recommended. (You can even cut and paste if your application is under the GPL.)

A.3.6 *GnomeAbout*

Library

Gnome

Header File

libgnomeui/gnome-about.h

Description

GnomeAbout is an About dialog, giving Gnome About dialogs a consistent look and feel. Chapter 7 covers the interface.

A.3.7 *GnomeMessageBox*

Library

Gnome

Header File

libgnomeui/gnome-messagebox.h

Description

GnomeMessageBox is simply a GnomeDialog with a prepacked label and a small icon. The icon corresponds to a message box type, such as a warning message, an error, or a question. This helps users rapidly determine the dialog's purpose. Section 7.4.3 explains the use of this widget.

A.3.8 *GnomePropertyBox*

Library

Gnome

Header File

libgnomeui/gnome-propertybox.h

Description

GnomePropertyBox is a dialog for application preferences or the properties of some user-visible object in your program. It has Apply, OK, Close, and Help buttons. OK is equivalent to Apply followed by Close. Section 7.4.2 describes it in more detail.

A.3.9   *GnomeScores*

Library

Gnome

Header File

`libgnomeui/gnome-scores.h`

Description

`GnomeScores` keeps track of and displays a high scores list. Most Gnome games use it.

A.3.10   *GnomeApp*

Library

Gnome

Header File

`libgnomeui/gnome-app.h`

Description

`GnomeApp` is a `GtkWidget` subclass specialized for main application windows. It has spaces for an optional toolbar, menubar, and statusbar. The application's "document" goes in a special slot in the center of the widget. Section 6.1 describes this widget.

A.3.11   *GtkDialog*

Library

GTK+

Header File

`gtk/gtkdialog.h`

Description

`GtkDialog` is a `GtkWindow` with three prepacked widgets: a `GtkVBox` for the dialog contents, a `GtkSeparator`, and a `GtkHBox` for the dialog's buttons. `GtkDialog` is not very useful; all Gnome programs should use `GnomeDialog` instead.

A.3.12 *GnomeFontSelector*

Library

Gnome

Header File

libgnomeui/gnome-font-selector.h

Description

GnomeFontSelector is an obsolete font-selection dialog, which is replaced by
GtkFontSelectionDialog. GtkFontSelectionDialog contains a GtkFontSelection.
Gnome programs should really use a GtkFontSelection inside a GnomeDialog because
GtkFontSelectionDialog doesn't use GnomeDialog. So, its look and feel is slightly
wrong. GnomeFontSelector shouldn't be used at all.

A.3.13 *GtkInputDialog*

Library

GTK+

Header File

gtk/gtkinputdialog.h

Description

GtkInputDialog is a dialog for selecting and setting up devices that use the X Input
Extension (such as drawing tablets). It predates Gnome and is not a GnomeDialog. So, it
looks a little funny in Gnome applications, but there is no reasonable workaround
without rewriting the widget.

A.3.14 *GtkColorSelectionDialog*

Library

GTK+

Header File

gtk/gtkcolorsel.h

Description

GtkColorSelectionDialog is a dialog containing a GtkColorSelection (see Figure A.1). Gnome applications should manually place the GtkColorSelection in a GnomeDialog or use GnomeColorPicker.

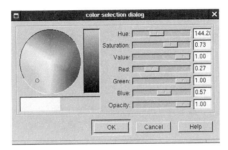

Figure A.1   GtkColorSelectionDialog.

A.3.15   *GtkFileSelection*

Library

GTK+

Header File

gtk/gtkfilesel.h

Description

GtkFileSelection (see Figure A.2) is a file selection dialog (unlike most of the other widgets ending in Selection, which are composite widgets meant to be placed inside a dialog). Unfortunately, there is no Gnome replacement for this dialog. So, Gnome applications typically use it despite its somewhat inconsistent look.

Figure A.2   GtkFileSelection.

A.3.16   *GtkFontSelectionDialog*

Library

GTK+

Header File

gtk/gtkfontsel.h

Description

GtkFontSelectionDialog is a dialog containing a GtkFontSelection (see Figure A.3). Gnome applications should use a GnomeDialog containing a GtkFontSelection instead.

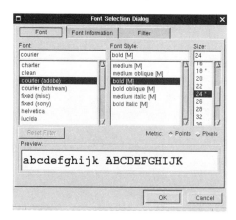

Figure A.3   GtkFontSelectionDialog.

A.3.17   *GtkPlug*

Library

GTK+

Header File

gtk/gtkplug.h

Description

GtkPlug is a top-level window that can be embedded in a GtkSocket widget running in a separate application. In other words, GtkSocket is a "hole" in one process that can contain a GtkPlug widget from another.

A.3.18   *GtkButton*

Library

GTK+

Header File

gtk/gtkbutton.h

Description

GtkButton, shown in Figure A.4, is a simple rectangular button. It's a container with one child. Usually it contains text or a pixmap, but it can contain any widget.

Figure A.4   A dialog filled with GtkButtons.

A.3.19 *GnomeColorPicker*

Library

Gnome

Header File

libgnomeui/gnome-color-picker.h

Description

GnomeColorPicker is a button containing a small colored square indicating the currently selected color. When clicked, it creates a color selection dialog to change the selected color.

A.3.20 *GnomeFontPicker*

Library

Gnome

Header File

libgnomeui/gnome-font-picker.h

Description

GnomeFontPicker is analogous to GnomeColorPicker. It's a button showing the currently selected font that displays a font selection dialog when clicked.

A.3.21 *GnomeHRef*

Library

Gnome

Header File

libgnomeui/gnome-href.h

Description

GnomeHRef is a borderless button with a hyperlink displayed on it. When the button is clicked, Gnome points the user's browser at the hyperlink's target URL or launches a new browser instance. The command used to go to the URL can be configured globally from the Gnome control center.

A.3.22   *GtkToggleButton*

Library

GTK+

Header File

gtk/gtktogglebutton.h

Description

GtkToggleButton, shown in Figure A.5, looks much like a regular GtkButton. However, it is intended to reflect a toggleable state: When the toggle is "active," the button appears to be depressed. GtkCheckButton should often be used instead of the toggle button. The check button usually looks nicer than GtkToggleButton, and it conveys that the button represents a toggleable state more clearly.

Figure A.5   Three GtkToggleButton widgets; the center one is "active."

A.3.23   *GtkCheckButton*

Library

GTK+

Header File

gtk/gtkcheckbutton.h

Description

The GtkCheckButton widget (see Figure A.6) works just like the GtkToggleButton, but it looks different (it looks like a label with small button to the left). In most cases, the check button is a better choice than the toggle button, because the toggle button doesn't give the user a visual hint that it represents a toggleable state.

Figure A.6   Three `GtkCheckButton` widgets; the center one is "active."

A.3.24   *GtkRadioButton*

Library

GTK+

Header File

gtk/gtkradiobutton.h

Description

A radio button represents one of several mutually exclusive options. Radio buttons are placed in "groups;" only one button in a group can be active at a given time (see Figure A.7). `GtkOptionMenu` can also be used to represent mutually exclusive options; an option menu is typically a better choice if there are more than a few options. A `GtkList` or `GtkCList` might be appropriate if there are a truly large number of options.

Figure A.7   A group of three `GtkRadioButtons`.

A.3.25 *GtkOptionMenu*

Library

GTK+

Header File

gtk/gtkoptionmenu.h

Description

GtkOptionMenu, shown in Figure A.8, displays the currently active item from among a number of options. When clicked, it displays a menu to allow the user to make a new item active.

Figure A.8 GtkOptionMenu.

A.3.26 *GnomeDockItem*

Library

Gnome

Header File

libgnomeui/gnome-dock-item.h

Description

GnomeDockItem is a container that allows its child to appear on a GnomeDock (see Figure A.9). Dock items can be detached from their parent window and placed anywhere on the desktop. They can also be moved around within the dock. GnomeDock lets users rearrange Gnome toolbars. GnomeDockItem provides the "handle" for dragging its child. GnomeApp uses GnomeDock internally, so Gnome toolbars can all be repositioned.

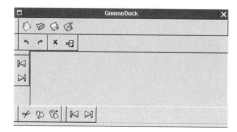

Figure A.9   GnomeDock with several GnomeDockItems.

A.3.27   *GtkAlignment*

Library

GTK+

Header File

gtk/gtkalignment.h

Description

GtkAlignment is an invisible container used to align a child widget within a space. It lets you set two factors, each in both the X and Y directions. The *alignment* is 0.0 for left-justified (or top-justified) and 1.0 for right-justified (or bottom-justified). An alignment of 0.5 centers the child in that direction. The *scale* factor determines how the child fills extra space it did not request; if 0.0, the child fills only its requisition. A scale of 1.0 means that the child always expands to fill all the available space. (Clearly, a 1.0 scale factor makes the alignment factor irrelevant.)

A.3.28   *GtkFrame*

Library

GTK+

Header File

gtk/gtkframe.h

Description

The frame widget draws a decorative frame around its child. It has an optional title describing the contents of the frame. To turn off the title, set it to NULL. It also has a configurable shadow style; the four possibilities are shown in Figure A.10. GTK_SHADOW_NONE is a fifth acceptable value for the shadow type; it turns the shadow off.

Figure A.10 GtkFrame with the four shadow types.

A.3.29 *GtkAspectFrame*

Library

GTK+

Header File

gtk/gtkaspectframe.h

Description

GtkAspectFrame is used to control the aspect ratio of its child. It also allows you to justify the child in both directions, similar to GtkAlignment. You can specify an aspect ratio or require that the ratio of the child's size request be preserved. Visually, GtkAspectFrame looks exactly like GtkFrame.

A.3.30 *GtkItem*

Library

GTK+

Header File

gtk/gtkitem.h

Description

GtkItem is an abstract base class for list items, tree items, and menu items. Items are widgets that can be selected, deselected, and toggled.

A.3.31 *GtkMenuItem*

Library

GTK+

Header File

gtk/gtkmenuitem.h

Description

A menu item is an invisible container; it is the only kind of widget that can appear in a GtkMenu. Typically, a label (or a label and a pixmap) are placed in the menu item to indicate its function. If a menu item has no child widget, it draws a separator line instead. This saves the overhead of adding a GtkSeparator to the menu item.

A.3.32 *GtkCheckMenuItem*

Library

GTK+

Header File

gtk/gtkcheckmenuitem.h

Description

GtkCheckMenuItem is a menu item that works like a GtkCheckButton. It has a small button next to its child widget, which is either active or inactive. Because it's a subclass of GtkMenuItem, it can appear in menus.

A.3.33   *GtkRadioMenuItem*

Library

GTK+

Header File

`gtk/gtkradiomenuitem.h`

Description

A radio menu item works like `GtkRadioButton`: It allows the user to choose from a set of mutually exclusive options. Because it's a subclass of `GtkMenuItem`, it can appear in menus.

A.3.34   *GtkPixmapMenuItem*

Library

Gnome

Header File

`libgnomeui/gtkpixmapmenuitem.h`

Description

`GtkPixmapMenuItem` is a Gnome widget despite its name. This widget solves a very specific problem: Namely, if a menu contains check or radio menu items, GTK+ indents the child widget of all the menu items in the menu to make room for the check or radio buttons (see Figure A.11). Gnome uses pixmaps next to some menu items; `GtkPixmapMenuItem` indents pixmaps in the same way GTK+ indents check or radio buttons. If you simply added a pixmap and a label to a `GtkMenuItem`, the pixmap would be incorrectly aligned with the plain labels in other menu items. This widget isn't really pixmap-specific; any widget can be placed in the unindented "pixmap" slot. Usually `GtkPixmapMenuItem` is created implicitly with the Gnome menu-creation functions.

Figure A.11   `GtkPixmapMenuItem` correctly positions pixmaps in a separate column to the left of the menu item texts.

A.3.35 *GtkTearoffMenuItem*

Library

GTK+

Header File

gtk/gtktearoffmenuitem.h

Description

GtkTearoffMenuItem is a "perforation" representing a spot where a menu can be "torn off" (that is, kept visible in a top-level window for easy access). Gnome menus all include a tear-off menu item by default, but users can globally disable them using the Gnome control center.

A.3.36 *GtkListItem*

Library

GTK+

Header File

gtk/gtklistitem.h

Description

GtkListItem is an invisible container that allows its child to appear in a GtkList. In other words, only list items can appear in a list.

A.3.37 *GtkTreeItem*

Library

GTK+

Header File

gtk/gtktreeitem.h

Description

GtkTreeItem is an invisible container that gives its child the ability to appear in a GtkTree. Only tree items can be placed in the tree widget.

A.3.38   *GtkEventBox*

Library

GTK+

Header File

`gtk/gtkeventbox.h`

Description

The event box widget may be the simplest container in GTK+; its only purpose is to have a `GdkWindow`. Certain operations work only on widgets with windows (such as setting the background color or capturing events). If you want to perform these operations on a windowless widget, you can place the widget in an event box and perform the operations on the event box, achieving much the same effect.

A.3.39   *GtkHandleBox*

Library

GTK+

Header File

`gtk/gtkhandlebox.h`

Description

The handle box widget (see Figure A.12) can be used to add a handle to a child widget. Dragging the handle removes the child from the window and repositions it on the user's desktop. The handle box is often used for toolbars. `GnomeDock` and `GnomeDockItem` offer a more flexible (but more elaborate) alternative.

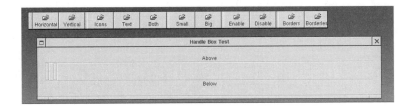

Figure A.12   A torn-off `GtkHandleBox` containing a toolbar alongside its original parent window.

A.3.40   *GtkScrolledWindow*

Library

GTK+

Header File

gtk/gtkscrolledwindow.h

Description

GtkScrolledWindow provides horizontal and vertical scrollbars for its child widget. Optionally, the scrollbars are hidden when the entire child is visible. If a child widget has a set_scroll_adjustments_signal in its GtkWidgetClass (see Section 11.2.2), the scrolled window uses it as the adjustment for the scrollbars. Otherwise, the scrolled window scrolls the entire widget using a GtkViewport. (Consider GtkCList, for example. The column titles aren't scrolled, only the list contents are. Thus, GtkCList provides scroll adjustment signals.)

A.3.41   *GtkViewport*

Library

GTK+

Header File

gtk/gtkviewport.h

Description

GtkViewport is more or less an implementation detail of GtkScrolledWindow. It contains a widget that doesn't provide a set_scroll_adjustments_signal. It provides such a signal on the child widget's behalf. See GtkScrolledWindow for more details.

A.3.42   *GtkBox*

Library

GTK+

Header File

gtk/gtkbox.h

Description

GtkBox is an abstract base class for GtkVBox, GtkHBox, and GtkButtonBox. It's an invisible layout container; Chapter 3 describes it in some detail.

A.3.43   *GtkHBox*

Library

GTK+

Header File

gtk/gtkhbox.h

Description

GtkHBox is a GtkBox that packs widgets from left to right. The left side is considered the "start" of the box.

A.3.44   *GnomeAppBar*

Library

Gnome

Header File

libgnomeui/gnome-appbar.h

Description

GnomeAppBar is a simple status bar with an optional progress meter (see Figure A.13). It doesn't have "contexts" like GtkStatusbar. Section 6.3.1 gives more details.

Figure A.13   GnomeAppBar with the optional progress bar turned on.

A.3.45 *GnomeDateEdit*

Library

Gnome

Header File

libgnomeui/gnome-dateedit.h

Description

GnomeDateEdit allows the user to edit a date and time, as shown in Figure A.14. The time-editing part can be turned off if you are only interested in the date.

Figure A.14 GnomeDateEdit.

A.3.46 *GtkCombo*

Library

GTK+

Header File

gtk/gtkcombo.h

Description

GtkCombo is a text entry box with a drop-down menu of "quick choices" (see Figure A.15). If you want to limit the user to a fixed set of options, GtkOptionMenu is more appropriate. GtkCombo allows the user to type in anything but offers some suggestions as well. GnomeEntry is a combo box that adds items the user types to the list of choices in the drop-down menu and automatically remembers the list from session to session.

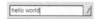

Figure A.15 GtkCombo.

A.3.47   *GnomeEntry*

Library

Gnome

Header File

libgnomeui/gnome-entry.h

Description

GnomeEntry is a GtkCombo extension that uses the drop-down menu as a history. If the user types something that isn't already in the history, GnomeEntry adds it and saves it in a configuration file to be loaded the next time the application starts up.

A.3.48   *GnomeFileEntry*

Library

Gnome

Header File

libgnomeui/gnome-file-entry.h

Description

GnomeFileEntry is a GnomeEntry that keeps filenames in its history. It also has a Browse button that displays a GtkFileSelection. It has a "directories only" mode as well.

A.3.49   *GnomeNumberEntry*

Library

Gnome

Header File

libgnomeui/gnome-number-entry.h

Description

GnomeNumberEntry allows the user to enter a number. It keeps a history of numbers entered in its drop-down menu. It also has a Calculator button to display a GnomeCalculator.

A.3.50   *GnomeProcBar*

Library

Gnome

Header File

`libgnomeui/gnome-procbar.h`

Description

`GnomeProcBar` is used in a Gnome panel applet that displays CPU and memory load, and in the GTop application (a graphical **top** clone). It displays a colored bar that can change length. It could be used to display any kind of constantly-changing value.

A.3.51   *GtkStatusbar*

Library

GTK+

Header File

`gtk/gtk.h`

Description

`GtkStatusbar` is described in Section 6.3.2. It's a status bar widget; it displays a line of text at the bottom of a window.

A.3.52   *GtkVBox*

Library

GTK+

Header File

`gtk/gtkvbox.h`

Description

`GtkVBox` is a `GtkBox` that packs widgets from top to bottom. The top is considered the "start" of the box.

A.3.53   *GnomeCalculator*

Library

Gnome

Header File

libgnomeui/gnome-calculator.h

Description

GnomeCalculator (see Figure A.16) is a simple calculator, implemented as a GtkWidget.

Figure A.16   GnomeCalculator.

A.3.54   *GnomeGuru*

Library

Gnome

Header File

libgnomeui/gnome-guru.h

Description

GnomeGuru was an attempt to implement a "wizard" widget (a series of pages representing steps in a task that the user can step through). It is an immature interface and should not be used. At the time this book was published, it appeared that a new widget called GnomeDruid would replace it in the next version of Gnome. GnomeDruid will most likely be available as an add-on module before that happens, so look for it if you need a wizard widget.

A.3.55 *GnomeIconEntry*

Library

Gnome

Header File

libgnomeui/gnome-icon-entry.h

Description

GnomeIconEntry is similar to GnomeColorPicker and GnomeFontPicker. It's a button displaying a currently-selected icon. When the button is clicked, an icon browser dialog allows the user to set a new icon. The widget used to have a text entry for typing an icon filename. That's why it's called GnomeIconEntry rather than GnomeIconPicker.

A.3.56 *GnomeIconSelection*

Library

Gnome

Header File

libgnomeui/gnome-icon-sel.h

Description

GnomeIconSelection browses icon files (see Figure A.17). It's used by GnomeIconEntry but can also be used directly.

Figure A.17 GnomeIconSelection.

A.3.57   *GnomeLess*

Library

Gnome

Header File

libgnomeui/gnome-less.h

Description

GnomeLess is a simple extension of GtkText that loads text from a file or file descriptor and displays it. It's probably a good idea to avoid this widget. Because it isn't very useful, it's likely to disappear from future versions of Gnome.

A.3.58   *GnomePaperSelector*

Library

Gnome

Header File

libgnomeui/gnome-paper-selector.h

Description

GnomePaperSelector is another widget worth avoiding. In the 1.0 release, it is strictly experimental. It allows the user to select the paper size for printing.

A.3.59   *GnomePixmapEntry*

Library

Gnome

Header File

libgnomeui/gnome-pixmap-entry.h

Description

GnomePixmapEntry has essentially the same purpose as GnomeIconEntry; it allows the user to select a pixmap. The only reason you might prefer one to the other is that GnomeIconEntry scales images to the standard Gnome icon size.

A.3.60 *GnomeSpell*

Library

Gnome

Header File

libgnomeui/gnome-spell.h

Description

GnomeSpell is a spell-checker interface. It uses the ispell program internally. This widget should be considered experimental and avoided in production code.

A.3.61 *GtkColorSelection*

Library

GTK+

Header File

gtk/gtkcolorsel.h

Description

GtkColorSelection allows the user to specify a color, using a color wheel or sliders. It makes up the contents of GtkColorSelectionDialog (refer to Figure A.1).

A.3.62 *GtkGammaCurve*

Library

GTK+

Header File

gtk/gtkgamma.h

Description

GtkGammaCurve, shown in Figure A.18, allows the user to edit a curve. It's a very specialized widget used in the GIMP. Few applications will have a use for it.

Figure A.18   `GtkGammaCurve`.

A.3.63   *GtkButtonBox*

Library

GTK+

Header File

`gtk/gtkbbox.h`

Description

`GtkButtonBox` is a special kind of `GtkBox` designed to store a dialog's buttons. It has horizontal and vertical variants. `GnomeDialog` creates a button box for you, so there is no need to use this widget directly when programming with Gnome.

A.3.64   *GtkHButtonBox*

Library

GTK+

Header File

`gtk/gtkhbbox.h`

Description

`GtkHButtonBox` is the horizontal variant of `GtkButtonBox`.

A.3.65   *gtk/gtkvbbox.h*

Library

GTK+

Header File

gtk/gtk.h

Description

GtkVButtonBox is the vertical variant of GtkButtonBox.

A.3.66   *GtkLayout*

Library

GTK+

Header File

gtk/gtklayout.h

Description

GtkLayout creates the illusion of a container with infinite size. Because X windows are limited to 32,768 pixels in size (2^{15}), most widgets also have a 32,768-pixel size limit (and child widgets must be positioned within the parent's X window). Naive widgets scroll by simply moving their GdkWindow. GtkLayout is more intelligent about this.

A.3.67   *GnomeCanvas*

Library

Gnome

Header File

libgnomeui/gnome-canvas.h

Description

GnomeCanvas, shown in Figure A.19, is discussed extensively in Chapter 12, "GnomeCanvas." It renders flicker-free structured graphics and is ideal for custom displays.

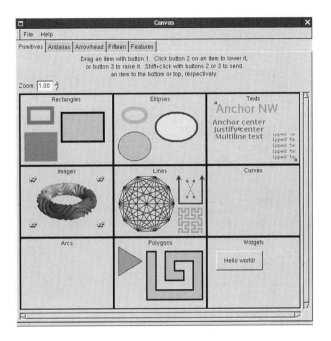

Figure A.19   GnomeCanvas.

A.3.68   *GnomeIconList*

Library

Gnome

Header File

`libgnomeui/gnome-icon-list.h`

Description

`GnomeIconList`, shown in Figure A.20, is used in the Gnome file manager. It displays icons and their names; users can select groups of icons by rubberbanding.

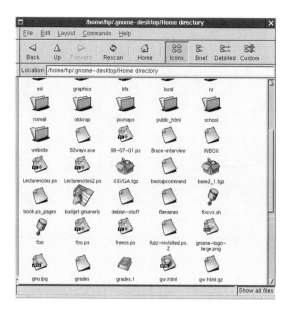

Figure A.20   Gnome file manager, demonstrating `GnomeIconList`.

A.3.69   *GnomeDockBand*

Library

Gnome

Header File

`libgnomeui/gnome-dock-band.h`

Description

GnomeDockBand contains one row or column of `GnomeDockItems`; a GnomeDock in turn contains one or more `GnomeDockBands`. See the `GnomeDockItem` entry (Section A.3.26) for details and a screen shot.

A.3.70   *GnomeDock*

Library

Gnome

Header File

libgnomeui/gnome-dock.h

Description

GnomeDock collects GnomeDockBands, which in turn hold GnomeDockItems. GnomeDock allows users to reposition toolbars and other application components. See the GnomeDockItem entry (Section A.3.26) for details and a screen shot.

A.3.71   *GtkCList*

Library

GTK+

Header File

gtk/gtkclist.h

Description

GtkCList (see Figure A.21) is a list-with-columns widget; it is also the base class for GtkCTree. GtkCList displays text and/or a pixmap in each cell; it *cannot* hold child widgets in its cells. GtkCList is only a container because it uses widgets for the column headings. You may prefer GtkList, which can have child widgets as list items but is less efficient and has a maximum list size of 32,768 pixels.

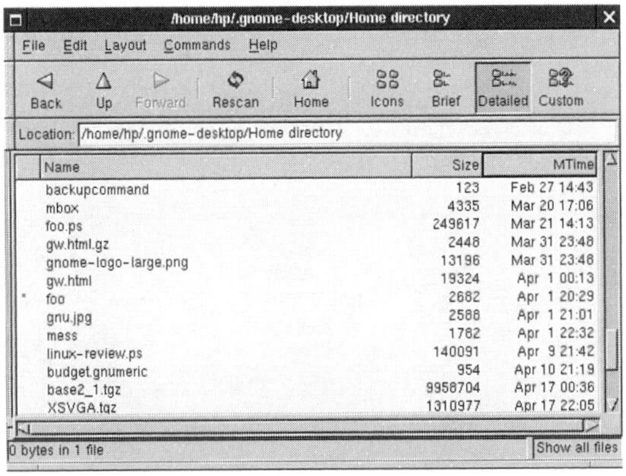

Figure A.21   The Gnome file manager's list view uses GtkCList.

A.3.72 *GtkCTree*

Library

GTK+

Header File

gtk/gtkctree.h

Description

GtkCTree is similar to GtkCList, but (unsurprisingly) it displays a tree with expandable nodes instead of a simple list (see Figure A.22). GtkTree is a more flexible tree widget (it can have arbitrary widgets in the tree cells), but it is less efficient and is limited to 32,768 pixels.

Figure A.22 GtkCTree.

A.3.73   *GtkFixed*

Library

GTK+

Header File

gtk/gtkfixed.h

Description

The GtkFixed container allows you to position child widgets at absolute coordinates. It always gives child widgets exactly their requested size. This widget is for masochists; it doesn't do anything automatically. You should almost always use another layout widget instead. (If you think you need the fixed widget, consider asking for help; a real layout widget can probably be made to work.)

A.3.74   *GtkNotebook*

Library

GTK+

Header File

gtk/gtknotebook.h

Description

A notebook widget presents the user with several pages. The user can move a page to the top by selecting its tab (see Figure A.23). Each child added to GtkNotebook becomes a page. You can also specify widgets to use for the tab labels. It is generally considered bad practice to have more than a single row of tabs, but GtkNotebook allows it. It is also possible to position the tabs on the left, right, or bottom of the notebook, but you should always leave them on top for interface consistency.

Figure A.23   GtkNotebook.

A.3.75   *GtkFontSelection*

Library

GTK+

Header File

gtk/gtkfontsel.h

Description

GtkFontSelection is a composite widget that allows the user to select a font from
among the fonts available on the system. GtkFontSelectionDialog contains an instance
of GtkFontSelection. Gnome applications should place a GtkFontSelection in a
GnomeDialog.

A.3.76   *GtkPaned*

Library

GTK+

Header File

gtk/gtkpaned.h

Description

The GtkPaned widget, shown in Figure A.24, divides an area into two user-resizable
sections. It has horizontal and vertical variants.

Figure A.24   Horizontal and vertical GtkPaned widgets.

A.3.77   *GtkHPaned*

Library

GTK+

Header File

gtk/gtkhpaned.h

Description

GtkHPaned is the horizontal variant of GtkPaned. It allows the user to divide a horizontal space between GtkHPaned's two child widgets.

A.3.78   *GtkVPaned*

Library

GTK+

Header File

gtk/gtkvpaned.h

Description

GtkVPaned is the vertical variant of GtkPaned. It allows the user to divide a vertical space between GtkVPaned's two child widgets.

A.3.79   *GtkList*

Library

GTK+

Header File

gtk/gtklist.h

Description

GtkList displays a list of items. Each item is a GtkListItem; GtkListItem is a container that can hold any kind of widget. The size of a GtkList is limited because list items are placed at fixed coordinates in the list's GdkWindow, and scrolling is achieved by moving the GdkWindow. GdkWindow has a maximum size of 32,768 pixels, and any list item positioned outside that range is invisible. GtkCList overcomes this limitation but is unable to contain arbitrary widgets.

A.3.80 *GtkMenuShell*

Library

GTK+

Header File

gtk/gtkmenushell.h

Description

GtkMenuShell is an abstract base class for widgets that contain GtkMenuItems. Its two subclasses are GtkMenu and GtkMenuBar.

A.3.81 *GtkMenuBar*

Library

GTK+

Header File

gtk/gtkmenubar.h

Description

GtkMenuBar is a menu bar. It contains one or more menu items. Normally, each menu item will have a submenu (that is, a GtkMenu with more menu items). For example, the menu bar might have a menu item called File, with a submenu containing the menu items Open and Quit.

A.3.82 *GtkMenu*

Library

GTK+

Header File

gtk/gtkmenu.h

Description

GtkMenu contains menu items. GtkMenu is unique because it shouldn't be shown (with gtk_widget_show()) by the programmer. Menus are displayed in response to user actions.

A.3.83   *GtkPacker*

Library

GTK+

Header File

gtk/gtkpacker.h

Description

GtkPacker is a layout container inspired by the Tk toolkit. If you're familiar with that toolkit, you might find it easier to use than the standard GTK+ layout containers.

A.3.84   *GtkSocket*

Library

GTK+

Header File

gtk/gtksocket.h

Description

GtkSocket is a "hole" in one application that allows a GtkPlug from a second application to be embedded.

A.3.85   *GtkTable*

Library

GTK+

Header File

gtk/gtktable.h

Description

Section 3.2.3 describes GtkTable in some detail. It's one of the most important GTK+ layout widgets.

A.3.86 *GtkTed*

Library

Gnome

Header File

libgnomeui/gtk-ted.h

Description

GtkTed is a relic from the early days of Gnome. "Ted" stands for "table editor." It's a kind of primitive GUI builder. There are at least two advanced projects to write good GUI builders (Glade and GLE), so this widget should be ignored. It will disappear in a future version of libgnomeui.

A.3.87 *GtkToolbar*

Library

GTK+

Header File

gtk/gtktoolbar.h

Description

No surprises here: GtkToolbar is a toolbar widget. Gnome applications will usually use the Gnome helper functions instead of creating a toolbar directly, as described in Chapter 6, "The Main Window: GnomeApp."

A.3.88 *GtkTree*

Library

GTK+

Header File

gtk/gtktree.h

Description

GtkTree is to GtkCTree as GtkList is to GtkCList. In other words, GtkTree is more flexible than GtkCTree—tree items can contain any widget—but it's also a bit slower than GtkCTree and holds only a limited number of items. The maximum number of items depends on the height of the rows. The total row height must fit inside a GdkWindow, which means 32,768 pixels. See Figure A.25.

Figure A.25   GtkTree.

A.3.89   *GnomeAnimator*

Library

Gnome

Header File

libgnomeui/gnome-animator.h

Description

GnomeAnimator displays a series of images, creating an animation. It has a "loop mode" and a "play once" mode. The GnomeAnimator API is marked "immature" in Gnome 1.0 and may change incompatibly in future versions; it is an experimental widget.

A.3.90 *GnomePixmap*

Library

Gnome

Header File

libgnomeui/gnome-pixmap.h

Description

GnomePixmap should be preferred to GtkPixmap even though it has the same purpose. GnomePixmap is a bit smarter about visuals. It can also load images from many different formats, using Imlib; so it's more convenient to use.

A.3.91 *GnomeStock*

Library

Gnome

Header File

libgnomeui/gnome-stock.h

Description

GnomeStock is a container that wraps a GnomePixmap. It automatically creates "insensitive" and "focused" copies of the pixmap to reflect the widget state. It can be set to one of the Gnome stock pixmap macros, such as GNOME_STOCK_PIXMAP_CUT (small picture of scissors), GNOME_STOCK_PIXMAP_PRINT (a little printer), and so on. You can also register new stock pixmaps specific to your application at runtime. Gnome uses this widget internally when creating menus and toolbars using a GnomeUIInfo template (see Section 6.2).

A.3.92 *GtkMisc*

Library

GTK+

Header File

gtk/gtkmisc.h

Description

The descriptively-named (or not) GtkMisc abstract base class allows you to set the alignment and padding of its subclasses. *Alignment* is a float between 0.0 and 1.0, where 0.0 is left-justified, 0.5 is centered, and 1.0 is right-justified. Alignment matters only if GtkMisc receives a size allocation larger than its size request. The alignment locates the natural bounding box of the widget within its actual bounding box. *Padding* is a number of pixels to add to the widget's size request. The widget will then leave those pixels blank.

You can make widgets that do not derive from GtkMisc "alignable" in the same way by placing them in a GtkAlignment container.

A.3.93   *GtkLabel*

Library

GTK+

Header File

gtk/gtklabel.h

Description

GtkLabel simply displays a text string. If the text string contains newlines, GtkLabel displays multiple lines. Labels honor the alignment parameter from their parent class (GtkMisc). You can use this to center the text or move it to the left or right. Alignment is not the same as justification. Justification defines the position of multiple lines with respect to each other. Left-justified means that each line starts in the same place. Right-justified means that each line ends in the same place. Center-justified means that each line is centered around the same imaginary vertical line. Justification has no meaning for one-line labels. Alignment set with gtk_misc_set_alignment() positions the entire block of text within its size allocation. Alignment matters only if the label receives more space than it requested (it will request just enough to hold the text block). Labels are GTK_NO_WINDOW widgets (which means that they don't receive events and draw on their parent's background).

A.3.94   *GtkAccelLabel*

Library

GTK+

Header File

gtk/gtkaccellabel.h

Description

GtkAccelLabel is associated with some other widget. It displays the accelerator key for that widget as part of the label.

A.3.95   *GtkClock*

Library

Gnome

Header File

libgnomeui/gtk-clock.h

Description

GtkClock is a label that displays the time. It can optionally update the time periodically (just like a clock!).

A.3.96   *GtkTipsQuery*

Library

GTK+

Header File

gtk/gtktipsquery.h

Description

GtkTipsQuery is a label that displays tooltips. It also has "What's this?" functionality. You call gtk_tips_query_start() to switch to query mode. In query mode, the cursor is changed to a question mark. As the mouse moves over widgets in the application, the GtkTipsQuery displays their tooltips. GtkTipsQuery emits a "widget_selected" signal if the user clicks a widget; you can use this to display more extensive help for that widget. You might store the more extensive help as the "private" component of a GtkTooltip, or you might use gtk_object_set_data() to store some kind of application-specific help information.

A.3.97   *GtkArrow*

Library

GTK+

Header File

gtk/gtkarrow.h

Description

GtkArrow displays an arrow. It's a very simple GTK_NO_WINDOW widget that doesn't even receive events. In the default theme, an arrow is simply a triangle.

A.3.98   *GtkImage*

Library

GTK+

Header File

gtk/gtkimage.h

Description

GtkImage displays a GdkImage in a widget. It's only useful if you already have a GdkImage. To display a fixed image, you usually want GnomePixmap.

A.3.99   *GtkPixmap*

Library

GTK+

Header File

gtk/gtkpixmap.h

Description

GtkPixmap displays a GdkPixmap. If you're using Gnome, use GnomePixmap for the reasons given in its description.

A.3.100   *GtkCalendar*

Library

GTK+

Header File

gtk/gtkcalendar.h

Description

GtkCalendar, shown in Figure A.26, displays a calendar page (one month). It allows users to select a date. GnomeDateEdit uses GtkCalendar in a pop-up menu.

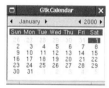

Figure A.26   GtkCalendar is Y2K-compliant!

A.3.101   *GtkDrawingArea*

Library

GTK+

Header File

gtk/gtkdrawingarea.h

Description

GtkDrawingArea is a thin wrapper around GdkWindow; it gives you a blank area to draw on. Normally, you would connect to its "configure_event" signal to catch changes in the size of the area and then do your drawing in an "expose_event" handler. To eliminate flicker, you might keep a GdkPixmap equal in size to the drawing area and draw to the pixmap. In your "expose_event" handler, simply copy the exposed region from the pixmap to the drawing area.

For high-level graphics, GnomeCanvas can be much more convenient to use.

A.3.102   *GtkCurve*

Library

GTK+

Header File

gtk/gtkcurve.h

Description

GtkCurve is used to display the curve in the GtkGammaCurve widget. It's a drawing area extension with curve-drawing capabilities. You probably won't find a use for this widget.

A.3.103   *GtkDial*

Library

GTK+

Header File

gtk/gtkdial.h

Description

GtkDial is a "speedometer" display (see Figure A.27). By default, the user can drag the "needle" around, changing the dial's value. GtkDial also has a "view only" mode.

Figure A.27   The GtkDial widget.

A.3.104 *GtkEditable*

Library

GTK+

Header File

gtk/gtkeditable.h

Description

GtkEditable is an abstract base class for widgets that allows the user to edit text. The base class interface allows cursor positioning, retrieving characters, and so on. It also includes the "changed" signal, which you can use to detect user input.

A.3.105 *GtkEntry*

Library

GTK+

Header File

gtk/gtkentry.h

Description

GtkEntry allows the user to enter a single line of text (see Figure A.28). It has a "password" mode in which the text in the entry is replaced by asterisks.

Figure A.28 GtkEntry allows the user to enter a line of text.

A.3.106 *GtkSpinButton*

Library

GTK+

Header File

gtk/gtkspinbutton.h

Description

GtkSpinButton is a GtkEntry customized to allow the user to enter a number. Spin buttons add up and down arrows to the entry, so the user can rapidly spin through the possible values (see Figure A.29).

Figure A.29   GtkSpinButton.

A.3.107   *GtkText*

Library

GTK+

Header File

gtk/gtktext.h

Description

GtkText, shown in Figure A.30, is a text widget. It can display text and offers simple text-editing facilities.

Two questions about the text widget are *very* frequently asked on the GTK+ mailing lists:

- Does the text widget support horizontal scrolling?
- The text widget doesn't seem very powerful. Are there plans to replace it?

The text widget doesn't support horizontal scrolling; instead, it wraps lines. It isn't very powerful, and the code is difficult to maintain; it will most likely be replaced in Gtk 1.4 as part of the move to Unicode.

```
gtk_clist_set_column_min_width (GTK_CLIST (clist), 3, 50);
gtk_clist_set_selection_mode (GTK_CLIST (clist), GTK_SELECTION_EXTE
NDED);
gtk_clist_set_column_justification (GTK_CLIST (clist), 1,
                                    GTK_JUSTIFY_RIGHT);
gtk_clist_set_column_justification (GTK_CLIST (clist), 2,
                                    GTK_JUSTIFY_CENTER);

for (i = 0; i < TESTGTK_CLIST_COLUMNS; i++)

  {
    texts[i] = text[i];
    sprintf (text[i], "Column %d", i);
  }

sprintf (text[1], "Right");
sprintf (text[2], "Center");

col1.red   = 56000;
col1.green = 0;
col1.blue  = 0;
col2.red   = 0;
col2.green = 56000;
col2.blue  = 32000;

style = gtk_style_new ();
```

Figure A.30   GtkText.

A.3.108 *GtkRuler*

Library

GTK+

Header File

gtk/gtkruler.h

Description

GtkRuler (see Figure A.31) is an abstract base class for the horizontal and vertical ruler widgets. The ruler widgets are used in the GIMP to display image dimensions.

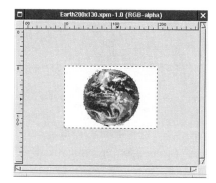

Figure A.31   GtkHRuler and GtkVRuler, as used in the GIMP.

A.3.109 *GtkHRuler*

Library

GTK+

Header File

gtk/gtkhruler.h

Description

This is the horizontal variant of GtkRuler.

A.3.110 *GtkVRuler*

Library

GTK+

Header File

gtk/gtkvruler.h

Description

This is the vertical variant of GtkRuler.

A.3.111 *GtkRange*

Library

GTK+

Header File

gtk/gtkrange.h

Description

GtkRange is an abstract base class for "slider" widgets. These widgets modify a numeric value as a "slider" is moved in a "trough." The two subclasses of GtkRange are GtkScale, used to allow the user to enter a numeric value, and GtkScrollbar, the GTK+ scrollbar widget.

A.3.112 *GtkScale*

Library

GTK+

Header File

gtk/gtkscale.h

Description

GtkScale allows the user to enter a numeric value by moving a slider (see Figure A.32). It can display the current value above the slider. You can turn this off if the exact value isn't relevant or if you want to provide feedback in some other way. GtkScale is an abstract base class; you must instantiate its vertical or horizontal variant.

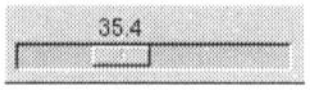

Figure A.32   The GtkScale widget.

A.3.113   *GtkHScale*

Library

GTK+

Header File

gtk/gtkhscale.h

Description

GtkHScale is the horizontal variant of GtkScale.

A.3.114   *GtkVScale*

Library

GTK+

Header File

gtk/gtkvscale.h

Description

GtkVScale is the vertical variant of GtkScale.

A.3.115   *GtkScrollbar*

Library

GTK+

Header File

gtk/gtkscrollbar.h

Description

GtkScrollbar is an abstract base class that gives horizontal and vertical scrollbars a
common interface.

A.3.116   *GtkHScrollbar*

Library

GTK+

Header File

gtk/gtkhscrollbar.h

Description

A horizontal scrollbar.

A.3.117   *GtkVScrollbar*

Library

GTK+

Header File

gtk/gtkvscrollbar.h

Description

A vertical scrollbar.

A.3.118   *GtkSeparator*

Library

GTK+

Header File

gtk/gtkseparator.h

Description

The GtkSeparator widget is a divider line that you can use to make your interface more attractive. For example, a GtkHSeparator is used to divide the contents of a GnomeDialog from its buttons.

A.3.119 *GtkHSeparator*

Library

GTK+

Header File

gtk/gtkhseparator.h

Description

This is the horizontal variant of GtkSeparator.

A.3.120 *GtkVSeparator*

Library

GTK+

Header File

gtk/gtkvseparator.h

Description

This is the vertical variant of GtkSeparator.

A.3.121 *GtkPreview*

Library

GTK+

Header File

gtk/gtkpreview.h

Description

GtkPreview displays an RGB image. The GIMP uses it to display a preview of the effects of an image transformation.

A.3.122 *GtkProgress*

Library

GTK+

Header File

gtk/gtkprogress.h

Description

GtkProgress is an abstract base class for progress displays. In GTK+ 1.2, only one concrete subclass exists (GtkProgressBar). Future versions of GTK+ may add additional progress widgets.

A.3.123 *GtkProgressBar*

Library

GTK+

Header File

gtk/gtkprogressbar.h

Description

GtkProgressBar is a flexible progress bar widget (see Figure A.33). It can display text over the progress bar. It has an "activity" mode to indicate "activity, but unknown total task size." In "activity" mode, a small block moves back and forth. GtkProgressBar is probably excessively configurable. You should try to use its default look and feel for consistency with other applications.

Figure A.33 GtkProgressBar.

A.3.124 *ZvtTerm*

Library

Zvt

Header File

zvt/zvtterm.h

Description

ZvtTerm, shown in Figure A.34, comes with gnome-libs but is not in libgnomeui. It's in a separate libzvt. ZvtTerm is simply a terminal emulator; you can spawn a child process to run inside the widget and interact with the user. ZvtTerm provides all the functionality of the gnome-terminal program that comes with the Gnome desktop environment.

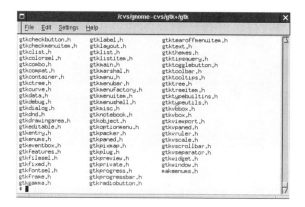

Figure A.34 gnome-terminal uses the ZvtTerm widget.

A.4   Canvas Items

A.4.1   *GnomeCanvasItem*

Library

Gnome

Header File

libgnomeui/gnome-canvas.h

Description

GnomeCanvasItem is the abstract base class for canvas items. Chapters 12 and 13 describe it in detail.

A.4.2   *GnomeCanvasRE*

Library

Gnome

Header File

libgnomeui/gnome-canvas-rect-ellipse.h

Description

GnomeCanvasRE is the base class for the rectangle and ellipse canvas items. In the future, it may also be the base class for a GnomeCanvasArc item. Section 12.4 details this canvas item.

A.4.3   *GnomeCanvasEllipse*

Library

Gnome

Header File

libgnomeui/gnome-canvas-rect-ellipse.h

Description

GnomeCanvasEllipse renders an ellipse on the canvas. See Section 12.4 for more details.

A.4.4   *GnomeCanvasRect*

Library

Gnome

Header File

`libgnomeui/gnome.h`

Description

`GnomeCanvasRect` renders a rectangle on the canvas. See Section 12.4 for more details.

A.4.5   *GnomeCanvasGroup*

Library

Gnome

Header File

`libgnomeui/gnome-canvas.h`

Description

`GnomeCanvasGroup` is a `GnomeCanvasItem` that contains other `GnomeCanvasItems`. It creates the hierarchical tree structure of the items on a `GnomeCanvas`. The `GnomeCanvas` creates a special `GnomeCanvasGroup` called the *root*; all user-created canvas items must be added below the root group. See Chapter 12 for more details.

A.4.6   *GnomeCanvasImage*

Library

Gnome

Header File

`libgnomeui/gnome-canvas-image.h`

Description

`GnomeCanvasImage` displays an image on the canvas (specifically, a `GdkImlibImage`). See Section 12.4 for details.

A.4.7   *GnomeCanvasLine*

Library

Gnome

Header File

libgnomeui/gnome.h

Description

GnomeCanvasLine displays a line segment or series of line segments on the canvas. It can also be used to display an unfilled polygon by joining the end of the last segment to the start of the first. Optionally, the line can have arrowheads at either end. See Section 12.4.

A.4.8   *GnomeCanvasPolygon*

Library

Gnome

Header File

libgnomeui/gnome-canvas-polygon.h

Description

GnomeCanvasPolygon displays a filled polygon. Use GnomeCanvasLine for hollow polygons. See Section 12.4 for more details.

A.4.9   *GnomeCanvasText*

Library

Gnome

Header File

libgnomeui/gnome-canvas-text.h

Description

GnomeCanvasText displays some text on the canvas. See Section 12.4 for more information.

A.4.10   *GnomeCanvasWidget*

Library

Gnome

Header File

libgnomeui/gnome-canvas-widget.h

Description

GnomeCanvasWidget emulates a GtkContainer; it holds a child widget and displays it on the canvas. See Section 12.4 for details.

A.4.11   *GnomeCanvasTextItem*

Library

Gnome

Header File

libgnomeui/gnome-icon-item.h

Description

GnomeCanvasTextItem is used internally by the GnomeIconList widget. You should never use it directly; it's considered an implementation detail and is subject to change in future versions of the library.

A.5   Miscellaneous Objects

A.5.1   *GnomeClient*

Library

Gnome

Header File

libgnomeui/gnome-client.h

Description

GnomeClient is a GtkObject that conceals the details of session management and provides a nice session-management API for Gnome applications. See Section 5.5 for more information.

A.5.2   *GnomeDEntryEdit*

Library

Gnome

Header File

```
libgnomeui/gnome-dentry-edit.h
```

Description

GnomeDEntryEdit is a very specialized object (see Figure A.35). It's a sort of "widget manager" that creates and keeps track of two child widgets—an "easy" and an "advanced" page. The two pages combine to let the user edit a Gnome .desktop entry, as described in Section 4.6.2. GnomeDEntryEdit is intended to be used in conjunction with a preexisting GtkNotebook. It isn't a GtkNotebook subclass itself, because you might want to use the GtkNotebook in a GnomePropertyBox. The Gnome panel and the Gnome menu editor use this widget.

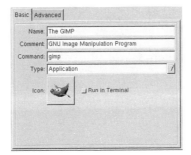

Figure A.35   The GnomeDEntryEdit object created the two widgets in this notebook.

A.5.3   *GnomeDockLayout*

Library

Gnome

Header File

```
libgnomeui/gnome-dock-layout.h
```

Description

GnomeDockLayout maintains information about the current position of items in a GnomeDock. It can load and save this information. GnomeDock uses this functionality to save and load toolbar positions. Recall that GnomeApp uses the GnomeDock widget for its layout.

A.5.4 *GnomeMDIChild*

Library

Gnome

Header File

libgnomeui/gnome-mdi-child.h

Description

GnomeMDIChild is an abstract interface. You must derive your own subclass or use GnomeMDIGenericChild in order to take advantage of the GnomeMDI object. GnomeMDI is a "multiple document interface" manager.

A.5.5 *GnomeMDIGenericChild*

Library

Gnome

Header File

libgnomeui/gnome-mdi-generic-child.h

Description

A generic implementation of GnomeMDIChild. For complex applications, you might need to write a custom implementation.

A.5.6 *GnomeMDI*

Library

Gnome

Header File

libgnomeui/gnome-mdi.h

Description

GnomeMDI keeps track of multiple documents. Users can configure how the documents are arranged in the application. They might be placed in a GtkNotebook in the same GtkWindow, or each document might have its own GtkWindow. Also, users can drag the notebook pages out of the GtkWindow, and they will be reparented into their own top-level window.

A.5.7 *GtkData*

Library

GTK+

Header File

gtk/gtkdata.h

Description

GtkData is an abstract base class for a piece of data that might be shared between multiple objects. Right now its interface is empty; in the future, there might be generic operations for all GtkData objects.

A.5.8 *GtkAdjustment*

Library

GTK+

Header File

gtk/gtkadjustment.h

Description

GtkAdjustment represents a numeric value. It can also store a maximum and minimum value, a "step increment," a "page increment," and a "page size." Some objects don't use all the fields in the adjustment, and some interpret them slightly differently. A GtkRange (including its GtkScale and GtkScrollbar subclasses) will allow the user to move the slider between the minimum and maximum values. Clicking the arrows on the end of a GtkScrollbar nudges the scroll bar by one "step increment"; clicking them with the middle button moves one "page increment." The "page size" determines the size of the scrollbar slider (it's the length of the "visible" page in the same units as the overall range). GtkAdjustment emits signals when its values change.

A.5.9   *GtkTooltips*

Library

GTK+

Header File

gtk/gtktooltips.h

Description

GtkTooltips associates some help text with a widget. If the user holds the mouse pointer over the widget for a short time, a tooltip will appear, displaying the help text. GtkTooltips can also store some "private" text; you might use this with a GtkTipsQuery to display more extensive help. Section 6.4.3 has more information on tooltips.

A.5.10   *GtkItemFactory*

Library

GTK+

Header File

gtk/gtkitemfactory.h

Description

GtkItemFactory is intended to simplify menu creation. Gnome applications should use GnomeUIInfo templates instead (see Section 6.2).

B

Table of Header Files

T HIS APPENDIX LISTS MOST OF THE HEADER FILES in GTK+ and Gnome, in alphabetical order, with a brief description of each one. Remember that Appendix A, "GTK+/Gnome Object Hierarchy," gives a slightly longer description of each widget and GtkObject.

Table B.1 **glib, GTK+, and Gnome Header Files**

Header File	Description
art_affine.h	Affine operations
art_alphagamma.h	Alphagamma tables
art_bpath.h	Bezier paths
art_filterlevel.h	"Filter levels" for image rendering
art_gray_svp.h	Renders sorted vector paths to a grayscale buffer
art_misc.h	Miscellaneous libart declarations
art_pathcode.h	Path operators (moveto, lineto, and so on)
art_pixbuf.h	Pixel buffers
art_point.h	Point data types (such as X,Y coordinate pairs)
art_rect.h	Rectangle data types
art_rect_svp.h	Bounding box computation for sorted vector paths
art_rect_uta.h	Bounding rectangles from a microtile array

continues

Table B.1   **Continued**

Header File	Description
art_rgb.h	Basic RGB drawing primitives (run-filling)
art_rgb_affine.h	Affine transformation of RGB buffers
art_rgb_bitmap_affine.h	Affine transformation of bitmaps
art_rgb_pixbuf_affine.h	Affine transformation of generic pixel buffers
art_rgb_rgba_affine.h	Affine transformation of RGBA buffers
art_rgb_svp.h	Rendering sorted vector paths to RGB buffers
art_svp.h	Sorted vector path data type
art_svp_ops.h	Sorted vector path set operations (union, intersection, and so on)
art_svp_render_aa.h	Antialiased sorted vector path rendering
art_svp_vpath.h	Sorts an unsorted vector path
art_svp_vpath_stroke.h	"Strokes" a vector path, yielding a sorted vector path
art_svp_wind.h	Winding rules for sorted vector paths
art_uta.h	Microtile array data type
art_uta_ops.h	Microtile array set operations (union, and so on)
art_uta_rect.h	Conversion from a rectangle to a microtile array
art_uta_svp.h	Conversion from a sorted vector path to a microtile array
art_uta_vpath.h	Conversion from a vector path to a microtile array
art_vpath.h	Vector path data type
art_vpath_bpath.h	Bezier-path-to-vector-path conversion
art_vpath_svp.h	Sorted vector-path-to-vector-path conversion
gdk.h	Gdk function declarations
gdkcursors.h	Gdk built-in cursor IDs
gdki18n.h	Portability wrappers for iswalnum() and iswspace()
gdkkeysyms.h	Gdk keysym names (GDK_space, GDK_Up, and so on)
gdkprivate.h	Private Gdk types
gdkrgb.h	Gdk's GdkRGB module
gdktypes.h	Gdk type declarations
gdkx.h	Declarations for Gdk-to-X mapping
glib.h	glib header
gnome.h	Includes all the public libgnome and libgnomeui headers
gnome-about.h	GnomeAbout widget
gnome-animator.h	GnomeAnimator widget
gnome-app.h	GnomeApp widget
gnome-appbar.h	GnomeAppBar widget
gnome-app-helper.h	GnomeApp add-ons, including GnomeUIInfo menu/toolbar generation

Header File	Description
gnome-app-util.h	User messages, via dialog or status bar
gnome-calculator.h	GnomeCalculator widget
gnome-canvas.h	GnomeCanvas widget, GnomeCanvasItem base class, and GnomeCanvasGroup item
gnome-canvas-image.h	GnomeCanvasImage canvas item
gnome-canvas-line.h	GnomeCanvasLine canvas item
gnome-canvas-load.h	Routine to load a PNG with alpha transparency
gnome-canvas-polygon.h	GnomeCanvasPolygon canvas item
gnome-canvas-rect-ellipse.h	GnomeCanvasRect and GnomeCanvasEllipse canvas items
gnome-canvas-text.h	GnomeCanvasText canvas item
gnome-canvas-util.h	Miscellaneous canvas–related routines
gnome-canvas-widget.h	GnomeCanvasWidget canvas item
gnome-client.h	GnomeClient session management interface
gnome-color-picker.h	GnomeColorPicker widget
gnome-config.h	Configuration file API
gnome-dateedit.h	GnomeDateEdit widget
gnome-defs.h	Miscellaneous libgnome macros
gnome-dentry.h	.desktop file handling
gnome-dentry-edit.h	GnomeDEntryEdit object
gnome-dialog.h	GnomeDialog widget
gnome-dialog-util.h	Dialog convenience functions
gnome-dns.h	Asynchronous DNS lookups
gnome-dock.h	GnomeDock widget
gnome-dock-band.h	GnomeDockBand widget
gnome-dock-item.h	GnomeDockItem widget
gnome-dock-layout.h	GnomeDockLayout object
gnome-entry.h	GnomeEntry widget
gnome-exec.h	Convenience wrappers to exec child processes
gnome-fileconvert.h	Routine that attempts to convert between MIME types
gnome-file-entry.h	GnomeFileEntry widget
gnome-font-picker.h	GnomeFontPicker widget
gnome-font-selector.h	GnomeFontSelector widget
gnome-geometry.h	Convenience functions for geometry strings (such as 1000×1000+0+0)
gnome-guru.h	Obsolete "wizard" widget
gnome-help.h	gnome_help_goto() and friends
gnome-history.h	Recently-used-file history
gnome-href.h	GnomeHRef widget
gnome-i18n.h	Gnome internationalization macros

continues

Table B.1   **Continued**

Header File	Description
gnome-i18nP.h	Library-internal internationalization (private)
gnome-ice.h	Code to handle an ICE connection
gnome-icon-entry.h	GnomeIconEntry widget
gnome-icon-item.h	GnomeIconTextItem canvas item (don't use; library-private)
gnome-icon-list.h	GnomeIconList widget
gnome-icon-sel.h	GnomeIconSelection widget
gnome-init.h	gnome_init() and variants
gnome-less.h	GnomeLess widget
gnome-mdi.h	GnomeMDI object
gnome-mdi-child.h	GnomeMDIChild object
gnome-mdi-generic-child.h	GnomeMDIGenericChild object
gnome-mdi-session.h	Session management support for GnomeMDI
gnome-messagebox.h	GnomeMessageBox widget
gnome-metadata.h	Facilities for associating data with files
gnome-mime.h	Determines a file's MIME type
gnome-mime-info.h	Gets information about registered MIME types
gnome-number-entry.h	GnomeNumberEntry widget
gnome-paper.h	Deprecated interface for paper size configuration (use gnome-print instead)
gnome-paper-selector.h	GnomePaperSelector widget
gnome-pixmap.h	GnomePixmap widget
gnome-pixmap-entry.h	GnomePixmapEntry widget
gnome-popt.h	Argument-parsing-related declarations
gnome-popup-help.h	Routine to add pop-up help to a widget
gnome-popup-menu.h	Convenience routines to create right-click pop-up menus
gnome-preferences.h	Routines to load and save certain Gnome-wide preferences
gnome-procbar.h	GnomeProcBar widget
gnome-properties.h	Experimental interface for handling preferences
gnome-property-entries.h	Auxiliary routines for experimental gnome-properties.h interface
gnome-propertybox.h	GnomePropertyBox widget
gnome-regex.h	Wrapper for regcomp() that caches compiled regular expressions
gnome-remote.h	Remote command execution (user configures the remote execution command on a per-host basis)
gnome-score.h	Routines to load and save high scores
gnome-scores.h	GnomeScores widget

Header File	Description
gnome-sound.h	Routines to play sounds
gnome-spell.h	GnomeSpell widget
gnome-startup.h	Routines to allow "locking" during session startup
gnome-stock.h	Gnome stock pixmap widgets and declarations
gnome-triggers.h	Registers events and actions to trigger when the events happen
gnome-types.h	Assorted type declarations
gnome-uidefs.h	Assorted macros
gnome-url.h	gnome_url_show() to display an URL using a user-configured method
gnome-util.h	Lots of useful utility functions
gnome-winhints.h	Gnome window manager hints
gnorba.h	libgnorba header file
gtk.h	Includes the public GTK+ headers and gdk.h
gtk-clock.h	GtkClock widget
gtk-ted.h	GtkTed widget
gtkaccelgroup.h	Accelerator key support
gtkaccellabel.h	GtkAccelLabel widget
gtkadjustment.h	GtkAdjustment object
gtkalignment.h	GtkAlignment widget
gtkarg.h	GtkArg type
gtkarrow.h	GtkArrow widget
gtkaspectframe.h	GtkAspectFrame widget
gtkbbox.h	GtkButtonBox widget
gtkbin.h	GtkBin widget
gtkbindings.h	Keybinding support for GTK_RUN_ACTION signals
gtkbox.h	GtkBox widget
gtkbutton.h	GtkButton widget
gtkcalendar.h	GtkCalendar widget
gtkcauldron.h	Experimental dialog-creation routines
gtkcheckbutton.h	GtkCheckButton widget
gtkcheckmenuitem.h	GtkCheckMenuItem widget
gtkclist.h	GtkCList widget
gtkcolorsel.h	GtkColorSelection widget
gtkcombo.h	GtkCombo widget
gtkcompat.h	Compatibility macros for renamed or removed functions
gtkcontainer.h	GtkContainer widget
gtkctree.h	GtkCTree widget
gtkcurve.h	GtkCurve widget
gtkdata.h	GtkData object

continues

Table B.1 **Continued**

Header File	Description
gtkdial.h	GtkDial widget
gtkdialog.h	GtkDialog widget
gtkdnd.h	GTK+ drag-and-drop interface
gtkdrawingarea.h	GtkDrawingArea widget
gtkeditable.h	GtkEditable widget
gtkentry.h	GtkEntry widget
gtkenums.h	Enumerations used in GTK+
gtkeventbox.h	GtkEventBox widget
gtkfeatures.h	Macros to identify GTK+ library version
gtkfilesel.h	GtkFileSelection widget
gtkfixed.h	GtkFixed widget
gtkfontsel.h	GtkFontSelection widget
gtkframe.h	GtkFrame widget
gtkgamma.h	GtkGammaCurve widget
gtkgc.h	Graphics context cache interface
gtkhandlebox.h	GtkHandleBox widget
gtkhbbox.h	GtkHButtonBox widget
gtkhbox.h	GtkHBox widget
gtkhpaned.h	GtkHPaned widget
gtkhruler.h	GtkHRuler widget
gtkhscale.h	GtkHScale widget
gtkhscrollbar.h	GtkHScrollbar widget
gtkhseparator.h	GtkHSeparator widget
gtkimage.h	GtkImage widget
gtkinputdialog.h	GtkInputDialog widget
gtkintl.h	GTK+ internationalization
gtkitem.h	GtkItem widget
gtkitemfactory.h	GtkItemFactory object
gtklabel.h	GtkLabel widget
gtklayout.h	GtkLayout widget
gtklist.h	GtkList widget
gtklistitem.h	GtkListItem widget
gtkmain.h	GTK+ main loop
gtkmarshal.h	GTK+ signal marshallers
gtkmenu.h	GtkMenu widget
gtkmenubar.h	GtkMenuBar widget
gtkmenufactory.h	GtkMenuFactory (use item factory instead)
gtkmenuitem.h	GtkMenuItem widget
gtkmenushell.h	GtkMenuShell widget
gtkmisc.h	GtkMisc widget

Header File	Description
gtknotebook.h	GtkNotebook widget
gtkobject.h	GtkObject base class
gtkoptionmenu.h	GtkOptionMenu widget
gtkpacker.h	GtkPacker widget
gtkpaned.h	GtkPaned widget
gtkpixmap.h	GtkPixmap widget
gtkpixmapmenuitem.h	GtkPixmapMenuItem widget
gtkplug.h	GtkPlug widget
gtkpreview.h	GtkPreview widget
gtkprogress.h	GtkProgress widget
gtkprogressbar.h	GtkProgressBar widget
gtkradiobutton.h	GtkRadioButton widget
gtkradiomenuitem.h	GtkRadioMenuItem widget
gtkrange.h	GtkRange widget
gtkrc.h	GTK+ rc file parsing
gtkruler.h	GtkRuler widget
gtkscale.h	GtkScale widget
gtkscrollbar.h	GtkScrollbar widget
gtkscrolledwindow.h	GtkScrolledWindow widget
gtkselection.h	Selection-handling routines
gtkseparator.h	GtkSeparator widget
gtksignal.h	Signal-related declarations
gtksocket.h	GtkSocket widget
gtkspinbutton.h	GtkSpinButton widget
gtkstatusbar.h	GtkStatusbar widget
gtkstyle.h	GtkStyle type and themed drawing routines
gtktable.h	GtkTable widget
gtktearoffmenuitem.h	GtkTearoffMenuItem widget
gtktext.h	GtkText widget
gtkthemes.h	Theme engine data type
gtktipsquery.h	GtkTipsQuery widget
gtktogglebutton.h	GtkToggleButton widget
gtktoolbar.h	GtkToolbar widget
gtktooltips.h	GtkTooltips object
gtktree.h	GtkTree widget
gtktreeitem.h	GtkTreeItem widget
gtktypebuiltins.h	GTK+ built-in type IDs
gtktypeutils.h	GTK+ type system routines
gtkvbbox.h	GtkVButtonBox widget
gtkvbox.h	GtkVBox widget
gtkviewport.h	GtkViewport widget

continues

Table B.1 **Continued**

Header File	Description
gtkvpaned.h	GtkVPaned widget
gtkvruler.h	GtkVRuler widget
gtkvscale.h	GtkVScale widget
gtkvscrollbar.h	GtkVScrollbar widget
gtkvseparator.h	GtkVSeparator widget
gtkwidget.h	GtkWidget base class
gtkwindow.h	GtkWindow widget
libgnome.h	Includes all public libgnome headers
libgnomeui.h	Includes all public libgnomeui headers
zvtterm.h	ZvtTerm widget

C

Frequently Asked Questions

THIS CHAPTER CONTAINS SOME COMMONLY ASKED questions and answers, with references to the rest of the book.

C.1 Index of Questions

- How do I make my application beep?   420
- When do I need to destroy my widgets?   421
- When I turn on memory profiling in glib, my application becomes unstable. What gives?   421
- To create a custom display, I want to place widgets in arbitrary locations, or move them around rapidly, or draw to them directly. How can I do this?   421
- Why does my memory debugging tool show memory leaks in glib?   421
- I get a bunch of `assertion failed` warnings from GTK+. What causes these?   422
- Why are some things in Gnome rather than GTK+?   422
- How can I center a window on the screen?   422
- Is there a widget that does printing?   423
- When I `fork()`, I get a bunch of warnings, and my program crashes. What's going on?   423

- When do I need to call `gtk_widget_realize()` versus `gtk_widget_show()`? 423
- When creating a pixmap, I get the warning `Creating pixmap from xpm with NULL window and colormap`. What's wrong? 424
- How can I separate the GUI from the rest of my application? 424
- I don't like the default appearance of [some widget]. How do I change its appearance? 425
- Why are signals specified as strings rather than integers or some sort of macro? 426
- Why is GTK+ written in C? 426
- My motion event handler is invoked only once. Why is that? 427
- Can I move the mouse pointer myself? 427
- How do I read the pixels out of a `GdkPixmap`? 427
- I'm drawing a lot of points to the screen with `gdk_draw_point()`, and it's unbelievably slow. What's wrong? How can I render image data to the screen? 428
- In the GTK+ and Gnome source code, many functions have two variants: one called `gtk_whatever_foo()`, and another called `gtk_whatever_real_foo()`. What's the difference? 428
- How do I "gray out" a widget so that the user can't select it? 428
- I'm trying to set the background of a `GtkLabel`, and it doesn't work. 428
- I'm connecting to `"button_press_event"` or some other event signal, but the callback is never invoked. 429
- I want to use the arrow keys as a control in my application, but GTK+ keeps stealing the key press events to move the focus around. 429
- Does GTK+ have multiple inheritance? 429
- I'm getting error messages from Gdk. How can I determine the cause of these? 430
- How do I update the GUI without returning control to the main loop? 430
- How should I format code to be included in GTK+ or Gnome? 430
- Is there a GUI builder for GTK+ and Gnome? 431
- How well do GTK+ and Gnome support internationalization? 431

C.2 Questions, with Answers

C.2.1 How do I make my application beep?

Call the `gdk_beep()` function.

C.2.2   When do I need to destroy my widgets?

See Section 3.3.1 for the simple answer, and Section 9.7 for more details.

C.2.3   When I turn on memory profiling in glib, my application becomes unstable. What gives?

Normally g_malloc() and g_free() are just wrappers around malloc() and free(), with a couple of extra features described in Section 2.1.4. However, when you turn on memory profiling, they are no longer interchangeable with malloc() and free(). So, anytime you incorrectly mix the two pairs of functions, your program will crash.

If you're using the GNU C library, which comes with nearly all Linux distributions, it has a special feature that can help you debug this. Set the MALLOC_CHECK_ environment variable to 2 before running your program, and then run the program in gdb. As soon as free() gets a pointer not created by malloc(), abort() will be called.

C.2.4   To create a custom display, I want to place widgets in arbitrary locations, or move them around rapidly, or draw to them directly. How can I do this?

You're probably fighting a losing battle. Most likely, widgets really aren't what you want. Consider using a GtkDrawingArea or the GnomeCanvas to create your custom display.

If you really need interactive widgets, such as a GtkEntry or GtkButton, you can try to use GtkLayout or GtkFixed.

If you have very specialized needs, you probably need to write your own widget. Chapter 11, "Writing a GtkWidget," tells you how to do so.

C.2.5   Why does my memory debugging tool show memory leaks in glib?

glib doesn't call malloc() every time it needs a new node in a data structure. If it did, building linked lists (for example) would be substantially slower. Instead, glib caches pools of equal-sized "memory chunks" for use in these data structures. Because the chunks are still available for recycling when your program exits, they are never free()d. (Of course, the operating system will reclaim the memory, but tools such as ccmalloc and Purify will report it as a memory leak.)

To get around this, you can plug a new GAllocator into most of the data structures. A GAllocator is a pool of memory, as just described. Just create an allocator manually so that you have a pointer to it; you can then free the allocator when you're finished. Function Listing C.1 summarizes the relevant functions for GList. A quick glance through glib.h will reveal the corresponding functions for other data structures.

The name argument to g_allocator_new() is used in debugging messages; the n_preallocs argument is passed through to g_mem_chunk_new().

Function Listing C.1 **Functions for replacing the *GList* memory allocator**
#include <glib.h>

```
void
g_list_push_allocator(GAllocator* allocator)

void
g_list_pop_allocator()

GAllocator*
g_allocator_new(gchar* name,
                guint n_preallocs)

void
g_allocator_free(GAllocator* allocator)
```

C.2.6 I get a bunch of *assertion failed* warnings from GTK+. What causes these?

These come from the `g_return_if_fail()` checks at the beginning of many GTK+ functions. (They will appear only if your copy of GTK+ was compiled with debugging turned on—and hopefully it was if you're writing an application.) You will need to look at the exact assertion that failed to see what causes the warning. Here's a common one: If you accidentally access a destroyed widget or object, you will have a pointer to memory garbage. Among other things, this means that the type tag will be invalid. So, GTK+'s runtime type checks will fail.

C.2.7 Why are some things in Gnome rather than GTK+?

Historical accident, mostly. Sometimes there is a reason. For example, GTK+ doesn't include `gdk_imlib`. Therefore, it doesn't include any widgets that rely on it. In very general terms, GTK+ imposes less "policy" than Gnome; some Gnome widgets are deliberately inflexible to keep people from creating an inconsistent user interface. GTK+ doesn't take this approach. Finally, some of the Gnome widgets were considered too "experimental" to go in GTK+ at the time. However, the core Gnome widgets discussed in this book are not in this category.

C.2.8 How can I center a window on the screen?

If the window is a `GnomeDialog`, this is user-configurable, and you should not do it. In most other cases it would be a bit strange, but there are exceptions, such as splash screens. The function you want is `gtk_window_set_position()`. You can leave the window's position up to the window manager (the default), ask to have it centered, or ask to have it appear wherever the mouse pointer is. An enumeration corresponds to these settings: `GTK_WIN_POS_NONE`, `GTK_WIN_POS_CENTER`, `GTK_WIN_POS_MOUSE`. For example:

```
gtk_window_set_position(GTK_WINDOW(window) GTK_WIN_POS_CENTER);
```

You should do this *before* calling `gtk_widget_show()`, because the function affects where the window appears when it is first placed on-screen.

C.2.9   Is there a widget that does printing?

No. When people ask this question, they're usually looking for an abstract interface that draws either to the screen or to a printer. There is nothing like that in GTK+ right now. `GnomeCanvas` will probably have a feature like this in a future version.

A `gnome-print` library is available. It handles many unpleasant low-level details when dealing with fonts and PostScript. It also comes with a printer-selection dialog.

C.2.10   When I *fork()*, I get a bunch of warnings, and my program crashes. What's going on?

There are two things to remember:

- The child process must not try to use the GUI. Because it shares file descriptors with the parent, including GTK+'s connection to the X server, GTK+ will become very confused.

- The child process must be terminated with `_exit()` rather than `exit()`; calling `exit()` will shut down GTK+ and confuse the parent process. (GTK+ registers a "cleanup" function using `atexit()`.)

C.2.11   When do I need to call *gtk_widget_realize()* versus *gtk_widget_show()*?

Section 3.3.2 goes into some detail about this. But here is a brief summary:

Showing a widget implies mapping it eventually. (To be precise, it schedules the widget to be mapped when its parent widgets are mapped.) Mapping a widget means calling `gdk_window_show()` to display the widget's `GdkWindow` on the screen (if it has a `GdkWindow`—some widgets don't). To map a widget, you must first realize it. Therefore, showing a widget implies realizing it. Thus, if you show a widget, you don't need to explicitly realize it with `gtk_widget_realize()` because it will be realized eventually anyway.

There's one exception, however. To *realize* a widget means to allocate X server resources for it—most notably a `GdkWindow`. Some things you might want to do require the `GdkWindow` to exist. So, you might want to force a widget to be realized immediately. `gtk_widget_realize()` does this. Since parent widgets must be realized before their children, `gtk_widget_realize()` will immediately realize all of a widget's parents as well. One of these parents must be a top-level window, or realization won't be possible.

If you force-realize a widget, you still have to call `gtk_widget_show()` because realization doesn't map the widget.

Here's a good, but not foolproof, rule of thumb: If you're using GTK_WIDGET (widget)->window, you will need widget to be realized.

However, it should be noted that force-realizing a widget is always a mildly bad idea. It is inefficient and uncomfortably low-level. In many cases you can work around the need to do so.

C.2.12   When creating a pixmap, I get the warning *Creating pixmap from xpm with NULL window and colormap.* What's wrong?

Creating a pixmap requires a colormap. gdk_pixmap_create_from_xpm_d() requires a GdkWindow argument in order to extract a colormap. You are probably trying to use the window field of an unrealized widget, which is NULL. You might try the newer function, gdk_pixmap_colormap_create_from_xpm_d(), which accepts a colormap argument. If you pass in a colormap, its window argument can be NULL. However, using Imlib instead is a still-better solution. Imlib's pixmap routines are faster anyway.

C.2.13   How can I separate the GUI from the rest of my application?

For a variety of reasons, an application's graphical user interface tends to be an exceptionally volatile and ever-changing piece of software. It's the focus of most user requests for change. It is difficult to plan and execute well the first time around. Often you will discover that some aspect of it is unpleasant to use only after you have written it. Making things worse, graphical interfaces aren't portable across machines. Gnome works on X windows, but if your application is useful, it won't be long before someone wants to run your application on another system, have a command-line version, or have a web-based interface. You might even want to have two interfaces in the same version—perhaps the GUI and a scripting language such as Guile.

In practical terms, this means that any large application should have a radical separation between its various *front ends,* or interfaces, and the *back end.* The back end should contain all the "hard parts:" your algorithms and data structures—the real work done by the application. Think of it as an abstract "model" being displayed to and manipulated by the user.

Each front end should be a "view" and a "controller." As a "view," the front end must note any changes in the back end and then change the display accordingly. As a "controller," the front end must allow the user to relay requests for change to the back end. (It defines how manipulations of the front end translate into changes in the model.)

There are many ways to discipline yourself to keep your application separated. Here are a couple of useful ideas:

- Write the back end as a library. If this becomes undesirable for any reason, you can always link statically.

- Write at least two front ends from the start. One or both can be ugly prototypes—you just want to get an idea of how to structure the back end. Remember, front ends should be easy; the back end has the hard parts.

If one of your front ends is Gnome- or GTK+-based, an excellent choice for the other is an interactive Guile terminal. Your nonexpert end users probably won't use it, but it's a great debugging tool. You can prototype and test the back end using easy-to-write Guile bindings and then add the graphical controls only when things are working. When you're done, you'll have a scriptable application almost for free.

If your application can potentially be run in batch mode, command-line and web interfaces are also relatively easy to write. They're also useful for debugging and will keep you disciplined.

Finally, if your project is large enough to justify the bother and complexity, consider using a cross-platform front end layer to share code between GUI front ends on different platforms. Mozilla (`http://www.mozilla.org`) and the AbiSource office suite (`http://www.abisource.com`) take this approach. It might be interesting to have a look at their code.

C.2.14   I don't like the default appearance of [some widget]. How do I change its appearance?

Don't program your preferences. GTK+ unfortunately has all sorts of look-and-feel settings that the programmer can affect. For example, you can change the appearance of the "expanders" in a `GtkCTree`: They can be triangles, squares, or circles. By default they are squares. You change them by calling `gtk_ctree_set_expander_style()`.

But there's no good reason to call this function in an application—ever. Think about why you would call it—because you happen to like that expander style better. It's a purely cosmetic issue. If you do call it, you've just made your application's look and feel different from that of every other application. This is *harmful* because it confuses users and gives them a sense that your application is "unprofessional" or "not quite right."

"But I want my favorite expanders!" you might complain. Don't despair. There is a correct way to handle this situation. Variable aspects of look and feel should be configurable *at runtime* by *users*. What's more, they should be configurable *globally* for *all applications at once*. GTK+ provides themes for precisely this purpose.

Unfortunately, themes do not yet cover all aspects of look and feel. So, the temptation remains to hard-code these in your application. You must resist. If you are dead-set against the default expander style, the default dialog position, or whatever, do the work to make it configurable on the library level, and submit that code to the GTK+ or Gnome maintainers.

You have to do this on the library level. Think about it. If you provide an application-specific way to configure look and feel, nothing has really been gained. If someone likes a particular expander style, she/he has to go through each program, deciding if and how the style can be changed. Some programs will invariably be "stuck" with the default, because the authors of those programs didn't make it configurable. The resulting mess is very annoying to users.

Gnome already has solutions for a number of common cases. For example, GTK+ lets you display a dialog at the mouse pointer, in the center of the screen, or wherever the window manager wants. There is no reason to pick your favorite and use it in your application. Thus, `GnomeDialog` loads a user preference for the dialog's initial position. This preference can be set from the Gnome control center.

C.2.15 Why are signals specified as strings rather than integers or some sort of macro?

Strings are nicer. They are easier to type and less stressful for `GtkObject` authors to maintain. They don't clutter the C namespace. Typing a string incorrectly will trigger a runtime error so that macros don't improve error checking. Finally, strings are internally converted to a numeric ID so there is no loss of efficiency.

Consider the maintenance headache of using enumerations instead: Both enumeration values and their names would have to be unique across GTK+, Gnome, and third-party extensions. What a nightmare!

C.2.16 Why is GTK+ written in C?

First and foremost, asking this question in any public forum is *strongly discouraged*. Don't do it. Check the archives for several extended off-topic flame fests if you're interested.

Here are some reasons:

- The original authors wanted to write it in C, and now many C-only applications are based on it. The current authors enjoy C.

- GTK+ handles types and objects much more flexibly than C++. It is runtime-oriented, more like Java or Objective C than C++. This is convenient for GUI builders and language bindings.

- C is the lingua franca of UNIX development; most people know how to code in it.

- There are already nice toolkits for languages such as Java and Objective C. There are C++ wrappers for GTK+—several, in fact.

- C is more portable than C++. ANSI C++ is not yet widely implemented, so only an ill-defined subset of C++ can actually be used.

- When GTK+ development first started, there was no free, working C++ compiler.

Again, do not ask this question on any mailing lists, because people will not be amused.

C.2.17 My motion event handler is invoked only once. Why is that?

If you specify `GDK_POINTER_MOTION_HINT_MASK`, you must call `gdk_window_get_pointer()` to get more motion events. One motion event is sent each time that you get the pointer location. See Section 10.5.6.

C.2.18 Can I move the mouse pointer myself?

There is an Xlib routine called `XWarpPointer()` that does this, but Gdk does not wrap it. It is almost certainly a bad idea to use this feature. (In fact, it is intended for window managers only.) You might consider writing to one of the GTK+ or Gnome mailing lists to ask for another way to achieve whatever you are trying to achieve. However, you can always use Xlib routines (such as `XWarpPointer()`) by including `gdk/gdkx.h` and `gdk/gdkprivate.h` and then manipulating the private parts of the Gdk data structures. If that sounds unsavory, it probably should.

C.2.19 How do I read the pixels out of a *GdkPixmap*?

First and foremost, remember that a pixmap is a server-side resource, possibly across a network and *definitely* across some kind of socket. Therefore, you don't want to request its pixels one by one. Iterating over a pixmap that way could easily take many seconds.

Gdk wraps an Xlib object called `XImage`. The wrapper is called `GdkImage`. A `GdkImage` is essentially a local copy of the data in a pixmap. You can copy a region of a pixmap or window into a `GdkImage` with the `gdk_image_get()` routine and then get and set pixels with `gdk_image_get_pixel()` and `gdk_image_put_pixel()`. You can also access the image's data structures directly, but this is quite complicated (due to visuals, depths, differences between host and network byte order, and so on). If you modify the image, you use `gdk_draw_image()` to copy it back to a server-side drawable.

Copying a pixmap to a `GdkImage` or vice versa still involves moving quite a bit of data over the network. However, because it's all in one burst, the speed can be tolerable in many cases. Also, if the client and the server are on the same machine, and the X shared memory extension is available, Gdk will automatically set up a shared memory segment to copy the data.

Most of the time, if you plan to do a lot of image manipulation, you are better off using RGB buffers as your primary data structure (see Section 10.9.8). The functions in gdk/gdkrgb.h allow you to copy an RGB buffer to a drawable. These functions use GdkImage internally, but they are tuned to be very fast and to handle all the complexities for you.

C.2.20   I'm drawing a lot of points to the screen with *gdk_draw_point()*, and it's unbelievably slow. What's wrong? How can I render image data to the screen?

See the preceding question. You should probably use the Gdk RGB functions (see Section 10.9.8).

C.2.21   In the GTK+ and Gnome source code, many functions have two variants: one called *gtk_whatever_foo()*, and another called *gtk_whatever_real_foo()*. What's the difference?

gtk_whatever_foo() is typically a public function that emits the "foo" signal, taking care of any necessary details before and after emission. (Remember that only GTK_RUN_ACTION signals can be emitted without special actions before and after.) gtk_whatever_real_foo() is the default handler for the signal, installed in the object's class struct. Chapter 11 has many examples of this.

C.2.22   How do I "gray out" a widget so that the user can't select it?

See Section 3.3.3. Here's the short answer:

```
gtk_widget_set_sensitive(widget, FALSE);
```

C.2.23   I'm trying to set the background of a *GtkLabel*, and it doesn't work.

GtkLabel is a windowless widget; it is "transparent" and draws on its parent container's background. If you want to set the background, place the label in a GtkEventBox. The same answer applies to other windowless widgets, such as GtkImage.

C.2.24   I'm connecting to *"button_press_event"* or some other event signal, but the callback is never invoked.

There are several possibilities:

- The widget has no GdkWindow (that is, the GTK_NO_WINDOW flag is set), so it doesn't receive events (other than synthesized expose events).

- The event you're trying to monitor isn't in the event mask for the widget's GdkWindow. Use gtk_widget_add_events() to add more events to the mask.

- The widget is a container, and some child widget is "handling" the event by returning TRUE from the event signal emission. Only "unhandled" events are propagated from child to parent.

See Section 10.5.3 for more details on events and how they are passed to widgets.

C.2.25   I want to use the arrow keys as a control in my application, but GTK+ keeps stealing the key press events to move the focus around.

Key press handling is somewhat complex. You might want to read Sections 10.5.6 and 3.3.3 for a brief overview. Section 10.5.3 is also relevant.

In short, key events are initially received by a top-level GtkWindow. GTK+'s key event behavior is more or less defined by the default key press event handler in gtkwindow.c (looking at this function is instructive). It works as follows:

- If there's a focus widget, the key event signal is emitted on the focus widget. If this emission returns TRUE, as described in Section 10.5.3, processing stops.

- If any of the accelerator groups attached to the window contain an accelerator matching the event, processing stops.

- If the key event hasn't been handled yet, there are some default bindings. The arrow keys move the focus around, for example.

Thus, to override the arrow key behavior, you can return TRUE from the focus widget's signal emission, install an accelerator for the arrow keys, or connect to "key_press_event" on the top-level window and use gtk_signal_emit_stop_by_name() to end the signal emission before the GtkWindow default handler runs.

C.2.26   Does GTK+ have multiple inheritance?

No, but "interfaces" (in Java terms) or "pure virtual classes" (in C++ terms) are planned for the next version. See Section 11.2.2 for a discussion of an ugly workaround used in GtkWidget to create "activateable" and "scrollable" interfaces.

C.2.27 I'm getting error messages from Gdk. How can I determine the cause of these?

First, run your program with the −sync option. This invokes XSynchronize() to turn off event buffering. It slows down the application but causes errors to be reported as soon as they occur. Alternatively, some Xlib implementations let you turn on synchronization by setting the global variable _Xdebug to TRUE in a debugger.

Once errors are being reported synchronously, just run your app in a debugger and wait for abort() to be called. For warnings, set a breakpoint at g_logv(), which is the function called by the g_warning() macro.

C.2.28 How do I update the GUI without returning control to the main loop?

Just do this:

```
while (gtk_events_pending())
  gtk_main_iteration();
```

This code will handle all pending events and then return control to you. You can also run nested instances of gtk_main(); each call to gtk_main_quit() exits one instance. gnome_dialog_run() uses this technique to block waiting for user input.

C.2.29 How should I format code to be included in GTK+ or Gnome?

The GTK+ coding style is basically the GNU coding style (http://www.gnu.org/prep/standards_toc.html). The Gnome libraries are less consistent but lean toward the Linux kernel coding style (documented in /usr/src/linux/Documentation/CodingStyle on many Linux systems).

The GTK+ style uses two-space indentation, puts all braces on a new line, and leaves one space between identifiers and opening parentheses, like this:

```
if (whatever)
  {
    foo (arg1, arg2);
  }
```

Emacs uses this style by default.

The Gnome style uses eight-space indentation and Kernighan and Ritchie braces, like so:

```
if (whatever) {
        foo (arg1, arg2);
}
```

It also leaves a space between identifiers and opening parentheses. To make Emacs use the Gnome style, add a line like this to the top of your source files:

```
/* -*- Mode: C; indent-tabs-mode: nil; c-basic-offset: 8 c-style: "K&R" -*- */
```

When preparing a patch for any piece of free software, it's polite to match the style of the preexisting code. It's customary to include a file called HACKING in source code distributions addressing this and similar issues; read it if it exists.

C.2.30   Is there a GUI builder for GTK+ and Gnome?

A very promising GUI builder called Glade is being developed. Glade can generate source code in several languages or an XML description of your widgets. An add-on module called libglade loads these XML descriptions at runtime and creates the described widgets. The next release of the Gnome libraries will very likely include or require libglade.

C.2.31   How well do GTK+ and Gnome support internationalization?

GTK+ 1.2 supports most European and Asian languages. Gdk contains an API for loading fontsets and rendering multibyte strings (although this book doesn't cover this topic). The stock GTK+ widgets that handle text use this API and will deal with multibyte strings correctly. GTK+ also supports input methods for Asian languages. GTK+ 1.2 does *not* support right-to-left scripts or scripts that require complex ligatures and unusual line breaks. However, support for these languages is a high priority for GTK+ 1.4. For details on future plans, Owen Taylor's white paper at http://www.gnome.org/white-papers/i18n/gtki18n/ is an excellent resource.

Both GTK+ and Gnome use the gettext message catalog system to translate user-visible strings, so any string that the toolkit knows how to render can be translated into foreign languages. Section 5.2 covers this topic.

Online Resources

THIS CHAPTER DOCUMENTS SOME USEFUL ONLINE resources for Gnome programmers.

D.1 Obtaining and Compiling the Libraries

Because the exact compilation instructions can change between releases, this book will not attempt to document them precisely. You should obtain the latest stable release of both GTK+ and Gnome from `http://www.gtk.org/` and `http://www.gnome.org`, respectively, and follow the instructions that come with the distribution.

It's a very good idea to compile the GTK+ and Gnome libraries yourself, for several reasons:

- You should have the source code handy—to learn from and to refer to when documentation is lacking.

- You should compile with debugging switched on so that preconditions and assertions will be triggered if you try to use the library incorrectly. Most prebuilt binaries turn these checks off for efficiency.

- You will probably want unstripped libraries so that you can see function names and so on in your debugger.

D.2   Web Sites

GTK+ and Gnome each have home pages—`http://www.gtk.org/` and `http://www.gnome.org`, respectively.

On the GTK+ site, take special note of these pages:

- `http://www.gtk.org/rdp/` is the GTK+ Reference Documentation Project; look here for reference materials on the GTK+ API.

- `http://www.gtk.org/faq/` has the GTK+ FAQ; asking these questions on the mailing list is discouraged. Appendix C, "Frequently Asked Questions," of this book supplements the official GTK+ FAQ with still more questions; check it out as well.

On the Gnome site, have a look at these pages:

- `http://www.gnome.org/lxr/` contains browsable, searchable, hypertext copies of all the code on the GTK+/Gnome CVS server. This includes GTK+ and Gnome, as well as many applications.

- `http://bugs.gnome.org/` enables you to browse GTK+ and Gnome bug reports and submit new ones. If you find a bug, you should submit it here so that the maintainers can keep track of it.

- `http://developer.gnome.org` contains comprehensive resources for Gnome developers.

D.3   Mailing Lists

Here are some of the mailing lists that cover GTK+ and Gnome development topics:

- `gtk-list@redhat.com` is appropriate for questions about using GTK+, reading the GTK+ source code, discussion of GTK+ bugs, and so on.

- `gnome-list@gnome.org` is very high-traffic; it is the general Gnome mailing list, for discussion of all things Gnome-related.

- `gnome-devel-list@gnome.org` is for questions about the Gnome libraries and how to write programs with them. It's also appropriate for discussing the development of the libraries themselves or submitting patches that modify the libraries.

- `gtk-app-devel-list@redhat.com` is an alternative to `gtk-list` that is more focused on application development. Most things appropriate for this list are also appropriate for `gtk-list`, but `gtk-app-devel-list` has less traffic if you're concerned about that.

- `gtk-devel-list@redhat.com` is for the discussion of developing the glib, Gdk, and GTK+ libraries. It is *not* for the discussion of *using* the libraries to develop applications.

- `gnome-announce-list@gnome.org` carries announcements related to Gnome and Gnome applications. It is relatively low-traffic.

To subscribe to any of these mailing lists, append `-request` to the list name and send a message with `subscribe` *my-address@wherever.net* in the subject. For example, I would subscribe to `gtk-list@redhat.com` by sending a message to `gtk-list-request@redhat.com` with `subscribe hp@pobox.com` in the subject line.

Please ask any and all questions about GTK+ and Gnome development on one of the mailing lists or on IRC. It is inappropriate to mail the developers privately, unless you have reason to believe they have special knowledge of some particular section of code. You'll almost certainly get a faster and better response from the list anyway.

D.4   Internet Relay Chat

The two main IRC channels related to GTK+ and Gnome development are both on `irc.gimp.org`; join `#gimp` or `#gnome` to ask questions. You can also meet the library developers and other participants in the GTK+/Gnome community.

D.5   This Book

This book has a web site with errata and other information; you can find it at:
`http://pobox.com/~hp/gnome-app-devel.html`

Code Listings

T HIS APPENDIX CONTAINS COMPLETE SAMPLE code listings.

E.1 The GnomeHello Application

GnomeHello is used as an example in Part II.

E.1.1 *hello.c*

```
#include <config.h>
#include <gnome.h>


#include "app.h"


static gint session_die(GnomeClient* client, gpointer client_data);

static gint save_session(GnomeClient *client, gint phase,
                         GnomeSaveStyle save_style,
                         gint is_shutdown, GnomeInteractStyle interact_style,
                         gint is_fast, gpointer client_data);
```

```
static int greet_mode = FALSE;
static char* message  = NULL;
static char* geometry = NULL;

struct poptOption options[] = {
  {
    "greet",
    'g',
    POPT_ARG_NONE,
    &greet_mode,
    0,
    N_("Say hello to specific people listed on the command line"),
    NULL
  },
  {
    "message",
    'm',
    POPT_ARG_STRING,
    &message,
    0,
    N_("Specify a message other than \"Hello, World!\""),
    N_("MESSAGE")
  },
  {
    "geometry",
    '\0',
    POPT_ARG_STRING,
    &geometry,
    0,
    N_("Specify the geometry of the main window"),
    N_("GEOMETRY")
  },
  {
    NULL,
    '\0',
    0,
    NULL,
    0,
    NULL,
    NULL
  }
};

int
main(int argc, char* argv[])
{
  GtkWidget* app;

  poptContext pctx;
```

```
char** args;
int i;

GSList* greet = NULL;

GnomeClient* client;

bindtextdomain(PACKAGE, GNOMELOCALEDIR);
textdomain(PACKAGE);

gnome_init_with_popt_table(PACKAGE, VERSION, argc, argv,
                           options, 0, &pctx);

/* Argument parsing */

args = poptGetArgs(pctx);

if (greet_mode && args)
  {
    i = 0;
    while (args[i] != NULL)
      {
        greet = g_slist_prepend(greet, args[i]);
        ++i;
      }
    /* Put them in order */
    greet = g_slist_reverse(greet);
  }
else if (greet_mode && args == NULL)
  {
    g_error(_("You must specify someone to greet."));
  }
else if (args != NULL)
  {
    g_error(_("Command line arguments are only allowed with —greet."));
  }
else
  {
    g_assert(!greet_mode && args == NULL);
  }

poptFreeContext(pctx);

/* Session Management */

client = gnome_master_client ();
gtk_signal_connect (GTK_OBJECT (client), "save_yourself",
                    GTK_SIGNAL_FUNC (save_session), argv[0]);
gtk_signal_connect (GTK_OBJECT (client), "die",
                    GTK_SIGNAL_FUNC (session_die), NULL);
```

```
  /* Main app */

  app = hello_app_new(message, geometry, greet);

  g_slist_free(greet);

  gtk_widget_show_all(app);

  gtk_main();

  return 0;
}

static gint
save_session (GnomeClient *client, gint phase, GnomeSaveStyle save_style,
              gint is_shutdown, GnomeInteractStyle interact_style,
              gint is_fast, gpointer client_data)
{
  gchar** argv;
  guint argc;

  /* allocate 0-filled, so it will be NULL-terminated */
  argv = g_malloc0(sizeof(gchar*)*4);
  argc = 1;

  argv[0] = client_data;

  if (message)
    {
      argv[1] = "—message";
      argv[2] = message;
      argc = 3;
    }

  gnome_client_set_clone_command (client, argc, argv);
  gnome_client_set_restart_command (client, argc, argv);

  return TRUE;
}

static gint
session_die(GnomeClient* client, gpointer client_data)
{
  gtk_main_quit ();
  return TRUE;
}
```

E.1.2 *app.h*

```
#ifndef GNOMEHELLO_APP_H
#define GNOMEHELLO_APP_H

#include <gnome.h>

GtkWidget* hello_app_new(const gchar* message,
                         const gchar* geometry,
                         GSList* greet);

void      hello_app_close(GtkWidget* app);

#endif
```

E.1.3 *app.c*

```
#include "app.h"
#include "menus.h"
#include <config.h>

/* Keep a list of all open application windows */
static GSList* app_list = NULL;

static gint delete_event_cb(GtkWidget* w, GdkEventAny* e, gpointer data);
static void button_click_cb(GtkWidget* w, gpointer data);

GtkWidget*
hello_app_new(const gchar* message,
              const gchar* geometry,
              GSList* greet)
{
  GtkWidget* app;
  GtkWidget* button;
  GtkWidget* label;
  GtkWidget* status;
  GtkWidget* frame;

  app = gnome_app_new(PACKAGE, _("Gnome Hello"));

  frame = gtk_frame_new(NULL);

  button = gtk_button_new();

  label = gtk_label_new(message ? message : _("Hello, World!"));

  gtk_window_set_policy(GTK_WINDOW(app), FALSE, TRUE, FALSE);
  gtk_window_set_default_size(GTK_WINDOW(app), 250, 350);
  gtk_window_set_wmclass(GTK_WINDOW(app), "hello", "GnomeHello");
```

```
gtk_frame_set_shadow_type(GTK_FRAME(frame), GTK_SHADOW_IN);

gtk_container_set_border_width(GTK_CONTAINER(button), 10);

gtk_container_add(GTK_CONTAINER(button), label);

gtk_container_add(GTK_CONTAINER(frame), button);

gnome_app_set_contents(GNOME_APP(app), frame);

status = gnome_appbar_new(FALSE, TRUE, GNOME_PREFERENCES_NEVER);

gnome_app_set_statusbar(GNOME_APP(app), status);

hello_install_menus_and_toolbar(app);


gtk_signal_connect(GTK_OBJECT(app),
                   "delete_event",
                   GTK_SIGNAL_FUNC(delete_event_cb),
                   NULL);

gtk_signal_connect(GTK_OBJECT(button),
                   "clicked",
                   GTK_SIGNAL_FUNC(button_click_cb),
                   label);

if (geometry != NULL)
  {
    gint x, y, w, h;
    if ( gnome_parse_geometry( geometry,
                               &x, &y, &w, &h ) )
      {
        if (x != -1)
          {
            gtk_widget_set_uposition(app, x, y);
          }

        if (w != -1)
          {
            gtk_window_set_default_size(GTK_WINDOW(app), w, h);
          }
      }
    else
      {
        g_error(_("Could not parse geometry string `%s'"), geometry);
      }
  }


if (greet != NULL)
```

```
    {
      GtkWidget* dialog;
      gchar* greetings = g_strdup(_("Special Greetings to:\n"));
      GSList* tmp = greet;

      while (tmp != NULL)
        {
          gchar* old = greetings;

          greetings = g_strconcat(old,
                                  (gchar*) tmp->data,
                                  "\n",
                                  NULL);
          g_free(old);

          tmp = g_slist_next(tmp);
        }

      dialog = gnome_ok_dialog(greetings);

      g_free(greetings);

      gnome_dialog_set_parent(GNOME_DIALOG(dialog), GTK_WINDOW(app));
    }

  app_list = g_slist_prepend(app_list, app);

  return app;
}

void
hello_app_close(GtkWidget* app)
{
  g_return_if_fail(GNOME_IS_APP(app));

  app_list = g_slist_remove(app_list, app);

  gtk_widget_destroy(app);

  if (app_list == NULL)
    {
      /* No windows remaining */
      gtk_main_quit();
    }
}

static gint
delete_event_cb(GtkWidget* window, GdkEventAny* e, gpointer data)
{
  hello_app_close(window);
```

```
        /* Prevent the window's destruction, since we destroyed it
         * ourselves with hello_app_close()
         */
        return TRUE;
}

static void
button_click_cb(GtkWidget* w, gpointer data)
{
  GtkWidget* label;
  gchar* text;
  gchar* tmp;

  label = GTK_WIDGET(data);

  gtk_label_get(GTK_LABEL(label), &text);

  tmp = g_strdup(text);

  g_strreverse(tmp);

  gtk_label_set_text(GTK_LABEL(label), tmp);

  g_free(tmp);
}
```

E.1.4 *menus.h*

```
#ifndef GNOMEHELLO_MENUS_H
#define GNOMEHELLO_MENUS_H

#include <gnome.h>

void hello_install_menus_and_toolbar(GtkWidget* app);

#endif
```

E.1.5 *menus.c*

```
#include "menus.h"
#include "app.h"
#include <config.h>

static void nothing_cb(GtkWidget* widget, gpointer data);
static void new_app_cb(GtkWidget* widget, gpointer data);
static void close_cb  (GtkWidget* widget, gpointer data);
static void exit_cb   (GtkWidget* widget, gpointer data);
static void about_cb  (GtkWidget* widget, gpointer data);
```

```
static GnomeUIInfo file_menu [] = {
  GNOMEUIINFO_MENU_NEW_ITEM(N_("_New Hello"),
                            N_("Create a new hello"),
                            new_app_cb, NULL),

  GNOMEUIINFO_MENU_OPEN_ITEM(nothing_cb, NULL),

  GNOMEUIINFO_MENU_SAVE_ITEM(nothing_cb, NULL),

  GNOMEUIINFO_MENU_SAVE_AS_ITEM(nothing_cb, NULL),

  GNOMEUIINFO_SEPARATOR,

  GNOMEUIINFO_MENU_CLOSE_ITEM(close_cb, NULL),

  GNOMEUIINFO_MENU_EXIT_ITEM(exit_cb, NULL),

  GNOMEUIINFO_END
};

static GnomeUIInfo edit_menu [] = {
  GNOMEUIINFO_MENU_CUT_ITEM(nothing_cb, NULL),
  GNOMEUIINFO_MENU_COPY_ITEM(nothing_cb, NULL),
  GNOMEUIINFO_MENU_PASTE_ITEM(nothing_cb, NULL),
  GNOMEUIINFO_MENU_SELECT_ALL_ITEM(nothing_cb, NULL),
  GNOMEUIINFO_MENU_CLEAR_ITEM(nothing_cb, NULL),
  GNOMEUIINFO_MENU_UNDO_ITEM(nothing_cb, NULL),
  GNOMEUIINFO_MENU_REDO_ITEM(nothing_cb, NULL),
  GNOMEUIINFO_MENU_FIND_ITEM(nothing_cb, NULL),
  GNOMEUIINFO_MENU_FIND_AGAIN_ITEM(nothing_cb, NULL),
  GNOMEUIINFO_MENU_REPLACE_ITEM(nothing_cb, NULL),
  GNOMEUIINFO_MENU_PROPERTIES_ITEM(nothing_cb, NULL),
  GNOMEUIINFO_END
};

static GnomeUIInfo help_menu [] = {
  GNOMEUIINFO_HELP ("gnome-hello"),

  GNOMEUIINFO_MENU_ABOUT_ITEM(about_cb, NULL),

  GNOMEUIINFO_END
};

static GnomeUIInfo menu [] = {
  GNOMEUIINFO_MENU_FILE_TREE(file_menu),
  GNOMEUIINFO_MENU_EDIT_TREE(edit_menu),
  GNOMEUIINFO_MENU_HELP_TREE(help_menu),
  GNOMEUIINFO_END
};
```

```
static GnomeUIInfo toolbar [] = {
  GNOMEUIINFO_ITEM_STOCK (N_("New"), N_("Create a new hello"), nothing_cb,
  ➥GNOME_STOCK_PIXMAP_NEW),

  GNOMEUIINFO_SEPARATOR,

  GNOMEUIINFO_ITEM_STOCK (N_("Prev"), N_("Previous hello"), nothing_cb,
  ➥GNOME_STOCK_PIXMAP_BACK),
  GNOMEUIINFO_ITEM_STOCK (N_("Next"), N_("Next hello"), nothing_cb,
  ➥GNOME_STOCK_PIXMAP_FORWARD),

  GNOMEUIINFO_END
};


void
hello_install_menus_and_toolbar(GtkWidget* app)
{
  gnome_app_create_toolbar_with_data(GNOME_APP(app), toolbar, app);
  gnome_app_create_menus_with_data(GNOME_APP(app), menu, app);
  gnome_app_install_menu_hints(GNOME_APP(app), menu);
}

static void
nothing_cb(GtkWidget* widget, gpointer data)
{
  GtkWidget* dialog;
  GtkWidget* app;

  app = (GtkWidget*) data;

  dialog = gnome_ok_dialog(_("This does nothing; it is only a demonstration."));

  gnome_dialog_set_parent(GNOME_DIALOG(dialog), GTK_WINDOW(app));
}

static void
new_app_cb(GtkWidget* widget, gpointer data)
{
  GtkWidget* app;

  app = hello_app_new(_("Hello, World!"), NULL, NULL);

  gtk_widget_show_all(app);
}

static void
close_cb(GtkWidget* widget, gpointer data)
{
  GtkWidget* app;
```

```c
  app = (GtkWidget*) data;

  hello_app_close(app);
}

static void
exit_cb(GtkWidget* widget, gpointer data)
{
  gtk_main_quit();
}

static void
about_cb(GtkWidget* widget, gpointer data)
{
  static GtkWidget* dialog = NULL;
  GtkWidget* app;

  app = (GtkWidget*) data;

  if (dialog != NULL)
    {
      g_assert(GTK_WIDGET_REALIZED(dialog));
      gdk_window_show(dialog->window);
      gdk_window_raise(dialog->window);
    }
  else
    {
      const gchar *authors[] = {
        "Havoc Pennington <hp@pobox.com>",
        NULL
      };

      gchar* logo = gnome_pixmap_file("gnome-hello-logo.png");

      dialog = gnome_about_new (_("GnomeHello"), VERSION,
                                "(C) 1999 Havoc Pennington",
                                authors,
                                _("A sample GNOME application."),
                                logo);

      g_free(logo);

      gtk_signal_connect(GTK_OBJECT(dialog),
                         "destroy",
                         GTK_SIGNAL_FUNC(gtk_widget_destroyed),
                         &dialog);

      gnome_dialog_set_parent(GNOME_DIALOG(dialog), GTK_WINDOW(app));

      gtk_widget_show(dialog);
    }
}
```

E.2   The *GtkEv* Widget

GtkEv is a widget that reports events on a subwindow, similar to the xev client that comes with X.

E.2.1   *gtkev.h*

```
#ifndef INC_GTK_EV_H
#define INC_GTK_EV_H

#include <gtk/gtkwidget.h>

#ifdef __cplusplus
extern "C" {
#endif /* __cplusplus */

#define GTK_EV(obj)        GTK_CHECK_CAST (obj, gtk_ev_get_type (), GtkEv)
#define GTK_EV_CLASS(klass) GTK_CHECK_CLASS_CAST (klass, gtk_ev_get_type (),
➥GtkEvClass)
#define GTK_IS_EV(obj)     GTK_CHECK_TYPE (obj, gtk_ev_get_type ())

typedef struct _GtkEv      GtkEv;
typedef struct _GtkEvClass GtkEvClass;

struct _GtkEv
{
  GtkWidget widget;

  GdkWindow*     event_window;

  GdkRectangle   event_window_rect;

  GdkRectangle   description_rect;

  GList*         buffer;
  GList*         buffer_end;
  gint           buffer_size;
};

struct _GtkEvClass
{
  GtkWidgetClass parent_class;


};


guint          gtk_ev_get_type       (void);
GtkWidget*     gtk_ev_new            (void);
```

```
#ifdef __cplusplus
}
#endif /* __cplusplus */

#endif /* __GTK_EV_H__ */
```

E.2.2   *gtkev.c*

```
#include "gtkev.h"

static void   gtk_ev_class_init   (GtkEvClass  *klass);
static void   gtk_ev_init         (GtkEv       *ev);


/* GtkObject functions */
static void   gtk_ev_destroy      (GtkObject   *object);


/* GtkWidget functions */

static gint   gtk_ev_event (GtkWidget          *widget,
                            GdkEvent           *event);

static void gtk_ev_realize      (GtkWidget        *widget);
static void gtk_ev_unrealize    (GtkWidget        *widget);
static void gtk_ev_size_request (GtkWidget        *widget,
                                 GtkRequisition   *requisition);
static void gtk_ev_size_allocate (GtkWidget       *widget,
                                 GtkAllocation    *allocation);

static void gtk_ev_draw         (GtkWidget        *widget,
                                 GdkRectangle     *area);
static void gtk_ev_draw_focus   (GtkWidget        *widget);

static gint gtk_ev_expose       (GtkWidget        *widget,
                                 GdkEventExpose   *event);
static gint gtk_ev_focus_in     (GtkWidget        *widget,
                                 GdkEventFocus    *event);
static gint gtk_ev_focus_out    (GtkWidget        *widget,
                                 GdkEventFocus    *event);

/* GtkEv-specific functions */

static void gtk_ev_paint        (GtkEv            *ev,
                                 GdkRectangle     *area);

static void gtk_ev_paint_event_window  (GtkEv         *ev,
                                        GdkRectangle  *area);

static void gtk_ev_push_text    (GtkEv            *ev,
                                 const gchar*     text);
```

```
/* Utility Functions */

static gchar* event_to_text (GdkEvent* event);

static GtkWidgetClass *parent_class = NULL;

guint
gtk_ev_get_type (void)
{
  static guint ev_type = 0;

  if (!ev_type)
    {
      static const GtkTypeInfo ev_info =
      {
        "GtkEv",
        sizeof (GtkEv),
        sizeof (GtkEvClass),
        (GtkClassInitFunc) gtk_ev_class_init,
        (GtkObjectInitFunc) gtk_ev_init,
        /* reserved_1 */ NULL,
        /* reserved_2 */ NULL,
        (GtkClassInitFunc) NULL,
      };

      ev_type = gtk_type_unique (gtk_widget_get_type (), &ev_info);
    }

  return ev_type;
}

static void
gtk_ev_class_init (GtkEvClass *klass)
{
  GtkObjectClass *object_class;
  GtkWidgetClass *widget_class;

  object_class = (GtkObjectClass*) klass;
  widget_class = (GtkWidgetClass*) klass;

  parent_class = gtk_type_class (gtk_widget_get_type ());

  object_class->destroy = gtk_ev_destroy;

  widget_class->realize = gtk_ev_realize;
  widget_class->unrealize = gtk_ev_unrealize;

  widget_class->size_request = gtk_ev_size_request;

  widget_class->size_allocate = gtk_ev_size_allocate;
```

```
  widget_class->draw = gtk_ev_draw;

  widget_class->event = gtk_ev_event;

  widget_class->draw_focus = gtk_ev_draw_focus;

  widget_class->expose_event = gtk_ev_expose;

  widget_class->focus_in_event = gtk_ev_focus_in;
  widget_class->focus_out_event = gtk_ev_focus_out;
}

static void
gtk_ev_init (GtkEv *ev)
{
  GTK_WIDGET_SET_FLAGS (GTK_WIDGET(ev), GTK_CAN_FOCUS);

  ev->event_window = NULL;
  ev->buffer       = NULL;
  ev->buffer_end   = NULL;
  ev->buffer_size  = 0;

  ev->event_window_rect.x = ev->event_window_rect.y = 0;
  ev->event_window_rect.width = ev->event_window_rect.height = 0;

  ev->description_rect.x = ev->description_rect.y = 0;
  ev->description_rect.width = ev->description_rect.height = 0;
}

GtkWidget*
gtk_ev_new (void)
{
  GtkEv *ev;

  ev = gtk_type_new (gtk_ev_get_type ());

  return GTK_WIDGET (ev);
}

/* GtkObject functions */
static void
gtk_ev_destroy      (GtkObject    *object)
{
  GtkEv* ev;
  GList* tmp;

  g_return_if_fail(object != NULL);
  g_return_if_fail(GTK_IS_EV(object));

  ev = GTK_EV(object);
```

```
    tmp = ev->buffer;
    while (tmp != NULL)
      {
        g_strfreev((gchar**)tmp->data);

        tmp = g_list_next(tmp);
      }

    g_list_free(ev->buffer);

    ev->buffer = NULL;
    ev->buffer_end = NULL;
    ev->buffer_size = 0;

    /* Chain up */
    if (GTK_OBJECT_CLASS(parent_class)->destroy)
      (* GTK_OBJECT_CLASS(parent_class)->destroy) (object);
}

/* GtkWidget functions */

static gint
gtk_ev_event (GtkWidget        *widget,
              GdkEvent         *event)
{
  GtkEv* ev;

  g_return_val_if_fail(widget != NULL, FALSE);
  g_return_val_if_fail(GTK_IS_EV(widget), FALSE);

  ev = GTK_EV(widget);

  if (event->any.window == widget->window)
    {
      if (GTK_WIDGET_CLASS(parent_class)->event)
        return (* GTK_WIDGET_CLASS(parent_class)->event) (widget, event);
      else
        return FALSE;
    }
  else
    {
      gchar* text;

      /* The event is either on ev->event_window, or it is a key event
       * passed down to us from the toplevel GtkWindow
       */

      text = event_to_text(event);

      gtk_ev_push_text(ev, text);
```

```
      g_free(text);

      /* If it was a motion event, make sure we get more */
      if (event->type == GDK_MOTION_NOTIFY)
        {
          gdk_window_get_pointer(ev->event_window, NULL, NULL, NULL);
        }

      /* We didn't "handle" the event, just listened in on it. */
      return FALSE;
    }
}

static void
gtk_ev_realize          (GtkWidget        *widget)
{
  GdkWindowAttr attributes;
  gint attributes_mask;
  GtkEv* ev;
  GdkCursor* cursor;

  g_return_if_fail(widget != NULL);
  g_return_if_fail(GTK_IS_EV(widget));

  ev = GTK_EV(widget);

  /* Set realized flag */

  GTK_WIDGET_SET_FLAGS (widget, GTK_REALIZED);

  /* Main widget window */

  attributes.window_type = GDK_WINDOW_CHILD;
  attributes.x = widget->allocation.x;
  attributes.y = widget->allocation.y;
  attributes.width = widget->allocation.width;
  attributes.height = widget->allocation.height;
  attributes.wclass = GDK_INPUT_OUTPUT;
  attributes.visual = gtk_widget_get_visual (widget);
  attributes.colormap = gtk_widget_get_colormap (widget);
  attributes.event_mask = gtk_widget_get_events (widget) | GDK_EXPOSURE_MASK;

  attributes_mask = GDK_WA_X | GDK_WA_Y | GDK_WA_VISUAL | GDK_WA_COLORMAP;

  widget->window = gdk_window_new (gtk_widget_get_parent_window (widget),
                                   &attributes, attributes_mask);
  gdk_window_set_user_data (widget->window, widget);

  /* Event window */
```

```
    cursor = gdk_cursor_new(GDK_CROSSHAIR);

    attributes.window_type = GDK_WINDOW_CHILD;
    attributes.x = ev->event_window_rect.x;
    attributes.y = ev->event_window_rect.y;
    attributes.width = ev->event_window_rect.width;
    attributes.height = ev->event_window_rect.height;
    attributes.wclass = GDK_INPUT_OUTPUT;
    attributes.visual = gtk_widget_get_visual (widget);
    attributes.colormap = gtk_widget_get_colormap (widget);
    attributes.event_mask = GDK_ALL_EVENTS_MASK;
    attributes.cursor = cursor;

    attributes_mask = GDK_WA_X ¦ GDK_WA_Y ¦ GDK_WA_VISUAL ¦
      GDK_WA_COLORMAP ¦ GDK_WA_CURSOR;

    ev->event_window = gdk_window_new (widget->window,
                                      &attributes, attributes_mask);
    gdk_window_set_user_data (ev->event_window, widget);

    gdk_window_show(ev->event_window);

    gdk_cursor_destroy(cursor);

    /* Style */

    widget->style = gtk_style_attach (widget->style, widget->window);

    gtk_style_set_background (widget->style, widget->window, GTK_STATE_NORMAL);

    gdk_window_set_background (ev->event_window,
                              &widget->style->base[GTK_STATE_NORMAL]);
}

static void
gtk_ev_unrealize (GtkWidget          *widget)
{
  GtkEv* ev;

  g_return_if_fail(widget != NULL);
  g_return_if_fail(GTK_IS_EV(widget));

  ev = GTK_EV(widget);

  /* Hide all windows */

  if (GTK_WIDGET_MAPPED (widget))
    gtk_widget_unmap (widget);

  GTK_WIDGET_UNSET_FLAGS (widget, GTK_MAPPED);
```

```
  /* Destroy our child window */

  if (ev->event_window)
    {
      gdk_window_set_user_data(ev->event_window, NULL);
      gdk_window_destroy(ev->event_window);
      ev->event_window = NULL;
    }

  /* This destroys widget->window and unsets the realized flag
   */
  if (GTK_WIDGET_CLASS(parent_class)->unrealize)
    (* GTK_WIDGET_CLASS(parent_class)->unrealize) (widget);
}

static void
gtk_ev_size_request  (GtkWidget       *widget,
                      GtkRequisition  *requisition)
{
  g_return_if_fail(widget != NULL);
  g_return_if_fail(GTK_IS_EV(widget));

  /*
   * GtkEv always wants to be the same fixed size.
   */

  requisition->width  = 450;
  requisition->height = 300;
}

static void
gtk_ev_size_allocate  (GtkWidget       *widget,
                       GtkAllocation   *allocation)
{
  static const gint spacing = 10;
  GtkEv* ev;

  g_return_if_fail(widget != NULL);
  g_return_if_fail(GTK_IS_EV(widget));

  ev = GTK_EV(widget);

  widget->allocation = *allocation;

  ev->event_window_rect.width =
    MAX(allocation->width - spacing*2, 0);
  ev->event_window_rect.height =
    MAX(allocation->height / 5 - spacing / 2, 0);

  ev->event_window_rect.x =
    (allocation->width - ev->event_window_rect.width)/2;
```

```
    ev->event_window_rect.y =
      MIN(spacing, allocation->height);

    ev->description_rect.x = ev->event_window_rect.x;
    ev->description_rect.y =
      ev->event_window_rect.y + ev->event_window_rect.height + spacing;
    ev->description_rect.width =
      ev->event_window_rect.width;
    ev->description_rect.height =
      MAX((allocation->height - ev->event_window_rect.height - spacing*3), 0);

    if (GTK_WIDGET_REALIZED (widget))
      {
        gdk_window_move_resize (widget->window,
                                allocation->x,
                                allocation->y,
                                allocation->width,
                                allocation->height);

        gdk_window_move_resize (ev->event_window,
                                ev->event_window_rect.x,
                                ev->event_window_rect.y,
                                ev->event_window_rect.width,
                                ev->event_window_rect.height);
      }
}

static void
gtk_ev_draw            (GtkWidget        *widget,
                        GdkRectangle     *area)
{
  GdkRectangle event_window_area;
  GdkRectangle intersection;
  GtkEv* ev;

  g_return_if_fail(widget != NULL);
  g_return_if_fail(GTK_IS_EV(widget));

  ev = GTK_EV(widget);

  gtk_ev_paint(ev, area);

  event_window_area = *area;

  if (gdk_rectangle_intersect(area, &ev->event_window_rect, &intersection))
    {
      /* Make the intersection relative to the event window */
      intersection.x -= ev->event_window_rect.x;
      intersection.y -= ev->event_window_rect.y;
```

```
      gtk_ev_paint_event_window(ev, &intersection);
    }
}

static void
gtk_ev_draw_focus      (GtkWidget        *widget)
{
  GdkRectangle rect;
  GtkEv* ev;

  g_return_if_fail(widget != NULL);
  g_return_if_fail(GTK_IS_EV(widget));

  ev = GTK_EV(widget);

  rect.x = 0;
  rect.y = 0;
  rect.width = widget->allocation.width;
  rect.height = widget->allocation.height;

  if (GTK_WIDGET_DRAWABLE (ev))
    gtk_ev_paint(ev, &rect);
}

static gint
gtk_ev_expose          (GtkWidget        *widget,
                        GdkEventExpose   *event)
{
  if (event->window == widget->window)
    gtk_ev_paint(GTK_EV(widget), &event->area);
  else if (event->window == GTK_EV(widget)->event_window)
    gtk_ev_paint_event_window(GTK_EV(widget), &event->area);
  else
    g_assert_not_reached();

  return TRUE;
}

static gint
gtk_ev_focus_in        (GtkWidget        *widget,
                        GdkEventFocus    *event)
{
  g_return_val_if_fail(widget != NULL, FALSE);
  g_return_val_if_fail(GTK_IS_EV(widget), FALSE);

  GTK_WIDGET_SET_FLAGS (widget, GTK_HAS_FOCUS);
  gtk_widget_draw_focus (widget);

  return FALSE;
}
```

```
static gint
gtk_ev_focus_out      (GtkWidget       *widget,
                       GdkEventFocus   *event)
{
  g_return_val_if_fail(widget != NULL, FALSE);
  g_return_val_if_fail(GTK_IS_EV(widget), FALSE);

  GTK_WIDGET_UNSET_FLAGS (widget, GTK_HAS_FOCUS);
  gtk_widget_draw_focus (widget);

  return FALSE;
}

/* GtkEv-specific functions */

static void
gtk_ev_paint          (GtkEv           *ev,
                       GdkRectangle    *area)
{
  GtkWidget* widget;

  g_return_if_fail(ev != NULL);
  g_return_if_fail(GTK_IS_EV(ev));

  widget = GTK_WIDGET(ev);

  if (!GTK_WIDGET_DRAWABLE (widget))
    return;

  gdk_window_clear_area (widget->window,
                         area->x,
                         area->y,
                         area->width,
                         area->height);

  gdk_gc_set_clip_rectangle(widget->style->black_gc, area);

  /* Draw a black rectangle around the event window */

  gdk_draw_rectangle(widget->window,
                     widget->style->black_gc,
                     FALSE,
                     ev->event_window_rect.x - 1,
                     ev->event_window_rect.y - 1,
                     ev->event_window_rect.width + 2,
                     ev->event_window_rect.height + 2);

  gdk_gc_set_clip_rectangle(widget->style->black_gc, NULL);

  /* Draw text in the description area, if applicable */
```

```
if (ev->buffer)
  {
    GdkRectangle intersection;

    if (gdk_rectangle_intersect(area,
                                &ev->description_rect,
                                &intersection))
      {
        static const gint space = 2;
        gint line;
        gint step;
        gint first_baseline;
        GList* tmp;

        step  = widget->style->font->ascent +
          widget->style->font->descent + space;

        first_baseline = ev->description_rect.y +
          widget->style->font->ascent + space;

        line = 0;

        tmp = ev->buffer;

        while (tmp != NULL)
          {
            gchar** this_event = tmp->data;
            gint i = 0;
            while (this_event[i])
              {
                gtk_paint_string (widget->style,
                                  widget->window,
                                  widget->state,
                                  &intersection, widget, "ev",
                                  ev->description_rect.x,
                                  first_baseline + line*step,
                                  this_event[i]);
                ++i;
                ++line;
              }

            /* Bail out if we're off the bottom; the "- 2*step" is
             * needed because the next baseline may be outside the
             * redraw area but we are interested in the whole row of
             * text, not the baseline. The 2* is because line is one
             * larger than we've actually drawn.
             */
            if ((first_baseline + line*step - 2*step) >
                (intersection.y + intersection.height))
              break;
```

```
                    tmp = g_list_next(tmp);
                }
            }
        }

    if (GTK_WIDGET_HAS_FOCUS (widget))
        {
            gtk_paint_focus (widget->style, widget->window,
                             area, widget, "ev",
                             widget->allocation.x, widget->allocation.y,
                             widget->allocation.width-1, widget->allocation.height-1);
        }
}

static void
gtk_ev_paint_event_window   (GtkEv           *ev,
                             GdkRectangle    *area)
{
    GtkWidget* widget;
    gint width;
    gint x, y;
    const char* title;

    g_return_if_fail(ev != NULL);
    g_return_if_fail(GTK_IS_EV(ev));

    widget = GTK_WIDGET(ev);

    if (!GTK_WIDGET_DRAWABLE (widget))
        return;

    title = _("Event Window");

    gdk_window_clear_area (ev->event_window,
                           area->x,
                           area->y,
                           area->width,
                           area->height);

    gdk_gc_set_clip_rectangle(widget->style->black_gc, area);

    /* Clearly it would be better to cache this */

    width = gdk_string_width(widget->style->font,
                             title);

    x = (ev->event_window_rect.width - width)/2;
    y = widget->style->font->ascent + 2;
```

```c
  gdk_draw_string(ev->event_window,
                  widget->style->font,
                  widget->style->black_gc,
                  x, y,
                  title);

  gdk_gc_set_clip_rectangle(widget->style->black_gc, NULL);
}

static void
gtk_ev_push_text (GtkEv           *ev,
                  const gchar*    text)
{
  if (text)
    {
      gchar** event;
      event = g_strsplit(text, "\n", 10);
      ev->buffer = g_list_prepend(ev->buffer, event);
      ev->buffer_size += 1;

      /* See if this was the first one we added */
      if (ev->buffer_end == NULL)
        {
          ev->buffer_end = ev->buffer;
        }

      /* See if we have too many to possibly fit on-screen */
      if (ev->buffer_size > 100)
        {
          GList* prev = ev->buffer_end->prev;

          prev->next = NULL;

          g_strfreev(ev->buffer_end->data);
          g_list_free_1(ev->buffer_end);

          ev->buffer_end = prev;

          ev->buffer_size -= 1;
        }
    }

  if (GTK_WIDGET_DRAWABLE (ev))
    gtk_widget_queue_draw_area(GTK_WIDGET(ev),
                               ev->description_rect.x,
                               ev->description_rect.y,
                               ev->description_rect.width,
                               ev->description_rect.height);
}

static gchar*
event_name_line(GdkEvent* event)
{
```

```c
switch (event->type)
  {
  case GDK_NOTHING:
    return g_strdup(_("Invalid event!\n"));
    break;

  case GDK_DELETE:
    return g_strdup(_("Delete\n"));
    break;

  case GDK_DESTROY:
    return g_strdup(_("Destroy\n"));
    break;

  case GDK_EXPOSE:
    return g_strdup(_("Expose\n"));
    break;

  case GDK_MOTION_NOTIFY:
    return g_strdup(_("Motion Notify\n"));
    break;

  case GDK_BUTTON_PRESS:
    return g_strdup(_("Button Press\n"));
    break;

  case GDK_2BUTTON_PRESS:
    return g_strdup(_("2 Button Press\n"));
    break;

  case GDK_3BUTTON_PRESS:
    return g_strdup(_("3 Button Press\n"));
    break;

  case GDK_BUTTON_RELEASE:
    return g_strdup(_("Button Release\n"));
    break;

  case GDK_KEY_PRESS:
    return g_strdup(_("Key Press\n"));
    break;

  case GDK_KEY_RELEASE:
    return g_strdup(_("Key Release\n"));
    break;

  case GDK_ENTER_NOTIFY:
    return g_strdup(_("Enter Notify\n"));
    break;
```

```
case GDK_LEAVE_NOTIFY:
  return g_strdup(_("Leave Notify\n"));
  break;

case GDK_FOCUS_CHANGE:
  return g_strdup(_("Focus Change\n"));
  break;

case GDK_CONFIGURE:
  return g_strdup(_("Configure\n"));
  break;

case GDK_MAP:
  return g_strdup(_("Map\n"));
  break;

case GDK_UNMAP:
  return g_strdup(_("Unmap\n"));
  break;

case GDK_PROPERTY_NOTIFY:
  return g_strdup(_("Property Notify\n"));
  break;

case GDK_SELECTION_CLEAR:
  return g_strdup(_("Selection Clear\n"));
  break;

case GDK_SELECTION_REQUEST:
  return g_strdup(_("Selection Request\n"));
  break;

case GDK_SELECTION_NOTIFY:
  return g_strdup(_("Selection Notify\n"));
  break;

case GDK_PROXIMITY_IN:
  return g_strdup(_("Proximity In\n"));
  break;

case GDK_PROXIMITY_OUT:
  return g_strdup(_("Proximity Out\n"));
  break;

case GDK_DRAG_ENTER:
  return g_strdup(_("Drag Enter\n"));
  break;

case GDK_DRAG_LEAVE:
  return g_strdup(_("Drag Leave\n"));
  break;
```

```c
    case GDK_DRAG_MOTION:
      return g_strdup(_("Drag Motion\n"));
      break;

    case GDK_DRAG_STATUS:
      return g_strdup(_("Drag Status\n"));
      break;

    case GDK_DROP_START:
      return g_strdup(_("Drop Start\n"));
      break;

    case GDK_DROP_FINISHED:
      return g_strdup(_("Drop Finished\n"));
      break;

    case GDK_CLIENT_EVENT:
      return g_strdup(_("Client Event\n"));
      break;

    case GDK_VISIBILITY_NOTIFY:
      return g_strdup(_("Visibility Notify\n"));
      break;

    case GDK_NO_EXPOSE:
      return g_strdup(_("No Expose\n"));
      break;

    default:
      g_assert_not_reached();
      return NULL;
      break;
    }
}

static gchar*
any_event_line(GdkEvent* event)
{
  guint32 event_time;

  event_time = gdk_event_get_time(event);

  if (event_time != GDK_CURRENT_TIME)
    return g_strdup_printf(_("Window: %p Time: %u send_event: %s\n"),
                           event->any.window,
                           event_time,
                           event->any.send_event ? _("True") : _("False"));
  else
    return g_strdup_printf(_("Window: %p send_event: %s\n"),
                           event->any.window,
                           event->any.send_event ? _("True") : _("False"));
}
```

```
#define MAX_STATES 30

static gchar*
event_state_line(GdkModifierType state)
{
  gchar** states;
  gint n_active;

  states = g_new(gchar*, MAX_STATES);

  n_active = 0;

  if (state & GDK_SHIFT_MASK)
    {
      states[n_active] = _("Shift");
      ++n_active;
    }
  if (state & GDK_LOCK_MASK)
    {
      states[n_active] = _("Lock");
      ++n_active;
    }
  if (state & GDK_CONTROL_MASK)
    {
      states[n_active] = _("Ctrl");
      ++n_active;
    }
  if (state & GDK_MOD1_MASK)
    {
      states[n_active] = _("Mod1");
      ++n_active;
    }
  if (state & GDK_MOD2_MASK)
    {
      states[n_active] = _("Mod2");
      ++n_active;
    }
  if (state & GDK_MOD3_MASK)
    {
      states[n_active] = _("Mod3");
      ++n_active;
    }
  if (state & GDK_MOD4_MASK)
    {
      states[n_active] = _("Mod4");
      ++n_active;
    }
  if (state & GDK_MOD5_MASK)
    {
      states[n_active] = _("Mod5");
      ++n_active;
```

```
        }
    if (state & GDK_BUTTON1_MASK)
      {
        states[n_active] = _("Button1");
        ++n_active;
      }
    if (state & GDK_BUTTON2_MASK)
      {
        states[n_active] = _("Button2");
        ++n_active;
      }
    if (state & GDK_BUTTON3_MASK)
      {
        states[n_active] = _("Button3");
        ++n_active;
      }
    if (state & GDK_BUTTON4_MASK)
      {
        states[n_active] = _("Button4");
        ++n_active;
      }
    if (state & GDK_BUTTON5_MASK)
      {
        states[n_active] = _("Button4");
        ++n_active;
      }
    if (state & GDK_RELEASE_MASK)
      {
        states[n_active] = _("Release");
        ++n_active;
      }

    if (n_active == 0)
      return NULL;
    else
      {
        /* Not efficient, but not important */

        gchar* str = NULL;
        gchar* tmp = NULL;

        guint i = 0;
        while (i < n_active)
          {

            if (str)
              {
                tmp = str;
                str = g_strconcat(str, " ¦ ", states[i], NULL);
                g_free(tmp);
              }
```

```
          else
            {
              str = g_strdup(states[i]);
            }

          ++i;
        }

      tmp = str;
      str = g_strconcat(str, "\n", NULL);
      g_free(tmp);

      return str;
    }
}

static gchar*
event_to_text (GdkEvent* event)
{
  gchar* any_line;
  gchar* name_line;
  gchar* entire_line;
  gchar* detail;
  gchar* state;

  name_line = event_name_line(event);
  any_line = any_event_line(event);

  entire_line = NULL;
  detail = NULL;
  state = NULL;

  switch (event->type)
    {
    case GDK_NOTHING:
      break;

    case GDK_DELETE:
      break;

    case GDK_DESTROY:
      break;

    case GDK_EXPOSE:
      detail = g_strdup_printf(_("Area: %d,%d  %dx%d Count: %d\n"),
                               event->expose.area.x,
                               event->expose.area.y,
                               event->expose.area.width,
                               event->expose.area.height,
                               event->expose.count);
      break;
```

```
        case GDK_MOTION_NOTIFY:
          detail = g_strdup_printf(_("x: %g y: %g\n"),
                                     event->motion.x,
                                     event->motion.y);
          state = event_state_line(event->motion.state);
          break;

        case GDK_BUTTON_PRESS:
        case GDK_2BUTTON_PRESS:
        case GDK_3BUTTON_PRESS:
        case GDK_BUTTON_RELEASE:
          detail = g_strdup_printf(_("Button: %d\n"),
                                     event->button.button);
          state = event_state_line(event->button.state);
          break;

        case GDK_KEY_PRESS:
        case GDK_KEY_RELEASE:
          detail = g_strdup_printf(_("Keyval: GDK_%s Text: %s\n"),
                                     gdk_keyval_name(event->key.keyval),
                                     event->key.string);
          state = event_state_line(event->key.state);
          break;

        case GDK_ENTER_NOTIFY:
          break;

        case GDK_LEAVE_NOTIFY:
          break;

        case GDK_FOCUS_CHANGE:
          break;

        case GDK_CONFIGURE:
          break;

        case GDK_MAP:
          break;

        case GDK_UNMAP:
          break;

        case GDK_PROPERTY_NOTIFY:
          break;

        case GDK_SELECTION_CLEAR:
          break;

        case GDK_SELECTION_REQUEST:
          break;
```

```
    case GDK_SELECTION_NOTIFY:
      break;

    case GDK_PROXIMITY_IN:
      break;

    case GDK_PROXIMITY_OUT:
      break;

    case GDK_DRAG_ENTER:
      break;

    case GDK_DRAG_LEAVE:
      break;

    case GDK_DRAG_MOTION:
      break;

    case GDK_DRAG_STATUS:
      break;

    case GDK_DROP_START:
      break;

    case GDK_DROP_FINISHED:
      break;

    case GDK_CLIENT_EVENT:
      break;

    case GDK_VISIBILITY_NOTIFY:
      break;

    case GDK_NO_EXPOSE:
      break;

    default:
      g_assert_not_reached();
      break;
    }

  if (entire_line == NULL)
    {
      /* Assumes we always have a detail if we have a state */

      entire_line = g_strconcat(name_line,
                                " ", any_line,
                                detail ? "  " : NULL, detail,
                                state ? "  " : NULL, state,
                                NULL);
    }
```

```
        g_free(name_line);
        g_free(any_line);
        g_free(detail);
        g_free(state);

        return entire_line;
    }
```

F

Open Publication License
Version 1.0

F.1 Requirements on Both Unmodified and Modified Versions

The Open Publication works may be reproduced and distributed in whole or in part, in any medium, physical or electronic, provided that the terms of this license are adhered to, and that this license or an incorporation of it by reference (with any options elected by the author(s) and/or publisher) is displayed in the reproduction.

Proper form for an incorporation by reference is as follows:

Copyright© <year> by <author's name or designee>. This material may be distributed only subject to the terms and conditions set forth in the Open Publication License, vX.Y or later (the latest version is presently available at http://www.opencontent.org/openpub/).

The reference must be immediately followed with any options elected by the author(s) and/or publisher of the document (see Section VI).

Commercial redistribution of Open Publication-licensed material is permitted.

Any publication in standard (paper) book form shall require the citation of the original publisher and author. The publisher and author's names shall appear on all outer surfaces of the book. On all outer surfaces of the book, the original publisher's name shall be as large as the title of the work and cited as possessive with respect to the title.

F.2 Copyright

The copyright to each Open Publication is owned by its author(s) or designee.

F.3 Scope of License

The following license terms apply to all Open Publication works, unless otherwise explicitly stated in the document.

Mere aggregation of Open Publication works or a portion of an Open Publication work with other works or programs on the same media shall not cause this license to apply to those other works. The aggregate work shall contain a notice specifying the inclusion of the Open Publication material and appropriate copyright notice.

- SEVERABILITY. If any part of this license is found to be unenforceable in any jurisdiction, the remaining portions of the license remain in force.
- NO WARRANTY. Open Publication works are licensed and provided "as is" without warranty of any kind, express or implied, including, but not limited to, the implied warranties of merchantability and fitness for a particular purpose or a warranty of non-infringement.

F.4 Requirements on Modified Works

All modified versions of documents covered by this license, including translations, anthologies, compilations, and partial documents, must meet the following requirements:

1. The modified version must be labeled as such.
2. The person making the modifications must be identified and the modifications dated.
3. Acknowledgement of the original author and publisher, if applicable, must be retained according to normal academic citation practices.
4. The location of the original unmodified document must be identified.
5. The original author's (or authors') name(s) may not be used to assert or imply endorsement of the resulting document without the original author's (or authors') permission.

F.5 Good-Practice Recommendations

In addition to the requirements of this license, it is requested from and strongly recommended of redistributors that:

1. If you are distributing Open Publication works on hardcopy or CD-ROM, you provide email notification to the authors of your intent to redistribute at least thirty days before your manuscript or media freeze, to give the authors time to provide updated documents. This notification should describe modifications, if any, made to the document.

2. All substantive modifications (including deletions) be either clearly marked up in the document or else described in an attachment to the document.

3. Finally, although it is not mandatory under this license, it is considered good form to offer a free copy of any hardcopy and CD-ROM expression of an Open Publication-licensed work to its author(s).

F.6 License Options

The author(s) and/or publisher of an Open Publication-licensed document may elect certain options by appending language to the reference to or copy of the license. These options are considered part of the license instance and must be included with the license (or its incorporation by reference) in derived works.

A. To prohibit distribution of substantively modified versions without the explicit permission of the author(s). "Substantive modification" is defined as a change to the semantic content of the document and excludes mere changes in format or typographical corrections.

   To accomplish this, add the phrase "Distribution of substantively modified versions of this document is prohibited without the explicit permission of the copyright holder." to the license reference or copy.

B. To prohibit any publication of this work or derivative works in whole or in part in standard (paper) book form for commercial purposes is prohibited unless prior permission is obtained from the copyright holder.

   To accomplish this, add the phrase "Distribution of the work or derivative of the work in any standard (paper) book form is prohibited unless prior permission is obtained from the copyright holder." to the license reference or copy.

F.7 Open Publication Policy Appendix

(This is not considered part of the license.)

Open Publication works are available in source format via the Open Publication home page at http://works.opencontent.org/.

Open Publication authors who want to include their own license on Open Publication works may do so, as long as their terms are not more restrictive than the Open Publication license.

If you have questions about the Open Publication License, please contact David Wiley and/or the Open Publication Authors' List at opal@opencontent.org, via email.

To subscribe to the Open Publication Authors' List: Send email to opal-request@opencontent.org with the word "subscribe" in the body.

To post to the Open Publication Authors' List: Send email to opal@opencontent.org or simply reply to a previous post.

To unsubscribe from the Open Publication Authors' List: Send email to opal-request@opencontent.org with the word "unsubscribe" in the body.

Index

A

AA mode. *See* antialiased mode
abstract base classes, 348
**Accessing Data in a Linked List
  (Function Listing 2.9), 23**
activate_signal, 250
**Adding Widgets to GnomeApp
  (Function Listing 6.2), 109**
**Affine Manipulation (Function
  Listing 12.3), 298**
affine transformations, 295
  GnomeCanvas, 297-301
affines
  composing, 297-298
  concatenating, 297-298
  inverting, 298
  multiplying, 297-298
  scaling, 297
  translating, 297
alignment
  GtkAlignment, 360
  GtkMisc, 388-389
allocation of space, container widgets, 45
animation, GnomeAnimator, 387
**antialiased (AA) mode, GnomeCanvas
  widget, 294, 299-300**
antialiased mode,
  render method, 331-333
applications
  beeping, 420
  Gnome
    features checklist, 137-138
    GTK+ features, 5
  GnomeHello code listings, 437-470
  menus, desktop entries, 83
  separating GUI, 424-425
arcs, drawing, GdkWindow, 233-234
arguments
  child, 288
  GnomeCanvasImage, 316
  GnomeCanvasLine, 313-314

  GnomeCanvasPolygon, 315-316
  GnomeCanvasRE, 312-313
  GnomeCanvasText, 318-319
  GnomeCanvasWidget, 319
  objects, 153
    reading arguments, 155
    runtime availability, 159-160
    setting arguments, 154-155
    subclasses, 156-159
  parsing, popt library, 88-94
arrow keys, 429
art_affine_identity( ) function, 299
art_affine_invert( ) function, 298
art_affine_multiply( ) function, 298
art_affine_rectilinear( ) function, 299
art_affine_scale( ) function, 299
art_affine_translate( ) function, 299
ascent metric (fonts), 221-224
assertion failed warnings, glib, 422
attaching data to objects, 179-180
**Attaching Key-Value Pairs to a
  GtkObject (Function Listing 9.54), 180**
**Attaching with Defaults (Function
  Listing 3.5), 55**
autoconf manual, 79
automake manual, 79

B

back ends, 424
backgrounds, GtkLabel, 428
base classes
  GtkBin, 348
  GtkContainer, 348
  GtkWidget, 245
  initialing, 145-148
baseline metric (fonts), 221-224
Bonobo library, 8
**bounds method, GnomeCanvasItem
  class, 338-339**
Bourne shell manual, 80

boxes
    container widgets
        homogeneous packing patterns, 49
        managing rows and columns, 45-48
        non-homogeneous packing patterns, 48-49
    error, 136
    GtBox, 366
    GtHBox, 367
    GtkButtonBox, 375
    GtkHButtonBox, 375
    GtkVButtonBox, 376
    info, 136
    warning, 136
buffer coordinates, GnomeCanvas, 296
built-in types (GTK+), 150
button events, GdkWindow, 201-203
    modifier masks, 203
buttons
    GnomeColorPicker, 356
    GnomeFontPicker, 356
    GnomeHRef, 356
    GtkButton, 355
    GtkCheckButton, 357-358
    GtkPixmapMenuItem, 363
    GtkRadioButton, 358
    GtkRadioMenuItem, 363
    GtkToggleButton, 357
    message boxes, 136

C

C programming language, compared to GTK+, 426-427
Calculators, GnomeCalculator, 3, 71
Calendar, GtkCalendar, 392
callbacks, 160-170
    GnomeCanvasItem, 305
    Hello, World, 42-43
    signal emission sequence, 173
Canvas Affines (Function Listing 12.4), 299
Canvas Constructors (Function Listing 12.5), 300
canvas coordinates, GnomeCanvas, 295
canvas items
    GnomeCanvas widget, 302-304
        callbacks, 305
        event signals, 305
        GnomeCanvasEllipse, 311-313
        GnomeCanvasImage, 316

        GnomeCanvasLine, 313-314
        GnomeCanvasPoints, 313
        GnomeCanvasPolygon, 315-316
        GnomeCanvasRect, 311-313
        GnomeCanvasText, 316-319
        GnomeCanvasWidget, 319
    GnomeCanvasItem
        draw method, 324-325
        overview, 321-323
        render method, 324-325
        update method, 325-331
    GnomeCanvasRect, 323-324
Canvas Scrolling (Function Listing 12.6), 301
canvas widgets, 293-294
    affine transformations, 297-301
    canvas items, 302-304
        callbacks, 305
        event signals, 305
        GnomeCanvasEllipse, 311-313
        GnomeCanvasImage, 316
        GnomeCanvasLine, 313-314
        GnomeCanvasPoints, 313
        GnomeCanvasPolygon, 315-316
        GnomeCanvasRect, 311-313
        GnomeCanvasText, 316-319
        GnomeCanvasWidget, 319
    coordinates, 295-297
    GnomeCanvasGroup, 294-295
    modes, 299-300
    scroll regions, 300-301
    zooming, 301
Canvas Zooming (Function Listing 12.7), 302
cells in tables, container widgets, 50-52
    example, 52-55
chaining up objects, 178-179
Changing sensitivity (Function Listing 3.11), 61
check buttons, GtkCheckButton, 357-358
child arguments, 288
class hints, 120
class structs
    GtkObject, 142
    GtkWidget, 246-249
    initializing new, 145-148
classes
    base, GtkWidget, 245
    GtkObject, arguments in subclasses, 156-159

client events, GdkWindow, 214-215
Closing GnomeDialog (Function Listing 7.2), 126
Code, debugging with macros, glib, 13, 16
coding styles, Gnome, compared to GTK+, 430-431
Color Allocation (Function Listing 10.3), 191
Colormaps, GdkWindow, 187-189, 193
  RGB values and pixels, 190, 193
colors
  GnomeColorPicker, 356
  GtkColorSelection, 374
  GtkColorSelectionDialog, 352-353
Columns, container widgets, managing, 45-50
Common Object Request Broker Architecture. *See* **CORBA**
composite widgets, 244
concatenating affines, 298
Configuration File Iterators (Function Listing 5.5), 102
configuration files, Gnome
  iterators, 99-102
  operations, 102-103
  reading, 96-98
  saving, 95, 98-99
  section iterators, 102
configure events, GdkWindow, 212
configure.in file, 74-77
connectors to signals, 160-170
  emission sequence, 173
containers
  GnomeAppBar, 367
  GnomeDateEdit, 368
  GnomeEntry, 369
  GnomeFileEntry, 369
  GnomeNumberEntry, 369
  GnomeProcBar, 370
  GtBox , 366
  GtHBox , 367
  GtkAlignment, 360
  GtkAspectFrame, 361
  GtkBin, 348
  GtkCheckMenuItem, 362
  GtkCombo, 368
  GtkContainer, 348
  GtkDockMenu, 359-360
  GtkEventBox, 365

  GtkFixed, 381
  GtkFrame, 360-361
  GtkPixmapMenuItem, 363
  GtkHandleBox, 365
  GtkItem, 362
  GtkListItem, 364
  GtkMenuItem, 362
  GtkPacker, 385
  GtkRadioMenuItem, 363
  GtkScrolled Window, 366
  GtkTearoffMenuItem, 364
  GtkTreeItem, 364
  GtkViewport Window, 366
  widgets, 44, 244
    controlling manually, 56-57
    defaults, 62
    dividing tables into cells, 50-52
    example, 52-55
    focus, 62
    grabbing, 62
    GtkButtonBox, 55
    GtkFixed, 55
    GtkLayout, 55
    GtkPacker, 55
    life cycle, 57-59
    managing rows or columns, 45-50
    mapped, 60-61
    realized, 60-61
    sensitivity, 61-62
    showing, 60-61
    size requisition, 44-45
    space allocation, 45
    states, 62-63
    visible, 60-61
Coordinate Conversions (Function Listing 12.2), 296-297
Coordinates, GnomeCanvas, 295-297
CORBA, 6
  libraries, libgnorba, 7
CORBA 2.2 ORB. *See* **ORBit**
crossing events, GdkWindow, 206-209
custom canvas items
  GnomeCanvasItem
    draw method, 324-325
    overview, 321-323
    render method, 324-325
    update method, 325-331
  GnomeCanvasRect, 323-324

D

date/time, GnomeDateEdit, 368

de Icaza, Miguel, Mexican Autonomous
  National University, 3

debugging code, macros, glib, 13, 16

Default Visual (Function
  Listing 10.2), 189

Default Window Size (Function
  Listing 3.7), 57

descent metric (fonts), 221-224

desktop, Gnome, 4

desktop entries, 83

destroy method, GtkObject, 174-177

destroying widgets, 57

destructing objects, GtkObject, methods
  destroy , 174-177
  finalize, 174-177
  shutdown, 174-177

development frameworks, Gnome, 4
  CORBA, 6
  Gtk, 5
  header files, 8
  libraries
    Bonobo, 8
    glib, 5
    gnome-print, 7
    gnome-xml, 8
    Guile, 8
    Imlib, 6
    libart_lgpl, 7
    libgnome, 6
    libgnomeui, 6-7
    libgnorba, 7
    libzvt, 7
    non-Gnome, 5
  ORBit, 6

dialog dialogs
  box routines, 7
  default buttons, 128
  example, 131-132
  GnomeAbout, 132-133, 350
  GnomeDialog, 124-125, 349
    completion steps, 127-129
    filling in, 125
    signals, 126-127
  GnomeFontSelector, 352
  GnomeMessageBox, 135-136
  GnomePropertyBox, 134-135, 350
  GtkColorSelectionDialog, 352-353
  GtkFileSelection, 353-354

GtkFontSelectionDialog, 354
GtkInputDialog, 352
modal, 129-131

DocBook, Gnome documentation, 81

documentation
  Gnome, help menus, 117-119
  installing, 81-83

drag-and-drop events, GdkWindow and
  proximity, 215

draw method, 324-325
  GnomeCanvasRect, 334-336

drawing, GdkWindow, 193-195
  arcs, 233-234
  lines, 232-233
  pixmaps, 236
  points, 232
  polygons, 234-235
  rectangles, 233
  RGB buffers, 236-238
  text, 235

Drawing Arcs (Function
  Listing 10.16), 234

Drawing Lines (Function
  Listing 10.14), 233

Drawing Pixmaps (Function
  Listing 10.19), 236

Drawing Points (Function
  Listing 10.13), 232

Drawing Polygons (Function
  Listing 10.17), 235

Drawing Rectangles (Function
  Listing 10.15), 233

Drawing Text (Function
  Listing 10.18), 235

E

emission hooks, 170

emissions, 160
  signals, 171-173

error boxes, buttons, 136

error messages, Gdk, 430

event handlers, motion, 427

event method, GnomeCanvasItem
  class, 336

event signals, 429
  GnomeCanvasItem, 305

events
  GdkWindow
    button, 201-204
    client, 214-215

configure, 212
drag-and-drop, 215
expose, 210-211
focus, 210
keyboard, 204, 206, 209
masks, 197, 199
mouse, 206-209
property, 213
proximity, 215
receiving in GTK+, 199-200
selection, 214
types, 195-197
visibility, 213
GtkWidget, 200-201
Hello, World in GTK+, 42
expose events, GdkWindow, 210-211
Extracting GtkProgress (Function
Listing 6.7), 115
EXTRA_DIST variable, 84

F

FAQs (frequently asked questions),
419-420
answers, 420-431
file selection, GtkFileSelection, 353-354
files
configure.in, 74-77
Makefile.am, 77-79
topic.dat, 81
filestopic.dat, 117
finalize method, GtkObject, 174-177
floating objects, 57
focus events
GdkWindow, 210
widgets, 62
Font Metrics (Function Listing 10.11),
223-224
fonts
GdkWindow, 221
metrics, 221-224
GnomeFontPicker, 356
GnomeFontSelector, 352
GtkFontSelection, 382
GtkFontSelectionDialog, 354
Forcing allocations (Function
Listing 3.6), 56
fork( ) function, 423
frames
GtkAspectFrame, 361
GtkFrame, 360-361

frameworks for development, Gnome, 4
CORBA, 6
Gnome, 4
Gtk, 5
header files, 8
libraries
Bonobo, 8
glib, 5
gnome-print, 7
gnome-xml, 8
Guile, 8
Imlib, 6
libart_lgpl, 7
libgnome, 6
libgnomeui, 6-7
libgnorba, 7
libzvt, 7
non-Gnome, 5
ORBit, 6
front ends, 424
functions
art_affine_identity( ), 299
art_affine_invert( ), 298
art_affine_multiply( ), 298
art_affine_rectilinear( ), 299
art_affine_scale( ), 299
art_affine_translate( ), 299
fork( ), 423
gdk_beep( ), 420
gdk_draw_point( ), 428
gnome-config, 95
gnome_app_set_statusbar, 113
gnome_canvas_item_new( ), 303
gnome_config_sync( ), 98-99
gnome_init( ), 85-86
GtkWidget, 246-249
gtk_button_get_type( ), 144
gtk_container_get_arg( ), 158
gtk_container_set_arg( ), 158
gtk_init( ), 145-149
gtk_object_add_arg_type( ), 156-159
gtk_object_class_add_signals( ), 162
gtk_object_destroy( ), 169, 175
gtk_object_finalize( ), 177
gtk_object_getv( ), 155
gtk_object_get_user_data( ), 179-180
gtk_object_query_args( ), 159-160
gtk_object_set( ), 154-155
gtk_object_setv( ), 155
gtk_object_set_user_data( ), 179-180

gtk_object_shutdown( ), 176-177
gtk_object_unref( ), 175-177
gtk_signal_connect_after( ), 169
gtk_signal_connect_full( ), 169
gtk_signal_connect_object( ), 168-169
gtk_signal_connect_while_alive( ), 169
gtk_signal_connect( ), 163, 168
gtk_signal_disconnect( ), 168
gtk_signal_emit_by_name( ), 171
gtk_signal_emit_stop( ), 170
gtk_signal_handler _block( ), 168
gtk_signal_handler _unblock( ), 168
gtk_signal_lookup( ), 166-169
gtk_signal_new( ), 161-165
gtk_signal_query( ), 170
gtk_type unique( ), 145
gtk_type_set_chunk_alloc( ), 144
gtk_whatever_foo( ), 428
gtk_whatever_real_foo( ), 428
gtk_widget_new( ), 155
gtk_widget_realize( ), 423-424
gtk_widget_show( ), 423-424
idle, 65-66
input, 66
quit, 64-65
timeout, 65
fundamental types (GTK+), 149-151

G

Games, GnomeScores, 351
GC (graphics context), GdkWindow, 224,
227-231
Gdk mode
error messages, 430
GnomeCanvas widget, 294, 299-300
Methods, draw, 334-336
relationship to Xlib, 181-182
GdkColor, 193
RGB values and pixels, 190, 193
GdkCursor (Function Listing 10.9), 218
GdkEventButton, 201-203
modifier masks, 203
GdkEventClient, 214-215
GdkEventConfigure, 212
GdkEventDND, 215
GdkEventEvents, 208-209
GdkEventExpose, 210-211
GdkEventFocus, 210

GdkEventKey, 204-206
focus flag, 209
GdkEventMotion, 207-208
GdkEventProperty, 213
GdkEventProximity, 215
GdkEventSelection, 214
GdkEventType, 195-196
values, 196-197
GdkEventVisibility, 213
GdkFont
fields, 220-221
metrics, 221-224
GdkFont (Function Listing 10.10), 221
GkGC (Function Listing 10.12), 225
GdkGCValues, 224, 227-231
GdkImage, 236-238
GdkPixmap, 193, 195
pixels, 427-428
GdkPixmap Constructor (Function
Listing 10.4), 194
GdkRBB (Function Listing 10.20), 237
GdkRGB, 236-238
GdkVisual struct, 189
GdkVisualType, values, 190
GdkWindow, 182-183
attributes, 184-188
colormaps, 187-189, 193
RGB values and pixels, 190, 193
compared to GtkWindow, 183
drawing, 193-195
arcs, 233-234
lines, 232-233
pixmaps, 236
points, 232
polygons, 234-235
rectangles, 233
RGB buffers, 236-238
text, 235
events
button, 201-204
client, 214-215
configure, 212
drag-and-drop, 215
expose, 210-211
focus, 210
keyboard, 204-206, 209
masks, 197-199
mouse, 206-209
property, 213
proximity, 215
receiving in GTK+, 199-200

selection, 214
types, 195-197
visibility, 213
fonts, 221
metrics, 221-224
graphics context, 224
values, 227-231
mouse pointers
changing cursors, 218-219
grabbing, 217-218
locating, 216
pixmaps, 193-195
reference counting, 238-239
relationhip to GtkWidget, 183
relationship to GtkStyle, 239-241
visuals, 187-189
types, 190
GdkWindow (Function Listing 10.1), 184
GdkWindow Event Mask (Function
Listing 10.5), 197
GdkWindowAttr object, 184
gdk_beep( ) function, 420
gdk_draw_point( ) function, 428
gettext manual, 79
gettext message catalog, 86-88
gettext package, internationalization, 73
GHashTable, 32-35
Gimp (GNU Image Manipulation
Program), 5
Gimp Drawing Kit, 5
Gimp Tool Kit. See GTK+
glib, 11
assertion failed warnings, 422
features, 35
hash tables, GHashTable, 32-35
header files, 411-418
linked lists, 21-25
macros, 12-13
debugging code, 13, 16
memory, 16-17
leaks, 421-422
memory profiling, 421
string handling, 17-20
trees
GNode, 28-32
GTree, 26-27
types, 12
glib library, 5
GList, 21
GNode, 28-32

Gnome (GNU Network Object Model
Environment), 3
applications, features checklist, 137-138
argument parsing with popt, 88-94
coding styles, 430-431
configuration files
iterators, 99-102
operations, 102-103
reading, 96-98
saving, 95, 98-99
section iterators, 102
desktop, 4
development framework, 4
Bonobo library, 8
CORBA, 6
glib library, 5
gnome-print library, 7
gnome-xml library, 8
Gtk, 5
Guile library, 8
header files, 8
Imlib, 6
libart_lgpl library, 7
libgnome library, 6
libgnomeui library, 6-7
libgnorba library, 7
libzvt library, 7
non-Gnome libraries, 5
ORBit, 6
gnome-session manager, 104
GnomeClient object, 104-106
GUI builders, 431
header files, 411-418
help
documentation, 117-119
menu hints, 119
menu tooltips, 119-120
history, 3-4
internationalization, 86-88, 431
IRC (Internet Relay Chat) channels, 435
libraries
initializing, 85-86
Web site, 433
mailing lists, 434-435
source trees, 72
checklist, 73-74
common characteristics of packages, 72-73
started by Miguel de Icaza, Mexican
Autonomous National University, 3
stock pixmaps, 7

Web site, 434

X session management specification, 104

GnomeClient object, 104-106

gnome-config functions, 95

gnome-libs package, libraries

libart_lgba, 7

libzvtpl, 7

libgnome, 6

libgnomeui, 6-7

libgnor, 7

gnome-print library, 7

gnome-session manager, 104

GnomeClient object, 104-106

gnome-xml library, 8

GnomeAbout dialogs, 132-133, 350

GnomeAnimator widget, 387

GnomeApp subclass, 351

GnomeApp Constructor (Function Listing 6.1), 108

GnomeApp widget, 7, 107-109

GnomeAppBar Constructor (Function Listing 6.5), 115

GnomeAppBar container, 367

GnomeAppBar widget, 114-116

GnomeCalculator widget, 371

GnomeCanvas, example program, 306-311

GnomeCanvas widget, 7, 293-294

coordinates, 295-301

GnomeCanvasGroup, 294-295

modes, 294, 299-300

scroll region, 300-301

zooming, 301

GnomeCanvasEllipse, 311-313

methods

render, 331-333

update, 327-328

GnomeCanvasEllipse widget, 403

GnomeCanvasGroup, 294-295

GnomeCanvasGroup widget, 404

GnomeCanvasImage, arguments, 316

GnomeCanvasImage widget, 404

GnomeCanvasItem

Methods, render, 324

overview, 321-323

GnomeCanvasItem (Function Listing 12.8), 302-303

GnomeCanvasItem base class, 302-304

callbacks, 305

event signals, 305

GnomeCanvasEllipse, 311-313

GnomeCanvasImage, 316

GnomeCanvasLine, 313-314

GnomeCanvasPoints, 313

GnomeCanvasPolygon, 315-316

GnomeCanvasRect, 311-313

GnomeCanvasText, 316-319

GnomeCanvasWidget, 319

methods

bounds, 338-339

draw, 324-325

event, 336

point, 336-338

realize, 339

render, 325

unrealize, 340

update, 325-331

GnomeCanvasItem widget, 293-294, 403

GnomeCanvasLine widget, 313, 405

arguments, 313-314

GnomeCanvasPoints, 313

GnomeCanvasPolygon widget, 405

arguments, 315-316

GnomeCanvasRE base class, arguments, 312-313

GnomeCanvasRE widget, 328, 403

GnomeCanvasRect class, 311-313, 323-324, 404

methods

draw, 334-336

render, 331-333

update, 325-328

GnomeCanvasText widget, 405

arguments, 318-319

GnomeCanvasTextItem widget, 406

GnomeCanvasWidget, arguments, 319

GnomeCanvasWidget, 406

GnomeClient widget, 104-106, 406

GnomeColorPicker button, 356

GnomeDateEdit container, 368

GnomeDEntryEdit widget, 407

GnomeDialog, 124-125

completion steps, 127-129

filling in, 125

signals, 126-127

GnomeDialog, 349

GnomeDialog Constructor (Function Listing 7.1), 124

GnomeDialog polish (Function Listing 7.3), 127

GnomeDock, 379

GnomeDockBand, 378
GnomeDockItem container, 359-360
GnomeDockLayout widget, 407
GnomeEntry container, 369
GnomeFileEntry container, 369
GnomeFontPicker button, 356
GnomeFontSelector dialog, 352
GnomeGuru widget, 371
GnomeHello application code listings, 437-470
GnomeHRef button, 356
GnomeIconEntry, 372
GnomeIconList, 377
GnomeIconSelection, 372
GnomeLess, 373
GnomeMDI widget, 408
GnomeMDIChild widget, 408
GnomeMDIGenericChild widget, 408
GnomeMessageBox dialog, 135-136, 350
GnomeNumberEntry container, 369
GnomePaperSelector widget, 373
GnomePixmap widget, 7, 388
GnomePixmapEntry, 373
GnomeProcBar container, 370
GnomePropertyBox dialog, 134-135, 350
GnomeScores, 351
GnomeSpell widget, 374
GnomeStock widget, 388
GnomeUIInfo struct, 109-112
    converting to widgets, 112-113
GnomeUIInfo templates, 109-112
GnomeUIInfoType, values, 111
gnome_app_set_statusbar function, 113
gnome_canvas_item_new( )function, 303
gnome_config_sync( ) function, 98-99
gnome_init( ) function, 85-86
GNU Coding Standards, Web site, 79
GNU manuals, Web site, 79
GNU Network Object Model
    Environment. *See* Gnome
GNU Project Coding Standards, Web
    site, 72
GNU Web site, 4
Grabbing the Pointer (Function
    Listing 10.8), 217
grabbing widgets, 62
graphics context, GdkWindow, 224
    values, 227-231
GSList, 21-25

GTK+, 5
    coding styles, 430-431
    GUI builders, 431
    header files, 411-418
    inheritance, 429
    internationalization, 431
    IRC (Internet Relay Chat) channels, 435
    Libraries, Web site, 433
    mailing lists, 434-435
    receiving Gdk events, 199-200
    Web site, 434
    written in C, 426-427
GtkAccelLabel widget, 390
GtkAdjustment widget, 409
GtkAlignment container, 360
GtkArg, 151-153
GtkArrow widget, 391
GtkAspectFrame container, 361
GtkBin abstract base class, 348
GtkBox container widget, 45-50, 366
GtkButton, 355
GtkButtonBox container widget, 55, 375
GtkCalendar widget, 392
GtkCheckButton button, 357-358
GtkCheckMenuItem container, 362
GtkCList widget, 379
GtkClock widget, 390
GtkColorSelection, 374
GtkColorSelectionDialog, 352-353
GtkCombo container, 348, 368
GtkCTree widget, 380
GtkCurve widget, 393
GtkData widget, 409
GtkDial widget, 393
GtkDialog, 351
GtkDrawingArea widget, 392
GtkEditable widget, 394
GtkEv widget, example, 250-267
GtkEventBox container, 365
GtkFileSelection dialog, 353-354
GtkFixed container widget, 55, 381
GtkFontSelection widget, 382
GtkFontSelectionDialog, 354
GtkFrame container, 360-361
GtkGammaCurve, 374
GtkHandleBox container, 365
GtkHBox constructor, 351, 367
    Function Listing 3.1, 46
GtkHButtonBox, 375
GtkHPaned widget, 383
GtkHRuler widget, 396

GtkHScale widget, 398

GtkHScrollbar widget, 399

GtkHSeparator widget, 400

GtkImage widget, 391

GtkInputDialog, 352

GtkItem container, 362

GtkItemFactory widget, 410

GtkLabel widget, 389

   backgrounds, 428

GtkLayout container widget, 55, 376

GtkList widget, 383

GtkListItem container, 364

GtkMenu widget, 384

GtkMenuBar widget, 384

GtkMenuItem container, 362

GtkMenuShell widget, 384

GtkMisc widget, 388-389

GtkNotebook widget, 381

GtkObject, 347

   arguments, 153

     reading, 155

     runtime availability, 159-160

     setting, 154-155

     subclasses, 156-159

   attaching data, 179-180

   methods, 340

     chaining up, 178-179

     destroy, 174-177

     finalize, 174-177

     shutdown, 174-177

   signals, 160-161

     adding, 161-165

     emitting, 171-172

     sequence, 173

     using, 166-170

   structs

     class, 142

     instance, 142

   types, identifiers, 142-145

GtkOptionMenu active option, 359

GtkPacker container widget, 55, 385

GtkPaned widget, 382

GtkPixmap widget, 391

GtkPixmapMenuItem container, 363

GtkPlug window, 355

GtkPreview widget, 400

GtkProgress widget, 401

GtkProgressBar widget, 401

GtkRadioButton, 358

GtkRadioMenuItem container, 363

GtkRange widget, 397

GtkRuler widget, 396

GtkScale widget, 397-398

GtkScrollbar widget, 398

GtkScrolledWindow container, 366

GtkSeparator widget, 351, 399

GtkSocket widget, 385

GtkSpinButton widget, 394-395

GtkStatusbar Functions (Function Listing 6.8), 116

GtkStatusbar widget, 116-117, 370

GtkStyle, relationship to GdkWindow, 239-241

GtkTable container widget, 50-52, 385

   example

     gtk_table_attach defaults( ), 55

     gtk_table_attach( ), 52-55

   Function Listing 3.4, 51

GtkTearoffMenuItem container, 364

GtkTed widget, 386

GtkText widget, 395

GtkTipsQuery widget, 390

GtkToggleButton, 357

GtkToolbar widget, 386

GtkTooltips widget, 410

GtkTree widget, 386-387

GtkTreeItem container, 364

GtkVBox constructor (Function Listing 3.2), 46

GtkVBox widget, 351, 370

   example, 281-292

GtkVButtonBox, 376

GtkViewport container, 366

GtkVPaned widget, 383

GtkVRuler widget, 397

GtkVScale widget, 398

GtkVScrollbar widget, 399

GtkVSeparator widget, 400

GtkWidget, 245, 347-348

   events, 200-201

   example, 268-281

   passing Gdk events to GTK+, 199-200

   relationhip to GtkWidget, 183

   signals, 250

   structs

     class, 246-249

     instance, 245-246

GtkWindow, 348-349

   compared to GdkWindow, 183

   subclasses, GnomeApp, 107-109

GTK_BUTTON( ) macro, 143

gtk_button_get_type( ) function, 144

gtk_container_get_arg( ) function, 158
gtk_container_set_arg( ) function, 158
gtk_init( ) function, 145-149
GTK_IS_BUTTON( ) macro, 143
gtk_object_add_arg_type( ) function,
    156-159
gtk_object_class_add_signals( )
    function, 162
gtk_object_destroy( ) function, 169, 175
GTK_OBJECT_DESTROYED( )
    macro, 176
gtk_object_finalize( ) function, 177
gtk_object_getv( ) function, 155
gtk_object_get_user_data( ) function,
    179-180
gtk_object_query_args( ) function,
    159-160
gtk_object_set( ) function, 154-155
gtk_object_setv( ) function, 155
gtk_object_set_user_data( ) function,
    179-180
gtk_object_shutdown( ) function, 176-177
GTK_OBJECT_TYPE( ) macro, 160
gtk_object_unref( ) function, 175-177
gtk_signal_connect after( ) function, 169
gtk_signal_connect full( ) function, 169
gtk_signal_connect object( ) function,
    168-169
gtk_signal_connect while_alive( )
    function, 169
gtk_signal_connect( ) function, 163, 168
gtk_signal_disconnect( ) function, 168
gtk_signal_emit_by_name( )
    function, 171
gtk_signal_emit_stop( ) function, 170
gtk_signal_handler block( ) function, 168
gtk_signal_handler disconnect( )
    function, 168
gtk_signal_handler unblock( )
    function, 168
gtk_signal_lookup( ) function, 166-168
gtk_signal_new( ) function, 161-165
gtk_signal_query( ) function, 170
gtk_type unique( ) function, 145
GTK_TYPE_SEQNO( ) macro, 143
gtk_type_set_chunk_alloc( ) function, 144
GTK_VALUE_ macro, 153
gtk_whatever_foo( ) function, 428
gtk_whatever_real_foo( ) function, 428

gtk_widget_new( ) function, 155
gtk_widget_realize( ) function, 423-424
gtk_widget_show( ) function, 423-424
GTree, 26-27
Guile library, 8
GUIs (graphical user interfacse)
    Gnome, 431
    separating from applications, 424-425
    updating, 430

H

handlers, 160-170
hash tables, GhashTable, glib, 32-35
header files, 8
    GTK+/Gnome, 411-418
height metric (fonts), 221-224
Hello, World in GTK+ code, 38-39
    callbacks, 42-43
    compiling, 39-40
    initialization, 40
    main loop, 42
    signals, 41-43
    widgets, 40-41
help files
    Function Listing 6.9, 119
    Gnome
        documentation, 117-119
        menu hints, 119
        tooltips, 119-120
    topic.dat, 81
history of Gnome, 3-4
hyperlinks, GnomeHRef, 356

I-J

identifiers of types, 142-145
idle functions, 65-66
Idle Functions (Function Listing 3.15), 66
Imlib (Image Library), 6
info boxes, buttons, 136
inheritance, GTK+, 429
Init with Argument Parsing (Function
    Listing 5.2), 89
initializing
    class structs, 145-148
    Gnome (Function Listing 5.1), 86
    Hello, World, 40
    libraries, Gnome, 85-86

input functions, 66
  Function Listing 3.16, 67
insensitive widgets, 61-62
installing
  documentation, 81-83
  pixmaps, 80-81
Installing a Statusbar (Function
  Listing 6.4), 114
Installing Menu Hints (Function
  Listing 6.10), 119
instance structs
  GtkObject, 142
  GtkWidget, 245-246
integer identifiers of types, 142-145
internal consistency of
  functions/libraries, 15
internationalization
  gettext package, 73
  Gnome, 86-88, 431
  GTK+, 431
Inverting affines, 298
IRC (Internet Relay Chat) channels,
  GTK+/Gnome development, 435
item coordinates, GnomeCanvas, 295
iterators, Gnome configuration files,
  99-102

K-L

KDE (K Desktop Environment)
  project, 3
key events, GdkWindow, modifier
  masks, 203
key press events, 429
keyboard events, GdkWindow, 204-206
  focus flag, 209

labels
  GtkAccelLabel, 390
  GtkLabel, 389
  GtkMenuItem, 362
libart_lgpl library, 7
libgnome library, 6
libgnomeui library, 6-7
libgnorba library, 7
libraries
  glib, 5
  Gnome
    initializing, 85-86
    popt argument parsing, 88-94
    Web site, 433

gnome-libs package
  libart_lgpl, 7
  libgnome, 6
  libgnomeui, 6-7
  libgnorba, 7
  libzvt, 7
GTK+, Web site, 433
non-Gnome, 5
non-gnome-libs package
  Bonobo, 8
  gnome-print, 7
  gnome-xml, 8
  Guile, 8
libtool manual, 79
libzvt library, 7
life cycle of widgets, 57-59
lines, drawing, GdkWindow, 232-233
linked lists, glib, 21-25
Linux Filesystem Hierarchy Standard,
  Web site, 72
Linux operating system, 3
list items, GtkItem, 362
listings
  function
    Accessing data in a linked list, 23
    Adding Widgets to GnomeApp, 109
    Affine Manipulation, 298
    Attaching Key-Value Pairs to a
      GtkObject, 180
    Attaching with defaults, 55
    Canvas Affines, 299
    Canvas Constructors, 300
    Canvas Scrolling, 301
    Canvas Zooming, 302
    Changing sensitivity, 61
    Closing GnomeDialog, 126
    Color Allocation, 191
    Configuration file iterators, 102
    Coordinate Conversions, 296-297
    Creating Widgets from GnomeUIInfo,
      112-113
    Default Visual, 189
    Default window size, 57
    Drawing Arcs, 234
    Drawing Lines, 233
    Drawing Pixmaps, 236
    Drawing Points, 232
    Drawing Polygons, 235
    Drawing Rectangles, 233
    Drawing Text, 235

Extracting GtkProgress, 115
Font Metrics, 223-224
Forcing allocations, 56
GdkCursor, 218
GdkFont, 221
GDkGC, 225
GdkPixmap Constructor, 194
GdkRBB, 237
GdkWindow, 184
GdkWindow Event Mask, 197
GnomeApp Constructor, 108
GnomeAppBar Constructor, 115
GnomeCanvasItem, 302-303
GnomeDialog constructor, 124
GnomeDialog polish, 127
Grabbing the Pointer, 217
GtkHBox constructor, 46
GtkStatusbar, 116
GtkTable, 51
GtkVBox constructor, 46
Help Files, 119
Idle Functions, 66
Init with Argument Parsing, 89
initializing Gnome, 86
Input Functions, 67
Installing a Statusbar, 114
Installing Menu Hints, 119
Main Loop, 64
Manipulating Object Arguments, 160
*Miscellaneous configuration file
   functions, 103*
Packing GtkBox, 46
Querying Pointer Location, 216
Querying Screen Size, 120
Quit Functions, 65
Reference counting, 58
*Retrieving data from configuration files,
   97-98*
Root Group Accessor, 294
Saving data to configuration files, 98-99
Setting Class Hints, 121
Setting GnomeAppBar Text, 115
Showing/realizing widgets, 60
Signal Emission, 172
Sorted lists, 25
Timeout Functions, 65
Using Signals, 166-168
Widget destruction, 57
Widget Event Mask, 198

macro
   *Macros for Accessing GtkArg Values,
      152-153*
   Sensitivity, 62
   State accessor, 63
   Translation Macros, 87
   Widget predicates, 61
lists
   glib, 21-25
   GnomeScores, 351
   GtkList, 383
   GtkListItem, 364
Loops, main, 63-64

M

m4 manual, 80
macros
   glib, 12-13
      debugging code, 13-16
   GTK_BUTTON( ), 143
   GTK_IS_BUTTON( ), 143
   GTK_OBJECT_DESTROYED( ), 176
   GTK_OBJECT_TYPE( ), 160
   GTK_TYPE_SEQNO( ), 143
   GTK_VALUE_, 153
   locating GTK+ and Gnome on user's
      system, 74-77
**Macros for Accessing GtkArg Values
   (Macro Listing 9.1), 152-153**
**mailing lists, GTK+/Gnome develop-
   ment, 434-435**
main loop, 63-64
   Hello, World, 42
Main Loop (Function Listing 3.12), 64
make manual, 80
make targets, 79
Makefile.am file, 77-79
**Manipulating Object Arguments
   (Function Listing 9.1), 160**
Mapping widgets, 60-61, 254, 268
marshallers, 164-170
masks, events
   GdkEventButton, 203
   GdkWindow, 197-199
memory
   glib, 16-17
   leaks, 421-422

memory profiling, glib, 421

menu bars, GtkMenuBar, 384

menus

desktop entries, 83

GnomeUIInfo template, 109-112

GtkMenuBar, 384

GtkTearoffMenuItem, 364

hints, Gnome, help menus, 119

menu items

GtkCheckMenuItem, 362

GtkItem, 362

GtkMenuItem, 362

message boxes, GnomeMessageBox, 350

methods

draw, 324-325

GnomeCanvasRect, 334-336

GnomeCanvasItem class

bounds, 338-339

event, 336

point, 336-338

realize, 339

unrealize, 340

GtkObject, 340

destroy, 174-177

finalize, 174-177

shutdown, 174-177

render, 324-325

GnomeCanvasEllipse, 331-333

GnomeCanvasRect, 331-333

RGB mode, 334

update, 325-331

metrics (fonts), 221-224

Miscellaneous Configuration File Functions (Function Listing 5.6), 103

modal dialogs, 129-131

modes, GnomeCanvas widget, 294, 299-300

motion events, GdkWindow, 206-209

motion event handlers, 427

mouse pointers, GdkWindow

changing cursors, 218-219

grabbing, 217-218

locating, 216

moving, 427

mouse events, GdkWindow, 206-209

multiplying affines, 297-298

Nodes, GNode, 28-32

non-container widgets, 244

Object Request Brokers. *See* ORBs

objects. *See also* widgets

GdkWindowAttr object, 184

GnomeClient, 104-106

GtkObject, 347

adding signals, 161-165

arguments, 153

arguments in subclasses, 156-159

arguments, runtime availability, 159-160

attaching data, 179-180

chaining up, 178-179

class structs, 142

destroy method, 174-177

emitting signals, 171-172

finalize method, 174-177

instance structs, 142

reading arguments, 155

sequence of signals, 173

setting arguments, 154-155

shutdown method, 174-177

signals, 160-161

type checking, 142-145

using signals, 166-170

online help. *See* help

operating systems, Linus, 3

ORBit, 6

ORBs (Object Request Brokers), 6

packing boxes, 47-48

homogeneous patterns, 49

non-homogeneous patterns, 48-49

Packing GtkBox (Function Listing 3.3), 46

Padding, GtkMisc, 388-389

padding parameters, box packing, 47-50

parents, dialogs, 127

paths, gnome-config functions, 95

pixels, GdkPixmap, 427-428

pixmaps

creating, 424

drawing, GdkWindow, 236

GdkWindow, 193-195

Gnome stock, 7

installing, 80-81

point method, GnomeCanvasItem class, 336-338

points, drawing, GdkWindow, 232

polygons, drawing, GdkWindow, 234-235

popt argument-parsing library, 88-94

portability string handling, glib, 17

printing widgets, 423

property boxes, GnomePropertyBox, 350

property events, GdkWindow, 213

Q-R

Querying Pointer Location (Function Listing 10.7), 216

Querying Screen Size (Function Listing 6.11), 120

quit functions, 64-65

Quit Functions (Function Listing 3.13), 65

radio buttons, GtkRadioButton, 358

realize method, GnomeCanvasItem class, 339

realized widgets, 60-61

realizing, widgets, 254, 268-271

rectangles, drawing, GdkWindow, 233

reference counting, GdkWindow, 238-239

Reference counting (Function Listing 3.9), 58

registered types (GTK+), 150

render method, 324-325
   GnomeCanvasEllipse, 331-333
   GnomeCanvasRect, 331-333
   RGB mode, 334

requisition of sizes, container widgets, 44-45

Retrieving Data from Configuration Files (Function Listing 5.3), 97-98

RGB buffers, drawing, GdkWindow, 236-238

RGB rendering, 334

Root Group Accessor (Function Listing 12.1), 294

root windows, 59

rotating affines, 297

rows, managing in container widgets, 45-50

rulers
   GtkHRuler, 396
   GtkRuler, 396
   GtkVRuler, 397

S

Saving Data to Configuration Files (Function Listing 5.4), 98-99

Screens, size, 120

scroll regions, GnomeCanvas widget, 300-301

scrollbars
   GtkHScrollbar, 399
   GtkScrollbar, 398
   GtkScrolled Window, 366
   GtkVScrollbar, 399

selection events, GdkWindow, 214

sensitive widgets, 61-62

Sensitivity (Macro Listing 3.2), 62

sequence numbers, types, 143

session-management.txt document, 104

session, gnome-session manager, 104
   GnomeClient object, 104-106

Setting Class Hints (Function Listing 6.12), 121

Setting GnomeAppBar Text (Function Listing 6.7), 115

set_scroll_adjustments_signal, 250

showing widgets, 60-61

Showing/realizing widgets (Function Listing 3.10), 60

shutdown method, GtkObject, 174-177

Signal Emission (Function Listing 9.3), 172

signals, 426
   callbacks, 160
   emissions, 160
   event, GnomeCanvasItem, 305
   GtkObject, 160-161
      adding, 161-165
      emission sequence, 173
      emitting, 171-172
      using, 166-170
   GtkWidget, 250
   handlers, 160
   Hello, World, 41-43

sinking floating objects, 57

sizes of container widgets
   managing rows or columns, 45-50
   requisition, 44-45
   space allocation, 45

Sorted lists (Function Listing 2.11), 25

sorted vector paths, 328

source trees, Gnome, 72
   checklist, 73-74
   common characteristics of packages, 72-73

space allocation, container widgets, 45
spacing parameters, box packing, 47-50
State accessor (Macro Listing 3.3), 63
states of widgets, 62-63
status bars
    GnomeAppBar, 367
    GnomeAppBar widget, 114-116
    gnome_app_set_statusbar function, 113
    GtkStatusbar, 370
    GtkStatusbar widget, 116-117
string handling, glib, 17-20
structs
    class, initializing, 145-148
    GdkVisual, 189
    GnomeUIInfo, 109-112
        converting to widgets, 112-113
    GtkObject
        class, 142
        instance, 142
    GtkWidget
        class, 246-249
        instance, 245-246
subclasses, GtkObject, arguments,
156-159

transformations (affine), 295
    GnomeCanvas, 297-301
translating affines, 299
translation catalogs, 86-88
Translation Macros (Macro
    Listing 5.1), 87
trees
    glib
        GNode, 28-32
        GTree, 26-27
    GtkTree, 386-387
    GtkTreeItem, 364
    items, GtkItem, 362
troubleshooting, FAQs (frequently asked
    questions), 419-420
    answers, 420-431
types (GTK+), 149-152
    built-in, 150
    fundamental, 149-151
    GdkWindow, 187
    glib, 12
    identifiers, 142-145
    registered, 150
    structs, class, 145-148

T

tables
    dividing into cells for container widgets,
        50-52
        example, 52-55
    GtkTable, 385
    GtkTed, 386
    Hash, GhashTable, glib, 32-35
targets, make, 79
templates, GnomeUIInfo, 109-112
text
    drawing, GdkWindow, 235
    GtkText, 395
text entry boxes, GtkCombo, 368
time, GtkClock, 390
time/date, GnomeDateEdit, 368
Timeout Functions (Function
    Listing 3.14), 65
toggle buttons, GtkToggleButton, 357
toolbars
    GnomeUIInfo template, 109-112
    GtkToolbar, 386
tooltips, Gnome, help menus, 119-120
topic.dat file, 81, 117

U-V

UNIX, popularity of Linux
    applications, 3
unrealize method, GnomeCanvasItem
    class, 340
unrealizing widgets, 270-271
update method, 325-331
Using Signals (Function Listing 9.2),
    166-168

Values, GnomeUIInfoType, 111
Variables, EXTRA_DIST, 84
visibility events, GdkWindow, 213
visible widgets, 60-61
visuals, GdkWindow, 187-189
    types, 190

W

warning boxes, buttons, 136
Web sites
    Gimp (GNU Image Manipulation
        Program), 5
    GNU, 4
        manuals, 79

GNU Coding Standards, 79
GNU Project Coding Standards, 72
GTK+/Gnome, 434
libraries, GTK+/Gnome, 433
Linux Filesystem Hierarchy Standard, 72
Windows with Cygnus \, 72
Widget Destruction (Function Listing 3.8), 57
Widget Event Mask (Function Listing 10.6), 198
Widget Predicates (Macro Listing 3.1), 61
widgets. *See also* **objects**
  abstract base classes, 348
  container, 44
    controlling manually, 56-57
    dividing tables into cells, 50-55
    GtkButtonBox, 55
    GtkFixed, 55
    GtkLayout, 55
    GtkPacker, 55
    managing rows or columns, 45-50
    size requisition, 44-45
    space allocation, 45
  defaults, 62
  destroying, 420
  focus, 62
  GnomeAnimator, 387
  GnomeApp, 7
  GnomeAppBar, 114-116
  GnomeCalculator, 371
  GnomeCanvas, 7, 293-294
    affine transformations, 297-301
    canvas items, 302-304
    canvas items, callbacks, 305
    canvas items, event signals, 305
    coordinates, 295-297
    example program, 306-311
    GnomeCanvasEllipse, 311-313
    GnomeCanvasGroup, 294-295
    GnomeCanvasImage, 316
    GnomeCanvasLine, 313-314
    GnomeCanvasPoints, 313
    GnomeCanvasPolygon, 315-316
    GnomeCanvasRect, 311-313
    GnomeCanvasText, 316-319
    GnomeCanvasWidget, 319
    modes, 299-300
    scroll region, 300-301
    zooming, 301
  GnomeCanvasEllipse, 403
  GnomeCanvasGroup, 404

GnomeCanvasImage, 404
GnomeCanvasItem, 403
GnomeCanvasLine, 405
GnomeCanvasPolygon, 405
GnomeCanvasRE, 403
GnomeCanvasRect, 404
GnomeCanvasText, 405
GnomeCanvasTextItem, 406
GnomeCanvasWidget, 406
GnomeClient, 406
GnomeDEntryEdit, 407
GnomeDockLayout, 407
GnomeGuru, 371
GnomeMDI, 408
GnomeMDIChild, 408
GnomeMDIGenericChild, 408
GnomeMessageBox, 350
GnomePaperSelector, 373
GnomePixmap, 7, 388
GnomeSpell, 374
GnomeStock, 388
GnomeUIInfo, 112-113
grabbing, 62
graying out, 428
GtkAccelLabel, 390
GtkAdjustment, 409
GtkArrow, 391
GtkCalendar, 392
GtkCList, 379
GtkClock, 390
GtkCTree, 380
GtkCurve, 393
GtkData, 409
GtkDial, 393
GtkDrawingArea, 392
GtkEditable, 394
GtkEv, example, 250-267
GtkFontSelection, 382
GtkHPaned, 383
GtkHRuler, 396
GtkHScale, 398
GtkHScrollbar, 399
GtkHSeparator, 400
GtkImage, 391
GtkItemFactory, 410
GtkLabel, 389
GtkList, 383
GtkMenu, 384
GtkMenuBar, 384
GtkMenuShell, 384
GtkMisc, 388-389

GtkNotebook, 381
GtkPaned, 382
GtkPixmap, 391
GtkPreview, 400
GtkProgress, 401
GtkProgressBar, 401
GtkRange, 397
GtkRuler, 396
GtkScale, 397-398
GtkScrollbar, 398
GtkSeparator, 399
GtkSocket, 385
GtkSpinButton, 394-395
GtkStatusbar, 116-117, 370
GtkTable, 385
GtkTed, 386
GtkText, 395
GtkTipsQuery, 390
GtkToolbar, 386
GtkTooltips, 410
GtkTree, 386-387
GtkVBox, 370
    example, 281-292
GtkVPaned, 383
GtkVRuler, 397
GtkVScale, 398
GtkVScrollbar, 399
GtkVSeparator, 400
GtkWidget, 245, 347-348
    class struct, 246-249
    example, 268-281
    instance struct, 245-246
    signals, 250
Hello, World, 40-41
implementation, 245
life cycle, 57-59
mapped widgets, 60-61
placing, 421
printing, 423
realized widgets, 60-61
sensitivity, 61-62
showing widgets, 60-61
states, 62-63

types
    composite, 244
    containers, 244
    non-container, 244
visible widgets, 60-61
ZvtTerm, 402
Widgets from GnomeUIInfo (Creating)
    (Function Listing 6.3), 112-113
width metric (fonts), 221-224
Windows, Cygnus, 72
windows
    centering, 422
    class hints, 120
    coordinates, GnomeCanvas, 296
    GnomeApp, 351
    GtkDialog, 351
    GtkEventBox, 365
    GtkHandleBox, 365
    GtkPlug, 355
    GtkViewport, 366
    GtkWindow, 348-349
    help, 117-119
        menus, 119
        tooltips, 119-120
    menus, 109-112
        tables, 112-113
    root, 59
    screens, size, 120
    status bars, 113-117
    toolbars, 109-112
world coordinates, GnomeCanvas,
    295, 301

X-Z

X session management specification
    (Gnome), 104
    GnomeClient object, 104-106
X Window System, 59
Xlib, relationship to Gdk, 181-182
Xlib Programming Manual, 221

Zooming, GnomeCanvas widget, 301
ZvtTerm widget, 402

Advanced Information to Solve Your Problems

New Riders Books Offer Advice and Experience

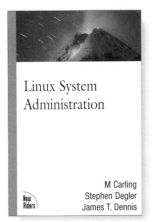

LANDMARK
Rethinking Computer Books

The *Landmark* series from New Riders targets the distinct needs of the working computer professional by providing detailed and solution-oriented information on core technologies. We begin by partnering with authors who have unique depth of experience and the ability to speak to the needs of the practicing professional. Each book is then carefully reviewed at all stages to ensure it covers the most essential subjects in substantial depth, with great accuracy, and with ease of use in mind. These books speak to the practitioner – accurate information and trustworthy advice, at the right depth, and at an attractive value.

ESSENTIAL REFERENCE
Smart, Like You

The *Essential Reference* series from New Riders provides answers when you know what you want to do but need to know how to do it. Each title skips extraneous material and assumes a strong base level of knowledge. These are indispensable books for the practitioner who wants to find specific features of a technology quickly and efficiently. Avoiding fluff and basic material, these books present solutions in an innovative, clean format – and at a great value.

MCSE CERTIFICATION
Engineered for Test Success

New Riders offers a complete line of test preparation materials to help you achieve your certification. With books like *MCSE Training Guide*, *TestPrep*, and *FastTrack*, and software like the acclaimed *MCSE Complete* and *Top Score*, New Riders offers comprehensive products built by experienced professionals who have passed the exams and instructed hundreds of candidates.

Books for Networking Professionals

Unix/Linux Titles

GTK+/Gnome Application Development
by Havoc Pennington
1st Edition Summer 1999
500 pages, $34.99
ISBN: 0-7357-0078-8

In *GTK+/Gnome Application Development* you'll find detailed and advanced coverage of the most popular programming toolkit for developing Linux applications. It fills the deep need in the Linux development community with comprehensive documentation on the free GTK+ programming toolkit. Covered in this book is information found no place else—information that Linux and X Windows developers need to one comprehensive development book. *GTK+/Gnome Application Development* provides the experienced programmer the knowledge to develop X Windows applications with the powerful GTK+ toolkit. The title also contains reference information for more experienced users already familiar with usage, but require function prototypes and detailed descriptions. It will assume knowledge of UNIX development and will cover a broader range of topics.

Solaris Essential Reference
By John Mulligan
1st Edition
304 pages, $24.95
ISBN: 0-7357-0230-7

Looking for the fastest, easiest way to find the Solaris command you need? Need a few pointers on shell scripting? How about advanced administration tips and sound, practical expertise on security issues? Are you looking for trustworthy information about available third-party software packages that will enhance your operating system? Author John Mulligan—creator of the popular Unofficial Guide to Solaris Web site (sun.icsnet.com)—delivers all that and more in one attractive, easy-to-use reference book. With clear and concise instructions on how to perform important administration and management tasks and key information on powerful commands and advanced topics, Solaris Essential Reference is the reference you need when you know what you want to do and you just need to know how.

Linux System Administration

By M Carling, Stephen Degler, & James T. Dennis
1st Edition Summer 1999
450 pages, $29.99
ISBN: 1-56205-934-3

As an administrator, you probably feel that most of your time and energy is spent in endless firefighting. If your network has become a fragile quilt of temporary patches and workarounds, then this book is for you. For example, have you had trouble sending or receiving your email lately? Are you looking for a way to keep your network running smoothly with enhanced performance? Are your users always hankering for more storage, more services, and more speed? Linux System Administration advises you on the many intricacies of maintaining a secure, stable system. In this definitive work, the author addresses all the issues related to system administration, from adding users and managing files permission to Internet services and Web hosting to recovery planning and security. This book fulfills the need for expert advice that will ensure a trouble-free Linux environment.

Linux Enterprise Security

By John S. Flowers
1st Edition Fall 1999
400 pages, $39.99
ISBN: 1-57870-197-X

New Riders is proud to offer the first book aimed specifically at Linux security issues. While there are a host of general UNIX security books, we thought it was time to address the practical needs of the Linux network. In this definitive work, author John Flowers takes a balanced approach to system security, from discussing topics like planning a secure environment to firewalls to utilizing security scripts. With comprehensive information on specific system compromises and advice on how to prevent and repair them, this is one book that every Linux administrator should have on the shelf.

KDE Application Development

by Uwe Thiem
1st Edition Winter 1999
450 pages, $39.99
ISBN: 1-57870-201-1

KDE Application Programming offers a head start into KDE and Qt. The book will cover the essential widgets available in KDE and Qt, and it offers a strong start without the "first try" annoyances which sometimes make strong developers and programmers give up. This book explains KDE and Qt by writing a real application from the very beginning stages, where it can't do anything but display itself and offer a button to quit. Then it will finally bring the user to a full-featured application. The process of developing such an application takes the potential KDE developer through all stages of excitement. In the end, the reader will be able to write any application he/she desires.

Developing Linux Applications with GTK+ and GDK
By Eric Harlow
1st Edition
400 pages, $34.99
ISBN: 0-7357-0214-7

We all know that Linux is one of the most powerful and solid operating systems in existence. And as the success of Linux grows, there is an increasing interest in developing applications with graphical user interfaces that really take advantage of the power of Linux. In this book, software developer Eric Harlow gives you an indispensable development handbook focusing on the GTK+ toolkit. More than an overview on the elements of application or GUI design, this is a hands-on book that delves deeply into the technology. With in-depth material on the various GUI programming tools and loads of examples, this book's unique focus will give you the information you need to design and launch professional-quality applications.

Linux Firewalls
by Robert Ziegler
1st Edition Winter 1999
350 pages, $29.99
ISBN: 0-7357-0900-9

An Internet-connected Linux machine is in a high-risk situation. This book details security steps that a small non-enterprise business user might take to protect themselves when dealing with what the attacker may gain and what a victim may lose. These steps include packet-level firewall filtering, IP masquerading, proxies, tcp wrappers, system integrity checking, and system security monitoring with an overall emphasis on filtering and protection. This book will provide a description of the need for security measures and solutions. The goal is to help people get their Internet security measures in place quickly, without the need to become an expert in security or firewalls.

Linux Essential Reference
Ed Petron
1st Edition Winter 1999
400 pages, $24.95
ISBN: 0-7357-0852-5

This book is all about getting things done as quickly and efficiently as possible by providing a structured organization to the plethora of available Linux information. We can sum it up in one word: VALUE. This book has it all: concise instruction on how to perform key administration tasks; advanced information on configuration; shell scripting; hardware management; systems management; data tasks; automation; and tons of other useful information. All coupled with an unique navigational structure and a great price. This book truly provides groundbreaking information for the growing community of advanced Linux professionals.

Samba Administration

by John Terpstra
1st Edition, Winter 1999
450 pages, $35.00
ISBN: 0-7357-0903-3

Samba Administration provides experienced insider information on the administration of Samba on your Linux/ UNIX and Windows NT network. The world of today's system administrators is filled with many different types of network operating systems, protocols, and hardware configurations all under the requirements of demanding and sometimes less than savvy users. Many administrators turn to the Samba product to help them share services between systems. *Samba Administration* provides the sysadmin with the necessary technical background on the SMB architecture, compiling the source & installation, managing clients & servers, and dealing with the inexplicable.

Gimp Essential Reference

by Alex Harford
1st Edition, Winter 1999
400 pages, $24.95
ISBN: 0-7357-0911-4

Gimp Essential Reference is designed to fulfill a need for the computer expert. It is made to bring someone experienced in computers up to speed with the GNU Image Manipulation Program. It provides essential information on using this program effectively. This book is targeted at the growing market of Linux users who want to efficiently use the Gimp. They may already be familiar with proprietary programs such as Adobe Photoshop or CorelDraw. *Gimp Essential Reference* will show users how to quickly become familiar with the advanced user interface using a table-heavy format that will allow users to find what they're looking for quickly. *Gimp Essential Reference* is for users working with the Gimp know what they want to accomplish, but don't know exactly how to do it.

Lotus Notes and Domino Titles

Domino System Administration

By Rob Kirkland
1st Edition Fall 1999
500 pages, $39.99
ISBN: 1-56205-948-3

Your boss has just announced that you will be upgrading to the newest version of Notes and Domino when it ships. As a Premium Lotus Business Partner, Lotus has offered a substantial price break to keep your company away from Microsoft's Exchange Server. How are you supposed to get this new system installed, configured, and rolled out to all of your end users? You understand how Lotus Notes works— you've been administering it for years. What you need is a concise, practical explanation about the new features, and how to make some of the advanced stuff really work. You need answers and solutions from someone like you, who has worked with the product for years, and understands what it is you need to know. Domino System Administration is the answer—the first book on Domino that attacks the technology at the professional level, with practical, hands-on assistance to get Domino running in your organization.

Lotus Notes and Domino Essential Reference
By Dave Hatter & Tim Bankes
1st Edition
704 pages, $45.00
ISBN: 0-7357-0007-9

You're in a bind because you've been asked to design and program a new database in Notes for an important client that will keep track of and itemize a myriad of inventory and shipping data. The client wants a user-friendly interface, without sacrificing speed or function-ality. You are experienced (and could develop this app in your sleep), but feel that you need to take your talents to the next level. You need something to facilitate your creative and techni-cal abilities, something to perfect your programming skills. Your answer is waiting for you: *Lotus Notes and Domino Essential Reference*. It's compact and simply designed. It's loaded with information. All of the objects, classes, functions, and methods are listed. It shows you the object hierarchy and the overlaying relationship between each one. It's perfect for you. Problem solved.

Programming Titles

Python Essential Reference
by David Beazley
1st Edition, Fall 1999
350 pages, $34.95
ISBN: 0-7357-0901-7

The *Python Essential Reference* concisely describes the Python programming language and its large library of standard modules, collectively known as the Python programming "environment." It is arranged into four major parts. First a brief tutorial and introduction is presented. Then, an informal language reference will cover lexical conventions, functions, statements, control flow, datatypes, classes, and execution models. The third part will cover the Python library, and the final section covers the Python C API that is used to write Python extensions.

This book is for the professional who has experience with other systems programming language such as C or C++ and is looking for content that is not embellished with basic introductory material on the Python programming environment.

Networking Titles

Cisco Router Configuration and Troubleshooting

By Pablo Espinosa and Mark Tripod
1st Edition
300 pages, $34.99
ISBN: 0-7357-0024-9

Want the real story on making your Cisco routers run like a dream? Why not pick up a copy of *Cisco Router Configuration and Troubleshooting* and see what Pablo Espinosa and Mark Tripod have to say? They're the folks responsible for making some of the largest sites on the Net scream, like Amazon.com, Hotmail, USAToday, Geocities, and Sony. In this book, they provide advanced configuration issues, sprinkled with advice and preferred practices. You won't see a general overview on TCP/IP—we talk about more meaty issues like security, monitoring, traffic management, and more. In the troubleshooting section, the authors provide a unique methodology and lots of sample problems to illustrate. By providing real-world insight and examples instead of rehashing Cisco's documentation, Pablo and Mark give network administrators information they can start using today.

DCE/RPC over SMB

by Luke Leighton
1st Edition
400 pages, $45.00
ISBN: 1-57870-150-3

This book describes how Microsoft has taken DCE/ RPC (Distributed Computing Environment / Remote Procedure Calls) and implemented it over SMB (Server Message Block) and TCP/IP. SMB itself runs over three transports: TCP/IP, IPX/SPX and NETBEUI. Luke Leighton presents Microsoft Developer NT system calls (including what some such calls would be, if they were documented) and shows what they look like over-the-wire by providing example C code to compile and use. This gives administrators and developers insights into how information flows through their network so that they can improve efficiency, security and heterogeneous transfers.

Implementing and Troubleshooting LDAP

By Robert Lamothe
1st Edition Spring 1999
400 pages, $34.99
ISBN: 1-56205-947-5

While there is some limited information available about LDAP, most of it is RFCs, white papers, and books about programming LDAP into your networking applications. That leaves the people who most need information—administrators—out in the cold. What do you do if you need to know how to make LDAP work in your system? You ask Bob Lamothe. Bob is a UNIX administrator with hands-on experience in setting up a corporate-wide directory service using LDAP. Bob's book is NOT a guide to the protocol; rather, it is designed to be an aid to administrators to help them understand the most efficient way to structure, encrypt, authenticate, administer, and troubleshoot LDAP in a mixed network environment. The book shows you how to work with the major implementations of LDAP and get them to coexist.

Implementing Virtual Private Networks
By Tina Bird and Ted Stockwell
1st Edition Spring 1999
300 pages, $29.99
ISBN: 0-73570-047-8

Tired of looking for decent, practical, up-to-date information on virtual private networks? *Implementing Virtual Private Networks*, by noted authorities Dr. Tina Bird and Ted Stockwell, finally gives you what you need—an authoritative guide on the design, implementation, and maintenance of Internet-based access to private networks. This book focuses on real-world solutions, demonstrating how the choice of VPN architecture should align with an organization's business and technological requirements. Tina and Ted give you the information you need to determine whether a VPN is right for your organization, select the VPN that suits your needs, and design and implement the VPN you have chosen.

Understanding Data Communications, Sixth Edition
By Gilbert Held
6th Edition Summer 1999
500 pages, $39.99
ISBN: 0-7357-0036-2

Updated from the highly successful fifth edition, this book explains how data communications systems and their various hardware and software components work. Not an entry-level book, it approaches the material in a textbook format, addressing the complex issues involved in internetworking today. This is a great reference book for the experienced networking professional, written by noted networking authority, Gilbert Held.

Windows NT Titles

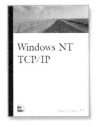

Windows NT TCP/IP
By Karanjit Siyan
1st Edition
480 pages, $29.99
ISBN: 1-56205-887-8

If you're still looking for good documentation on Microsoft TCP/IP, then look no further—this is your book. *Windows NT TCP/IP* cuts through the complexities and provides the most informative and complete reference book on Windows-based TCP/IP. Concepts essential to TCP/IP administration are explained thoroughly, and then related to the practical use of Microsoft TCP/IP in a real-world networking environment. The book begins by covering TCP/IP architecture, advanced installation and configuration issues. Then, it moves on to routing with TCP/IP, DHCP Management, and WINS/DNS Name Resolution.

Windows NT DNS

By Michael Masterson,
Herman L. Knief, Scott
Vinick, and Eric Roul
1st Edition
340 pages, $29.99
ISBN: 1-56205-943-2

Have you ever opened a Windows NT book looking for detailed information about DNS only to discover that it doesn't even begin to scratch the surface? DNS is probably one of the most complicated subjects for NT administrators, and there are few books on the market that really address it in detail. This book answers your most complex DNS questions, focusing on the implementation of the Domain Name Service within Windows NT, treating it thoroughly from the viewpoint of an experienced Windows NT professional. Many detailed, real-world examples illustrate further the understanding of the material throughout. The book covers the details of how DNS functions within NT and then explores specific interactions with critical network components. Finally, proven procedures to design and set up DNS are demonstrated. You'll also find coverage of related topics, such as maintenance, security, and troubleshooting.

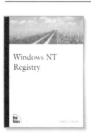

Windows NT Registry

By Sandra Osborne
1st Edition
564 pages, $29.99
ISBN: 1-56205-941-6

The NT Registry can be a very powerful tool for those capable of using it

wisely. Unfortunately, there is very little information regarding the NT Registry, due to Microsoft's insistence that their source code be kept secret. If you're looking to optimize your use of the registry, you're usually forced to search the Web for bits of information. This book is your resource. It covers critical issues and settings used for configuring network protocols, including NWLink, PTP, TCP/IP, and DHCP. This book approaches the material from a unique point of view, discussing the problems related to a particular component, and then discussing settings, which are the actual changes necessary for implementing robust solutions.

Windows NT Performance

By Mark Edmead and
Paul Hinsberg
1st Edition
288 pages, $29.99
ISBN: 1-56205-942-4

Performance monitoring is a little like preventative medicine for the administrator: no one enjoys a checkup, but it's a good thing to do on a regular basis. This book helps you focus on the critical aspects of improving the performance of your NT system, showing you how to monitor the system, implement benchmarking, and tune your network. The book is organized by resource components, which makes it easy to use as a reference tool.

Windows NT Terminal Server and Citrix MetaFrame

By Ted Harwood
1st Edition
416 pages, $29.99
ISBN: 1-56205-944-0

It's no surprise that most administration headaches revolve around integration with other networks and clients. This book addresses these types of real-world issues on a case-by-case basis, giving tools and advice on solving each problem. The author also offers the real nuts and bolts of thin client administration on multiple systems, covering such relevant issues as installation, configuration, network connection, management, and application distribution.

Windows NT Security

By Richard Puckett
1st Edition Fall 1999
600 pages, $29.99
ISBN: 1-56205-945-9

Swiss cheese. That's what some people say Windows NT security is like. And they may be right, because they only know what the NT documentation says about implementing security. Who has the time to research alternatives; play around with the features, service packs, hot fixes and add-on tools, and figure out what makes NT rock solid? Well, Richard Puckett does. He's been researching Windows NT Security for the University of Virginia for a while now, and he's got pretty good news. He's going to show you how to make NT secure in your environment, and we mean really secure.

Windows NT Network Management: Reducing TCO

By Anil Desai
1st Edition Spring 1999
400 pages, $34.99
ISBN: 1-56205-946-7

Administering a Windows NT network is kind of like trying to herd cats—an impossible task characterized by constant motion, exhausting labor and lots of hairballs. Author Anil Desai knows all about it—he's a Consulting Engineer for Sprint Paranet, and specializes in Windows NT implementation, integration and management. So we asked him to put together a concise manual of best practices, a book of tools and ideas that other administrators can turn to again and again in managing their own NT networks.

Planning for Windows 2000

By Eric K. Cone, Jon Boggs and Sergio Perez
1st Edition Spring 1999
400 pages, $29.99
ISBN: 0-73570-048-6

Windows 2000 is poised to be one of the largest and most important software releases of the next decade, and you are charged with planning, testing, and deploying it in your enterprise. Are you ready? With this book, you will be. *Planning for Windows 2000* lets you know what the upgrade hurdles will be, informs you how to clear them, guides you through effective Active Directory design, and presents you with detailed rollout procedures. Eric K. Cone give you the benefit of their extensive experiences as Windows 2000 Rapid Deployment Program members, sharing problems and solutions they've encountered on the job.

MCSE Core NT Exams Essential Reference

By Matthew Shepker
1st Edition
256 pages, $19.99
ISBN: 0-7357-0006-0

You're sitting in the first session of your Networking Essentials class and the instructor starts talking about RAS and you have no idea what that means. You think about raising your hand to ask about RAS, but you reconsider—you'd feel pretty foolish asking a question in front of all these people. You turn to your handy *MCSE Core NT Exams Essential Reference* and find a quick summary on Remote Access Services. Question answered. It's a couple months later and you're taking your Networking Essentials exam the next day. You're reviewing practice tests and you keep forgetting the maximum lengths for the various commonly used cable types. Once again, you turn to the *MCSE Core NT Exams Essential Reference* and find a table on cables, including all of the characteristics you need to memorize in order to pass the test.

BackOffice Titles

Implementing Exchange Server

By Doug Hauger, Marywynne Leon, and William C. Wade III
1st Edition
400 pages, $29.99
ISBN: 1-56205-931-9

If you're interested in connectivity and maintenance issues for Exchange Server, then this book is for you. Exchange's power lies in its ability to be connected to multiple email subsystems to create a "universal email backbone." It's not unusual to have several different and complex systems all connected via email gateways, including Lotus Notes or cc:Mail, Microsoft Mail, legacy mainframe systems, and Internet mail. This book covers all of the problems and issues associated with getting an integrated system running smoothly, and it addresses troubleshooting and diagnosis of email problems with an eye toward prevention and best practices.

Exchange Server Administration

By Janice K. Howd
1st Edition Spring 1999
400 pages, $34.99
ISBN: 0-7357-0081-8

OK, you've got your Exchange Server installed and connected, now what? Email administration is one of the most critical networking jobs, and Exchange can be particularly troublesome in large, heterogeneous environments. So Janice Howd, a noted consultant and teacher with over a decade of email administration experience, has put together this advanced, concise handbook for daily, periodic, and emergency administration. With in-depth coverage of topics like managing disk resources, replication, and disaster recovery, this is the one reference book every Exchange administrator needs.

SQL Server System Administration

By Sean Baird,
Chris Miller, et al.
1st Edition
352 pages, $29.99
ISBN: 1-56205-955-6

How often does your SQL Server go down during the day when everyone wants to access the data? Do you spend most of your time being a "report monkey" for your co-workers and bosses? *SQL Server System Administration* helps you keep data consistently available to your users. This book omits the introductory information. The authors don't spend time explaining queries and how they work. Instead they focus on the information that you can't get anywhere else, like how to choose the correct replication topology and achieve high availability of information.

Internet Information Server Administration

By Kelli Adam, et al.
1st Edition Fall 1999
300 pages, $29.99
ISBN: 0-73570-022-2

Are the new Internet technologies in Internet Information Server giving you headaches? Does protecting security on the Web take up all of your time? Then this is the book for you. With hands-on configuration training, advanced study of the new protocols in IIS, and detailed instructions on authenticating users with the new Certificate Server and implementing and managing the new e-commerce features, *Internet Information Server Administration* gives you the real-life solutions you need. This definitive resource also prepares you for the release of Windows 2000 by giving you detailed advice on working with Microsoft Management Console, which was first used by IIS.

SMS Administration

1st Edition Summer 1999
350 pages, $34.99
ISBN: 0-7357-0082-6

Microsoft's new version of its Systems Management Server (SMS) is starting to turn heads. While complex, it's allowing administrators to lower their total cost of ownership and more efficiently manage clients, applications and support operations. So if your organization is using or implementing SMS, you'll need some expert advice. Wayne Koop and Brian Steck can help you get the most bang for your buck, with insight, expert tips, and real-world examples. Brian and Wayne are consultants specializing in SMS, having worked with Microsoft on one of the most complex SMS rollouts in the world, involving 32 countries, 15 languages, and thousands of clients.

Other Books By New Riders Press

Windows Technologies

Windows NT Network Management:
Reducing Total
Cost of Ownership
1-56205-946-7
Windows NT DNS
1-56205-943-2
Windows NT Performance
Monitoring, Benchmarking
and Tuning
1-56205-942-4
Windows NT Registry:
A Settings Reference
1-56205-941-6
Windows NT TCP/IP
1-56205-887-8
Windows NT Terminal Server and
Citrix MetaFrame
1-56205-944-0
Implementing Exchange Server
1-56205-931-9
Exchange Server Administration
0-7357-0081-8
SQL Server System Administration
1-56205-955-6

Networking

Cisco Router Configuration and
Troubleshooting
0-7357-0024-9
Network Intrusion Detection:
An Analyst's Handbook
0-7357-0864-9
Understanding Data Communications,
Sixth Edition
0-7357-0036-2

Certification

A+ Certification TestPrep
1-56205-892-4
A+ Certification Top Score Software
0-7357-0017-6
A+ Certification Training Guide
1-56205-896-7
A+ Complete v 1.1
0-7357-0045-1
A+ Fast Track
0-7357-0028-1
MCSE Essential Reference:
Core NT Exams
0-7357-0006-0
MCSD Fast Track: Visual Basic 6, Exam
70-176
0-7357-0019-2
MCSE Fast Track: 6-in-1 Bundle 1-
56205-909-2
MCSE Fast Track: Internet Information
Server 4
1-56205-936-X
MCSE Fast Track:
Networking Essentials
1-56205-939-4

MCSE Fast Track: TCP/IP
1-56205-937-8
MCSD Fast Track: Visual Basic 6, Exam
70-175
0-7357-0018-4
MCSE Fast Track: Windows 98
0-7357-0016-8
MCSE Fast Track: Windows NT Server
4
1-56205-935-1
MCSE Fast Track: Windows NT Server
4 Enterprise
1-56205-940-8
MCSE Fast Track: Windows NT
Workstation 4
1-56205-938-6
MCSE Simulation Guide: Windows
NT Server 4 & Enterprise
1-56205-914-9
MCSE Simulation Guide: Windows
NT Workstation 4
1-56205-925-4
MCSE TestPrep:
Core Exam Bundle, 2E
0-7357-0030-3
MCSE TestPrep: Networking Essentials
Second Edition
0-7357-0010-9
MCSE TestPrep: TCP/IP,
Second Edition
0-7357-0025-7
MCSE TestPrep: Windows 95 Second
Edition
0-7357-0011-7
MCSE TestPrep: Windows 98
1-56205-922-X
MCSE TestPrep: Windows NT Server
4 Enterprise Second Edition 0-7357-
0009-5
MCSE TestPrep: Windows NT Server
4 Second Edition
0-7357-0012-5
MCSE TestPrep: Windows NT
Workstation 4 Second Edition
0-7357-0008-7
MCSD TestPrep: Visual Basic 6 Exams
0-7357-0032-X
MCSE Training Guide: Core Exams
Bundle, Second Edition
1-56205-926-2
MCSE Training Guide: Networking
Essentials Second Edition
1-56205-919-X
MCSE Training Guide: TCP/IP
Second Edition
1-56205-920-3
MCSE Training Guide: Windows
98 1-56205-890-8
MCSE Training Guide: Windows NT
Server 4 Second Edition
1-56205-916-5

MCSE Training Guide: Windows NT
Server Enterprise Second Edition
1-56205-917-3
MCSE Training Guide: Windows NT
Workstation 4 Second Edition
1-56205-918-1
MCSD Training Guide: Visual Basic 6
Exams
0-7357-0002-8
MCSE Top Score Software:
Core Exams
0-7357-0033-8
MCSE + Complete, v1.1
0-7897-1564-3
MCSE + Internet Complete, v1.2
0-7357-0072-9

Graphics

Inside 3D Studio MAX 2 Volume I
1-56205-857-6
Inside 3D Studio MAX 2 Volume II:
Modeling and Materials
1-56205-864-9
Inside 3D Studio MAX 2 Volume III:
Animation
1-56205-865-7
Inside 3D Studio MAX 2
Resource Kit
1-56205-953-X
Inside AutoCAD 14 Limited Edition
1-56205-898-3
Inside Softimage 3D
1-56205-885-1
HTML Web Magic, 2nd Edition
1-56830-475-7
Dynamic HTML Web Magic
1-56830-421-8
Designing Web Graphics.3
1-56205-949-1
Illustrator 8 Magic
1-56205-952-1
Inside trueSpace 4
1-56205-957-2
Inside Adobe Photoshop 5
1-56205-884-3
Inside Adobe Photoshop 5,
Limited Edition
1-56205-951-3
Photoshop 5 Artistry
1-56205-895-9
Photoshop 5 Type Magic
1-56830-465-X
Photoshop 5 Web Magic
1-56205-913-0

We Want to Know What You Think

To better serve you, we would like your opinion on the content and quality of this book. Please complete this card and mail it to us or fax it to 317-581-4663.

Name _____

Address _____

City_____State_____Zip _____

Phone _____

Email Address _____

Occupation _____

Operating System(s) that you use _____

What influenced your purchase of this book?

❑ Recommendation   ❑ Cover Design
❑ Table of Contents   ❑ Index
❑ Magazine Review   ❑ Advertisement
❑ New Rider's Reputation ❑ Author Name

How would you rate the contents of this book?

❑ Excellent   ❑ Very Good
❑ Good   ❑ Fair
❑ Below Average   ❑ Poor

How do you plan to use this book?

❑ Quick reference   ❑ Self-training
❑ Classroom   ❑ Other

What do you like most about this book?
Check all that apply.

❑ Content   ❑ Writing Style
❑ Accuracy   ❑ Examples
❑ Listings   ❑ Design
❑ Index   ❑ Page Count
❑ Price   ❑ Illustrations

What do you like least about this book?
Check all that apply.

❑ Content   ❑ Writing Style
❑ Accuracy   ❑ Examples
❑ Listings   ❑ Design
❑ Index   ❑ Page Count
❑ Price   ❑ Illustrations

What would be a useful follow-up book to this one for you?_____

Where did you purchase this book? _____

Can you name a similar book that you like better than this one, or one that is as good? Why?

_____

_____

How many New Riders books do you own? _____

What are your favorite computer books?_____

_____

What other titles would you like to see us develop? _____

_____

Any comments for us? _____

_____

_____

_____

GTK+/Gnome Application Development, 0-7357-0078-8

www.newriders.com • Fax 317-581-4663

Fold here and tape to mail

New Riders Publishing
201 W. 103rd St.
Indianapolis, IN 46290

New Riders | How to Contact Us

Visit Our Web Site

www.newriders.com

On our Web site you'll find information about our other books, authors, tables of contents, indexes, and book errata. You can also place orders for books through our Web site.

Email Us

Contact us at this address:

newriders@mcp.com

editors@newriders.com

- If you have comments or questions about this book
- To report errors that you have found in this book
- If you have a book proposal to submit or are interested in writing for New Riders
- If you would like to have an author kit sent to you
- If you are an expert in a computer topic or technology and are interested in being a technical editor who reviews manuscripts for technical accuracy

sales@newriders.com

- To find a distributor in your area, please contact our international department at the address above.

pr@newriders.com

- For instructors from educational institutions who wish to preview New Riders books for classroom use. Email should include your name, title, school, department, address, phone number, office days/hours, text in use, and enrollment in the body of your text along with your request for desk/examination copies and/or additional information.

Write to Us

New Riders Publishing

201 W. 103rd St.

Indianapolis, IN 46290-1097

Fax Us

(317) 581-4663